Praise for Edward Glaeser's *Triumph of the City*

"If you live in a city, if you're planning on living in a city, if you ever lived in a city—this is a great book to read to give yourself a nice feeling of what you're accomplishing. It's a tremendous book."
—Jon Stewart, host of *The Daily Show*

"[A] terrific new book." —David Brooks, *The New York Times*

"Although liberally sprinkled with statistics, *Triumph of the City* is no dry work. Mr. Glaeser writes lucidly and spares his readers the equations of his trade. This is popular economics of the best sort." —*The Economist*

"Glaeser loves an argument, and he's a wonderful guide into one. *Triumph of the City* is bursting with insights and policy proposals to debate.... You'll ... walk away dazzled by the greatness of cities and fascinated by this writer's nimble mind." —*The New York Times Book Review*

"Deeply researched ... his book convincingly argues that concentrated populations can have 'magical consequences.'" —*Bloomberg BusinessWeek*

"Glaeser's new book, *Triumph of the City,* is a probing look at what makes and breaks cities—which, Glaeser argues, represent the pinnacle of human achievement and the best hope for the future of the species. It is a vindicating read for urbanites." —*New York Magazine*

"Whatever the city under discussion, Mumbai or Woodlands, Texas, Glaeser is discerning and independent.... Thought-provoking material." —*Booklist*

"An authority on the subject within the academic world and without ... Glaeser's latest book ... is a tour of his greatest insights about urban economics, written for a general audience." —*National Review Online*

"A popular treatment of Glaeser's main findings in urban economics ... engaging and entertaining." —*Washington Monthly*

"[*Triumph of the City*] succeeds at challenging our assumptions about the relation between individual cities and the larger world in which we live." —*San Francisco Chronicle*

"Provocative." —*The New York Observer*

"One book you *can* judge by its cover. The title and cover art—a gleaming nighttime cityscape—convey the author's enthusiasm for his topic. And Glaeser . . . delivers one idea after another that debunks the conventional urban wisdom of cities' 'antiurbanite' critics." —*Pittsburgh Tribune-Review*

"Provocative and lively."   —*The Berkshire Eagle*

"Ed Glaeser is one of the nation's most influential thinkers on urban affairs— and rightly so. . . . His writing is vigorous; his perspective, fresh."
—*Governing*

"Edward Glaeser's recent book *Triumph of the City* is both a manifesto on behalf of the best cities and a self-affirmation book for confirmed urbanites who may just once have considered cheating with a suburb."
—*Next American City*

"Glaeser is a clear-eyed observer, and he offers plenty of enlightening history along with some useful policy recommendations. . . . If you want to learn more about cities, *Triumph of the City* is a useful book." —*Dissent* magazine

"Glaeser's book arrives at just the right moment. . . . [It] is a lively recitation of economic insights and counterintuitive observations that should provoke thought and discussion among citizens and policy makers."
—MinnPost.com

"A broad, intelligent survey of an important, misunderstood subject."
—*A. V. Club*

"Terrific . . . a brisk and accessible tour through a series of real-life experiments deeply grounded in data."   —FutureOfCapitalism.com

"A thrilling ride around the world's great cities."
—*The Independent* (London)

"A thrilling and very readable hymn of praise to an invention so vast and so effective that it is generally taken for granted . . . this is a tremendous book."
—*The Literary Review*

"Fascinating . . . [Glaeser] is established as one of the leading economic thinkers about the city."   —*The Telegraph* (London)

"Glaeser's enthusiasm for cities is catching . . . and for a book bursting with statistics, *Triumph of the City* is never dull. . . . Glaeser has provided a timely reminder of the benefits of urbanization." —*London Evening Standard*

"Smart." —*The Globe and Mail* (Toronto)

"Excellent." —*Hindustan Times*

"Edward Glaeser is one of the world's most brilliant economists, and *Triumph of the City* is a masterpiece. Seamlessly combining economics and history, he explains why cities are 'our species' greatest invention.' This beautifully written book makes clear how cities have not only survived but thrived, even as modern technology has seemingly made one's physical location less important."
—Steven D. Levitt, coauthor of *Freakonomics* and *Superfreakonomics* and professor of economics at the University of Chicago

"If you would like to improve slums, turn poverty into prosperity, or get a grip on urban sprawl, read this thoughtful and thought-provoking book."
—Simon Johnson, author of *13 Bankers* and professor of entrepreneurship at MIT Sloan School of Management

"A magisterial book from the world's leading authority on why and how cities work. Comprehensive, compelling and strongly recommended."
—Tim Harford, author of *The Undercover Economist* and *Adapt* and columnist for *Financial Times*

"Ed Glaeser is an economist's economist—as smart as they come, driven by empiricism, with something interesting to say about nearly anything."
—Stephen Dubner, *Freakonomics* blog

"The overarching theme of Glaeser's book is that cities make us smarter, more productive, and more innovative. To put it plainly, they make us richer. And the evidence in favor of this point is very, very strong."
—Ezra Klein, TheWashingtonPost.com

ABOUT THE AUTHOR

Edward Glaeser is the Fred and Eleanor Glimp Professor of Economics at Harvard University, where he directs the Taubman Center for State and Local Government and the Rappaport Institute for Greater Boston. He is also a senior fellow at the Manhattan Institute and a contributing editor to *City Journal*. He studies the economics of cities, housing, segregation, obesity, crime, innovation, and other subjects, and writes about many of these issues as a columnist for Bloomberg View.

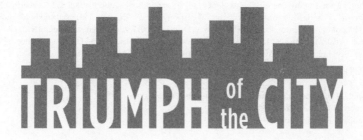

TRIUMPH of the CITY

How Our Greatest Invention Makes Us Richer,
Smarter, Greener, Healthier, and Happier

Edward Glaeser

PENGUIN BOOKS

PENGUIN BOOKS
Published by the Penguin Group
Penguin Group (USA) Inc., 375 Hudson Street, New York, New York 10014, U.S.A. · Penguin Group (Canada), 90 Eglinton Avenue East, Suite 700, Toronto, Ontario, Canada M4P 2Y3 (a division of Pearson Penguin Canada Inc.) · Penguin Books Ltd, 80 Strand, London WC2R 0RL, England · Penguin Ireland, 25 St. Stephen's Green, Dublin 2, Ireland (a division of Penguin Books Ltd) · Penguin Books Australia Ltd, 250 Camberwell Road, Camberwell, Victoria 3124, Australia (a division of Pearson Australia Group Pty Ltd) · Penguin Books India Pvt Ltd, 11 Community Centre, Panchsheel Park, New Delhi—110 017, India · Penguin Group (NZ), 67 Apollo Drive, Rosedale, Auckland 0632, New Zealand (a division of Pearson New Zealand Ltd) · Penguin Books (South Africa) (Pty) Ltd, 24 Sturdee Avenue, Rosebank, Johannesburg 2196, South Africa

Penguin Books Ltd, Registered Offices: 80 Strand, London WC2R 0RL, England

First published in the United States of America by The Penguin Press, a member of Penguin Group (USA) Inc. 2011
Published in Penguin Books 2012

20   19   18   17   16

THE LIBRARY OF CONGRESS HAS CATALOGED THE HARDCOVER EDITION AS FOLLOWS:

Glaeser, Edward L. (Edward Ludwig), ———.
    Triumph of the city : how our greatest invention makes us richer, smarter, greener, healthier, and happier / Edward L. Glaeser.
        p.   cm.
    Includes bibliographical references and index.
    ISBN 978-1-59420-277-3 (hc.)
    ISBN 978-0-14-312054-4 (pbk.)
    1. Urbanization.   2. Cities and towns—Growth.   3. Urban economics.   4. Urban sociology.   I. Title.
    HT361.G53   2011
    307.76—dc22   2010034609

Printed in the United States of America
DESIGNED BY NICOLE LAROCHE

To Nancy,

for All the Days

CONTENTS

TRIUMPH of the CITY

Our Urban Species

T wo hundred forty-three million Americans crowd together in the 3 percent of the country that is urban. Thirty-six million people live in and around Tokyo, the most productive metropolitan area in the world. Twelve million people reside in central Mumbai, and Shanghai is almost as large. On a planet with vast amounts of space (all of humanity could fit in Texas—each of us with a personal townhouse), we choose cities. Although it has become cheaper to travel long distances, or to telecommute from the Ozarks to Azerbaijan, more and more people are clustering closer and closer together in large metropolitan areas. Five million more people every month live in the cities of the developing world, and in 2011, more than half the world's population is urban.

Cities, the dense agglomerations that dot the globe, have been engines of innovation since Plato and Socrates bickered in an Athenian marketplace. The streets of Florence gave us the Renaissance, and the streets of Birmingham gave us the Industrial Revolution. The great prosperity of contemporary London and Bangalore and Tokyo comes from their ability to produce new thinking. Wandering these cities—whether down cobblestone sidewalks or grid-cutting cross streets, around roundabouts or under freeways—is to study nothing less than human progress.

In the richer countries of the West, cities have survived the tumultuous end of the industrial age and are now wealthier, healthier, and more alluring than ever. In the world's poorer places, cities are expanding enormously because urban density provides the clearest path from poverty to prosperity. Despite the technological breakthroughs that have caused the death of distance, it turns out that the world isn't flat; it's paved.

The city has triumphed. But as many of us know from personal experience, sometimes city roads are paved to hell. The city may win, but too often its citizens seem to lose. Every urban childhood is shaped by an onrush of extraordinary people and experiences—some delicious, like the sense of power that comes from a preteen's first subway trip alone; some less so, like a first exposure to urban gunfire (an unforgettable part of my childhood education in New York City thirty-five years ago). For every Fifth Avenue, there's a Mumbai slum; for every Sorbonne, there's a D.C. high school guarded by metal detectors.

Indeed, for many Americans, the latter half of the twentieth century—the end of the industrial age—was an education not in urban splendor but in urban squalor. How well we learn from the lessons our cities teach us will determine whether our urban species will flourish in what can be a new golden age of the city.

My passion for the urban world began with the New York of Ed Koch, Thurman Munson, and Leonard Bernstein. Inspired by my metropolitan childhood, I've spent my life trying to understand cities. That quest has been rooted in economic theory and data, but it has also meandered through the streets of Moscow and São Paulo and Mumbai, through the histories of bustling metropolises and the everyday stories of those who live and work in them.

I find studying cities so engrossing because they pose fascinating, important, and often troubling questions. Why do the richest and poorest people in the world so often live cheek by jowl? How do once-mighty cities fall into disrepair? Why do some stage dramatic comebacks? Why do so many artistic movements arise so quickly in particular cities at particular moments? Why do so many smart people enact so many foolish urban policies?

There's no better place to ponder these questions than what many consider to be the archetypal city—New York. Native New Yorkers, like myself, may occasionally have a slightly exaggerated view of their city's importance, but New York is still a paradigm of urbanity and therefore an appropriate place to start our journey to cities across the world. Its story encapsulates the past, present, and future of our urban centers, and provides a springboard for many of the themes that will emerge from the pages and places ahead.

If you stand on Forty-seventh Street and Fifth Avenue this Wednesday afternoon, you'll be surrounded by a torrent of people. Some are rushing uptown for a meeting or downtown to grab a drink. Others are walking east to enter the great subterranean caverns of Grand Central Terminal, which has more platforms than any other train station in the world. Some people may be trying to buy an engagement ring—after all, Forty-seventh Street is the nation's premier market for gems. There will be visitors gazing upward—something New Yorkers never do—on their way from one landmark to another. If you imitate a tourist and look up, you'll see two great ridges of skyscrapers framing the shimmering valley that is Fifth Avenue.

Thirty years ago, New York City's future looked far less bright. Like almost every colder, older city, Gotham seemed to be a dinosaur. The city's subways and buses felt archaic in a world being rebuilt around the car. The city's port, once the glory of the Eastern seaboard, had sunk into irrelevance. Under the leadership of John Lindsay and Abe Beame, the city's government had come near default despite having some of the highest taxes in the nation. Not just Jerry Ford, but history itself seemed to be telling New York City to drop dead.

New York, or more properly New Amsterdam, was founded during an earlier era of globalization as a distant outpost of the Dutch West India Company. It was a trading village where a hodgepodge of adventurers came to make fortunes swapping beads for furs. Those mercantile Dutch settlers clustered together because proximity made it easier to exchange goods and ideas and because there was safety behind the town's protective wall (now Wall Street).

In the eighteenth century, New York passed Boston to become the English colonies' most important port; it specialized in shipping wheat and flour south to feed the sugar and tobacco colonies. During the first half of the nineteenth century, with business booming, New York's population grew from sixty thousand to eight hundred thousand, and the city became America's urban colossus.

That population explosion was partly due to changes in transportation technology. At the start of the nineteenth century, ships were generally small—three hundred tons was a normal size—and, like smaller airplanes today, ideal for point-to-point trips, like Liverpool to Charlestown or Boston to Glasgow. Between 1800 and 1850, improvements in technology and finance brought forth larger ships that could carry bigger loads at faster speeds and lower cost.

There was no percentage in having these jumbo clipper ships traveling to every point along the American coast. Just like today's Boeing 747s, which land at major hubs and transfer their passengers onto smaller planes that take them to their final destinations, the big clipper ships came to one central harbor and then transferred their goods to smaller vessels for delivery up and down the Eastern seaboard. New York was America's superport, with its central location, deep, protected harbor, and river access far into the hinterland. When America moved to a hub-and-spoke shipping system, New York became *the* natural hub. The city's position was only strengthened when canals made Manhattan the eastern end of a great watery arc that cut through the Midwest all the way to New Orleans.

Shipping was the city's economic anchor, but New Yorkers were more likely to work in the manufacturing industries—sugar refining, garment production, and publishing—that grew up around the harbor. Sugar producers, like the Roosevelt family, operated in a big port city, because urban scale enabled them to cover the fixed costs of big, expensive refineries and to be close enough to consumers so that refined sugar crystals wouldn't coalesce during a long, hot water voyage. The garment industry similarly owed its concentration in New York to the vast cargoes of cotton and textiles that came through the city and sailors' need for ready-made clothes. Even New York's publishing preeminence ultimately reflected the city's central place on transatlantic trade routes, as the big money in nineteenth-century books came from being the first printer out with pirated copies of English novels. The Harper brothers really arrived as publishers when they beat their Philadelphia competitors by printing the third volume of Walter Scott's *Peveril of the Peak* twenty-one hours after it arrived in New York by packet ship.

In the twentieth century, however, the death of distance destroyed the transport-cost advantages that had made New York a manufacturing mammoth. Why sew skirts on Hester Street when labor is so much cheaper in China? Globalization brought fierce competition to the companies and cities that made anything that could be easily shipped across the Pacific. New York's economic decline in the midtwentieth century reflected the increasing irrelevance of its nineteenth-century advantages.

But of course, as anyone standing on Fifth Avenue today must notice, the story didn't end there. New York didn't die. Today, the five zip codes that occupy the mile of Manhattan between Forty-first and Fifty-ninth streets employ six hundred thousand workers (more than New Hampshire or Maine), who earn on average more than $100,000 each, giving that tiny piece of real estate a larger annual payroll than Oregon or Nevada.

Just as globalization killed off New York's advantages as a manufacturing hub, it increased the city's edge in producing ideas. While there isn't much sewing left in New York, there are still plenty of Calvin Kleins and Donna Karans, producing designs that will often be made on the other side of the planet. Honda may have brought heartache to Detroit's Big Three, but managing the international flow of finance has earned vast sums for New York's bankers. A more connected world has brought huge returns to the idea-producing entrepreneurs who can now scour the earth in search of profits.

New York reinvented itself during the bleak years of the 1970s when a cluster of financial innovators learned from each other and produced a chain of interconnected ideas. Academic knowledge about trading off risk and return made it easier to evaluate and sell riskier assets, like Michael Milken's high-yield (junk) bonds, which made it possible for Henry Kravis to use those bonds to get value out of underperforming companies through leveraged buyouts. Many of the biggest innovators acquired their knowledge not through formal training but by being close to the action, like mortgage-backed security magnate Lewis Ranieri of *Liar's Poker* fame, who started in the Salomon Brothers mailroom. Today, 40 percent of Manhattan's payroll is in the financial services industry, the bulwark of a dense and still-thriving city. And even though some of these financial wizards helped give us the Great Recession, the city that housed them has weathered that storm, too. Between 2009 and 2010, as the American economy largely stagnated, wages in Manhattan increased by 11.9 percent, more than any other large county. In 2010, the average weekly wage in Manhattan was $2,404, which is 170 percent more than the U.S. average, and 45 percent more than in Santa Clara County, home of Silicon Valley, which pays the highest wages outside of Greater New York.

The rise and fall and rise of New York introduces us to the central paradox of the modern metropolis—proximity has become ever more valuable as the cost of connecting across long distances has fallen. New York's story is unique in its operatic grandeur, but the key elements that drove the city's spectacular rise, sad decline, and remarkable rebirth can be found in cities like Chicago and London and Milan, as well.

In this book, we'll look closely at what makes cities our species' greatest invention. We'll also unpack their checkered history, which is relevant now because so many cities in the developing world struggle with the vast challenges that once plagued today's urban stars like San Francisco, Paris, and Singapore. And we'll examine the often surprising factors that shape the success of today's cities—from winter temperatures to the Internet to misguided environmentalism.

Cities are the absence of physical space between people and companies. They are proximity, density, closeness. They enable us to work and play together, and their success depends on the demand for physical connection. During the middle years of the twentieth century, many cities, like New York, declined as improvements in transportation reduced the advantages of locating factories in dense urban areas. And during the last thirty years, some of these cities have come back, while other, newer cities have grown because technological change has increased the returns to the knowledge that is best produced by people in close proximity to other people.

Within the United States, workers in metropolitan areas with big cities earn 30 percent more than workers who aren't in metropolitan areas. These high wages are offset by higher costs of living, but that doesn't change the fact that high wages reflect high productivity. The only reason why companies put up with the high labor and land costs of being in a city is that the city creates productivity advantages that offset those costs. Americans who live in metropolitan areas with more than a million residents are, on average, more than 50 percent more productive than Americans who live in smaller metropolitan areas. These relationships are the same even when we take into account the education, experience, and industry of workers. They're even the same if we take individual workers' IQs into account. The income gap between urban and rural areas is just as large in other rich countries, and even stronger in poorer nations.

In America and Europe, cities speed innovation by connecting their smart inhabitants to each other, but cities play an even more critical role in the developing world: They are gateways between markets and cultures. In the nineteenth century, Mumbai (then called Bombay) was a gateway for cotton. In the twenty-first century, Bangalore is a gateway for ideas.

If you mentioned India to a typical American or European in 1990, chances are that person would mutter uncomfortably about the tragedy of Third World poverty. Today, that person is more likely to mutter uncomfortably about the possibility that his job might be outsourced to Bangalore. India is still poor, but it's growing at a feverish pace, and Bangalore, India's fifth-largest city, is among the subcontinent's greatest success stories. Bangalore's wealth comes not from industrial might (although it still makes plenty of textiles) but from its strength as a city of ideas. By concentrating so much talent in one place, Bangalore makes it easier for that talent to teach itself and for outsiders, whether from Singapore or Silicon Valley, to connect easily with Indian human capital.

Echoing antiurbanites throughout the ages, Mahatma Gandhi said that "the true India is to be found not in its few cities, but in its 700,000 villages" and "the growth of the nation depends not on cities, but [on] its villages." The great man was wrong. India's growth depends almost entirely on its cities. There is a near-perfect correlation between urbanization and prosperity across nations. On average, as the share of a country's population that is urban rises by 10 percent, the country's per capita output increases by 30 percent. Per capita incomes are almost four times higher in those countries where a majority of people live in cities than in those countries where a majority of people live in rural areas.

There is a myth that even if cities enhance prosperity, they still make people miserable. But people report being happier in those countries that are more urban. In those countries where more than half of the population is urban, 30 percent of people say that they are very happy and 17 percent say that they are not very or not at all happy. In nations where more than half of the population is rural, 25 percent of people report being very happy and 22 percent report unhappiness. Across countries, reported life satisfaction rises with the share of the population that lives in cities, even when controlling for the countries' income and education.

So cities like Mumbai and Kolkata and Bangalore boost not only India's economy, but its mood. And certainly they are not un-Indian, any more than New York is un-American. These cities are, in so many ways, the places where their nation's genius is most fully expressed.

The urban ability to create collaborative brilliance isn't new. For centuries, innovations have spread from person to person across crowded city streets. An explosion of artistic genius during the Florentine Renaissance began when Brunelleschi figured out the geometry of linear perspective. He passed his knowledge to his friend Donatello, who imported linear perspective in low-relief sculpture. Their friend Masaccio then brought the innovation into painting. The artistic innovations of Florence were glorious side effects of urban concentration; that city's wealth came from more prosaic pursuits: banking and cloth making. Today, however, Bangalore and New York and London all *depend* on their ability to innovate. The spread of knowledge from engineer to engineer, from designer to designer, from trader to trader is the same as the flight of ideas from painter to painter, and urban density has long been at the heart of that process.

The vitality of New York and Bangalore doesn't mean that all cities will succeed. In 1950, Detroit was America's fifth-largest city and had 1.85 million people. In 2008, it had 777 thousand people, less than half its former size, and was continuing to lose population steadily. Eight of the ten largest American cities in 1950 have lost at least a fifth of their population since then. The failure of Detroit and so many other industrial towns doesn't reflect any weakness of cities as a whole, but rather the sterility of those cities that lost touch with the essential ingredients of urban reinvention.

Cities thrive when they have many small firms and skilled citizens. Detroit was once a buzzing beehive of small-scale interconnected inventors—Henry Ford was just one among many gifted entrepreneurs. But the extravagant success of Ford's big idea destroyed that older, more innovative city. Detroit's twentieth-century growth brought hundreds of thousands of less-well-educated workers to vast factories, which became fortresses apart from the city and the world. While industrial diversity, entrepreneurship, and education lead to innovation, the Detroit model led to urban decline. The age of the industrial city is over, at least in the West.

Too many officials in troubled cities wrongly imagine that they can lead their city back to its former glories with some massive construction project—a new stadium or light rail system, a convention center, or a housing project. With very few exceptions, no public policy can stem the tidal forces of urban change. We mustn't ignore the needs of the poor people who live in the Rust Belt, but public policy should help poor *people*, not poor places.

Shiny new real estate may dress up a declining city, but it doesn't solve its underlying problems. The hallmark of declining cities is that they have *too much* housing and infrastructure relative to the strength of their economies. With all that supply of structure and so little demand, it makes no sense to use public money to build more supply. The folly of building-centric urban renewal reminds us that cities aren't structures; cities are people.

After Hurricane Katrina, the building boosters wanted to spend hundreds of billions rebuilding New Orleans, but if $200 billion had been given to the people who lived there, each of them would have gotten $400,000 to pay for moving or education or better housing somewhere else. Even before the flood, New Orleans had done a mediocre job caring for its poor. Did it really make sense to spend billions on the city's infrastructure, when money was so badly needed to help educate the children of New Orleans? New Orleans' greatness always came from its people, not from its buildings. Wouldn't it have made more sense to ask how federal spending could have done the most for the lives of Katrina's victims, even if they moved somewhere else?

Ultimately, the job of urban government isn't to fund buildings or rail lines that can't possibly cover their costs, but to care for the city's citizens. A mayor who can better educate a city's children so that they can find opportunity on the other side of the globe is succeeding, even if his city is getting smaller.

While the unremitting poverty of Detroit and cities like it clearly reflects urban distress, not all urban poverty is bad. It's easy to understand why a visitor to a Kolkata slum might join Gandhi in wondering about the wisdom of massive urbanization, but there's a lot to like about urban poverty. Cities don't make people poor; they attract poor people. The flow of less advantaged people into cities from Rio to Rotterdam demonstrates urban strength, not weakness.

Urban structures may stand for centuries, but urban populations are fluid. More than a quarter of Manhattan's residents didn't live there five years ago. Poor people constantly come to New York and São Paulo and Mumbai in search of something better, a fact of urban life that should be celebrated.

Urban poverty should be judged not relative to urban wealth but relative to rural poverty. The shantytowns of Rio de Janeiro may look terrible when compared to a prosperous Chicago suburb, but poverty rates in Rio are far lower than in Brazil's rural northeast. The poor have no way to get rich quick, but they can choose between cities and the countryside, and many of them sensibly choose cities.

The flow of rich and poor into cities makes urban areas dynamic, but it's hard to miss the costs of concentrated poverty. Proximity makes it easier to exchange ideas or goods but also easier to exchange bacteria or purloin a purse. All of the world's older cities have suffered the great scourges of urban life: disease, crime, congestion. And the fight against these ills has never been won by passively accepting the way things are or by mindlessly relying on the free market. American cities became much healthier in the early twentieth century because they were spending as much on water as the federal government spent on everything except the military and the postal service. The leaps made by European and American cities will likely be repeated in the developing cities of the twenty-first century, and that will only make the world more urban. New York City, where boys born in 1901 were expected to live seven years fewer than their American male counterparts, is now considerably healthier than America as a whole.

The urban victories over crime and disease made it possible for cities to thrive as places of pleasure as well as productivity. Urban scale makes it possible to support the fixed costs of theaters, museums, and restaurants. Museums need large expensive exhibits and attractive, often expensive structures; theaters need stages, lighting, sound equipment, and plenty of practice. In cities, these fixed costs become affordable because they're shared among thousands of museum visitors and theatergoers.

Historically, most people were far too poor to let their tastes in entertainment guide where they chose to live, and cities were hardly pleasure zones. Yet as people have become richer, they have increasingly chosen cities based on lifestyle—and the consumer city was born.

During much of the twentieth century, the rise of consumer cities like Los Angeles seemed to be yet another force battering the Londons and New Yorks of the world. Yet as older cities have become safer and healthier, they, too, became reinvigorated as places of consumption, through restaurants, theaters, comedy clubs, bars, and the pleasures of proximity. Over the past thirty years, London and San Francisco and Paris have all boomed, in part, because people have increasingly found them fun places to live. These metropolises have their pricey treats, like Michelin Guide three-star meals, but they also have their more affordable enjoyments, like sipping a coffee while admiring the Golden Gate Bridge or the Arc de Triomphe, or downing a real ale in a wood-paneled pub. Cities enable us to find friends with common interests, and the disproportionately single populations in dense cities are marriage markets that make it easier to find a mate. Today successful cities, old or young, attract smart entrepreneurial people, in part, by being urban theme parks.

The rise of reverse commuting may be the most striking consequence of successful consumer cities. In the dark days of the 1970s, few were willing to live in Manhattan if they didn't work there. Today, thousands of people choose to live in the city and travel to jobs outside it. Middle Eastern millionaires aren't the only people buying pieds-à-terre in London and New York, and Miami has done well by selling second homes to the rich of Latin America.

Robust demand, created by economic vitality and urban pleasures, helps explain why prices in attractive cities have risen so steadily, but the supply of space also matters. New York, London, and Paris have increasingly restricted new building activity, which has made those cities harder to afford.

Many of the ideas in this book draw on the wisdom of the great urbanist Jane Jacobs, who knew that you need to walk a city's streets to see its soul. She understood that the people who make a city creative need affordable real estate. But she also made mistakes that came from relying too much on her ground-level view and not using conceptual tools that help one think through an entire system.

Because she saw that older, shorter buildings were cheaper, she incorrectly believed that restricting heights and preserving old neighborhoods would ensure affordability. That's not how supply and demand work. When the demand for a city rises, prices will rise unless more homes are built. When cities restrict new construction, they become more expensive.

Preservation isn't always wrong—there is much worth keeping in our cities—but it always comes at a cost. Think of the ordered beauty of Paris. Its tidy, charming boulevards are straight and wide, lined with elegant nineteenth-century buildings. We can relish the great monuments of Paris because they're not hidden by nearby buildings. A big reason for those sight lines is that any attempt to build in Paris must go through a byzantine process that puts preservation first. Restrictions on new construction have ensured that Paris—once famously hospitable to starving artists—is now affordable only to the wealthy.

Like Paris, London has a strong attachment to its nineteenth-century edifices. The Prince of Wales himself took a strong stand against tall, modernist buildings that might compromise a single sight line of St. Paul's Cathedral. And the British seem to have exported their antipathy to height to India, where limits on construction are less justified and more harmful.

Mumbai has had some of the most extreme land-use restrictions in the developing world; for much of Mumbai's recent history, new buildings in the central city had to average less than one-and-a-third stories. What insanity! This bustling hub of India enforces suburban density levels in its urban core. This self-destructive behavior practically ensures prices that are too high, apartments that are too small, and congestion, sprawl, slums, and corruption. Despite an economy that is even hotter than Mumbai's, Shanghai remains far more affordable because supply has kept pace with demand. Like other progrowth autocrats, from Nebuchadnezzar to Napoléon III, China's leaders like building.

At the start of the twentieth century, visionaries like Fritz Lang imagined a world of increasingly vertical cities with streets darkened by the shadows of immense towers. Brilliant architects, like William Van Alen, designed great skyscrapers like the Chrysler Building, and others, like Le Corbusier, planned a world built at staggering heights. But twentieth-century urban America didn't belong to the skyscraper; it belonged to the car.

Transportation technologies have always determined urban form. In walking cities, like central Florence or Jerusalem's old city, the streets are narrow, winding, and crammed with shops. When people had to use their legs to get around, they tried to get as close as possible to each other and to the waterways that provided the fastest way into or out of the city. Areas built around trains and elevators, like midtown Manhattan and the Chicago Loop, have wider streets often organized in a grid. There are still shops on the streets, but most of the office space is much further from the ground. Cities built around the car, like much of Los Angeles and Phoenix and Houston, have enormous, gently curving roads and often lack sidewalks. In those places, shops and pedestrians retreat from the streets into malls. While older cities usually have an obvious center, dictated by an erstwhile port or a rail station, car cities do not. They just stretch toward the horizon in undifferentiated urban sprawl.

Places like Atlanta and Houston remind us that there are places that lie between hyperdense Hong Kong and rural Saskatchewan. Living and working in car-oriented Silicon Valley offers plenty of proximity, at least to people in the computer industry. The threat that these places pose to traditional cities reflects the fact that they offer some of the old advantages of urban access along with plenty of land and the ability to drive everywhere.

While the rise of car-based living was bad for many older cities, it wasn't bad for everyone. Excoriating the exurbs is a popular intellectual pastime, but the people who moved to the suburbs weren't fools. The friends of cities would be wiser to learn from Sunbelt sprawl than to mindlessly denigrate its inhabitants.

Speed and space are the two big advantages of car-based living. The average commute by public transportation in the United States is forty-eight minutes; the average commute by car is twenty-four minutes. Cars enable mass-produced housing at moderate densities that give ordinary Americans a lifestyle that is extraordinarily opulent by world standards.

But acknowledging the upside of sprawl doesn't mean that sprawl is good or that American policies that encourage sprawl are wise. The environmental costs of sprawl should move government to put the brakes on car-based living, but American policies push people to the urban fringe. The spirit of Thomas Jefferson, who liked cities no more than Gandhi did, lives on in policies that subsidize home ownership and highways, implicitly encouraging Americans to abandon cities.

One problem with policies that subsidize sprawl is that car-based living imposes environmental costs on the entire planet. The patron saint of American environmentalism, Henry David Thoreau, was another antiurbanite. At Walden Pond, he became so "suddenly sensible of such sweet beneficent society in Nature" that "the fancied advantages of human neighborhood" became "insignificant." Lewis Mumford, the distinguished architectural critic and urban historian, praised the "parklike setting" of suburbs and denigrated the urban "deterioration of the environment."

Now we know that the suburban environmentalists had it backward. Manhattan and downtown London and Shanghai, not suburbia, are the real friends of the environment. Nature lovers who live surrounded by trees and grass consume much more energy than their urban counterparts, as I painfully discovered when, after thirty-seven years of almost entirely urban living, I recklessly experimented with suburban life.

If the environmental footprint of the average suburban home is a size 15 hiking boot, the environmental footprint of a New York apartment is a stiletto-heel size 6 Jimmy Choo. Traditional cities have fewer carbon emissions because they don't require vast amounts of driving. Fewer than a third of New Yorkers drive to work, while 86 percent of American commuters drive. Twenty-nine percent of all the public-transportation commuters in America live in New York's five boroughs. Gotham has, by a wide margin, the least gas usage per capita of all American metropolitan areas. Department of Energy data confirms that New York State's per capita energy consumption is next to last in the country, which largely reflects public transit use in New York City.

Few slogans are as silly as the environmental mantra "Think globally, act locally." Good environmentalism requires a worldwide perspective and global action, not the narrow outlook of a single neighborhood trying to keep out builders. We must recognize that if we try to make one neighborhood greener by stopping new building, we can easily make the world browner, by pushing new development to someplace far less environmentally friendly. The environmentalists of coastal California may have made their own region more pleasant, but they are harming the environment by pushing new building away from Berkeley suburbs, which have a temperate climate and ready access to public transportation, to suburban Las Vegas, which is all about cars and air-conditioning. The stakes are particularly high in the developing world, where urban patterns are far less set and where the number of people involved is much larger. Today, most Indians and Chinese are still too poor to live a car-oriented lifestyle. Carbon emissions from driving and home energy use in America's greenest metropolitan areas are still more than ten times the emissions in the average Chinese metropolitan area.

But as India and China get richer, their people will face a choice that could dramatically affect all our lives. Will they follow America and move toward car-based exurbs or stick with denser urban settings that are far more environmentally friendly? If per capita carbon emissions in both China and India rise to U.S. per capita levels, then global carbon emissions will increase by 139 percent. If their emissions stop at French levels, global emissions will rise by only 30 percent. Driving and urbanization patterns in these countries may well be the most important environmental issues of the twenty-first century.

Indeed, the most important reason for Europe and the United States to get their own "green" houses in order is that, without reform, it will be awfully hard to convince India and China to use less carbon. Good environmentalism means putting buildings in places where they will do the least ecological harm. This means that we must be more tolerant of tearing down the short buildings in cities in order to build tall ones, and more intolerant of the activists who oppose emissions-reducing urban growth. Governments should encourage people to live in modestly sized urban aeries instead of bribing home buyers into big suburban McMansions. If ideas are the currency of our age, then building the right homes for those ideas will determine our collective fate.

The strength that comes from human collaboration is the central truth behind civilization's success and the primary reason why cities exist. To understand our cities and what to do about them, we must hold on to those truths and dispatch harmful myths. We must discard the view that environmentalism means living around trees and that urbanites should always fight to preserve a city's physical past. We must stop idolizing home ownership, which favors suburban tract homes over high-rise apartments, and stop romanticizing rural villages. We should eschew the simplistic view that better long-distance communication will reduce our desire and need to be near one another. Above all, we must free ourselves from our tendency to see cities as their buildings, and remember that the real city is made of flesh, not concrete.

CHAPTER 1

What Do They Make in Bangalore?

A high fence of trees and shrubs surrounds the MindTree campus in Bangalore's aptly named office park, Global Village. Outside that leafy barrier, the streets churn with hawkers and auto rickshaws and the energy of messy urban life. Inside the wall, elegant buildings rise from manicured gardens, and peace reigns amid palm trees, glass, and cool gray stone. MindTree is one of Bangalore's many successful information technology companies, cofounded by Subroto Bagchi, who bounds around its campus in immaculate ivory sneakers and a polo shirt. Bagchi looks like a Silicon Valley mogul, speaks like a management guru, and seems equally at ease with investors from Singapore, software engineers from India's poorest regions, and even a socially awkward Harvard professor.

Bagchi's openness is reflected in the obstruction-free plan of his company's compound, which encourages employees to mingle. The entire staff gathers to eat the buffet lunch on the roof and take in the view over the sprawl of one of Asia's most productive cities. Smaller Bangalore start-ups locate in less pristine space, perhaps a cramped apartment in an older building in a crowded neighborhood. In these less formal settings, there's a computer here, a computer there, and sometimes a mattress in the corner for those who work late. But however different their office space, the shoestring start-up and the established IT enterprise share the same remarkable energy and the same focus on selling their products worldwide.

India's poor roads and weak electricity grid make life difficult for big manufacturing firms, which explains why the country seems to be leapfrogging straight from agriculture to information technology. Anyone who builds a large factory and employs unskilled workers must contend with India's powerful labor unions. The information technology business is less fettered by these constraints. There are few unions in IT, ideas don't need roads to move across continents, and every successful Internet firm can afford a backup generator.

There's still plenty of hunger in rural India today, but the software entrepreneur has joined the starving peasant and the caste-conscious Brahmin in the roster of Indian stereotypes. Ruban Phukan is one of Bangalore's Internet entrepreneurs whose path illustrates how Bangalore educates and empowers the young and talented. He grew up in Guwahati, in eastern India far from Bangalore, then went to Karnataka Regional Engineering College. In 2001, he became the fifteenth employee of Yahoo!'s Bangalore operation, where he studied rival Internet search engines. At Yahoo! he met a business partner, and Yahoo! stock options gave him enough cash to become an entrepreneur.

In 2005, he established www.bixee.com (meant to sound like big sea), an Indian job-search engine that aggregates information from different sites like monster.com. Phukan and his partner developed their software on a shoestring, then sold it to MIH Holdings, for a substantial sum (by Bangalore standards). One ranking agency claimed that Bixee had over a hundred thousand unique visitors each day in 2010. At MIH, Phukan worked to develop ibibo .com, initially a social-networking and video-sharing site that allows ordinary people to showcase their talent and Bollywood film producers to showcase their movies. He has since left MIH to develop new social media software.

In the nineteenth century, cities like Buenos Aires and Chicago were conduits across continents for beef and grain. Today, Bangalore is a conduit for ideas, an urban education hub where private firms train thousands of young Indians like Phukan. New technologies have made it easy to connect between Yahoo!'s Silicon Valley headquarters and a Bangalore subsidiary, but easy international connections haven't flattened India. Globalization has made some places, like Bangalore, far more important and successful than others. Phukan could never have become a software entrepreneur if he'd stayed in Guwahati.

Ports of Intellectual Entry: Athens

More than 2,500 years before Ruban Phukan started working for Yahoo! in Bangalore, cities were gateways between cultures. Ports on the Pearl River, cities on the Silk Road, and other ancient imperial entrepôts all encouraged world travelers to meet and exchange ideas. The great dance of civilizations, in which knowledge moved from East to West and back again, has unfolded largely in cities. Bangalore is simply the latest venue for that age-old dance.

In the sixth century B.C., Athens was hardly the intellectual center of the world. The most exciting Greek thinkers lived on the edges of the Greek diaspora in Asia Minor, where they learned from the older civilizations of the Near East. Miletus, a wool-making port in western Turkey, produced the first philosopher, Thales, and the father of European urban planning, Hippodamus, whose gridlike plans provided a model for the Romans and countless cities since then.

Athens grew by trading wine, olive oil, spices, and papyrus. The city cemented its power by leading the Greek resistance to the Persian invasions that had already ravaged places like Miletus. Just as rich, ebullient post–World War II New York attracted writers and painters from battle-scarred Europe, fifth-century-B.C. Athens pulled in the best minds of battle-scarred Asia Minor. Hippodamus came from Miletus to plan the city's harbor. Others came to tutor wealthy Athenians. This first generation of Athenian scholars then influenced their friends and students, like Pericles and Socrates. Socrates generated his own innovations and taught Plato, who taught Aristotle.

This remarkable period saw the birth not only of Western philosophy but also of drama and history, as artists and scholars from all over the Mediterranean world converged in a single spot that gave them the proximity and the freedom to share their ideas. Athens flowered because of small random events that then multiplied through urban interaction. One smart person met another and sparked a new idea. That idea inspired someone else, and all of a sudden something really important had occurred. The ultimate cause of Athenian success may seem mysterious, but the process is clear. Ideas move from person to person within dense urban spaces, and this exchange occasionally creates miracles of human creativity.

The Greeks' knowledge was preserved and enhanced for almost a millennium in the hubs of the classical world, like Alexandria, Rome, and Milan, as well as the cities of Persia and northern India, where Alexander the Great's successors established Hellenistic states. The Roman cities of Western Europe—London, Marseilles, Trier, Tarragona—were marvels of the age that brought civilization to once savage places. Roman engineering made cities possible by delivering that great urban necessity, clean water.

But while the Roman Empire had a good long run—far longer than the British Empire or, so far, the American republic—it did decline and ultimately fell to a wave of external invaders. In the fifth century, it still seemed possible that the barbarians who conquered Rome would leave its urban areas intact. Many of them, like Theodoric, saw the advantage of cities like Ravenna. But while the Goths and Huns and Vandals and Burgundians were strong enough to smash the Roman Empire, they were not strong enough to maintain and protect its roads and infrastructure, and cities starve without well-functioning transport networks to deliver food and water.

The urban world of the Roman Empire, which had produced so much culture and technology, was replaced by rural stagnation. As cities disappeared, knowledge itself moved backward. The Roman cities prized skills, while the world of rural warriors and peasants rewarded a strong arm more than a trained mind. At the peak of Rome's power, Europe was on the world's technological frontier, a worthy competitor with the advanced societies of China and India. No such claims of European eminence could be made in the centuries after Rome fell. In the eighth century, Charlemagne, the master of Europe, connected with Hārūn ar-Rashīd, the caliph of the Islamic world. The Frank was a semi-literate warlord, while his Arab counterpart was the urbane overlord of a sophisticated civilization. In the great metropolises of Asia, urban proximity was pushing humanity forward while rural Europe stood still.

A thousand years ago, Europe had only four cities with more than fifty thousand people, one of which was the last vestige of Roman power, Constantinople. The other three—Seville, Palermo, and Córdoba—were all Islamic. The Islamic caliphates, which stretched from Persia to Portugal, created a new trading network that exchanged both goods and ideas over vast distances, and great cities emerged under the protection of powerful emirs and caliphs.

Under their aegis, a renaissance began 1,200 years ago, not in Italy but in Arab cities. In these places, Greek and Indian and even Chinese knowledge passed to Islamic scholars. Eventually, these places would pass their knowledge back to the West.

Baghdad's House of Wisdom

In fifth-century-B.C. Athens and twentieth-century New York, independent thinkers created innovations by competing and collaborating in a free market of ideas. But in the Islamic world, rulers created intellectual connection by imperial fiat. The Abbasid caliphs established their capital in Baghdad, about fifty miles north of ancient Babylon, and they wanted to adorn the new city with physical and human marvels. They collected scholars as if they were valuable baubles and eventually massed those minds in the House of Wisdom, a sort of research institution whose first job was to import the world's knowledge and translate it into Arabic. The scholars there translated, among many other works, Hippocrates' *Aphorisms,* Plato's *Republic,* Aristotle's *Physics,* the Old Testament, and the Sindhind, a compendium of Indian mathematical knowledge. At the start of the ninth century, Muhammad al-Khwārizmī drew from the Sindhind to develop algebra, which he essentially named. Al-Khwārizmī also brought Indian numerals into the Arab world. The philosopher Yaqūb al-Kindī wrote one of the first treatises on environmentalism, and made Greek philosophy compatible with Islamic theology. Medical knowledge came to Baghdad from the Persians; paper-making was brought there by Chinese prisoners of war. Over a golden six decades, a chain of brilliance made Baghdad the intellectual center of the Middle East and perhaps the world.

In the medieval era, Eastern understanding trickled westward through Europe's cities. Venice, Italy's great eastern port, served as the gateway for ideas, as well as spices, throughout the Middle Ages. When the Spanish retook Toledo in 1085, its library became accessible to Christian scholars, who translated its classics into Latin. Thirteen years later, crusaders captured Antioch and gave European translators access to its stock of Arabic medical and science texts. In the Islamic cities of Spain, the largest urban areas in Western Europe, ancient texts were rediscovered, retranslated, and transferred to Christendom.

Those texts came to the new universities of Padua and Paris, where a growing body of Europeans, such as Albertus Magnus and his student Thomas Aquinas, built on Greek and Islamic philosophy.

Europe slowly became safer and more prosperous, and its cities gradually grew once again. The minds of the medieval world connected with each other as Europe urbanized anew, and the continent's rate of innovation increased. In monasteries, Benedictine monks rediscovered the advantages of intellectual proximity. They recovered classic texts and experimented with agricultural innovations, like the waterwheel. Merchants congregated in trade fairs, which had some of the advantages of urban agglomeration without the fixed and vulnerable infrastructure. Eventually urban powerhouses like Bruges and Florence emerged, growing as centers of skill and commerce, protected by forces of armed artisans or mercenaries.

Many factors help explain the rise of the West—the development of military prowess and technology through constant warfare, the painful acquisition of immunity to infectious disease through centuries of exposure, the consolidation of powerful nation-states—but the growing commercial cities of Italy, England, and the Low Countries did more than their share. The growth of cities run by merchants was considerably greater than the growth of cities led by princes and monarchs. These dense places were havens for innovation and were the nodes of a global trading network that brought in the knowledge of the East. The commercial cities developed the legal rules regarding private property and commerce that still guide us today; the Great Revolt that started in the trading and wool-making towns of the Low Countries established in Holland the first modern republic. Commercial cities and trading companies were directly responsible for many of the military victories—from the fall of Constantinople in 1204 to the Battle of Plassey 553 years later—that established Western Europe's hegemony over the rest of the world.

Westerners ultimately surpassed Asians in the development of originally Chinese ideas like printing and gunpowder. By the eighteenth century, Western technology and thought had come to dominate the world. Gradually, European learning started moving back east, and cities were, once again, the points through which knowledge passed.

Learning in Nagasaki

By the middle of the nineteenth century, European military might had proven its technological superiority over most of Asia, but one nation, Japan, remained almost completely independent of European control. When American ships showed up in 1853, Japan agreed to open itself to trade with outsiders, but still more or less on its own terms, and within forty years, Japan had thoroughly mastered Western ways and become a formidable power on the world stage. Between 1894 and 1910, the Japanese beat up the Chinese, just like a European colonial power, defeated Russia, and conquered Korea. By the middle of the twentieth century, the Japanese were building ships and airplanes as good as, and sometimes better than, their American counterparts. How could the Japanese catch up to the West so fast?

One answer to this question lies in a city: Nagasaki. The first contacts between Japan and the West took place there in 1543, when Portuguese ships landed on the nearby island of Tanegashima. Over the next three hundred years, Nagasaki would be the conduit for all Western technology coming into Japan. The xenophobic Japanese policy of concentrating foreigners in one spot made it easy for Japanese to seek out Western learning. In 1590, Portuguese Jesuits set up East Asia's first metal printing press in Nagasaki. Forty-six years later, the Jesuits were kicked out for their political meddling and religious proselytizing and were replaced by the Dutch East India Company, which would never let such matters get in the way of a profitable trading opportunity.

But the Dutch would soon give their hosts more than mere commerce. Western medicine entered Japan in the 1640s, as high officials and even the shogun himself sought care from the East India Company's resident physician. Soon Japanese students were being trained and certified in Nagasaki, bringing European medical techniques to Japan. By the start of the nineteenth century, a Japanese doctor would perform the world's first surgery under general anesthesia. The operation, a mastectomy, followed European procedures except that the doctor used a mixture of Eastern herbs to produce unconsciousness. By combining Eastern and Western knowledge, the Japanese had pulled ahead in medicine, and it would take forty years for Europeans to catch up.

In addition to Western medicine, the Dutch brought the Japanese telescopes, barometers, camera obscuras, magic lanterns, and even sunglasses through Nagasaki. In 1720, an inquisitive shogun started allowing Western books in Japan; his interest in the West also led to "the gradual emergence of Edo [now Tokyo] as a new focus of Dutch Studies." When the American gunboats showed up in 1853, the Japanese could quickly catch up to their new adversaries because they had many engineers trained in the "Dutch Studies." In 1855, the Dutch gave the Japanese their first steamship, which would reside at the new Nagasaki Naval Training Station. As the Japanese started aggressively copying European military techniques, Nagasaki continued to be the port of entry for knowledge as well as goods. That military and technological know-how enabled Japan, within a hundred years, to conquer much of Asia and surprise the American Navy at Pearl Harbor.

How Bangalore Became a Boom Town

From classical Athens to eighth-century Baghdad to Nagasaki, cities have always been the most effective way to transfer knowledge between civilizations. This isn't mere happenstance. Urban proximity enables cross-cultural connection by reducing the curse of communicating complexity, the fact that the possibility of a garbled message increases with the amount of information that is being transferred. It's easy to get across a simple yes or no but much harder to teach someone astrophysics—or economic theory, for that matter.

Cross-cultural communications are always complicated; things are always lost in translation. New ideas from different continents can be so unlike our current knowledge that we need to make huge intellectual leaps, which invariably means that we need plenty of coaching. We may understand the context of ideas in our society, but we are often adrift when confronted with thoughts that came from a totally different society, like the translators of the Sindhind, who didn't understand the Euclidean math that lay behind it.

Cities, and the face-to-face interactions that they engender, are tools for reducing the complex-communication curse. Long hours spent one-on-one enable listeners to make sure that they get it right. It's easy to mistakenly offend someone from a different culture, but a warm smile can smooth conflicts that could otherwise turn into flaming e-mails. Cities like Nagasaki, Baghdad, or Bangalore, which specialize in international connection, develop communications experts who become adept at importing information. Such cities are convenient spots for foreigners to sample a host society's science, art, and commerce, and vice versa.

The success of places like Bangalore is not only about international intellectual connections. These cities create a virtuous cycle in which employers are attracted by the large pool of potential employees and workers are drawn by the abundance of potential employers. So firms come to Bangalore for the engineers, and engineers come for the firms. Urban scale also makes it easier for workers to move from job to job. In highly entrepreneurial industries, workers get ahead by hopping from firm to firm. Young people become more productive and better paid as they switch employers and acquire new skills. An abundance of local employers also provides implicit insurance against the failure of any particular start-up. In Bangalore, there'll always be another software company. Moreover, dense concentrations of entrepreneurial talent encourage the growth of related industries, like the venture capitalists who work near Silicon Valley.

The forces that compel concentration in a single city are clear, but it isn't obvious why any particular city should emerge as a hub of information transfer. Why did Bangalore, out of all Indian cities, achieve this status? Bangalore does have a relatively benign climate—drier than Mumbai and much less oppressive than Delhi. But skills, not geography, are the source of Bangalore's strength. An initial kernel of engineering expertise attracted companies like Infosys, and a virtuous circle was born, wherein smart firms and smart workers flock to Bangalore to be near each other.

Few have gotten more out of Bangalorean proximity than the city's three Infosys billionaires. Infosys was founded in 1981 and moved to Bangalore in 1983. In the summer of 2008, the company had close to a hundred thousand employees, and its market capitalization exceeded $30 billion. Today Infosys is a flat-world phenomenon, with vast operations in software, banking services, and consulting. In essence, Infosys is selling intelligence—whether provided by humans or machines—at lightning speed around the world, and it takes its employees' skills seriously, educating thousands of people each year in its training center in Mysore. Fewer than 2 percent of Infosys's job applicants get a place in that training center, making it far more competitive than any Ivy League school.

Narayana Murthy, one of the Infosys founders, received engineering degrees from the University of Mysore and the Indian Institute of Technology at Kanpur. But Murthy may have picked up his most valuable skills in the 1970s at Patni Computers. Patni was a bridge company, an early connector between the United States and India, whose Indian founders had lived in America. They saw the opportunities for Indian software and set up a back office in Pune. Murthy worked there with the six other founders of Infosys, where they learned how to link Indian talent with American markets.

In 1981, they left Patni to found their own company selling software to foreign clients. Murthy borrowed $250 from his wife to cover expenses. In 1982, they acquired their first American client, a software company. In 1983, they moved to Bangalore to provide software for a German spark plug producer that had located there back in 1954 and wanted Infosys close by so that information could flow readily between the two companies. Infosys was also attracted to Bangalore because it was near top-notch engineering schools.

Over the past twenty-five years, Infosys has opened offices in the United States, Canada, Latin America, and Europe, but it remains rooted in Bangalore. The rise of Infosys may seem to suggest that distance is dead, but it can just as easily be interpreted as evidence that proximity matters as much as ever. By concentrating so much talent in one place, Bangalore makes it easier for outsiders, whether from St. Louis or Shanghai, to do business with Indian entrepreneurs. Bangalore may be luckier than any other Indian city, but only because it made its luck. Its current abundance of engineers reflects decisions made long ago by its leaders, the maharajas of Mysore and their ministers. Mysore had a long tradition of embracing new technologies. In the eighteenth century, its sultan dealt the British a fearsome defeat with the help of imported cannons, manned by imported sailors. Throughout the Raj, Mysore stood out among the princely states for its competence, but the savviest of its leaders was Sir Mokshagundam Visvesvaraya, or Sir MV, the state's prime minister during the early twentieth century.

Sir MV was born about thirty-five miles from Bangalore and came to the city for high school. After an illustrious career as a civil engineer, he returned to Bangalore and in 1908 became the prime minister of Mysore. Along with the maharaja, who was both fabulously wealthy and remarkably progressive, Sir MV pushed through a sweeping modernization program, including dams, hydroelectricity, steel mills, and, most important, schools. Sir MV's motto was

"Industrialize or perish," but instead of just pushing big construction projects, he emphasized the education needed to build projects efficiently. Infrastructure eventually becomes obsolete, but education perpetuates itself as one smart generation teaches the next.

In the United States and Europe, industrialization rarely encouraged education. Much of factories' appeal for owners and workers alike was that they gave jobs to unskilled labor, not skilled artisans. But for Sir MV, industrialization meant training the engineers who could import technology from the West, just as he had done. He founded both the University of Mysore and Bangalore's engineering college, which now bears his name. Those schools first generated a cluster of engineers that persists to this day.

By the middle of the twentieth century, Mysore was fully industrialized. Its probusiness government brought Hindustan Aeronautics Limited, Hindustan Machine Tools, Bharat Heavy Electricals, and Indian Telephone Industries to Bangalore. It also attracted the German spark plug producer that would later bring Infosys there. Those early companies were important not because Bangalore's future lay with heavy industry (it did not), but because they nurtured that cluster of engineers. Starting in 1976, Bangalore also paved (sometimes literally) the path to IT dominance by launching an extensive program to improve roads, electricity, and other utilities that would attract international IT firms.

Education and Urban Success

Human capital, far more than physical infrastructure, explains which cities succeed. Typically, in the United States, the share of the population with a college degree is used to estimate the skill level of a place. Admittedly, this yardstick is imperfect at the individual level. Using a college degree as a measure would classify Bill Gates, surely among the world's most skilled people, as unskilled. But despite its coarseness, no other measure does better in explaining recent urban prosperity. A 10 percent increase in the percentage of an area's adult population with a BA in 1980 predicts 6 percent more income growth between 1980 and 2000. As the share of the population with college degrees increases by 10 percent, per capita gross metropolitan product rises by 22 percent.

People have flocked to skilled areas because of higher incomes, and education in 1970 does an impressive job of explaining which of America's older, colder cities have managed to successfully reinvent themselves. Between 1970 and 2000, the population of counties where more than 10 percent of the adult population had college degrees grew by 72 percent while the population of those areas where fewer than 5 percent of people had college degrees grew by 37 percent.

We live in an age of expertise, when earnings and knowledge are closely linked. For each worker, an extra year of schooling typically leads to about 8 percent higher earnings. On average, an extra year of schooling for a country's entire population is associated with a more than 30 percent increase in per capita gross domestic product. The striking correlation between education and a country's GDP may reflect what economists call human capital externalities, a term for the idea that people become more productive when they work around other skilled people. When a country gets more educated, people experience both the direct effect of their own extra learning plus the benefits that come from everyone around them being more skilled.

The connection between urban skills and urban productivity has grown steadily stronger throughout the developed world since the 1970s. In those days, less-skilled places that were filled with highly paid, unionized factory workers often earned more than more-skilled areas. In 1970, per capita incomes were higher in industrial areas like Cleveland and Detroit than in better-educated metropolitan areas like Boston and Minneapolis. Over the past thirty years, however, the less-skilled manufacturing cities have faltered while the more-skilled idea-producing cities have thrived. In 1980, men with four years of college earned about 33 percent more than high school graduates, but by the mid-1990s, that earnings gap had increased to nearly 70 percent. Over the past thirty years, American society has become more unequal, partly because the marketplace increasingly rewards people with more skills.

While no one disputes the robust increase in the value of skills, there are competing theories about why they've become more valuable. One school of thought emphasizes technological change. Some new technologies, like computers, have increased the returns for being better educated. Other new technologies, like robots in car factories, have decreased the need for unskilled labor. Not just the technologies themselves, but the rate of technological change also favors the skilled. Many studies have shown that skilled people are better at adapting to new circumstances, like the introduction of hybrid corn and computers. Like skilled people, skilled cities also seem to be better at reinventing themselves during volatile times.

A second school of thought emphasizes international trade and globalization. According to this view, declining transportation costs made it possible to outsource less-skilled labor. Detroit's carmakers once had a near-monopoly on American auto purchases, but today those companies face intense competition from Japan, Europe, and Korea, and this makes it much harder to sustain high wages for less-skilled workers.

Of course, more skilled jobs are being outsourced as well. That's one reason for Bangalore's success. Yet so far at least, skilled Americans and Europeans seem to have gotten more from the ability to work the world market than they've lost from foreign competition. The most-skilled people in the rich countries have thrived by selling their ideas to the world and by using worldwide labor to produce their inventions more cheaply. The software producers in Bangalore haven't made Silicon Valley obsolete. Instead, they've made it cheaper—and thus easier—for Silicon Valley firms to develop software.

The Rise of Silicon Valley

America's greatest information technology hub is Santa Clara County, California, which most people know better as Silicon Valley. Much like Bangalore, the Valley achieved this status by making its luck with education. A century ago, when New York and Nagasaki were old, computers didn't exist, and Santa Clara County was covered in orchards and farms. This agricultural community became a world capital of high technology because Senator Leland Stanford, a railroad magnate, decided to build a university on his eight-thousand-acre horse farm.

Founding universities was, like breeding horses, a way for nineteenth-century millionaires to spend their surplus money. My University of Chicago diploma displays, in appropriately gilt letters, the name of the school's Gilded Age founder, John D. Rockefeller. But while Rockefeller envisioned a Baptist college and hired a classicist as president, Leland Stanford opened Stanford declaring that "life is, above all, practical; that you are here to fit yourselves for a useful career." He wanted leaders who were committed to the real world, to developing the American West, and to spreading useful knowledge.

Stanford University's first major high-tech start-up had its roots in the unschooled genius of Francis McCarty, the son of Senator Stanford's head coachman. McCarty left school at twelve to work as an apprentice electrician. In 1904, at the age of sixteen, he had crafted a "spark telephone" that could send a voice seven miles over water. McCarty wasn't the first to send words by wireless, but he was close, and his brilliance brought financial backing. Tragically, in 1906, McCarty died in a traffic accident, smashing his head against a telephone pole. He wasn't even eighteen.

But his backers hadn't lost their appetite for radio, and they asked a Stanford engineering professor to recommend a suitable replacement for McCarty. He pointed them to Cyril Elwell, a bright Stanford student who had written his dissertation on electric smelting. Elwell proved an inspired choice. He worked for a year on McCarty's design and concluded that it couldn't provide reliable wireless service. But instead of giving up, Elwell opted for an even newer technology: Valdemar Poulsen's arc transmitter. Elwell sailed to Copenhagen and came back to Palo Alto with a Poulsen transmitter. With financial backing from the president of Stanford, Elwell then set up the Poulsen Wireless Telephone and Telegraph company, soon renamed the Federal Telegraph Corporation.

FTC was the pioneer firm of Silicon Valley's radio industry, attracting talent and producing spin-offs. Lee De Forest, the inventor of the audion transmitter, came to FTC in 1910 when his own company went bankrupt. There he developed the first vacuum tube, a critical part of radio technology until 1947, when another product of Palo Alto, William B. Shockley, led the group that invented its replacement, the transistor. Even after De Forest left, FTC thrived with navy contracts and access to Stanford's talented students. Stanford's first PhD in electrical engineering was awarded on the basis of work done at FTC.

Like later Silicon Valley firms, FTC produced distinguished progeny. Two Danes who had come to Palo Alto to help with Poulsen's arc transmitter left to form Magnavox. Another FTC employee invented the first metal detector and started Fisher Research Laboratories. Litton Industries, which grew large by producing vacuum tubes for the military during World War II, was yet another FTC offspring.

But no FTC employee did more to make Silicon Valley what it is today than Frederick Terman, who connected with the company as a kid and worked there during his college summers. His father was a Stanford professor who specialized in gifted children like his own son. The elder Terman became famous for developing the Stanford-Binet IQ test. The younger Terman went to Palo Alto High and Stanford, then headed east to get his doctorate in electrical engineering at MIT in 1924. He became a Stanford institution, serving for forty years as professor, dean of engineering, and provost, but his greatest gift was turning Palo Alto into the center of the computer industry.

One advantage enjoyed by a university surrounded by orchards is an abundance of available land, and Terman got the idea to start an industrial park right next to Stanford. His vision, which would inspire technology-intensive clusters in Bangalore and throughout the world, was to create an area packed with technology businesses. His students David Packard and William Hewlett were two early tenants in Terman's industrial park, but he couldn't achieve critical mass relying solely on his own protégés. He sought tenants like Lockheed, General Electric, and Westinghouse. Most important, he convinced the new Shockley Semiconductor Laboratory to come to the valley.

William Shockley was already a legend in the mid-1950s. Like Terman, his father had taught at Stanford. The young Shockley actually did poorly on an IQ test given by Terman's father, which says something about the fallibility of IQ tests. Shockley was educated at MIT and then worked at Bell Labs in New Jersey. After earning a medal for his wartime work using technology to fight U-boats, Shockley was put in charge of Bell Labs' new solid-state physics research group. This group collectively invented the transistor, and in 1956, Shockley and two of his co-workers shared the Nobel Prize in Physics.

By that time, Shockley had left Bell Labs and headed out to California, where his enormous abilities—and a fatal flaw—would both assert themselves and both contribute to the success of Silicon Valley. Like Pericles and the Abbasid caliphs, he had a rare talent for attracting geniuses. In his first years, he searched America's campuses and brought great young minds eager to come to Silicon Valley and work with the Nobel laureate. But Shockley was a capricious and dictatorial manager who couldn't keep the talent that he had attracted. In one notorious incident, he made his workers take lie detector tests in order to establish who was responsible for a secretary's cutting her hand on a pin. By attracting and then repelling genius, Shockley both brought talented people to Silicon Valley and ensured that they would be starting their own firms instead of just working for him.

At one point, eight of his best young scientists collectively quit. A camera-making magnate named Sherman Fairchild bankrolled them, and Fairchild Semiconductor was born. The firm stayed in Silicon Valley. Why would the "traitorous eight" want to leave a paradise packed with Terman-trained engineers? In 1959, Fairchild Semiconductor patented the first integrated circuit. Eventually, the talent also tired of Fairchild's management. Two of them left Fairchild in 1968 to form Intel. Another left to form the venture capital giant Kleiner Perkins, which would bankroll many of the Valley's next wave of innovators.

The Fairchildren gave the Valley a new set of entrepreneurs, and others soon joined them. Many of the companies formed near Stanford focused on hardware, including Intel, Cisco, and Sun Microsystems. Two former Hewlett-Packard employees, both members of Silicon Valley's Homebrew Computer Club, mixed hardware and software innovations when they started Apple Computer. A former Apple employee started eBay in the 1990s, when Silicon Valley also became the place for pioneering the Internet. Both Yahoo! and Google were formed by Stanford graduates not far from their alma mater.

In some ways, Silicon Valley is like a well-functioning traditional city. It attracts brilliant people and then connects them. Walker's Wagon Wheel played a legendary role as a place where smart entrepreneurs shared ideas with one another outside the confines of their various day jobs. Silicon Valley's concentration is also a response to the curse of communicating complexity; all that cutting-edge technology can be pretty complicated, and geographic proximity helps the flow of information. Like all of today's successful cities, its strength lies in its human capital, which is nurtured by Stanford University and attracted by economic opportunity and a pleasant climate.

Yet in some ways Silicon Valley looks completely different from any older city. It is built almost entirely around the car. While there are some areas, particularly in downtown Palo Alto, where you can walk a few pleasant blocks to get an ice cream or buy a book, feet are generally useless for getting from one company to another. A few companies, like Google, run their own bus services, but public transportation is minimal. Only 3.7 percent of the people living in Santa Clara County take mass transit to work. Car-based living goes together with low density levels. There are only about 2.14 people per acre living in Santa Clara County. There is a lot of action in the Valley, but you have to drive a ways to find it.

Santa Clara County's economy makes little room for poorer, less skilled people. Even after the housing bust, the median housing price in the San Jose metropolitan areas remains over $550,000, making it very hard for someone who isn't a successful computer person to buy a home. Some of the most attractive areas in the Valley have completely priced out less skilled people and the businesses that employ them. Only 22.2 percent of Palo Alto's residents over the age of twenty-five lack a college degree.

The Valley's other major drawback is that it's a one-industry town; over half the county's payroll in its export-related sectors, such as manufacturing, information, and even wholesaling, appears to come from computer-related firms. Traditionally, single-industry cities, like Detroit and Manchester, haven't done well in the long run because their industrial monocultures discourage the growth of new ideas and companies. Jane Jacobs explained this phenomenon by pointing out that new ideas are formed by combining old ideas. Even in information technology, some of the most successful entrepreneurs of the last thirty years have been hybrids, merging ideas from multiple industries. Michael Bloomberg created his enormously successful IT company by knowing exactly what Wall Street traders wanted to know and how technology could help them. Facebook started on a college campus, and its founders knew what kind of information undergraduates wanted to share. Proximity to customers or related industries provides valuable information that can be a wellspring of innovation.

When eBay wanted to expand its customer base, it had to reach outside Silicon Valley in order to find a CEO, Meg Whitman, who had amassed experience selling to the American public at Procter & Gamble, Stride Rite, Walt Disney, and Hasbro. Can the Valley's software experts continue to offset their isolation from the rest of American industry by occasionally importing smart, experienced outsiders? The Valley was a great place to develop faster and faster semiconductors, but it might not be the best place to connect technology with other businesses.

But perhaps those connections aren't necessary. The Internet revolution was about making technology accessible for ordinary Americans, who can search the Web with Google, use e-mail, or buy and sell on eBay. Software engineers are people, too, and they can look to their families and friends—as the Facebook founders did—to understand the needs and desires of ordinary mortals.

In the long run, Silicon Valley will likely be hurt by concentrating too much on a single industry and by allowing too much space between its innovators. But despite the poor track record of single-industry cities, like Detroit, there are good reasons to be more optimistic about the Valley. Unlike Detroit, Silicon Valley is not concentrated in a few big firms, and that helps keep the area entrepreneurial. It has superb educational institutions and continues to invest in its schools and universities. It has arguably the best climate in the United States, and that will continue to attract rich, smart people, who are willing to pay some of the country's highest housing prices to live in that climate surrounded by many of the world's most innovative companies.

The Cities of Tomorrow

Silicon Valley and Bangalore remind us that electronic interactions won't make face-to-face contact obsolete. The computer industry, more than any other sector, is the place where one might expect remote communication to replace person-to-person meetings; computer companies have the best tele-conferencing tools, the best Internet applications, the best means of connecting far-flung collaborators. Yet despite their ability to work at long distances, this industry has become the world's most famous example of the benefits of geographic concentration. Technology innovators who could easily connect electronically pay for some of America's most expensive real estate to reap the benefits of being able to meet in person.

A wealth of research confirms the importance of face-to-face contact. One experiment performed by two researchers at the University of Michigan challenged groups of six students to play a game in which everyone could earn money by cooperating. One set of groups met for ten minutes face-to-face to discuss strategy before playing. Another set of groups had thirty minutes for electronic interaction. The groups that met in person cooperated well and earned more money. The groups that had only connected electronically fell apart, as members put their personal gains ahead of the group's needs. This finding resonates well with many other experiments, which have shown that face-to-face contact leads to more trust, generosity, and cooperation than any other sort of interaction.

The very first experiment in social psychology was conducted by a University of Indiana psychologist who was also an avid bicyclist. He noted that "racing men" believe that "the value of a pace," or competitor, shaves twenty to thirty seconds off the time of a mile. To rigorously test the value of human proximity, he got forty children to compete at spinning fishing reels to pull a cable. In all cases, the kids were supposed to go as fast as they could, but most of them, especially the slower ones, were much quicker when they were paired with another child. Modern statistical evidence finds that young professionals today work longer hours if they live in a metropolitan area with plenty of competitors in their own occupational niche.

Supermarket checkouts provide a particularly striking example of the power of proximity. As anyone who has been to a grocery store knows, checkout clerks differ wildly in their speed and competence. In one major chain, clerks with differing abilities are more or less randomly shuffled across shifts, which enabled two economists to look at the impact of productive peers. It turns out that the productivity of average clerks rises substantially when there is a star clerk working on their shift, and those same average clerks get worse when their shift is filled with below-average clerks.

Statistical evidence also suggests that electronic interactions and face-to-face interactions support one another; in the language of economics, they're complements rather than substitutes. Telephone calls are disproportionately made among people who are geographically close, presumably because face-to-face relationships *increase* the demand for talking over the phone. And when countries become more urban, they engage in *more* electronic communications.

Certainly some people still work alone, handling customer complaints or airline reservations, perhaps, over the phone in some spot far from any city. However, most of those jobs require less skill and accordingly pay less. In the average U.S. county with less than one person per acre, 15.8 percent of adults have college degrees. In the average county with more than two people per acre, 30.6 percent of adults have college degrees. The Internet and long-distance calling make it possible to perform basic tasks at home, but working alone makes it hard to actually accumulate the most valuable forms of human capital.

Innovations cluster in places like Silicon Valley because ideas cross corridors and streets more easily than continents and seas. Patent citations demonstrate the intellectual advantage of proximity. In 1993, three economists found that patents had a remarkable tendency to cite other patents that were geographically close. More than one fifth of all corporate patent citations were to older patents in the same metropolitan area, and more than one quarter of these citations were to patents in the same state. Correcting for the tendency of people to cite patents from the same firm, the propensity to cite patents from the same metropolitan area is about twice as likely as it should have been if citations were determined by luck. The geographic pattern becomes looser as patents age, because ideas do eventually spread across space, but even in our age of information technology, ideas are often geographically localized. More recent research continues to find that patent citations are geographically close to one another. Recent research also finds that productivity is significantly higher for firms that locate near the geographic center of inventive activity in their industry. Just as proximity speeds the flow of the most important inventions, it also enables the more mundane learning that turns neophytes into experts. More than a century ago, the great English economist Alfred Marshall described how in dense concentrations "the mysteries of the trade become no mystery but are, as it were, in the air." Hanging around successful older engineers helps make younger engineers more successful themselves.

Data backs up Marshall's claim. Workers in big cities earn about 30 percent more than their nonurban equivalents, but people who come to urban areas don't experience higher wage gains overnight. Year-by-year, workers in cities have higher wage growth, as they accumulate the skills that make them successful. Wage growth is particularly faster in cities with more skilled workers. Two decades of extra job-market experience is associated with 10 percent more wage growth in skilled metropolitan areas than in nonmetropolitan America, but only 3 percent more wage growth in less skilled metropolitan areas.

For over a century, pundits have been predicting that new forms of communication would make urban life irrelevant. One hundred years ago, the telephone was supposed to make cities unnecessary. That didn't happen. More recently, faxes, e-mail, and videoconferencing were all supposed to eliminate the need for face-to-face meetings, yet business travel has soared over the last twenty years. To defeat the human need for face-to-face contact, our technological marvels would need to defeat millions of years of human evolution that has made us into machines for learning from the people next to us.

Better audio and higher-definition screens have enabled videoconferences to seem more like real live encounters, but will technology ever be able to simulate the full range of sensory inputs—eye contact, olfactory cues, the warmth of a handshake—that help make live meetings work? Furthermore, much of the value of a dense work environment comes from unplanned meetings and observing the random doings of the people around you. Fancy videoconferences will never give a young assistant the ability to learn by watching the day-to-day operations of a successful mentor. Facebook is another Internet technology that makes face-to-face interactions more valuable and effective. Studies find that Facebook typically connects people who have met in person at a party or in the same class, and that Facebook is disproportionately used by people who are good at real-life conversation. Moreover, the initial idea for an Internet social network seems to have come out of a series of murky meetings between members of a real live network of smart, ambitious Harvard students.

Today, information technology is changing the world, making it more idea-intensive, better connected, and ultimately more urban. Improvements in information technology seem to have increased, rather than reduced, the value of face-to-face connections, which might be called Jevons's Complementarity Corollary. The nineteenth-century English economist William Stanley Jevons noted that more fuel-efficient steam engines didn't lead to less coal consumption. Better engines made energy use effectively less expensive, and helped move the world to an industrial era powered by coal. The term Jevons's paradox has come to refer to any situation in which efficiency improvements lead to more, not less, consumption—one reason why low-calorie cookies can lead to larger waistlines and fuel-efficient cars can end up consuming more gas. Jevons's paradox applied to information technology means that as we acquire more efficient means of transmitting information, like e-mail or Skype, we spend more, not less, time transmitting information.

One might think that better information technology would reduce the need to learn from other sources, like face-to-face meetings in cities. But

Jevons's Complementarity Corollary, which follows naturally from Jevons's paradox, predicts that improvements in information technology can lead to more demand for face-to-face contact, because face time complements time spent communicating electronically. All those electronic interactions are creating a more relationship-intensive world, just as improvements in steam engines led to a more coal-intensive economy, and those relationships need both e-mail and interpersonal contact. Better connections between people create far-ranging opportunities for trade and commerce. Information technology, from the book to the Internet, has enormously increased the scope of human knowledge and consequently made it more difficult to master. Better information technology has made the world more information intensive, which in turn has made knowledge more valuable than ever, and that has increased the value of learning from other people in cities.

It takes time to see the far-reaching, systemic effects of new technologies, so it makes sense to look at the long path of history, over which increases in the ability to communicate at long distances have generally made cities more important. No modern innovation can equal the printing press in its impact on long-distance communication. The ability to put words on paper cheaply and in great quantities was a seismic shift in mankind's ability to communicate with people who weren't in the same room. Yet there is no reason to think that books hurt cities and every reason to believe that the printing press helped to create a more urban world.

The most obvious reasons that books helped cities are that printing technology was developed in cities and cities are natural centers of publishing. Gutenberg, who grew up in the first years of the fifteenth century, set out to create a printing press with the secrecy of a medieval alchemist, but a piece of machinery as bold and as expensive as a printing press could never have been created by a solitary genius. Gutenberg needed financial backers and assistants, and they were found in cities. After his breakthrough, the technology of movable-type printing soon spread from town to town, carried by itinerant merchants, and by the 1480s, Venice had become the world center of printing. Cities have an edge whenever a technology, like printing, relies on expensive forms of infrastructure, like a printing press. Large urban markets make it easier to cover the fixed costs of these new technologies, which is one reason why telephones and broadband technology, as well as printed books, became available in cities first.

The city's rich, literate population provided plenty of local demand for books, but Venice also thrived because it had a ready supply of material worth printing. The city's position at the crossroads of East and West gave it a ready supply of scholars, like the Byzantines who fled to Venice after Constantinople fell to the Ottomans in 1453 and started translating for its presses. In later centuries, New York came to dominate printing in the United States because it had access to pirated English novels coming into its port and because the city attracted a vast number of writers and artists.

But the book didn't help cities just by boosting their publishing industries. The printed word also made the world more urban in subtler, deeper ways. One direct effect of the printing press was allowing far-flung farmers to read the Bible, but indirectly the printing press helped make the world more knowledge intensive, more democratic, more commercial, and ultimately more urban. Martin Luther described the printing press as "God's highest and extremest act of grace," because the Bible, translated into German by Luther himself, provided a source of religious authority other than Catholic tradition and played a crucial role in the Reformation: "Between 1517 and 1520, Luther's thirty publications probably sold well over 300,000 copies.... Altogether in the spread of religious ideas, it seems impossible to exaggerate the significance of the Press." The Reformation, then, supported economic, political, and social changes that made commerce in cities more attractive. Max Weber famously connected Protestantism with the spirit of capitalism and the ethical values of urban merchants and artisans. Personally, I don't think that Protestantism has an inherent superiority in supporting cities, trade, or democracy, which all flourish today in many Catholic nations. Instead, I believe that the post-Reformation rise of cities, trade, and democracy reflects the value of religious competition, which meant more choice over church rules and doctrine and led to reforms, like the erosion of usury laws, that aided the rise of global commerce.

The printing press both directly and indirectly—through the Reformation—also supported revolutions that created a more republican and more urban Europe. The great Dutch revolt started in 1566 near the Flemish cloth-producing town of Steenvoorde when a Calvinist mob destroyed the statues of a local Catholic church. In 1581, using language that would be familiar to later English, American, and French revolutionaries, the Dutch declared that King Philip of Spain had acted illegally and thereby lost his right to rule Holland. This revolutionary Act of Abjuration drew on a recently published Protestant (Huguenot) tract. The Act itself was printed and widely posted throughout the Low Countries to bolster opposition to Spain. After almost seventy years of fighting, Holland became an independent republic, the most urban nation in Europe, and the center of a global trading network that would reach as far east as Nagasaki, Japan, and as far west as the island of Manhattan.

Books, the first form of information technology for the masses, did not hurt cities. Over two centuries, books helped generate revolutionary changes in religion and politics that made the world more connected, more commercial, and ultimately more urban. There is every reason to think that globalization and modern changes in technology will have the same effect.

Cities—Bangalore, San Francisco, Singapore—are the nodes that connect our increasingly globalized world. Urban areas, like Athens and Baghdad, have always played this role, but as the world becomes ever more tightly knit, cities are becoming even more important. Silicon Valley brings together native-born engineers and brilliant immigrants, including the founders of both Yahoo! and Google, then links them to other hubs of engineering excellence, like Bangalore. As America continues to represent an ever smaller share of the global market, it will rely more heavily on its urban connectors to the growing economies of India, China, and elsewhere, where the spread of knowledge makes the difference between promise and poverty.

Some places will, however, be left behind. Not every city will succeed, because not every city has been adept at adapting to the age of information, in which ideas are the ultimate creator of wealth. While some historic metropolises specialized in connections and commerce, which continue to be sources of success, other urban areas rose as vast centers for the mass production of goods. These places had their roots in the brilliant ideas of urban entrepreneurs, but they evolved into places that thrived by keeping costs down through the economies of specialization and scale. The unusual era of the industrial city is over, at least in the West, and we are left with the problems of former manufacturing giants that have been unable to reinvent themselves in the new era.

CHAPTER 2

Why Do Cities Decline?

The corner of Elmhurst Street and Rosa Parks Boulevard in Detroit feels as far from New York's Fifth Avenue as urban space can get in America. Though this intersection lies in the heart of Detroit, much of the nearby land is empty. Grass now grows where apartment buildings and stores once stood. The Bible Community Baptist Church is the only building at the intersection; its boarded-up windows and nonworking phone number suggest that it doesn't attract many worshippers.

If you walk down Elmhurst, you'll see eleven low-rise homes; four of them are vacant. There are also two apartment buildings—one is less than a third occupied, the other is empty. There are also another ten or so vacant lots and a parking lot, blank spaces that once held homes and apartment buildings. Despite its ruinous condition, the area feels perfectly safe because there isn't enough humanity to create a threat. The open spaces give this neighborhood the feel of a ghost town, where the spirits of Detroit's past bemoan the plight of what was once America's fourth-largest city.

Between 1950 and 2008, Detroit lost over a million people—58 percent of its population. Today one third of its citizens live in poverty. Detroit's median family income is $33,000, about half the U.S. average. In 2009, the city's unemployment rate was 25 percent, which was 9 percentage points more than any other large city and more than 2.5 times the national average. In 2008, Detroit had one of the highest murder rates in America, more than ten times higher than New York City's. Many American cities endured a collapse in housing prices between 2006 and 2008. But Detroit was unique in both missing the boom early in the decade *and* suffering a 25 percent price drop since the bust.

Detroit's decline is extreme, but it's hardly unique. Eight of the ten largest U.S. cities in 1950 have lost at least a sixth of their population since then. Six of the sixteen largest cities in 1950—Buffalo, Cleveland, Detroit, New Orleans, Pittsburgh, and St. Louis—have lost more than half their population since that year. In Europe, cities like Liverpool, Glasgow, Rotterdam, Bremen, and Vilnius are all much smaller than they once were. The age of the industrial city is over, at least in the West, and it will never return. Some erstwhile manufacturing towns have managed to evolve from making goods to making ideas, but most continue their slow, inexorable declines.

But we shouldn't see the exodus from the Rust Belt as an indictment of urban living; the manufacturing cities fell because they had abandoned the most vital features of city life. The old commercial towns, like Birmingham and New York, specialized in skills, small enterprises, and strong connections with the outside world. Those attributes, which also create urban prosperity today, made cities successful long before a single bolt of cloth left a textile mill in Manchester or a single car rolled off an assembly line in Detroit. The industrial town was unlike either those old commercial cities or the modern capitals of the information age. Its vast factories employed hundreds of thousands of relatively unskilled workers. Those factories were self-sufficient and isolated from the world outside, except that they were providing the planet with vast quantities of cheap, identical products.

That model served the West extremely well for about a century. Detroit's car factories provided good wages to hundreds of thousands of people, but over the past fifty years, areas with abundant small firms have grown more quickly than places dominated by enormous enterprises. Skilled cities have been more successful than less educated places, and only 11 percent of Detroit's adults have college degrees. People and firms have moved to warmer areas and away from the chilly Midwest, whose waterways first nurtured the cities that now comprise the Rust Belt. Industrial diversity has been more conducive to growth than manufacturing monocultures, and Detroit practically defined the one-industry town.

While it would be wrong to attribute too much of these places' problems to politics, political mismanagement was often a feature of Rust Belt decline. Perhaps the most common error was thinking that these cities could build their way back to success with housing projects, grandiose office towers, or fanciful high-tech transit systems. Those mistakes came out of the all-too-common error of confusing a city, which is really a mass of connected humanity, with its structures.

Reviving these cities requires shedding the old industrial model completely, like a snake sloughing off its skin. When a city reinvents itself successfully, the metamorphosis is often so complete that we forget that the place was once an industrial powerhouse. As late as the 1950s, New York's garment industry was the nation's largest manufacturing cluster. It employed 50 percent more workers than the auto industry did in Detroit. America's Industrial Revolution practically began in greater Boston, but now nobody associates smokestacks with that city. These places have reinvented themselves by returning to their old, preindustrial roots of commerce, skills, and entrepreneurial innovation.

If Detroit and places like it are ever going to come back, they will do so by embracing the virtues of the great pre- and postindustrial cities: competition, connection, and human capital. The Rust Belt will be reborn only if it can break from its recent past, which has left it with a vast housing stock for which there is little demand, a single major industry that is dominated by a few major players, and problematic local politics. Beneath these cities' recent history lies an instructive older story of connection and creativity, which provide the basis for reinvention. To understand Detroit's predicament and its potential, we must compare the city's great and tragic history with the story of other cities, like New York, that have successfully weathered industrial decline.

How the Rust Belt Rose

Detroit is French for strait, and like New York and Chicago, it began as a hub of waterborne commerce. In 1900, all twenty of America's largest cities were on major waterways. Water reduces resistance, and for millennia, this meant that boats were the best means of moving goods from place to place. New York's entire existence had once depended on a gift of nature: a superb port connected to a deep, long river, near the center of the Eastern seaboard. Detroit was founded as a French fort, on high ground overlooking the narrowest part of the river connecting Lake Erie to the western Great Lakes. That narrowness enabled the guns of the French commander, Antoine Cadillac, to control river traffic, and it would later make Detroit an ideal spot to cross the water barrier between Canada and the United States, perhaps with a shipment of bootleg whiskey in tow.

Nineteenth-century advances in waterborne commerce—the globalization of that era—sped the growth of cities like Detroit, New York, and Chicago. In 1816, it cost as much to ship goods thirty miles overland as it did for those goods to cross the Atlantic. Because moving thirty miles away from the water would double the cost of getting goods to and from the Old World, America's population perched on the Eastern seaboard, clustered around ports from Boston to Savannah. In the eighteenth century, the Atlantic Ocean was America's highway, the lifeline through which we traded with the markets of Europe and the Caribbean.

America's founders understood that it could become a cohesive nation only if people and goods could easily move around its interior, from one state to another. Before he became the president of the United States, George Washington was president of the Potowmack Canal Company. He dreamed of connecting the Potomac and Ohio rivers even before the battles of Lexington and Concord. Unfortunately, in the eighteenth century, no private entrepreneur in the United States had access to enough capital to fund such a large, long-term, risky endeavor as building a vast waterway, and Washington proved more successful with cannons than with canals. The great liquid highway—the Erie Canal—would be built farther north by New Yorkers, and it would connect the Hudson River to the Great Lakes. New York's victory reflected both its geographical advantages and the willingness of its government to bet vast sums of public money on a canal. They were right to bet; the canal turned a profit almost immediately because of the huge demand for east-west transport.

Cities soon sprang up along the Erie Canal's path, creating the trading network that would make it possible for farmers to move west. Syracuse initially specialized in shipping nearby salt. Rochester became America's flour city, milling wheat produced by nearby farmers and sending it down the canal. Buffalo was the waterway's western terminus, where goods were transferred between the larger boats that traversed the Great Lakes and the flatboats that plied the canal. American cities like Buffalo and Chicago, and New York itself, grew on spots where goods had to be shifted from one form of transportation to another. The need to lift all that grain led one Buffalo merchant to start using elevators, a technology that would later transform cities.

A second waterway, the Illinois and Michigan Canal, completed a great arc that ran all the way from New Orleans to New York by way of St. Louis, Chicago, Detroit, and Buffalo. From 1850 until 1970, at least five of the ten largest American cities were along that route. Chicago's speculators realized that the Illinois and Michigan Canal would make their city the keystone of the arc— the spot where the canal boats coming along the Chicago River hit the Great Lakes—and the city's land market exploded in the 1830s while the canal was being built. Between 1850 and 1900, Chicago experienced a fiftyfold population increase, from fewer than thirty thousand to more than 1.5 million inhabitants, as trains followed waterways.

The cities that grew up as nodes along America's nineteenth-century transport network enabled vast numbers of people to access the wealth of the U.S. hinterland. Then, as now, Iowa's rich, dark soil made it a farmer's dream. In 1889, Iowa corn yields were 50 percent higher than the yields in older areas such as Kentucky. Corn may have been easier to grow out west, but its low value per ton made it relatively expensive to ship. Canal boats and railcars played their part in moving calories westward, but so did cities, which helped make produce easier to ship.

Before the Ohio and Erie canals, the high cost of moving grain led farmers to transform it into whiskey, which is durable and contains more than twice as many calories per ounce as raw corn, making it lighter, and some might say tastier, on a per-calorie basis. As transport costs fell with canals and railroads, it became cost-effective to ship corn in porcine form, because ham lies between corn and whiskey in both calories per ounce and durability. Cities like America's Porkopolis, Cincinnati, and Chicago, specialized in slaughtering and salting the animals that were brought there by nearby farmers. Chicago's stockyards switched from pigs to beef when Gustavus Swift introduced a refrigerated railcar that could keep slaughtered beef from spoiling in transit. Like many important innovations, Swift's great idea now seems blindingly obvious. He put the ice on top, instead of on the bottom, so it melted down onto the sides of beef and kept them cool.

Like Chicago, Detroit grew as a node of the great rail and water network long before Henry Ford made his first Model T. Between 1850 and 1890, the city's population increased tenfold, from 21,000 to 206,000 people. Detroit's growth was again intimately tied to its waterway, the Detroit River, which was part of the path from Iowa's farmland to New York's tables. By 1907, 67 million tons of goods were moving along the Detroit River, more than three times as much as the total amount going through the ports of New York or London.

In Europe, as well, industrial cities sprang up along waterways. The industrial heartland of Germany, the Ruhr, is named after the river that gave access to that coal-mining region. The great English industrial cities of Liverpool and Manchester were tied together by the river Mersey and by canals built in the eighteenth century. Canal building during the Georgian era likewise connected Birmingham with the port of Bristol. In the 1830s, rail would complement waterways and ensure that these industrial areas had even easier access to each other and to global markets.

In New York and Chicago and Detroit, entrepreneurs came, eager for access to harbors, other manufacturers, and urban consumers. The money that industries save on transport costs when they locate near each other and their customers is an example of *agglomeration economies*—the benefits that come from clustering in cities. The growing city's large home market and its waterborne access to other customers also enabled industrialists to take advantage of what economists call *returns to scale,* a term for the fact that per unit costs are cheaper in bigger plants that produce more units, like large sugar refineries or car factories.

Detroit Before Cars

Some of Detroit's largest and most successful businesses, like Detroit Dry Dock, catered directly to the vast numbers of boats floating by the city. Detroit Dry Dock was incorporated in 1872, and over the next thirty years, its engine works would become one of the most important shipbuilders on the Great Lakes. Henry Ford came to Detroit Dry Dock in 1880. Ford had already worked as a machinist, at a smaller firm that had, according to Ford's biographer Allan Nevins, "probably offered better opportunities for a comprehensive training than most of the larger plants," but the Dry Dock was Ford's first major exposure to technologically sophisticated engine production. Detroit had ready access to wood and iron ore, and its shipyards were at the center of the Great Lakes system. It was natural for this city to specialize in building ship engines, and its expertise in building and repairing engines would make Detroit a natural place to build cars.

The car was a new idea that combined two old ideas: the carriage and the engine. Both carriages and engines had long been made in Detroit. The engines were being built and serviced for the ships on the Great Lakes; the carriages were made from the plentiful wood of Michigan's forests. Henry Ford got his start in the engine business, while Billy Durant, the entrepreneur behind General Motors, began making horse-drawn carriages in nearby Flint.

At the end of the nineteenth century, Detroit looked a lot like Silicon Valley in the 1960s and 1970s. The Motor City thrived as a hotbed of small innovators, many of whom focused on the new new thing, the automobile. The basic science of the automobile had been worked out in Germany in the 1880s, but the German innovators had no patent protection in the United States. As a result, Americans were competing furiously to figure out how to produce good cars on a mass scale. In general, there's a strong correlation between the presence of small firms and the later growth of a region. Competition, the "racing men" phenomenon, seems to create economic success.

After Ford left Detroit Dry Dock in 1882, he returned to his family farm and kept experimenting with engines. He got more experience operating a neighbor's Westinghouse threshing machine and used his expertise to get a job at Westinghouse working on their engines, while experimenting in his free time with steam engines, even building a proto-tractor. In 1891 he jumped ship and joined Westinghouse's archrival, the Edison Illuminating Company. In 1893, he was promoted to chief engineer in the Detroit plant and when Ford explained his ideas about cars to Edison, the great inventor supposedly replied, "Young man, that's the thing!"

Ford used the experience and know-how he got at Edison to start tinkering with motor vehicles. In 1896, after toiling for two years in a workshop behind his home, he produced the Ford Quadricycle. The Quadricycle was a simple vehicle that ran on bicycle tires, but its 20-miles-per-hour top speed was fast enough to impress a lumber baron who bankrolled Ford's first car company in 1899. Ford's early cars were expensive and of low quality, not a winning combination, and he had left the firm he had founded by 1901. The lumber baron didn't give up so easily; he brought in another engineer and renamed his company after Detroit's founder: Cadillac.

New York City actually had a larger share of the nation's automobile producers than Detroit in 1900, but there was an explosion in automotive entrepreneurship in Detroit in the early 1900s. Detroit seemed to have had a budding automotive genius on every street corner. Ford, Ransom Olds, the Dodge brothers, David Dunbar Buick, and the Fisher brothers all worked in the Motor City. Some of these men made cars, but Detroit also had plenty of independent suppliers, like the Fisher Brothers, who could cater to start-ups. Ford was able to open a new company with backing from the Dodge brothers, who were making engine and chassis components. They supplied Ford with both financing and parts.

Gradually, Ford's cars became cheaper and faster. In 1906, Ford produced his Model N, a 1,050-pound car that he sold for the bargain price of $500, and he sold so many of them (over 8,500) that he leaped into the front ranks of the automotive industry. In 1908, Ford introduced his Model T at the bargain price of $825 (about $19,000 in 2010 currency). Five years later, Ford started producing the Model T on a moving assembly line, which increased his factory's speed and efficiency. Of course, the process of mass industrialization—dividing complicated manufacturing processes into small, straightforward tasks—long predated Ford. In 1776, Adam Smith was extolling the efficiencies created by the division of labor in a pin factory. Ford simply took this process one step further, using machines to move parts along and making sure that his workers' actions meshed perfectly.

The last chapter discussed Jevons's complementarity corollary, according to which more efficient information technology makes information learned face-to-face more valuable, but not all new technologies increase the returns from knowledge. Henry Ford's assembly lines are an example of that strange creature, the knowledge-destroying idea. While information technology seems to increase the returns from being smart, machines that reduce the need for human ingenuity work in the opposite direction. By turning a human being into a cog in a vast industrial enterprise, Ford made it possible to be highly productive without having to know all that much. But if people need to know less, they also have less need for cities that spread knowledge. When a city creates a powerful enough knowledge-destroying-idea, it sets itself up for self-destruction.

The irony and ultimately the tragedy of Detroit is that its small, dynamic firms and independent suppliers gave rise to gigantic, wholly integrated car companies, which then became synonymous with stagnation. Ford figured out that massive scale could make his cars cheap, but supersize, self-contained factories were antithetical to the urban virtues of competition and connection. Ford figured out how to make assembly lines that could use the talents of poorly educated Americans, but making Detroit less skilled hurt it economically in the long run.

Successful car companies bought up their suppliers, like Fisher Body, and their competitors. By the 1930s, only the most foolhardy and well-financed businessman would have dared take on General Motors and Ford. The intellectually fertile world of independent urban entrepreneurs had been replaced by a few big companies that had everything to lose and little to gain from radical experimentation.

Henry Ford and Industrial Detroit

As the car companies got out of innovation and into mass production, they no longer saw any advantages to locating in the city. Dense urban centers are ideal places to come up with new ideas, but not ideal places to make millions of Model T's. Ford's desire for massive scale required a factory too large for any city to accommodate. In 1917, he began building his River Rouge plant in suburban Dearborn, southwest of Detroit. At River Rouge, he erected a ninety-three-building complex with 7 million square feet of workspace. River Rouge had its own docks, rail lines, and power plant. Raw materials could be turned into cars within a single facility.

Ford's River Rouge plant began the process of suburbanizing manufacturing that would continue throughout the twentieth century. While the car may have been born in the city, it ended up being a very rebellious child. Automobiles enabled Americans to live in distant suburbs away from streetcars or sidewalks. Trucks enabled factories to locate far away from rail lines. The car and the truck both enabled space-hungry people and firms to leave dense urban areas.

By the 1950s, both New York and Detroit started shrinking as the advantages they once got from their ports and rail yards became far less important because other areas had also acquired easy access to world markets. Between 1890 and today, the real cost of moving a ton a mile by rail dropped from twenty cents to two, so it didn't matter nearly as much whether or not your factory was close to a transport hub. Before World War II, companies put up with high labor costs in Northern cities because the transport network made it so much easier to buy raw materials and ship final products. As transport costs plummeted, it became cost-effective to locate in cheaper places: suburban factories, like River Rouge, Southern right-to-work states, and China. At the same time, the rise of the car made older cities built around trains and elevators seem obsolete.

America's union movement had grown up in those older cities. Samuel Gompers, the founder of the American Federation of Labor, was a cigar maker from New York City. Tens of thousands of New York's garment workers organized themselves into unions and forced their employers to raise wages and improve working conditions through massive strikes like the Great Revolt of 1910.

Cities also spread stories of corporate faults that helped build public support for labor in the early twentieth century. On a May afternoon in 1937, labor organizers who had been trying to unionize Ford's workers gathered on a pedestrian overpass at River Rouge. They were handing out leaflets denouncing Ford and posing for a photograph for the *Detroit News*. During the photo op, Ford's security men attacked the peaceful organizers. The *Detroit News* captured images of these men smashing organizers' faces against concrete and beating women up. It was a public relations disaster for Ford, and it made heroes out of the union men. It would take another four years, but eventually Ford caved and signed a contract with the United Auto Workers that would usher in a half century of union power in Northern industrial cities.

Around the same time, the federal government also helped strengthen the unions' hand. The National Labor Relations Act, passed in 1935, made it more difficult to fire striking workers and led to the formation of closed shops, where unions and firms agreed that all workers in a given facility must join the union. In these closed shops, it was impossible to hire nonunion strikebreakers, which gave workers greater power to press their demands on manufacturers. A company that has invested millions or billions in fixed infrastructure can't easily move if its workers press for higher wages, more benefits, shorter hours, or other concessions. If striking workers take control of that valuable infrastructure, as they do during a sit-down strike, they can cause such financial pain that management will often give in. In the short term, union power meant high wages for New York's garment workers and Detroit's auto workers, but those wages ultimately prompted manufacturers to abandon these cities.

The industrialization of the Sunbelt was helped—and Northern cities like Detroit and New York were hurt—by the Taft-Hartley Act of 1947, which allowed states to pass right-to-work laws that forbid the formation of closed shops. In right-to-work states, which were often in the South, unions had much less bargaining power because firms could always turn to nonunion workers. Unsurprisingly, manufacturers have steadily drifted to right-to-work states, away from America's older industrial regions. One classic paper compared the effect of right-to-work laws on factory jobs in neighboring counties, on either side of a right-to-work border. It found that manufacturing grew 23.1 percent faster between 1947 and 1992 on the anti-union side of the divide.

High union wages didn't seem like such a drag on Detroit during the first decades after World War II. When the UAW whipsawed the Big Three automakers into raising wages, higher costs were mostly passed along to consumers. The automakers were so profitable that they could withstand some of the most expensive labor costs on the planet. Of course, the car companies weren't above trying to open new plants in states with lower labor costs, which is why Detroit was losing people even before the car industry began to decline.

Industrial decline ultimately hit every older city. Boston's maritime industries, which had grown great on the clipper ships and China trade in the first half of the nineteenth century, became obsolete with the rise of steam-powered ships. New York's garment industry imploded in the late 1960s and 1970s, and the city lost more than three hundred thousand manufacturing jobs between 1967 and 1977. The exodus of urban manufacturing was not inherently a bad thing—making goods in cheap locales made those goods less expensive for ordinary people—but it posed a mortal challenge for the world's industrial cities.

The same forces that decimated America's manufacturing cities created similar Rust Belts in Europe. In 1937, three years before John Lennon was born, Liverpool had 867,000 residents. Liverpool had been, and is, a great port, linking England with the rest of the world. The raw cotton used in Manchester's giant textile mills was shipped into Liverpool, and finished cloth left England through the same port. Just as in New York, and for the same reasons, sugar refining was once a booming business in Liverpool. But since 1937, like Detroit, Liverpool has lost about half of its population. Labor-saving technologies like containerization put thousands of stevedores out of work. Lower transport costs enabled industry to move to less expensive areas. Labor unions in Britain were more powerful than even the UAW, and the cost of running a factory there is a lot higher than in China. London reinvented itself, with the help of idea-intensive sectors like finance, but goods-producing areas, like Liverpool and England's old industrial north, remain troubled.

After centuries spent in rural somnolence, Spain was among the last European nations to industrialize, but even there, the age of the industrial city is over. In 1959, Franco belatedly empowered a new technocratic economic team that opened up the Spanish economy. From 1960 to 1975, Spain rapidly urbanized, and its GDP grew faster than that of any country in the world except Japan. Low wages and proximity to European markets made its ports, like Bilbao, natural places for heavy industries like steel. But just like Detroit, Bilbao suffered in the 1970s as oil prices spiked, the world went into recession, and other, lower-cost countries began competing with its industries. Bilbao's population fell by 14 percent between 1981 and 1995.

Why Riot?

Cities suffer from economic downturns directly, because of the loss of jobs and decline in wages, but negative shocks also have indirect consequences, like social upheaval and falling tax revenues, that can be just as harmful. The collapse of the industrial city was the backdrop for the crime waves and riots of the 1960s, and for an increasingly impotent public sector that was just trying to stay solvent. In the bright, optimistic days of the early 1960s, many American cities turned from old-style machine politicians to young, charismatic leaders. In Detroit and New York, an alliance of liberals and African Americans elected Jerome Cavanagh and John Lindsay respectively. While his predecessors had been seen as abettors of police brutality, Cavanagh promised fairer law enforcement. He launched affirmative-action programs and marched with Martin Luther King Jr. John Lindsay also fought police brutality and supported affirmative action. Lindsay's finest hour may have been in the aftermath of King's shooting, when he walked the streets of Harlem and cooled tempers with warmth and compassion.

But ultimately neither mayor could control the forces that were convulsing his city. Neither can be blamed for failing to halt the manufacturing exodus from his city—the economic headwinds were just too strong. Neither can be blamed for the social unrest that erupted in America's cities during the 1960s, in the wake of economic distress, expanding but unmet expectations, and a breakdown in traditional means of social control. But both mayors made mistakes that contributed to their cities' distress.

Lindsay's besetting sin was his inability to rein in costs, especially when faced with tough municipal unions and transit strikes. Lindsay, initially a Republican, hoped to limit union pay raises, but his background as the congressman from Manhattan's silk-stocking district hardly prepared him to win a brutal street fight with the transit workers. He ended up preferring pay raises to strikes, and the increasing costs of city government were then hidden with increasingly creative bookkeeping, which led straight to New York's near bankruptcy in 1975. Cavanagh's fatal flaw was his penchant for razing slums and building tall structures with the help of federal urban-renewal dollars. Detroit's housing market had peaked in the 1950s and was already depressed when Cavanagh took office. The city was shedding people and had plenty of houses. Why subsidize more building? Successful cities must build in order to accommodate the rising demand for space, but that doesn't mean that building *creates* success.

Urban renewal, in both Detroit and New York, may have replaced unattractive slums with shiny new buildings, but it did little to address urban decline. Those shiny new buildings were really Potemkin villages spread throughout America, built to provide politicians with the appearance of urban success. But Detroit had plenty of buildings; it didn't need more. What Detroit needed was human capital: a new generation of entrepreneurs like Ford and Durant and the Dodge brothers who could create some great new industry, as Shockley and the Fairchildren were doing in Silicon Valley. Investing in buildings instead of people in places where prices were already low may have been the biggest mistake of urban policy over the past sixty years.

Both mayors also failed at fighting crime. New York's murder rate quadrupled between 1960 and 1975, and Detroit experienced a similarly disturbing trend. But racial discrimination and police brutality in both cities led both mayors to emphasize accountability more than enforcement. African Americans were no longer willing to take abuse from white thugs, whether in or out of police uniform. In Detroit, a 93 percent white police force didn't seem all that integrated in a city that was close to 50 percent black. While later mayors, like Rudy Giuliani, would reduce crime with rigorous policing, in the 1960s, it wasn't obvious that aggressive enforcement could keep the peace.

Less than a mile down Rosa Parks Boulevard from the Elmhurst Street corner, a dilapidated park occupies the corner at Clairmount Street. This is the site of an event from which Detroit has still not recovered almost half a century later. In the wee hours of Sunday morning, July 23, 1967, a club on that corner was hosting a party for some returning veterans, when Detroit's police department staged a raid. The vice squad, which had a robust reputation for brutality toward the city's blacks, took a while to cart off the eighty-five partygoers. A jeering crowd of two hundred gathered and began throwing bottles at the cops, who fled. The mob grew and grew, and soon Detroit was ablaze.

Riots are a classic tipping-point phenomenon. Being one of three rioters is dangerous business—the cops are likely to get you—but the chances of arrest are far lower if you're one of three thousand rioters. In Detroit, over a thousand police officers failed to control the thousands of rioters who burned and looted. Cavanagh completely lost control of his city. The riot didn't end until after Tuesday, when thousands of paratroopers from the 82nd and 101st airborne divisions showed up with armed vehicles. By the time this surge quelled the violence, there had been forty-three deaths, 1,400 burned buildings, 1,700 looted stores, and seven thousand arrests.

It's easy to see why Detroit's African-American citizens were moved to riot. They'd been brutalized by a police force full of whites recruited from the South. They'd been systematically excluded from white jobs in the auto industry for decades, and the jobs they did get typically either paid lower wages or offered worse working conditions. Statistics show that Detroit was hardly the only city that had fomented this sort of black anger, and riots were most common in those cities with larger numbers of young, unemployed African Americans.

Cities with more cops actually had smaller riots. Unfortunately, draconian enforcement seems to be the only effective way to stop a riot once it starts. Three of the great experts on civil unrest summarized their research on the link between dictatorship and rioting with the pithy phrase "repression works." Brutal regimes that severely punish rioting have fewer riots, which may explain why democracies see more rioting than dictatorships, and the more progressive cities of the North had far more riots than the Jim Crow South.

Riots are one example of the collective action enabled by cities that may seem to be an unmitigated urban curse, but riots near Steenvoorde began the Dutch Revolt that led to Europe's first modern republic, and unruly mob action in Boston was a critical part of America's road to revolution and republic. Thomas Jefferson wrote that "I view great cities as pestilential to the morals, the health and the liberties of man," but his own liberties owed much to urban agitators like Sam Adams and John Hancock, who succeeded at creating conflict with England precisely because the great port of Boston enabled them to conjure up a mob.

Just like King George III, the leaders of America's cities in the 1960s had two plausible responses to rioting. One was to beef up law enforcement and make the streets safer by locking people up. The other response was to empathize with the rioters and to try to create a more just society. There's much to be said for the second approach, which attracted both Lindsay and Cavanagh. In the 1960s and 1970s, many reform-minded leaders strove to bring greater racial and social equality to their cities. Unfortunately, those leaders only showed how hard it is to right great social wrongs at the city level.

The awful history of American racism helps explain why so many African Americans felt like rioting in the 1960s, but that history doesn't change the fact that those riots did tremendous harm to America's cities, especially to their African-American residents. After all, the rioters weren't burning the homes of prosperous white suburbanites. Those riots and rising crime rates helped create the sense that civilization had fled the city. As a result, many of those who could leave Detroit did.

Urban Reinvention: New York Since 1970

As recently as the 1970s, pretty much every older industrial city seemed similarly doomed. Both New York and Detroit were reeling from the decline of their core industries, and if anything, New York seemed worse off because the car industry remained more tightly tied to Motown than the garment sector did to Gotham. In 1977, workers in Wayne County, Michigan, which includes Detroit, were paid more than workers in Manhattan. New York City's government didn't seem any better than Detroit's. In 1975, New York State established the Municipal Assistance Corporation to take over the city's finances and stop it from falling into bankruptcy, despite having some of the nation's highest taxes.

But while Detroit has continued to decline, New York came back.

There's no shortage of explanations for New York's rebirth. Some Yankee fans think that Reggie Jackson's home runs brought back the city's mojo. Hipper urbanists look to Andy Warhol and the arts. Mayor Giuliani credits himself. There is a bit of truth to all of these views, but New York's resurrection was primarily tied to an explosion of entrepreneurship, much of which was in financial services. In 2008, more than $78.6 billion was paid to employees in the sector that the U.S. Census Bureau quaintly calls Securities, Commodity Contracts, and Other Financial Investments and Related Activities. And that doesn't even include all the really big payouts to the people who own financial firms.

Sixty years ago, New York's resilience was already something of a puzzle, and the economist Benjamin Chinitz then argued that the city owed its strength to a tradition of entrepreneurship, which the small firms of the apparel industry had encouraged. Chinitz suggested that the salaried employees of large steel companies in Pittsburgh taught their children to obey their boss and keep their noses clean, but the garment manufacturers of New York taught their kids to take risks. Certainly, financial billionaire Sandy Weill's father, who started as a dressmaker and then switched to importing steel, produced a son who was more comfortable running a company than working for someone else.

Cities have long created intellectual explosions, in which one smart idea generates others. The artistic renaissance in Florence was one such explosion; the industrial revolution in Birmingham and Manchester was another. The growth of finance in late-twentieth-century New York was encouraged by just such an innovation, the ability to quantify the trade-off between risk and return, which made it easier to sell investors riskier assets, from junk bonds to mortgage-backed securities, which in turn enabled riskier, high-return activities, like leveraged buyouts of underperforming companies such as RJR/Nabisco. Today's hedge-fund billionaires are only the latest links in a long chain of connected innovators.

For the millions worldwide who look askance at all of New York's financial innovation, Michael Bloomberg's story, in which a smart trader became an entrepreneur in another sector, might be easier to embrace. In the 1970s, Bloomberg had been riding high at Salomon Brothers, running the firm's trading floor, until he was exiled into the geeky world of systems development before being fired in 1981. Bloomberg then got into information technology, and over the next three decades he grew his company into a behemoth by supplying exactly what increasingly quantitative Wall Street traders wanted—jargon-free keyboards and a vast stream of information that was updated constantly.

But while Bloomberg made his fortune moving information electronically, he knows the value of working face-to-face. He set up his offices in an "open plan," which followed the pattern of Wall Street trading floors like the one he'd run at Salomon, and the unimpeded flow of information within the firm helped his success. In most of the world, rich people surround themselves with big offices and decorated walls, but on trading floors, some of the world's wealthiest people work right on top of each other. Rich traders are forgoing privacy for the knowledge that comes from proximity to other people. In a sense, trading floors are just the city writ small. When Bloomberg switched careers yet again in 2002 to become mayor of New York, he took the open plan with him to City Hall.

While New York was rising as a financial phoenix, Detroit continued its inexorable decline. The Motor City's failure was, in many ways, the legacy of Henry Ford's success. Urban reinvention is made possible by the traditional urban virtues that were to be found in nineteenth-century Detroit: educated workers, small entrepreneurs, and a creative interplay among different industries. Late-twentieth-century Detroit was dominated by a single industry that employed hundreds of thousands of less-skilled workers in three vast vertically integrated firms. What a toxic mixture!

Cities like Detroit with big firms have suffered weaker employment growth than cities with more and smaller employers. In metropolitan areas, a 10 percent increase in the number of firms per worker in 1977 is associated with 9 percent more employment growth between 1977 and 2000. This relationship holds, no matter what types of industries are involved, how old the companies are, or how big the cities are.

Big, vertically integrated firms may be productive in the short run, but they don't create the energetic competition and new ideas that are so necessary for long-term urban success. No small entrepreneur, even with the experience and panache of John DeLorean, could successfully compete with the Big Three. Detroit had stifled the diversity and competition that encourage growth. Moreover, the city of the assembly line had never invested in the educational institutions that enabled more diverse places, like Boston, Milan, and New York, to come back.

Meanwhile, declining transportation costs made it easier for European and Japanese competitors to sell cars in the U.S. market. While Detroit's Big Three had long lost their appetite for radical risk, Soichiro Honda was building fuel-efficient little cars. Detroit's automobile industry stayed afloat with occasional innovations like the minivan and the SUV, but its days of dominance were over. In the 1970s, as high gas prices dampened Americans' appetites for Cadillac Eldorados and Chrysler Imperials, Detroit had nowhere else to go. As the car industry declined, Detroit fell further and further. The age of the industrial city—with its vast factories and powerful unions—was over.

The Righteous Rage of Coleman Young

Detroit's fall has more to do with economics than politics, but the political response to the city's decline only made things worse. New York responded to the crisis of the 1970s by giving up the dream of ending social injustice at the local level and instead electing centrist, workmanlike mayors—Koch, Dinkins, Giuliani, Bloomberg—who were determined to make the city as attractive as possible to employers and middle-class residents. Detroit was led by a passionate crusader whose anger was understandable but unhelpful.

Coleman Young's family had moved from Alabama to Detroit in the 1920s. He got a job working for Henry Ford but was ultimately blacklisted from the auto industry because of his involvement with labor and civil rights issues. In World War II, Young joined the Tuskegee Airmen as a bombardier. This all-black unit gave African Americans their first opportunity to fly for their country. In 1943, Detroit's simmering racial antipathies exploded in a massive riot, which seems to have started when white youths began attacking blacks in the parks of Belle Isle. White police officers responded by shooting and killing seventeen blacks and no whites. The federal government thought it wise to move Young's all-black bombing outfit, which had been outside Detroit, first to Kentucky and then to Freeman Field in Indiana.

Freeman Field had two officers' clubs, separate but not equal, for the white instructors and the black trainees. Young put his skills as a labor organizer, learned on the streets of Detroit, to work integrating these clubs. En masse, the black officers entered the white club and were arrested. Eventually, after pressure from African-American groups, they were released and transferred back to Kentucky, where the officers' club was open to all but where the white officers could also use another club at Fort Knox.

For eighteen years after the war, Young worked his way up Detroit's political ladder. In 1951 he founded the National Negro Labor Council, whose radicalism attracted the scrutiny of the House Un-American Activities Committee during the McCarthy era. When questioned about his associates, Young refused to answer, explaining that "I am not here as a stool pigeon." Finally in 1963, the times had begun to catch up with his radicalism, and he was elected to the state senate. Three years later, he became the senate minority leader. He pushed through open-housing laws that limited segregation, and he also helped pass Detroit's first income tax.

Local income taxes illustrate the problem of trying to create a just society city by city. The direct effect of Young's income tax was to take money from the rich to fund services that helped the poor. The indirect effect of a local income tax is to encourage richer citizens and businesses to leave. Research by four economists found that in three out of four large cities, higher tax rates barely increase tax revenues because economic activity dissipates so quickly in response to higher tax rates. In a declining place like Detroit, well-meaning attempts at local redistribution can easily backfire by speeding the exodus of wealthier businesses and people, which only further isolates the poor.

After the riot destroyed Jerome Cavanagh's career, he retired, and finally, in

1973, as the black share of Detroit's population continued to rise, Young was elected mayor. His outspoken views gave voice to the long frustrated hopes of Detroit's black community, and he went on to win his next four mayoral elections easily, as Detroit changed from a city that was 55.5 percent white in 1970 to a city that was 11.1 percent white in 2008.

Young's brash style dominated headlines during his twenty years in office. He thought profanity was useful: "You can express yourself much more directly, much more exactly, much more succinctly, with properly used curse words." He argued that whites didn't even know the extent of their racism: "The victim of racism is in a much better position to tell you whether or not you're a racist than you are." Some people thought that Young was urging criminals to suburbanize when he invited them "to leave Detroit" and "hit the eight-mile road," the highway that separates Detroit from its northern suburbs. The mayor certainly had no time for his enemies and was happy to see them leave the city.

Young's bellicosity gave his many supporters the sense that they had a fearless champion fighting for them in City Hall. After years of being treated as second-class citizens, Detroit's African Americans could hold their heads up. Young's bitter experience with racial injustice made him unwilling to whisper sweetly to the city's white population. Moreover, his political interests were only helped by the continuing exodus of Detroit's whites.

The Curley Effect

Economists have long argued that the ability of citizens to "vote with their feet" creates competition among local governments that provides some of the same benefits as competition among companies. But there are real limits to that rosy picture. Sometimes, as the story of Coleman Young and Detroit shows, the possible flight of voters can create perverse political incentives that make government worse. I've named this phenomenon the Curley Effect, after Boston's colorful mayor James Michael Curley.

Curley had much in common with Young, and if anything, he was even more argumentative. Curley cast himself as the champion of a poor ethnic minority (the Irish) and rode to victory promising to right old wrongs. Curley frequently made pronouncements that infuriated Boston Brahmins, like calling Anglo-Saxons "a strange and stupid race." He was elected mayor of Boston four times, not quite Young's five terms, but Curley also won a term as governor. Also unlike Young, Curley spent two terms in jail, serving sentences for mail fraud and for taking a Civil Service exam for someone else.

One day in 1916, during Curley's first term as mayor, a British recruiting officer had asked the mayor whether he could invite Bostonians of British extraction to fight on Britain's side during the Great War. Curley replied: "Go ahead, Colonel. Take every damn one of them." After all, Protestant Bostonians of English descent overwhelmingly opposed Curley. The more Boston became a city of poor Irishmen, the more likely it was to reelect James Michael Curley.

The Curley Effect illustrates the danger of ethnic politics, especially in cities where exit is easy. Boston's economy would have benefited if wealthier Yankees had stayed in the city, but Curley did all he could to get rid of them. Likewise, Detroit's economy was hurt by the vast exodus of wealthier whites. Young may never have explicitly told them to leave, but he did little that encouraged them to stay. It's hard not to empathize with the mayor's anger, given the injustices he'd suffered, but righteous anger rarely leads to wise policy.

The mobility of the prosperous limits the ability of any city government to play Robin Hood. The well-off can, with relative ease, walk away from a depressed and declining city. Detroit's middle class escaped Coleman Young by moving to the suburbs.

The Edifice Complex

Young did have an economic strategy for Detroit, but it pursued the wrong objective. Instead of trying to attract smart, wealthy entrepreneurial people, he built structures—making the same error as Jerome Cavanagh, mistaking the built city for the real city. For centuries, leaders have used new buildings to present an image of urban success. The Emperor Vespasian, who ruled Rome in the first century, created an aura of legitimacy with vast construction projects like the Colosseum. Seventeen hundred years later, according to legend, General Grigory Potemkin created a prosperous-looking fake village to impress Empress Catherine the Great. Today urban leaders love to pose at the opening of big buildings that seem to prove that their municipality has either arrived or come back. For decades, the federal government has only exacerbated this tendency by offering billions for structures and transportation and far less for schools or safety.

The tendency to think that a city can build itself out of decline is an example of the edifice error, the tendency to think that abundant new building leads to urban success. Successful cities typically do build, because economic vitality makes people willing to pay for space and builders are happy to accommodate. But building is the result, not the cause, of success. Overbuilding a declining city that already has more structures than it needs is nothing but folly.

In the 1970s, the Detroit Red Wings hockey team threatened to leave for the suburbs. Young responded by building the Joe Louis Arena for $57 million ($205 million in 2010 dollars) and renting it to the Red Wings at bargain rates. The city kept its sports team—but at an enormous cost. In 1987, Detroit opened a monorail system, the People Mover, at a cost of over $200 million (more than $425 million in 2010 dollars). The three-mile system carries about 6,500 people each day and requires about $8.5 million a year in subsidies to operate. It is perhaps the single most absurd public transit project in the country. While it was sold to the public with wildly optimistic ridership projections, it fills only a tiny fraction of its seats. Detroit never needed a new public transit system. The streets below the People Mover are generally empty and could accommodate fleets of buses.

The great hope of the 1970s was the Renaissance Center. The center did receive tax breaks, as well as the enthusiastic support of both Cavanagh and Young, but it was really an example of private rather than public folly. Henry Ford II somehow thought that Detroit could be saved by a vast structure with millions of square feet of new office space. Unfortunately, new space was not what Detroit needed in those years. The Center cost $350 million to build but was sold to General Motors for less than $100 million in 1996. General Motors now occupies Henry Ford II's giant white elephant.

In 1981, Coleman Young and General Motors teamed up for yet another construction project. Young used eminent domain to destroy 1,400 homes in the ethnic neighborhood of Poletown. Activists protested and took the case to the Michigan Supreme Court, but Young still got the land and gave it to General Motors to build a new, high-tech factory inside the city limits. The plant still functions, employing about 1,300 people on its 465 acres, but it's hard to see the benefit of moving more than 4,000 people to create such a land-intensive enterprise within city borders.

Detroit's construction projects certainly changed the look of the city. The Renaissance Center dominates the skyline. Riding on the People Mover feels like a trip to Disney World, if Disney World were in the middle of a desperate city. But as in other declining places, billions were spent on infrastructure that the city didn't need. Unsurprisingly, providing more real estate in a place that was already full of unused real estate was no help at all. The failures of urban renewal reflect a failure at all levels of government to realize that people, not structures, really determine a city's success.

Could an alternative public policy have saved Detroit? By the time Young was elected, Detroit was far gone, and I suspect that even the best policies could only have eased the city's suffering. But it is possible to imagine a different path, if it was taken during earlier decades, when the city was far richer. Perhaps if the city had used its wealth and political muscle, starting in the 1920s, to invest in education at all levels, it could have developed the human capital that has been the source of survival for postindustrial cities.

Remaining in the Rust Belt

That harsh reality of industrial decline and political failures meant that by 2008 Detroit's per capita income was $14,976, only 54.3 percent of the U.S. average. Even before the recession hit, in 2006, Detroit's unemployment rate was 13.7 percent, which was far higher than that of the next largest city. The city's winters are cruel—January temperatures average 24.7 degrees—and Americans do seem to love warm weather. Over the last century, no variable has been a better predictor of urban growth than temperate winters. Given these fundamentals of cold and poverty, perhaps we shouldn't be asking why Detroit declined. Perhaps we should be asking why 777,000 people remain as of 2008.

There are as many different answers to that question as there are people left in Detroit, and each one of them could tell you something that they value about the place. But there is one force that helps explain why most of them stay—cheap, durable housing. Any area's population is linked closely to the number of homes in that area, and homes don't disappear overnight. They are also too valuable to abandon, at least immediately. Their prices drop precipitously, but they remain occupied, often for many decades. According to the Census Bureau, 86 percent of central-city Detroit's housing stock was built before 1960. The average house in the city is valued at $82,000, which is far below the cost of new construction.

When cities are doing well, they can grow very quickly as long as homes can be speedily constructed to house new residents. When cities decline, they decline very slowly, because people are loath to abandon something as valuable as a home. In a sense, the durability of housing is a blessing, because it provides cheap space to people with few resources. The downside of cities kept alive through cheap housing is that they overwhelmingly attract the poor, creating centers of extreme deprivation that cry out for social justice.

Shrinking to Greatness

Many cities around the world have experienced some version of Detroit's fate, and politicians have implemented many approaches to urban decline. U.S. cities have mainly tried to build their way out of decline. Spain has turned to transportation, spending tens of billions of dollars on high-speed rail, partly as a way to boost economic growth in poorer areas. Other places, like Italy, have used large tax subsidies to encourage enterprise in poorer regions. Many European cities have tried cultural strategies like the Guggenheim Museum in Bilbao. In 2008, Liverpool had a flurry of new construction to celebrate its one-year stint as Europe's capital of culture. Which of these strategies can actually reverse urban decline? Which strategies generate benefits that cover their costs?

In the nineteenth century, when moving goods was enormously expensive, places with good transportation links, like New York or Liverpool, enjoyed a huge edge. Today, moving goods and people is pretty cheap almost everywhere, so further improvements in transportation provide far less of an edge.

Transportation investments are most effective when they radically increase the speed at which a poor area can access a booming, space-starved metropolis. In Spain, a spate of investment in high-speed rail has radically reduced travel times between Madrid and other cities, such as Barcelona and Ciudad Real. The high-speed rail connection shortened the 140-mile trip between

Madrid and Ciudad Real to fifty minutes, and presto, people can live in Ciudad Real and work in Spain's largest city. The population of Ciudad Real does seem to have increased since getting the rail connection. In compact England, cities like Birmingham, Manchester, and Liverpool could also grow significantly as a result of extremely fast rail connections to London.

Yet the very things that have helped Ciudad Real benefit from high-speed rail are absent in much of America's Rust Belt. Flying to New York from Buffalo or Cleveland or Detroit will always be faster than taking a train. There's a lot of empty space between New York and these cities, so why would those relatively distant places be natural spots for back-office overflow? Faster links to New York can certainly benefit nearby places like Philadelphia or New Haven, but America's wide-open spaces are just too big for faster ground transportation to revitalize more distant areas.

Another way to bring places back is to give businesses tax cuts when they locate in a disadvantaged area. Research has found that tax breaks significantly increased employment in troubled areas, but it took $100,000 in tax breaks to generate just one job. But regardless of cost, should the national government even be using the tax code to shuffle economic activity around? Would it have made sense to tax nineteenth-century Chicago or Detroit to keep the population of Salem, Massachusetts, growing? Why should national policy encourage firms to locate in unproductive places?

National policy should strive to enrich and empower everybody, not to push people to live in any particular spot. The federal government has no business trying to encourage economic development in the foothills of the Rockies, and it is hard to see the case for spending billions to encourage people to move to politically favored cities. Expensive efforts to renew cities often do more for well-connected businesses than for the poor people living in those declining areas. Even if building a museum in a depressed neighborhood raises property values and brings in a stream of artsy visitors, that won't help the renter who doesn't care for art and now has to pay more for her apartment.

The success of Bilbao's Guggenheim Museum has lent credence to the view that cultural institutions can be successful urban renewal strategies. Frank Gehry's iconic structure has certainly spurred tourism, which rose from 1.4 million visitors in 1994 to 3.8 million in 2005; the museum alone attracts a million visitors annually. There are certainly Bilbao skeptics, however. One study attributed only about nine hundred new jobs to the museum, a project that cost the Basque treasury $240 million. But the bigger problem with drawing lessons from Bilbao is that its experience is far from standard. For every Guggenheim, there are dozens of expensive failures, like the National Centre for Popular Music, built in Sheffield, England, with the hope of four hundred thousand new visitors each year. It attracted a quarter of that number when it opened in 1999 and closed the same year. Leipzig also has a beautiful art museum, with splendid soaring rooms that unfortunately emphasize the museum's paucity of visitors.

Leipzig is worthy of emulation less for its cultural strategy than for its hardheaded policy of accepting decline and reducing the empty housing stock. In 2000, one fifth of the city's homes stock was vacant, a total of 62,500 units. After refusing to accept the reality of decline for decades, the city government finally recognized that those units would never again house anybody and that it made more sense to demolish them and replace them with green space. Bulldozing vacant homes reduces the costs of city services, eliminates safety hazards, and turns decaying eyesores into usable space. Leipzig set a target of destroying 20,000 vacant units.

In the United States, Youngstown, Ohio, which has lost more than half of its 1970 population, has also embraced this vision of shrinking to greatness. In 2005, the city's newly elected mayor immediately earmarked funds for demolishing abandoned homes. Many of these homes are being destroyed. Parks, open space, and large lots will replace once-dense neighborhoods. This strategy won't bring Youngstown's population back, but it will make the city more attractive, less dangerous, and cheaper to maintain. And finally Detroit has itself found a mayor, David Bing, who understands that the people aren't coming back and that empty homes should be replaced with some more reasonable use of space. Mayor Bing is not short on compassion, but he also understands the edifice error. He knows Detroit can be a great city if it cares for its people well even if it has far fewer structures.

Museums and transportation and the arts do have an important role in place-making. Yet planners must be realistic and expect moderate successes, not blockbusters. Realism pushes toward small, sensible projects, not betting a city's future on a vast, expensive roll of the dice. The real payoff of these investments in amenities lies not in tourism but in attracting the skilled residents who can really make a city rebound, especially if those residents can connect with the world economy.

The path back for declining industrial towns is long and hard. Over decades, they must undo the cursed legacy of big factories and heavy industry. They must return to their roots as places of small-scale entrepreneurship and commerce. Apart from investing in education and maintaining core public services with moderate taxes and regulations, governments can do little to speed this process. Not every city will come back, but human creativity is strong, especially when reinforced by urban density.

While poverty and urban failure are often linked in people's minds, particularly because declining places attract poor people with cheap housing, there's nothing intrinsically wrong with urban poverty. In fact, as we'll see in the next chapter, poverty is usually a sign of a city's success.

CHAPTER 3

What's Good About Slums?

There are few pleasures simpler or purer than drinking a plastic cup of cool, cheap beer on Ipanema Beach in Rio de Janeiro at sunset. Rio's beaches are among the most hedonistic of urban spaces. The weather is generally sublime. The beach is usually adorned with beautiful people. Looking eastward toward the sea, one takes in a spectacular coastline graced by the Sugar Loaf hill. Landward, a row of impressive structures takes advantage of the oceanfront views. It has been forty years since Rio was Brazil's capital, and its political and economic importance has waned over that time, but the city remains the most pleasurable place in a pleasurable nation. Beautiful older buildings and great natural beauty are the physical bones on which Rio's natives, the Cariocas, create an exciting urban space. That space is a mecca for tourists, but the Cariocas usually seem to be having even more fun than the foreigners.

If you look from Ipanema Beach into the hills, your eye will be drawn by the vast statue of Christ the Redeemer, the Corcovado. But look carefully, and you'll spy a blot upon this urban arcadia. The hills surrounding Rio are filled with shantytowns, favelas, that often lack electricity or sewers. Their presence in those hills seems puzzling, incongruous. Rio's hills have some of the best views in the world, so why are they occupied by disheveled huts, where rule of law is as rare as decent infrastructure? The sight of the favelas reminds the beachgoer that Rio is not just a playground for the prosperous, but a city where more than a million poor people crowd into dilapidated housing.

Twenty-five hundred years ago, Plato noted that "any city, however small, is in fact divided into two, one the city of the poor, the other of the rich." Almost every city in every developing country has its concentrations of poverty, its shantytowns. In some places, like Kolkata or Lagos, the suffering can be so extensive and extreme that observers can't help but see the entire city as hellish. Even in the developed world, cities are disproportionately poor. In America, the poverty rate is 17.7 percent within cities and 9.8 percent in suburbs.

The terrible prevalence of urban poverty seems to indict cities as places of inequality and deprivation. Many urban analysts see a great crisis in the problem of the megacity, which usually means the vast numbers of poor people living in Mumbai or Mexico City. It seems wise to many to limit the growth of these megacities, whose crowds and squalor doom millions to harsh, dead-end lives. In the developed world, cozy, homogeneous suburbs can appear far more egalitarian than the extraordinary urban gulfs that separate a Fifth Avenue billionaire from a ghetto child.

But the preceding paragraph is filled with nonsense. The presence of poverty in cities from Rio to Rotterdam reflects urban strength, not weakness. Megacities are not too big. Limiting their growth would cause significantly more hardship than gain, and urban growth is a great way to reduce rural poverty. The seemingly equal world of the suburb is in many ways more of a problem for society as a whole, especially those people who can't afford its pleasures, than the unequal world of the city.

Cities aren't full of poor people because cities make people poor, but because cities *attract* poor people with the prospect of improving their lot in life. The poverty rate among recent arrivals to big cities is higher than the poverty rate of long-term residents, which suggests that, over time, city dwellers' fortunes can improve considerably. The poorer people who come to cities from other places aren't mad or mistaken. They flock to urban areas because cities offer advantages they couldn't find in their previous homes. The great problem of urban slums is not that there are too many people living in a city, but that those residents are often too disconnected from the economic heart of the metropolis. The great masses of the urban poor do create challenges that must be faced, and those are the topic of the next chapter, but it's far better to hope for a world where cities can accommodate millions more of the rural poor than to wish that those potential migrants would end their days in agricultural isolation.

Rio's slums are densely packed because life in a favela beats stultifying rural poverty. Rio has long offered more economic opportunity, public services, and fun than the desolate areas of Brazil's hinterland. America's ghettos were filled by immigrants fleeing pogroms or poverty and by African Americans fleeing the hardships of agricultural work in the Jim Crow South. The great economic engine of nineteenth-century Manchester was associated with vast amounts of poverty, not because the city was failing but because its mills were attracting rural folk eager for work. Indeed, we should worry more about places with too little poverty. Why do they fail to attract the least fortunate?

In a free society, people choose where to live, either explicitly by moving or implicitly by staying in the place of their birth. A city's population tells you about what the city offers. Salt Lake City is full of Mormons because it's a good place to be a Mormon. London has many bankers because it's a good place to manage money. Cities like Rio have plenty of poor people, because they're relatively good places to be poor. After all, even without any cash, you can still enjoy Ipanema Beach.

The free movement of people means that certain types of urban success can make a place poorer. Economics emphasizes the power of incentives. When the payoff for doing something goes up, more people will do that something. The absence of poor people in an area is a signal that it lacks something important, like affordable housing or public transportation or jobs for the least skilled. The great urban poverty paradox is that if a city improves life for poor people currently living there by improving public schools or mass transit, that city will attract more poor people.

When American cities have built new rapid-transit stops over the last thirty years, poverty rates have generally increased near those stops. This doesn't mean that mass transit was making people poor, but rather that poor people value being able to get around without a car. The fact that public transit disproportionately carries and attracts the poor is a benefit, not a flaw.

What forces draw the poor to urban areas? Above all, they come for jobs. Urban density makes trade possible; it enables markets. The world's most important market is the labor market, in which one person rents his human capital to people with financial capital. But cities do more than merely allow laborer and capitalist to interact. They provide a wide range of jobs, often thousands of them; a big city is a diversified portfolio of employers.

If one employer in a city goes belly-up, there's another one (or two or ten) to take its place. This mixture of employers may not provide insurance against the global collapse of a great depression, but it sure smooths out the ordinary ups and downs of the marketplace. A one-company town like Hershey, Pennsylvania, depends on a single employer, and workers' lives depend on whether that employer rises or falls. Not so in New York City or Rio de Janeiro, where there's a plethora of factories in different industries. A classic study by two economists found that unemployment rates were almost 3 percent higher in the downturns of the 1970s and 1980s in places that lacked a diverse range of employers.

The sheer variety of urban jobs also allows people to figure out what they can and can't do well. For millennia, most humans toiled on farms regardless of whether or not they had any aptitude for tilling the soil. In a city, people can hop from firm to firm and industry to industry. As people job-hop, they learn what they like and can do well. How much would the world have lost if Thomas Edison or Henry Ford had been forced to spend all his days farming?

Rio's Favelas

Rio's shantytowns began in the late nineteenth century, when Brazil was lurching out of its quasi-feudal past. In the 1870s and 1880s, when other New World countries, like Argentina and the United States, elected their rulers, Brazil was ruled by an emperor, a scion of Portugal's ancient house of Braganza, and slavery was still legal.

By the middle of the nineteenth century, about 40 percent of Rio's population—eighty thousand people—were slaves. As abolitionism grew as a political force, slaves increasingly ran away to the city to escape plantation life. Runaway slaves in Rio formed shantytowns called *quilombos* in the nineteenth century, which were the ancestors of favelas. Emperor Pedro II disliked slavery, but fear of a political backlash may have kept him from trying to emancipate the rest of the country. Finally, in 1888, when the emperor was out of the country, his daughter, acting as regent, signed Brazil's emancipation proclamation, making it the last country in the Americas to end slavery. The emperor had been right to fear a backlash. In the next year, a military coup, backed by oligarchs outraged by losing their human chattels, toppled the Braganza dynasty.

The first true favela had its roots not in urban Rio but in the impoverished countryside of northeastern Brazil, where an itinerant preacher and erstwhile abolitionist, Antonio the Counselor, founded a town called Canudos, populated by former slaves, and started a tax rebellion. Canudos had grown to thirty thousand people by 1895, so the Counselor's refusal to pay taxes was no mere whiskey rebellion. In 1896, open war broke out, and the government sent thousands of soldiers to take the town. Before Canudos finally fell, about fifteen thousand people were killed.

While the Brazilian army won, the parsimonious government opted not to pay the soldiers. They responded by setting up their own village, unconsciously aping the Counselor they had just defeated, in the hills outside Rio. That shantytown became the Morro da Providência, the ur-favela. Over the next seventy years, hundreds of thousands of poor peasants, many of them freed slaves, came to Rio. The dilapidated dwellings may not look like much, but they beat working on a plantation for one's former master. Just like the freed American slaves who populated U.S. cities in the twentieth century, the freed Brazilians chose urban promise over rural poverty.

Foreign visitors tend to compare the poor in Rio with other people they've seen, perhaps poor residents of America's ghettoes, who are almost invariably better off, but that's a mistake. The favela's residents don't usually have the option of living in Los Angeles, and they should be compared with the people, largely unseen by foreign eyes, living in the poor rural areas of *Brazil*. Rio has plenty of poverty, but it's nothing like Brazil's rural northeast. One recent study reported that while 90 percent of Rio residents earned more than $85 a month in 1996, only 30 percent of people in the rural northeast were above that poverty line.

Even when compared with the most dire urban poverty, conditions in rural areas are usually worse. Lagos, Nigeria, is often depicted as a place of profound deprivation, but in fact the extreme-poverty rate in Lagos, when corrected for higher prices in the city, is less than half the extreme-poverty rate in rural Nigeria. About three quarters of Lagos residents have access to safe drinking water, a proportion that is horribly low but that is far higher than anyplace else in Nigeria, where the norm is less than 30 percent. Kolkata is also considered a place of great deprivation, but the poverty rate in that city is 11 percent, while the poverty rate in rural West Bengal is 24 percent. In recent years, more than 10 percent of West Bengal's rural residents have faced food shortages; the comparable figure for urban residents is less than 1 percent.

Cities and urbanization are not only associated with greater material prosperity. In poorer countries, people in cities also say that they are happier. Throughout a sample of twenty-five poorer countries, where per capita GDP levels are below $10,000, where I had access to self-reported happiness surveys for urban and nonurban populations, I found that the share of urban people saying that they were very happy was higher in eighteen countries and lower in seven. The share of people saying that they were not at all happy was higher in the nonurban areas in sixteen countries and lower in nine.

And unlike the hinterlands, urban slums often serve as springboards to middle-class prosperity. The Lower East Side of Manhattan, for example, despite high levels of poverty, produced a string of dazzling successes. The Jews who settled in the Lower East Side came from a culture with a long devotion to learning and lived in a country that was rapidly expanding its commitment to schooling. The situation for Brazil's slaves and their descendants was less promising. They went for centuries without schools, and Brazil has been bad at investing in human capital. Still, the favelas have produced some remarkable success stories.

Leila Velez, a janitor's daughter who grew up in a Rio favela, was working at a McDonald's when she was fourteen. She and her sister-in-law, a hairdresser, were determined to find a way to make their hair less frizzy. They understood the size of the market for such a product; they were surrounded by people who wanted frizzless hair. The two budding entrepreneurs lacked any scientific background, but Leila's husband let his hair be used to test many strange concoctions cooked up by his sister and wife. He repeatedly went bald, but eventually trial and error produced an effective hair straightener.

Velez patented the concoction and sold her Volkswagen Beetle for $3,000 to get the capital to open a salon. They knew their customers, and the product sold well. From there, she expanded the number of salons, generally hiring former customers as employees. Her firm currently sells $30 million a year of beauty products. She is in some ways a modern version of the early twentieth-century entrepreneur Madam C. J. Walker, whose "wonderful hair grower" brought her out of poverty and made her the most successful African-American businessperson and the world's most successful female entrepreneur of her time.

The occasional success story doesn't mean that urban poverty isn't awful. It is. Few readers of this book would want to spend a week, let alone a lifetime, in a favela. Yet urban poverty, despite its terrors, can offer a path toward prosperity both for the poor and for the nation as a whole. Brazil, China, and India are likely to become far wealthier over the next fifty years, and that wealth will be created in cities that are connected to the rest of the world, not in isolated rural areas.

It is natural to see the very real problems of poorer megacities and think that the people should go back to their rural villages, but cities, not farms, will save the developing world. Many poor nations suffer from poor soil quality—that's one reason why they're poor—so it's unlikely that they'll ever be leaders in global agriculture. Improvements in agricultural productivity typically involve new technology that reduces the number of people working on farms. That fact alone makes it unlikely that better farming will deliver widespread prosperity. And developing rural areas of poor countries is inherently difficult because it's so expensive to provide infrastructure across large distances.

Poor rural villages can seem like a window into the distant past, where little has changed for millennia. Cities are dynamic whirlwinds, constantly changing, bringing fortunes to some and suffering to others. A city might bring a bullet, but it also offers a chance of a richer, healthier, brighter life that can come from connecting with the planet. Life in a rural village might be safer than life in a favela, but it is the safety of unending poverty for generations. The status quo in the world's poorest places is terrible, which is why the urban roller coaster has so much to offer, especially because cities can transmit the knowledge countries need to take part in the global economy.

The vast flow of migrants to cities certainly stresses urban infrastructure; that's one of the familiar arguments against allowing the growth of megacities. But while an influx of new migrants worsens the quality of roads and water for a city's longtime residents, the new arrivals go from having virtually no infrastructure to enjoying all the advantages that come from access to decent transport and utilities. It is wrong to keep the quality of urban infrastructure high by preventing people from enjoying that infrastructure. It's more ethical—and more economically beneficial for the country as a whole—to invest more in urban infrastructure so more people can benefit from it.

Traditionally, governments have done more—if not always enough—to address urban poverty than rural poverty. This pattern has held true in Brazil for more than a century. After all, Rio was the nation's capital until 1960, and the favelas are still close to the mansions of the country's elite. Starting in the early 1900s, Brazil began a public health campaign to make Rio's favelas healthier.

The government began with a vaccination campaign and eventually brought schools and some health care to the favelas. The "City of God" that inspired a movie about Rio's poverty was a governmental attempt to improve housing quality for favela dwellers. Policing has been a trickier problem, but at least crime in the favelas is viewed as a national problem to be addressed by the national government. As a result, some resources get targeted at improving the lives of the urban poor, while the rural poor, who are less visible, get less.

The ironic result of attempts to improve life for Rio's poor is that still more poor people come to the favelas, which is the urban poverty paradox in action. If a government provides health care and education in the city but not in the countryside, then those services will attract more poor to urban areas. Any attempt to fix the poverty level in a single city may well backfire and increase the level of poverty in a city by attracting more poor people.

Moving On Up

Americans who are shocked by the favelas' squalor have forgotten their own urban past. Such extremes of wealth and poverty were standard in nineteenth-century American cities. Irish immigrants who fled starvation often lived in shantytowns like New York's Hell's Kitchen, the area of far western Manhattan from Thirty-fourth to Fifty-ninth streets, which has since become a trendy, sought-after neighborhood. The Upper East Side of Manhattan, stretching from Fifty-ninth Street to Ninety-sixth Street between Fifth Avenue and the East River, now includes some pricey real estate, but was also full of Irish shanties in the nineteenth century. The Upper East Side Armory occupies its incongruous location, surrounded by tony apartment buildings on Park Avenue, because its bourgeois soldiers were originally meant to protect urban elites from unruly immigrants.

Even more than New York, Boston is considered the mother city of Irish America. New York actually received more Irish immigrants than Boston did during the 1840s, but New York's Irish were later swamped by vast numbers of immigrants from Eastern Europe and elsewhere. Boston received a large influx of Irish during the potato famine, but much smaller numbers of the different ethnicities that dominated later immigrations. Boston's Irish character is essentially a gift of its strength during the era of sail. In the 1840s, during the famine, it was still faster, if not cheaper, to get to Boston than New York. If you were a poor Irish family, short on food, it often made sense to just get to Boston and stay there. Thirty years later, when steam had replaced sail, relatively fewer ships were coming to Boston, and late-nineteenth-century immigration came overwhelmingly through New York. The absence of those waves in Boston meant the city would be defined for decades by the conflict between Yankees and Irish.

Boston's fame as an Irish-American city is particularly associated with a single family, the Kennedys, whose story shows how urban poverty can beget opportunity. Patrick Kennedy was born in 1823 in Ireland's County Wexford. He got little schooling. Poor rural areas have generally offered little education, and when he was born, rules preventing Catholic education in Ireland were still in force. Young Kennedy worked on his older brother's farm, planting potatoes and harvesting grain. The one nonagricultural skill he acquired came from a more urban friend, Patrick Barron, who worked in a brewery and taught him how to make barrels.

The potato famine hit the Kennedys' meager farm hard. Facing the prospect of starvation, Patrick Kennedy followed Barron to Boston, where Barron got him a job as a cooper in East Boston. Boston offered economic opportunity, because it had a market where Kennedy could sell his labor to an employer who had capital. Boston provided a ready market for barrels because of its role as a center for transportation, and of course brewing.

Just as in Rio's favelas, in East Boston the density that enabled poor people to sell their labor enabled bacteria to flow, and Patrick Kennedy died of cholera. Kennedy's son, however, also named Patrick, thrived. He started off working on the docks and saved enough to buy a saloon. He soon owned a second and then a third drinking establishment, catering increasingly to wealthier Bostonians. He vertically integrated his business—by importing whiskey.

Patrick Kennedy followed the example of former Massachusetts governor Sam Adams, combining alcohol and politics. He was first elected to the Massachusetts legislature in 1884 and served several terms as a state representative and then state senator. In 1888, this son of a poor immigrant rose high enough to give a speech at the Democratic national convention. His growing wealth enabled him to send his bright son, Joseph, to Harvard. Patrick Kennedy's political connections made it natural that his son would marry the beautiful daughter of Boston's mayor John F. "Honey Fitz" Fitzgerald. Joe Kennedy started out working for the government as a bank examiner, then took over a bank in which his father had substantial holdings. He made a fortune on Wall Street in the 1920s, by more and less savory means. Just as important, he got out in time and found other lucrative pursuits, like investing in real estate and importing British liquor. His sons, of course, became America's great political dynasty.

Cities have an enduring attraction for immigrants like Patrick Kennedy; as of 2008, 36 percent of New Yorkers are foreign-born, and 48 percent speak a language other than English at home. The comparable numbers for the United States as a whole are 13 percent and 20 percent. Just as cities are good for immigrants, immigrants are good for cities. Boston owes much to the Kennedys, as New York does to immigrants ranging from Andrew Carnegie to Al Jolson to Zubin Mehta. Indeed, for all but 12 of the 118 years between 1891 and 2009, the New York Philharmonic has depended on foreign-born music directors. Needless to say, more populist elements of New York culture, like bagels and pizza and Kung Pao chicken, are also the gifts of immigrants.

America and its cities have benefited enormously from the influx of immigrant talent. German Americans, like Dwight Eisenhower and Chester Nimitz, led the war against Germany and Japan. Scots, like Andrew Carnegie and Andrew Mellon, helped build our industry. Irish Americans, like the Kennedys, Al Smith, and Chicago's Daley dynasty have been important political leaders. The son of a Kenyan sits in the Oval Office. America is not an Anglo-Saxon nation but an agglomeration of people from around the globe who've made their contributions primarily in our big urban areas.

And America is hardly the only country whose immigrants have made fortunes. Robert Cain and his family left poverty in Ireland for Liverpool when he was a young child, and as a young man he went to sea working as a cooper. In the 1840s, he settled in Liverpool and used his savings to open a modest brewery. He made millions, and his son ended up in the House of Lords. Carlos Slim, who may be the world's richest man, was the son of a Lebanese immigrant to Mexico City who started out running a dry goods store. As these and many less famous examples attest, cities everywhere allow people to move from destitution to phenomenal wealth—and to any number of promising points in between.

Urban labor markets have long made it easier to work without owning a farm or animals or equipment. The Kennedys were on both sides of this bargain. When penniless Patrick Kennedy arrived, he could sell his labor to people with capital. His son did the same thing when he was young, but as he aged and saved, he could switch to the hiring side of the model. Capitalists and workers are often seen as enemies, as they are, for example, during a strike. But more generally, capital increases the returns to labor, and it is urban capital that made cities such magnets for the poor.

Cities don't just connect capital-less workers with capital-rich employers; they offer a huge variety of job opportunities that allow poor people (indeed, everybody) to find talents they might otherwise never know they had. The great University of Chicago economist George Stigler once wrote that "in a regime of ignorance, Enrico Fermi would have been a gardener, von Neumann a checkout clerk in a drugstore." Stigler's vision of two of the finest minds of the twentieth century working dead-end jobs is frightening. Luckily, both men grew up in large cities and came from relatively privileged backgrounds, and their mathematical and scientific talents were spotted at a young age. Similarly, Boston brought forth Patrick Kennedy's talents in a way that rural Ireland could not.

Richard Wright's Urban Exodus

The great swaths of America's cities that are almost entirely African American and almost entirely poor illustrate what can go wrong when neighborhoods get cut off from the economic heart of their cities. But even those neighborhoods should be viewed in light of the even worse conditions endured in the rural South. The great African-American writer Richard Wright was born in Natchez, Mississippi. He and his mother moved north, first to Memphis and then to Chicago, seeking to escape Jim Crow laws as much as to find economic opportunity. As Wright wrote in his autobiographical *Black Boy,* "I headed north full of a hazy notion that life could be lived with dignity, that the personalities of others should not be violated, that men should be able to confront other men without fear or shame, and that if men were lucky in their living on earth they might win some redeeming meaning for their having struggled and suffered here beneath the stars."

Wright's northern exodus may have freed him from the harsh racial laws of Mississippi, but it didn't immediately bring him "redeeming meaning." In Chicago, he started off working as a porter, then an errand boy and a dishwasher. Like Coleman Young and thousands of other talented African Americans during that period, he sought a better life by working for the post office, but malnutrition had left him 15 pounds below the government's 125-pound minimum. Finally, in the spring of 1929, he made weight and got a full-time job working the night shift at Chicago's central post office, then the world's largest.

The job was a good one that allowed him to do some writing. Even more important, it connected him with a left-wing literary salon. He was brought into a group of ten in the South Side of Chicago that met to argue current events. As Wright recounts in a brilliant and funny memoir, "I Tried to Be a Communist," he "was amazed to discover that many of them had joined the Communist Party." Soon enough, "Sol" asked Wright to come to a meeting of the Moscow-affiliated John Reed Club. Wright responded with a certain amount of cynicism: "I don't want to be organized." Sol dangled the bait Wright craved most in the world: "They can help you to write."

Wright was laid off when the Great Depression drastically reduced the business of Chicago's mail-order houses, and he began a peripatetic stream of jobs, selling life insurance on commission, cleaning streets, digging ditches, and eventually working for the Michael Reese Hospital. He apparently got that job because he had caught the eye of the wife of the great urban sociologist Louis Wirth. She also got him work writing the history of Illinois for the New Deal

Works Progress Administration. He moved to New York in 1937, working on the WPA publication *New York Panorama,* which remains a wonderful description of big-city living.

In 1938, the year after he came to New York, he won a $500 prize for a short story. His first book, a collection of stories called *Uncle Tom's Children,* was published by Harper and Company. He won a Guggenheim Fellowship to write *Native Son,* and with that, he became a literary lion. In nine years, Chicago and then New York had brought him from struggling porter to successful writer during the depths of the Great Depression. Talent and the urban ability to match talent to task won out.

Richard Wright's move north made him part of the vast exodus of African Americans who fled the Jim Crow South. The economic advantages that came from moving north were immense. A Southern sharecropper in the 1920s would be lucky to earn $445 a year. A black worker in one of Henry Ford's plants would earn $5 a day, more than three times that income. Yet like Richard Wright, the African Americans who came north found more than just higher incomes. They found freedom.

The Harlem Renaissance brought together a dizzying array of writers, such as Langston Hughes and Zora Neale Hurston, and performers like Ella Fitzgerald and Billie Holiday. All of America benefited as black talents like Duke Ellington burst into the white world. For these famous figures and for millions of more obscure African Americans, urban density enabled upward mobility.

This history suggests that areas should be judged not by their poverty but by their track record in helping poorer people move up. If a city is attracting continuing waves of the less fortunate, helping them succeed, watching them leave, and then attracting new disadvantaged migrants, then it is succeeding at one of society's most important functions. If an area has become the home of default for poor people who are staying poor, then that area is failing.

Rise and Fall of the American Ghetto

The African-American migration north is as great an epic as America has experienced. In the early twentieth century, African Americans were rare in Northern cities. Only 2 percent of New York's population and 1.8 percent of

Chicago's population were African American in 1900. Decade after decade, these percentages grew as blacks chose urban opportunity. They came north to experience freedom and pursue prosperity, but when they arrived, they found color barriers that, while less obvious than those in the South, could still be terrible. Just like building a factory, enacting a law has fixed costs, so Northern racists didn't bother to enact laws when there were only a handful of urban blacks, but as their numbers increased, so did discriminatory legislation, and Northern cities increasingly found ways to isolate their growing African-American populations.

George W. F. McMechen would seem to be the ultimate upwardly mobile African American at the start of the last century. He graduated from Morgan College and Yale Law School and came to Baltimore, where he formed a successful legal practice with another African American, W. Ashbie Hawkins. McMechen wanted to live in one of Baltimore's more affluent neighborhoods, which were in those days overwhelmingly white. In 1910, Hawkins bought a house at 1834 McCulloh Street and leased it to McMechen.

This formerly all-white neighborhood rose up in arms. Local kids threw bricks through McMechen's windows. A neighborhood improvement association was formed specifically to get rid of him. Whites tried to buy the property from McMechen's partner, who demanded three times his purchase price. The white neighbors balked and decided to rewrite the law instead. One of McMechen's neighbors was an attorney—"eminent" according to the *New York Times,* "briefless" according to Hawkins—who dug up a copy of Baltimore's city charter and decided that it was well within the city's rights to pass a race-based zoning ordinance. He drafted such a law and had no problem getting it passed by the city council and signed by the mayor, who implausibly announced that the law's supporters were "the best friends that the colored people have."

Similar measures were soon passed in Richmond, Atlanta, Louisville, and other Southern cities. Yet despite the fact that segregation had become law in so many areas of Southern life, there was still doubt about the legality of zoning by race. McMechen argued that it was "unconstitutional, unjust and discriminatory against the negro." Hawkins took Baltimore to court and won, invalidating the segregationist laws in state court. Finally, in 1917, the National Association for the Advancement of Colored People (NAACP) achieved its first great triumph when the Supreme Court made zoning by race illegal, in what probably was the greatest courtroom victory for black America up to that time.

But the Supreme Court's ruling barely held back the white desire to isolate blacks. In some cities, like Atlanta and Chicago, rioters terrorized blacks who ventured into white areas. Restrictive covenants in deeds prevented the sale of property to classes of people deemed undesirable. One 1947 study found that there were racially restrictive covenants in 72 percent of developments built in New York between the world wars.

These restrictions meant that African Americans not only lived in isolated neighborhoods but often also paid more for their housing. Almost forty years ago, a study by economists John Kain and John Quigley found that blacks paid more than whites for comparable housing in St. Louis. This finding squared well with earlier claims that African-American "residents of the black belt in Chicago pay as much per cubic foot per room as that paid by wealthy residents for equivalent space on the Lakeside drive." Throughout the country, blacks paid more, relative to whites, in cities that were more segregated.

But cities also produced the legal champions who slowly brought down the ghetto walls. Two Baltimore attorneys, Thurgood Marshall and Philip Perlman, one black and one white, one representing the NAACP and the other representing the U.S. government, came together to fight restrictive covenants. Swayed by their arguments, in 1948 the Supreme Court ruled that racial covenants were not prohibited, but state power could not be used to enforce them, effectively ending their usefulness. There is a beautiful irony in this: An activist court promoted racial equality by telling the government not to act. Ten years later, in New York City, a powerful coalition of blacks, Jews, and other ethnicities pioneered the nation's first fair-housing law that banned discrimination on the basis of religion or race in private dwellings. Other areas followed New York's lead, and after another ten years, a week after the assassination of Martin Luther King Jr., Congress passed the Civil Rights Act of 1968, which barred discrimination in all American housing.

These legal triumphs made it possible for upwardly mobile African Americans to leave the ghetto and to move to previously all-white neighborhoods. Between 1970 and 2000, segregation declined almost everywhere in America, primarily because formerly lily-white areas acquired a few mostly well-off

African Americans. Between 1970 and 1990, the segregation level of African-American college graduates declined by about 25 percent, while the segregation level of high school dropouts declined by less than 10 percent.

The nature of segregation also changed. Before the 1960s, it reflected hard barriers against black mobility, which limited African Americans' housing choices and caused them to pay more for housing in more segregated cities. Today, segregation is more likely to reflect the workings of a free housing market, in which whites are often simply more willing than many blacks to pay a premium to live in mostly white neighborhoods. As a result, housing today is particularly cheap for African Americans in more segregated areas—the exact opposite of the situation half a century ago.

The end of laws enforcing segregation was a triumph for American society, but segregation persists, and tragically the triumph of integration seems to have made segregation increasingly harmful. Studies in the 1960s and 1970s found little difference in outcomes between African Americans who grew up in more segregated cities and those who lived in less segregated areas. That changed as more prosperous African Americans left the ghetto. By 1990, blacks between the ages of twenty and twenty-four who grew up in more segregated cities were 5.5 percent less likely than similarly aged African Americans in less segregated areas to have a high school degree and 6.2 percent more likely to be out of school and out of work. The African Americans in less segregated areas were earning 17 percent more. There were no significant differences among whites living in more and less segregated metropolitan areas. Young black women were 3.2 percent more likely to be single mothers in more segregated cities.

Thirty years ago, William Julius Wilson argued that when the most well-educated African Americans stayed in segregated communities, they provided role models and leadership for the entire community. When they left, those communities became rudderless. A mass of evidence has accrued since then to support his argument. Here we see the wisdom in sociologist Robert Merton's law of unintended consequences, which so often attend even the most well-meaning public actions. Merton understood the complexity of society and the fact that public action may bring unexpected and undesired aftereffects. No one wants to return to a world where blacks who moved into a white suburb faced death threats, yet the exodus of skilled minorities has meant that ghettos are now worse places for the children of those left behind. The sad fact is that too many segregated cities have changed from being places of upward mobility to places of perpetual poverty.

The Inner City

The fight against the terrible segregation that remains in American cities is so difficult, in part, because there are economic forces that pull the rich and poor apart. There is a hidden logic behind the concentrated poverty that results from the tendency of the poor to live at the physical center of American cities. That tendency reflects, in part, the power of transportation to shape cities. All forms of travel involve two types of cost: money and time. The cash cost of commuting is the same for rich and poor, but rich people with higher wages give up more income when they spend more time commuting and less time working. As a result the rich are generally willing to pay more for faster trips to work. Why are the centers of Manhattan and Rio richer than more distant areas? Richer people can pay more for the privilege of having shorter commutes.

Yet in most American cities, there are also reversals where the poor live closer to the center than the rich. When a single transportation mode, like driving or taking the subway, dominates, then the rich live closer to the city center and the poor live farther away. But when there are multiple modes of transit, then the poor often live closer in order to gain access to public transit. The U.S. poverty line for a four-person household in 2009 is $22,050. In 2008, a typical nonurban household spent $9,000 on car-related transportation. How in the world could a two-adult family with $22,000 of income afford two cars?

New York, Boston, and Philadelphia have four transit and income zones: an inner zone (like central Manhattan or Beacon Hill) where the rich commute by foot or public transit, a second zone (the edges of New York's outer boroughs, or Roxbury in Boston) where the poor commute by public transit, a third zone (Westchester County or Wellesley) where the rich drive, and an outer zone comprising distant areas where less wealthy people live and drive.

Paris likewise has excellent public transportation and consequently has an inner zone where the rich use the Métro or walk. The next zone has the poor living in more distant areas that are still connected to the city by train.

Newer cities, like Los Angeles, are far less oriented toward public transit and as a result have no inner walking or public-transit zone used by the wealthy. The prosperous all drive, and there are just three zones: an inner area where the poor take public transit (South Central L.A.), a middle area where the rich drive (Beverly Hills), and an outer area where the less wealthy have horrendous commutes.

Transportation isn't the only force pulling the poor to the center of American cities. Above all, prosperous parents suburbanize to get access to better schools. Central areas are often historic, and as a result they usually have older homes that have depreciated in quality and in price. Just as richer people buy new cars and then sell them to less wealthy people, typically new housing is built for more prosperous people and then as the housing depreciates, it comes to house the less fortunate. Just as an abundance of cheap used cars is a boon for poorer people, the abundance of cheap used housing in places like Detroit or St. Louis also benefits the poor.

The connection between poverty and inner-city transportation reminds us that some places are poor for a reason and that we shouldn't expect them to quickly get rich. When an area offers amenities like mass transit or cheaper, older housing that poor people particularly value, then the place will likely remain poor.

How Policy Magnifies Poverty

For decades, public policies have tried to alleviate the costs of segregation, but many of these well-meaning interventions have done more to prove the weakness of Washington than to fix urban suffering. One line of attack offers businesses tax breaks for locating in disadvantaged areas, called Empowerment Zones in the United States and Enterprise Zones in England. As we saw in the last chapter, Empowerment Zones do bring jobs to poor areas, but they're expensive; it takes about $100,000 in tax breaks to generate one job. Moreover, we still don't know if this employment translates into long-term success for the children growing up in these areas.

An alternative view argues that such approaches are just "gilding the ghetto," as my former colleague John Kain once wrote. In this view, only greater mobility, such as that created by housing vouchers, can relieve the suffering of segregation. In the 1990s, the Department of Housing and Urban Development tried a social experiment, called Moving to Opportunity, that randomly distributed vouchers among a pool of single-parent families eager for aid. One third of the subjects got nothing; they were the control group. One third got a standard-issue voucher that could pay for housing anywhere in the city. The remaining third got a voucher that could only be used in a low-poverty neighborhood. This restriction was an attempt to put poor people in wealthier neighborhoods and gauge the effects of place on those people. By comparing the control groups with the voucher recipients, it was possible to get an estimate of the impact of various neighborhoods on parents and kids.

The results were strikingly mixed. Parents whose vouchers enabled them to move to low-poverty neighborhoods were happier, healthier, and less likely to be crime victims, but they weren't any better off financially. After all, the old ghettos were actually pretty close to jobs. The impact on children's achievement was quite mixed as well. Girls did much better academically and seemed to be settling well into their new environments. The boys did poorly, and if anything had more behavioral problems if they moved to a low-poverty environment, which is another example of the unforeseen consequences that are so common in social policy. These mixed results for girls and boys mirror a broader pattern over the last three decades: African-American women have been much more successful than men.

Housing vouchers are good at what they were designed to do—using public dollars to put poorer people into better homes. They actually get resources to the people who need them, instead of lining contractors' pockets and building white-elephant projects. But they are not the solution to cities' larger social problems. The Moving to Opportunity study shows that we can't solve the problems of urban poverty by just giving people money to move to richer neighborhoods.

Bad policy puts place-making above helping people, but sometimes social entrepreneurs can do great good by focusing on just one place. For almost forty years, the Harlem Children's Zone has fought for the children of Manhattan's best-known African-American community. They've created a dense web of social activities, such as the Baby College, which teaches parenting skills, aimed at improving academic outcomes and reducing crime. In one sense, they may be "gilding the ghetto," but in another sense, they are giving Harlem's children the skills they need to thrive and even leave Harlem if they want to.

In 2004, as New York began to allow more experimentation in its schools, the Harlem Children's Zone opened its own charter school, the Promise Academy. The school's curriculum is intense, requiring long hours from its students, and it offers financial incentives for success. The school's leaders worked aggressively to lure the best teachers available, and the academy fired almost 50 percent of its teachers in its first year. Entrance into the school is determined by lottery, which led my colleague Roland Fryer to perform a true natural experiment comparing similar lottery winners and losers. He and his co-author found that the school had strong, positive effects on its students: the Promise Academy eliminated the black-white achievement gap in mathematics. The teachers had particular success with boys, which is unusual and remarkable.

The Harlem Children's Zone proves that investing in segregated areas can work, as long as that investment targets children, not stadiums or monorails. But does its success mean that President Obama was right in 2007 to promise that "when I'm President, the first part of my plan to combat urban poverty will be to replicate the Harlem Children's Zone in twenty cities across the country"? Can the federal government successfully replicate the social entrepreneurship that sprang up in New York City? Can other cities attract the same remarkable pool of leaders, teachers, and benefactors that came to the zone in New York, especially if they have to play by rules laid down in Washington? I hope so, but I fear that the success of the zone and the relative failure of most nationwide interventions suggest that the solution to urban problems is more likely to come from local initiative than from federal policy. When a city attracts enough skilled people, some of them will be willing to work on the city's problems and find solutions for even the most seemingly intractable ones.

The case for federal action is strongest when that action is reducing the artificial separation of rich and poor created by the government itself. Whenever public services are radically different in two adjacent areas, those differences will influence where people choose to live. Some of that sorting is perfectly benign: One suburban school may have a better football team than its neighbor and attract more sports-oriented parents. Given the athletic incompetence that my children may inherit from me, I'm happy to have an option of less sports-oriented schools. But there is far more reason to worry when differences in school quality lead to the isolation of the poor.

East St. Louis provides an extreme example of the urban poverty paradox, whereby public policy that helps the poor in one area can lead to a massive concentration of poverty. East St. Louis lies across the Mississippi River, in Illinois, from St. Louis, Missouri. In 1989, the annual Aid to Families with Dependent Children payment was 20 percent higher in Illinois than in Missouri. If you were out of work, it made sense to move to Illinois, and so in 1990 the poverty rate in East St. Louis was 43 percent—higher than in St. Louis or Buffalo or Detroit or any other declining Rust Belt city. Since welfare reform in 1996, the gap in welfare payments has essentially disappeared, and the poverty-rate gap between St. Louis and East St. Louis has narrowed considerably.

Welfare disparities have diminished, but differences in school quality remain, and they help explain why some central cities, like Detroit, are poor while others, like Paris, are not. Paris has some of the best public high schools in the world, and prosperous Parisian parents dream of getting their children into lycées like Henri-IV and Louis le Grand. But in the United States, public school monopolies have ensured that central cities often have poorly functioning school districts. Suburbs are smaller and more competitive, attracting more prosperous parents.

Nowhere was the power of schools to cause segregation made clearer than in the strange case of busing. In the wake of the 1964 Civil Rights Act, federal and state authorities started requiring busing among districts to achieve a constant proportion of blacks and whites within each school district. Proponents of busing saw it as a means of breaking down the intellectual isolation of the ghetto and improving opportunity for African Americans. Enemies of busing, and that included more than 90 percent of America, saw it as an intrusion that destroyed neighborhood schools and forced kids to travel long distances.

It's easy to sympathize with both arguments but hard to see any wisdom in the Supreme Court's decision in the case of *Milliken v. Bradley,* which limited busing to the borders of school districts. That decision essentially meant that people within cities were forced to integrate their public schools, but suburban kids were exempt. If an antiurban fiend had tried to cause a mass exodus from the older cities, he couldn't have done better. White neighborhoods abandoned cities like Boston en masse for suburbs like Scituate outside the boundaries of the school district. They didn't want their children to be bused, and the Supreme Court had set things up so that they could avoid the whole thing just by leaving the city. The result isolated the urban poor even more.

The odd fact is that America's school system could decrease segregation if it moved either to the socialist left or to the free-market right. If America imitated the best aspect of European socialism and invested enough in public schools so that they were all good, then there would be little reason for the rich to leave cities to get better schooling. If America allowed vouchers or charter schools that would foster more competition in urban school districts, then their quality would rise and might even become a draw for prosperous parents. The American system of local public school monopolies has done little to help cities and much to ensure that those cities are poorer than they should be.

Urban poverty is not pretty—no poverty is pretty—but the favelas of Rio, the slums of Mumbai, and the ghettos of Chicago have long provided pathways out of destitution for the poor. In some cases, the dream of upward mobility is not coming true, but that is a reason to continue fighting for our cities, not to place our hope in rural life, especially in the developing world. Cities bring change—for society and for individuals—and the status quo is no friend of those without food or health care or a future. The part of the world that is rural and poor moves glacially—only occasionally shocked by famine or civil war or, very rarely, something as helpful as the Green Revolution—while the part of the world that is urban and poor is changing rapidly. There is opportunity in change.

But there is a reason why people promote the myth that cities are bad for the poor. The flow of millions of poor people into cities may be a hopeful sign for those migrants, but it won't necessarily improve the quality of life for the middle-income people who are already living in those areas. Policies aimed at reducing migration into cities, like Mumbai's draconian limitations on building, appeal to current city dwellers who know that crowding and congestion won't make their lives better. Density has costs as well as benefits.

Urban growth will be palatable to everyone when cities do a better job of defeating the demons that come with density. Over the last three centuries, wealthier countries have spent billions on the fights against urban disease and crime. The cities of the developing world have yet to win those battles, which are the topic of the next chapter.

CHAPTER 4

How Were the Tenements Tamed?

The Dharavi neighborhood of Mumbai houses between six hundred thousand and a million people on around 530 acres. It is a teeming mass of humanity and entrepreneurship. People aren't sitting around Dharavi waiting for their chance to be on *Who Wants to Be a Millionaire.* In one small, dirt-floored windowless room, a couple of guys are recycling cardboard boxes—tearing them open, turning them inside out, and then stapling them up again so the printing is on the inside. The space does double duty as a dormitory, for old boxes make an adequate resting spot. Right next door, a couple of tailors are making brassieres, which can take your mind back to the Lower East Side a century ago.

Nearby, dozens of potters work in ill-lit rooms off unpaved streets. They transform freshly delivered clay into pots, which are then fired in a large outdoor smoke-bellowing kiln. In another room, seven or eight women are sorting through used plastic goods. All this recycling makes Dharavi feel pretty green, but I'm not sure even the most ardent environmentalist can take much pleasure in the recycling of syringes.

While Dharavi's entrepreneurial energy illustrates the upside of urban poverty—ambitious people working hard and benefiting from proximity to urban customers and inputs—the area's dirty air and contaminated water emphasize the costs of urban concentration. The streets are unpaved. Sewage lines, when they exist, often spill into water lines. There are supposedly more than a thousand inhabitants for every working toilet, so it is common to see people defecating in the streets. In such conditions, disease is inevitable, taking the lives of far too many poor Indians. According to one study, tuberculosis is the second leading cause of death in Mumbai, and its ravages help make the life expectancy there seven years lower than in the rest of India.

In 1962, the psychologist John B. Calhoun published an article in *Scientific American* describing horrific consequences that followed when he created massively overcrowded rat colonies. The rats' problems included high levels of infant mortality, cannibalism, "frenetic overactivity," and "pathological withdrawal." One can reasonably doubt whether hypercrowded rats have much to tell us about human life in cities, and experiments on others species, like the rhesus monkey, have found that density can lead to kindness rather than killing. Still, Calhoun's work is a warning that reminds us that density can have considerable downsides.

Mumbai's traffic congestion can be excruciating—taxis come to a standstill behind a bullock-drawn cart. While Dharavi is pretty safe—thanks to a well-functioning social system in which neighbors look after each other—Mumbai in general has its share of criminals, like the infamous gangsters who prey on Bollywood stars. These problems are not unique to Mumbai or to India. Every older city has battled the scourges of disease and crime. Every crowded city faces a potential congestion problem. The same density that spreads ideas can spread disease.

These problems are not intractable, but they often require the intervention of an active, even aggressive, public sector. Public-sector incompetence is often cited as an excuse for promoting rural poverty—the awful logic is that because the cities aren't clean, people should stay in their agricultural huts. This is wrong for both moral and practical reasons. Urban governments in developing countries must do what the cities of the West did in the nineteenth and early twentieth centuries: provide clean water while safely removing human waste. They must make ghettos safe. They must even do what too many American cities have failed to do: break the isolation that can rob poor children of the advantages that most people get from living in a big city. The Western world's fights against urban disease, corruption, crime, and segregation over the past two centuries offer many lessons for the developing world today, but unfortunately one of those lessons is that these fights are never easy.

The Dharavi slum simultaneously displays all that is great in the Indian people and all that is rotten in the state government of Maharashtra. Though it's unsettling to people who, like me, have a taste for free markets, the solution to Dharavi's problems is not for the government to disappear. There are, in fact, plenty of areas, like land use controls and business licensing, where the Indian government could and should intervene less, but there's no free-market solution for the great urban problems facing slums like Dharavi. Cities desperately need forceful, capable governments to provide clean water, safe neighborhoods, and fast-moving streets.

It's easy to idolize democracy, but effective city governments usually need leaders who govern with a firm hand, unencumbered by checks and balances and free from the need to heed the wishes of every disgruntled citizen. When describing his fight against crime in New York City, Teddy Roosevelt noted that "in most positions, the 'division of powers' theory works unmitigated mischief." I'm not going that far—separation of powers can play a very useful role in restraining bad leaders—but TR's attempts at curbing corruption were certainly stymied by his fellow police commissioners' ability to veto his actions. Teddy Roosevelt's rule for unrestrained reform seems to have been that undivided power helps prevent the forces that benefit from the status quo from blocking change. Just as we entrust our leaders with more authority in time of war, we may have to trust them more when our streets are unsafe or when every sip of water carries disease.

I have great admiration for India's remarkable democratic institutions, which are unique among the world's poorer nations, but that robust democracy, with its various entrenched constituencies, often impedes the forceful action that must be taken to substantially improve urban life. One of the worst aspects of Indian democracy is that power is often lodged at the state rather than the city level, and states are often dominated by rural voters who, just as in the U.S. Senate, have far more representation per capita. India's cities need more control over their own destinies.

The Plight of Kinshasa

Dharavi exemplifies the human capacity to persevere in difficult conditions, but some cities, like Kinshasa, the capital of the Democratic Republic of the Congo, are so dysfunctional that they seem to thwart even the most dogged effort to live a decent life. When the public sector completely fails to address the consequences of millions of poor people clustering in a single metropolis, cities can become places of horror, where criminals and disease roam freely. This failure prevents the city from fulfilling its core purpose, lifting the country by connecting talented people with each other and with the outside world. Who, other than the most dedicated humanitarians, would want to come to a place that offers so much risk for so little reward?

Kinshasa had bad beginnings. It was founded and named Léopoldville by the adventurer Henry Morton Stanley in 1881 to provide a trading post for King Leopold of Belgium, whose name became synonymous with a barbarous colonialism that forced African labor to extract resources from the earth and used mass killings as a management tool. Over time, Belgian government improved, and by the 1950s, the city had become almost pleasant, but Kinshasa deteriorated drastically after independence. For thirty-two years, Mobutu Sese Seko ruled with a rampantly corrupt regime that impoverished Zaire (as he renamed the country) by nationalizing industries, engaging in foreign military escapades, and failing to invest in either human or physical capital. Mobutu reminds us of the crucial shortcoming of Roosevelt's rule for unrestrained reform—undivided power is only good when that power is in the right hands, and that is never guaranteed. The years after Mobutu's ouster have hardly been better for the country (now called Congo again), as hundreds of thousands died in war, and corruption continued unabated.

As a result of protracted unrest in the Congo, Kinshasa grew rapidly even though there was no functioning state to mitigate its problems. Since 1960, the city has grown from 446,000 to an urban agglomeration of 10.4 million people.

A hallmark of one-man rule is that power radiates out from the dictator, and as a result, the capital cities in dictatorships are on average more than 30 percent larger than capital cities in stable democracies. A study of corruption in Indonesia found that the stock prices of companies whose leaders stood closest to that country's dictator in photographs suffered most when the leader fell ill. If you wanted a share in Zaire's kleptocracy, you would have to come to Kinshasa, to be close to Mobutu.

Some studies have found that more than one third of children in Kinshasa are infected with the malaria parasite. Hundreds died and thousands were infected in a typhoid fever outbreak in 2004–2005. On top of Kinshasa's other problems, the city has long been at the epicenter of the AIDS epidemic. The earliest HIV-positive blood samples come from residents of Leopoldville in 1959. By 1985, one random sample found that 5 percent of the population was infected. CNN recently listed Kinshasa as one of the world's ten most dangerous cities.

Conditions in Kinshasa are awful, but the situation in the rest of the Congo has often been even worse. The U.S. State Department notes that traveling in Kinshasa is "generally safe during daylight hours" but "remote areas are less secure because of high levels of criminal activity." The wars that tormented Central Africa's interior between 1996 and 2003 drove many thousands to the relative safety of Congo's capital. Seventy-three out of every thousand children born in the Kinshasa Province die before their first birthday. That's about ten times the U.S. average, but less than the figure for rural Congo. A survey in 2001 found that more than 10 percent of the children in some Kinshasa districts were suffering from malnutrition, which sounds bad, except when compared with rates outside the capital, which sometimes exceed 30 percent. The state-run water agency has failed miserably to provide clean water. Three tenths of the Congo's urbanites have to travel more than thirty minutes for potable water, but even that hasn't deterred migration from the country's interior.

Kinshasa, built by a brutal colonial regime and then ruled by an evil despot, was dealt a terrible hand. The city's problems may seem unsolvable from the perspective of London or New York today, but New York and London once had to solve similar problems. Every one of the world's older cities once fought epidemics of disease and violence. The ultimate success of those hard-fought battles should bring hope even to Kinshasa.

Healing Sick Cities

Plague came to Athens in 430 B.C. through its port of Piraeus and may have killed one out of every four Athenians. The city's leader, Pericles, was one of its victims. Plague came to Constantinople about 970 years later and, according to the historian Procopius, killed more than ten thousand people every day at its height. For more than three centuries after 1350, plague routinely slaughtered the city dwellers of Western Europe. In the seventeenth century, death rates were much higher in urban areas when compared with the

English countryside. Plague vanished from Europe (though not from Asia) in the early eighteenth century, but yellow fever invaded, and cholera began devastating Western cities by 1830.

While earlier public health actions against disease were mostly limited to quarantine, increasingly sophisticated urbanites like John Snow were acquiring the knowledge needed to battle the spread of pestilence. Snow was a coal worker's son from York who was apprenticed at the age of fourteen to the doctor of railroad pioneer George Stephenson. Nine years later, Snow walked two hundred miles alone to London to get the skills he needed to become a surgeon. Two years later, he received his license and became a successful doctor and medical researcher, one who learned much from the city around him. His greatest success came from observing the pattern of cholera deaths in the outbreak of 1854.

London was Snow's laboratory, and with the help of a local clergyman, he interviewed residents and produced a remarkable map of the cholera outbreak. Street by street, case by case, the map showed the geography of the disease. By examining the layout of the affliction, Snow saw that a particular water pump lay at the epicenter of the outbreak. His interviews led him to conclude "there has been no particular outbreak or prevalence of cholera in this part of London except among the persons who were in the habit of drinking the water of the above-mentioned pump well." Nearby ale imbibers remained healthy; alcohol's ability to kill waterborne bacteria had long helped city dwellers avoid illness.

The well appears to have been polluted by a nearby cesspit that contained infected feces. When Snow got the pump's handle removed, the outbreak subsided. The doctor didn't quite understand the bacterial origins of cholera, but he correctly determined that the malady was being spread by infected water. Snow's research offered early proof of a fact that now seems obvious: Cities must provide clean water to ensure urban health. Snow also provides us with an example of *self-protecting urban innovation,* cities' ability to generate the information needed to solve their own problems.

In the United States, city governments, driven more by intuition than by Snow's science, had begun the Herculean job of providing clean water at the start of the nineteenth century. Somehow they grasped that foul water played a role in disease outbreaks, and for years they fought for cleaner water. After yellow fever struck America's cities in 1793 and 1798, Philadelphia and New York both decided to provide their citizens with water uncontaminated by nearby cesspools. Philadelphia, guided by the English architect and engineer Benjamin Latrobe, went the public route. Expenses for both construction and operation were far higher than Latrobe's original estimate, but eventually the city had a well-functioning public system that drew from the upper reaches of the Schuylkill River.

New York followed a private path, but its attempts to save money only meant that decades would pass before clean water came to Manhattan. After the yellow fever outbreak, the city's Common Council initially proposed a public system, but state assemblyman and failed vice-presidential candidate Aaron Burr had different plans. To sway his political opponents, the Federalists on the Common Council, he enlisted his archrival, Mr. Federalism himself, Alexander Hamilton, as an ally. Hamilton cautioned against the "burthensome" taxes needed to fund a public system and convinced the Common Council to accept Burr's vision of privately supplied water.

Burr then used his own considerable political skills to shepherd a new private water company's charter through the state legislature. The charter's key provisions allowed the company to raise $2 million, and use any surplus capital in "monied transactions not inconsistent with the constitution and laws of this state, or of the United States." This seemingly innocuous provision meant that Burr could do whatever he wanted with the company, as long as it produced some water. He saw more financial and political profit in banking than in water provision. Hamilton had unwittingly created a competitor for his own Bank of New York. The Bank of the Manhattan Company has had more than two solid centuries of success, evolving later into Chase Manhattan and now JPMorgan Chase, but it certainly didn't solve New York's water problem.

To save capital that Burr badly wanted for its banking operations, the company used an old well and built an undersize reservoir. The Manhattan Company seems to have broken its promise to bring in clean, fresh water from the Bronx and instead filled its tanks with *aqua obscura*, water of unknown, questionable origin.

Private water provision works in plenty of places, but it has two potential problems. Consumers can't easily verify their water quality, which means that suppliers can cut corners without losing sales. And even if a private provider could guarantee clean water, customers aren't always willing or able to spend enough to make such purity profitable. Both of these issues disappear in a wealthy economy in which people can be counted on to pay plenty of money for drinking water and, generally speaking, providers can be counted on to provide healthy water, especially given the lawsuits they might face if they don't. But in the age of Hamilton and Burr, even if a prosperous burgher was able to send servants uptown for fresh water, that burgher could be sure that the people in the poorer wards were using cheaper, dirtier, downtown water. Bad water could still kill that burgher or his family, despite their own precautions, because a citywide epidemic could still start in those poor wards, spread by inexpensive, filthy water.

This is what economists call an *externality,* an impact that one person's actions have on someone else that doesn't work through a voluntary transaction. For more than a century, economists have argued that externalities require some form of state intervention, and so it was with water. Since the Manhattan Company didn't solve New York's clean-water problem, waterborne diseases kept reappearing. New York City would occasionally lose more than a half percent of its population to an epidemic during a given year, double the death rate in a normal year, as it did during the 1832 cholera epidemic.

Finally, New York City followed Philadelphia and spent millions, as Hamilton had warned, on public water provision. The Croton Aqueduct, built at a cost of $9 million (more than $170 million in 2010 dollars), provided New York's water after 1842, and that clean water quickly had an impact. After 1860, the mortality rate experienced a remarkable sixty-year decline, from more than thirty deaths per thousand at the end of the Civil War to around ten per thousand during the 1920s.

By 1896, there were almost 1,700 public water systems in the United States, and municipalities were spending as much on water as the federal government spent on everything except the military and the postal service. In Paris, Baron Georges-Eugène Haussmann had used his virtually unlimited authority as the agent of Napoléon III to create a sewage system that still serves the city and attracts tourists to its tunnels.

Economic historian Werner Troesken has done an enormous amount of research, which shows that investments in municipal waterworks significantly reduced deaths from typhoid fever and other diseases. Clean water has even re-duced deaths from diseases that aren't carried by water. Echoing century-old research on the impact of clean water in Massachusetts, Troesken and his coauthor Joseph Ferrie found that, starting in 1850, lower rates of typhoid fever in Chicago generally went along with larger reductions in other diseases. Deaths from other ailments may have fallen because waterborne diseases were being mistaken for other diseases or because waterborne illnesses were weakening immune systems, which then failed when other ailments attacked them. Whatever the reason, Ferrie and Troesken believe that "the introduction of pure water explains between 30 and 50 percent of Chicago's mortality decline" between 1850 and 1925.

Clean water came to cities only because of massive public investments in infrastructure. It will take similar efforts, either by government or by suitably subsidized and regulated private companies, to make the slums of Dharavi as free from waterborne disease as the streets of Paris.

Street Cleaning and Corruption

Despite the huge reductions in disease that came from cleaner water, as late as 1901 life expectancy at birth was seven years lower in New York than in the rest of the county, primarily because of the prevalence of infectious diseases. A century ago, America was just as corrupt as many developing countries today, and just as corruption today limits the efficacy of public services in the developing world, corruption made American cities far less healthy in the nineteenth century.

New York got clean streets thanks to a police scandal that temporarily pushed the notorious Tammany Hall machine out of power. There is a lot to dislike in political systems that lodge too little power in local hands, but the right answer isn't complete autonomy, either. When things work right, multiple layers of government—federal, state, and city—can check each other, especially when different parties hold power at different layers. African Americans in the South wouldn't have gotten civil rights if the federal government hadn't intervened in state matters, and New York City got clean streets sooner because a Republican state senator led an investigation of the Democratic city government's police department.

The rampant corruption detailed in the senator's ten-thousand-page report would stun even the most jaded reader. When investigators asked the infamous policeman "Clubber" Williams how he could afford his New York townhouse, his Connecticut country house, and his yacht, all on a policeman's pay, Williams replied that "I bought real estate in Japan and it has increased in value." That report was the backdrop for New York's 1894 election, which ousted Tammany Hall and put a Republican businessman, William L. Strong, into the mayor's office.

Strong originally wanted to put Theodore Roosevelt in charge of street cleaning, but Roosevelt wanted to be police commissioner instead. So Strong tapped Colonel George Waring, who turned out to be, as Roosevelt said in a rare burst of modesty, "a far better man for his purpose." Certainly Waring shared Roosevelt's enthusiasm for unrestrained reform. Waring had gotten his start in sanitation forty years earlier as a twenty-something overseeing the drainage of Central Park. He raised six cavalry regiments for the Union Army, introduced Jersey cattle to the United States, helped develop the toilet, and built Memphis's sewer system after a series of waterborne epidemics made the city a national cause célèbre. In 1895, this engineer, farmer, and first-rate horseman took charge of New York's street cleaning.

He immediately became a lightning rod. He went 25 percent over budget during his first year. A political firestorm arose when Waring supposedly called the Grand Army of the Republic "a dammed lot of drunken bums," roughly equivalent to calling the AARP "a bunch of lazy welfare cheats" today. Waring responded that he had only called the nation's most powerful lobbying group "pension bummers" and that he wasn't backing down, even after the New York State Assembly called for his removal. He insisted on seizing vehicles left idle on city streets, creating a "riot in Mott Street" between street cleaners "who were sent out to seize trucks and a mob of Italians who tried to prevent the trucks from being taken." He stayed up nights planning his department's response to snowstorms. Even with all the ruckus, the New York Times reported that in his first seven months, "marvels have been done toward the sanitation of the city."

Waring's energy, honesty, and competence earned him public support that overwhelmed his detractors. He also had the benefit of a new technology—

asphalt. In the 1880s, New York's streets were typically paved with oblong granite blocks laid on a bed of gravel. Sweeping those streets was easier than keeping cobblestones clean, but dirt and dust were still ubiquitous. Slowly, asphalt—a sticky tarlike substance used to bind together small stones and gravel—was adopted for paving streets. When Baron Haussmann built his grand boulevards through Paris in the 1860s, he found that asphalt provided a smooth, manageable surface. By the 1890s, New York City had also turned to asphalt paving. There were numerous charges of corrupt ties between Tammany Hall and the private asphalt companies, but the streets were smoothly paved, making them far easier for Waring's men to clean.

Waring resigned his post in 1898 to improve sanitation in Cuba at the end of the Spanish-American War, where he caught the yellow fever that killed him, but he left behind a cleaner—and healthier—city. Between 1901 and 1910, New York's male life expectancy increased by 4.7 years, and the gap between it and the nation's fell by half. The biggest gains in life expectancy came from reductions in infant mortality, which reflected the spread of medical knowledge, improvements in sanitation, and better hospitals.

Mayor Strong's administration didn't end urban corruption in New York. Strong was eventually replaced by a Tammany man, who earned a fortune by creating an ice monopoly in the city. But municipal corruption had become less extreme than in the days of Boss Tweed, as the population became better educated and more politically effective. Typically, corruption decreases as education levels rise, because citizens become less dependent on the informal safety net that machine bosses provide and better able to organize opposition to corruption. But machine politics wouldn't abate in most American cities until the New Deal brought better bookkeeping, which again showed that multiple layers of government can have positive effects.

The old model of machine politics had local bosses doling out jobs and favors to their constituents in exchange for votes. An immigrant family who supported the machine could rely on help getting a young man a job or aid during a fire or a turkey on Thanksgiving. Those services were provided from city coffers overseen by machine bosses. The New Deal vastly strengthened the federal safety net and weakened the power of local politicians to buy support with occasional handouts. To get money, local leaders had to scrupulously document their cash flows. The era of the boss became the age of the bureaucrat, many of whom followed in the professional path of officials like Colonel George Waring.

More Roads, Less Traffic?

Contagious diseases turn the great urban advantage—connecting people—into a cause of death. Traffic congestion eliminates that advantage altogether by making it too hard to get around in a city. Too much trash turns city streets into a health hazard; too many drivers turn city streets into a parking lot. Providing clean water requires an engineering solution, but providing uncongested streets requires more than just technical know-how. Our streets only become usable when people don't overuse them, and that calls for the tools of the economist. Driving creates a negative externality, because each driver typically considers only his own private costs and benefits. Drivers don't usually take into account the fact that their driving slows everyone else down. The best way to fix that externality is to charge people for using roads.

Moving water into cities and sewage out was a vast undertaking, which tested the very limits of engineering know-how. Traffic congestion is also an engineering challenge but a psychological one as well, mainly because each improvement changes drivers' behaviors in a way that actually offsets the improvement. For decades, we've tried to solve the problem of too many cars on too few lanes by building more roads, but each new highway or bridge then attracts more traffic. Economists Gilles Duranton and Matthew Turner have found that vehicle miles traveled increases essentially one-to-one with the number of miles of new highway, and have called this phenomenon the fundamental law of road congestion.

The traffic problem essentially reflects the impossibility of sating the demand for anything that's free. Roads are expensive to build and valuable to use, yet American motorists seem to think that a right to drive for free was promised them by the Bill of Rights. Soviet Russia used to charge artificially low prices for consumer goods, and the result was empty shelves and long lines. That is basically what happens when people are allowed to drive on city streets for free.

The best way to reduce traffic congestion was dreamed up by a Nobel

Prize–winning Canadian-born economist, William Vickrey. Vickrey first pondered the puzzles of public transportation when, in 1951, he joined a mayor's committee to improve New York's finances. He was assigned the problem of pricing subways, and he noted that "users of private cars and taxis, and perhaps also of buses, do not, by and large, bear costs commensurate with the increment of costs that their use imposes." When we drive, we consider the private costs to ourselves of the time, gas, and automobile depreciation, but we don't usually consider the costs—the lost time—we impose on every other driver. We don't consider the congestion we create, and as a result, we overuse the highways.

The natural economists' solution to this problem is to charge drivers for the full cost of their commute—which means adding a fee that charges drivers for the impact that their car imposes on the rest of the road. Vickrey followed up his core insight in the late 1950s in a report on the Washington, D.C., bus system, in which he first advocated charging drivers for the congestion they create. Vickrey's insight, inspired by the city around him, is another example of self-protecting urban innovation. Decades before E-ZPass, Vickrey recommended an electronic system for imposing these congestion charges, and he suggested that charges rise during rush hours, when congestion is worse.

Decades of experience have proven Vickrey right. Building more roads almost never eliminates traffic delays, but congestion pricing does. In 1975, Singapore adopted a simple form of congestion pricing, charging motorists more for driving in the central city. Now the system is electronic and sophisticated and keeps that city traffic-jam free. In 2003, London adopted its own congestion charge and also saw traffic drop significantly.

So why is congestion pricing so rare in the United States? Because politics trumps economics. Imposing a new fee on thousands of motorists is unpopular, and as a result, millions of hours of valuable time are needlessly lost by drivers stalled in traffic. Vickrey himself died of a heart attack, slumped over the wheel of his car, traveling late at night. I've always imagined that he was driving at that hour to avoid congestion.

In America, congestion wastes billions of dollars' worth of lost time, but its consequences can seem even more severe in the cities of the developing world, where crowding is more extreme and where alternative traffic options, like subways, are typically underdeveloped. Buildings are shorter and consequently more spread out, and that, along with terrible sidewalks, makes the pedestrian option less practical. In cities like Mumbai, congestion can bring the business of urban life to a standstill, which is why fighting congestion is not about convenience; it is a fight to ensure that the city can fulfill its most basic function of bringing people together.

Making Cities Safer

The urban edge in connecting people can be compromised just as much by crime as by congestion. Fear keeps people behind locked doors, cut off from each other and from the advantages of city life. And fear has been an all-too-common by-product of bringing thousands of people together in a dense urban cluster. Just as urban proximity enables the spread of ideas and disease, it can also enable crime.

For centuries, the threat of urban disorder has pushed citizens to pay taxes and sacrifice liberty in search of safety. The first modern police force was formed in Paris during the reign of Louis XIV, when that city was probably Europe's largest and certainly filled with violent disorder. Indeed, Paris first became a City of Light in the seventeenth century because the man who ran its police force launched a vast street-lighting project to make the city less dangerous at night.

Willie Sutton said he robbed banks because "that's where the money is," but in most cases, crime means poor people robbing other poor people. Crime victims are more likely to be poor, young, and male—just like criminals. One major reason people join criminal gangs is the promise of protection from other criminals.

In much of the world, crime is disproportionately urban. In 1989, more than 20 percent of people living in cities with more than a million people had been crime victims during the previous year, while fewer than a tenth of residents in towns with under ten thousand people were victims. In 1986, murder rates increased, on average, 25 percent as city populations doubled.

Cities are crime-prone mostly because the poor people who come to cities bring the social problems of poverty, like crime, with them. Cities also encourage crime because urban areas present a dense concentration of potential victims. While it's hard to earn a living as a thief on a lonely country road, the crowds on a subway provide a plethora of pockets to pick. I once estimated that the financial returns to an average crime are about 20 percent higher within metropolitan areas than outside them.

The city-crime connection also reflects the difficulty of law enforcement in big, often anonymous cities. In the game of Clue, players solve a murder by progressively eliminating all the possible suspects. Real cops often do the same thing, but this process is much harder in cities because there are a lot more suspects to consider. As a result, the probability of being arrested for any given crime drops by about 8 percent as city population doubles.

Crime rates have been reliably correlated with city size, but the differences in crime rates among cities and over time often have little to do with law enforcement, income, or anything else that can be measured. Rio's slums are famous for their trigger-happy gangs, but Mumbai's slums are usually quite safe. Despite the prevalence of criminals in the movie *Slumdog Millionaire,* the overall crime rate in Mumbai is much lower than in urban India as a whole. Mumbai's slums lack the dangerous feeling I have felt in Rio's favelas or New York's poorer areas in the 1970s. This discrepancy isn't because Mumbai's police are doing a great job, and Mumbai is poorer than Rio.

The best explanation for the safety of Mumbai's slums is that, while these places may be poor, they're also well-functioning social spaces, like the Greenwich Village described by Jane Jacobs in her masterpiece *The Death and Life of Great American Cities* fifty years ago. In these areas, residents watch the streets and alleys. Misbehavior is quickly noticed and dealt with, not by the police, but by the community.

Within cities too, crime rates move up and down for reasons that are hard to fathom. Murder is the only crime that can be reliably used to measure long-term changes in public safety, because other crimes are often underreported for various reasons. Official crime rates can actually decrease when a police force is particularly inept or corrupt, because people stop reporting most crimes altogether.

The crime historian Eric Monkkonen assembled data on more than two hundred years of murders in New York. Murder fell from 1800 to 1830 and then rose again, peaking during the Civil War. During the nineteenth century, when street gangs held sway over immigrant neighborhoods and New York's police were infamously corrupt, there were generally between three and six murders per hundred thousand New Yorkers every year. There does appear to be a weak link between corruption and homicide. Between 1865 and 1961, there were about 12 percent more homicides during years when Tammany Hall was in power than during reform administrations.

Murders then fell in the late nineteenth century, rose after 1900, and peaked during the Roaring Twenties at 5.4 murders per hundred thousand before falling to a low of 4.1 in the 1950s. The national homicide rate fell by about 29 percent between 1939 and 1959. Between 1960 and 1975, all of the gains that were made during the 1930–1960 period evaporated, and cities became more lawless than ever. The murder rate in New York increased fourfold, to 22 murders per hundred thousand people in 1975.

Many of the fluctuations in crime rates have no obvious causes. America and New York were getting richer and bigger during all these time periods; poverty or city size can't explain why crime rose or fell during particular decades. The crime explosion from 1960 and 1975 has been extensively analyzed, but no consensus has emerged. One might guess that this increase can be explained by the rising number of young people during those years (crimes are disproportionately committed by the young), but Steven Levitt estimates that the increase in the number of young people can explain, at most, one fifth of the rise in crime during this period. Other explanations include worsening economic conditions in urban industrial economies or a decline in police effectiveness, but again no measurable variable can really explain the change.

The inexplicable changes in crime over time and space are, in a sense, the damaging counterpart of the inexplicable explosions in art and creativity that occasionally appear in cities. Both phenomena are examples of the power of social interactions. One artist—Brunelleschi, Haydn—can set off a chain of innovation in his or her city. Likewise, a handful of urban criminals can break down the social norms that keep cities safe, thereby making crime more attractive. The Crips, the vast gang that now supposedly contains more than thirty thousand members, was founded by a few young men. Because cities enhance the influence of individuals—for good and ill—and because the choices and talents of individuals are enormously unpredictable, urban phenomena like crime waves are similarly hard to understand.

Crime waves may be hard to explain, but their impact can be painfully obvious. Between 1940 and 1960, New York was about as healthy as the rest of the United States. Life expectancies for white men were never more than six months different between New York and the nation as a whole. But between 1960 and 1990, a 2.7-year gap opened up between life expectancy for men in New York and life expectancy for men elsewhere. Men in the country as a whole were getting healthier than those in New York. This gap didn't appear for women, in part, because the great majority of murder victims are men.

Plenty of factors contributed to the increasing numbers of dead men in New York. AIDS arrived and started slaying New Yorkers, again mostly men. Death rates from heart disease also increased in New York between the 1960s and 1980s, perhaps because of drug use or stress. New York's Central Park became a kind of no-man's-land that only the brave or foolhardy would enter at night. In 1925, the lyricist Lorenz Hart had described the city as a "wond'rous toy just made for a girl and boy." Fifty years later, the city seemed made for muggers—and was anything but "wond'rous."

Then between 1975 and 2005, New York's murder rate declined from nearly twenty-two to slightly over six deaths per hundred thousand residents. This decline was accompanied by similar drops in the numbers of rapes, robberies, and almost all serious crimes. Just as there is much that was inexplicable about the rise in crime rates, much about the drop in crime reflects social forces beyond measurement or control. John Donohue and Steven Levitt have persuasively argued that the legalization of abortion played some role in the crime drop.

Moreover, even though crime rates can often change for reasons wholly unrelated to the police, policing does matter. The economics of crime and punishment, pioneered by Gary Becker, starts with the premise that criminals aren't totally irrational. They respond—just like the rest of us—to incentives. There will be less crime if the expected punishment from crime increases, and the expected punishment depends on the probability of arrest and the severity of punishment after arrest. The rationality of crime actually makes sense of recidivism rates that are often above 90 percent. If criminals are rational and know what to expect from prison before going to jail, then a stint in the slammer shouldn't change their thinking about their life's work. No one expects professional basketball players who foul out of a few games to suddenly change their style of play. If crime seemed like a good idea to someone before arrest, why should it look like a bad idea afterward?

Plenty of statistical work supports the intuitive idea that crime falls as punishments increase, although many studies have found that crime falls more in response to higher arrest rates than in response to longer sentence lengths. The sky-high murder rates in South American cities like Rio and Bogotá can be explained by the low conviction rates for murders. In the United States, about 50 percent of murders lead to a conviction. In Bogotá and Rio, fewer than 10 percent of murderers end up with jail time. It's not surprising that these places have such extreme crime problems when the costs of committing crime are so low. In Latin America, the more popular response to high crime rates was trying to fix the poverty that accompanies crime. Unfortunately, that strategy has been no more successful there than it was in the United States.

After America's cities exploded in crime and rioting in the 1960s, an early consensus argued that we could make our cities safer by making them more prosperous. As long as America focused on solving its poverty problem, the crime problem would automatically be solved. In response to the riots, the Kerner Commission recommended that America "take immediate action to create 2,000,000 new jobs over the next three years—one million in the public sector and one million in the private sector—to absorb the hard-core unemployed and materially reduce the level of underemployment for all workers, black and white."

Unfortunately, no one really knew how to create 2 million new jobs for the urban unemployed, how to solve the poverty problem more generally, or how to stem the decline in urban manufacturing during this era. Moreover, it was far from obvious that rising incomes alone would radically reduce crime. As the 1960s turned into the 1970s, even liberals started arguing for a more direct law-and-order approach to crime prevention.

In 1973, Nelson Rockefeller, once considered the liberal hope of the Republican Party, signed the Rockefeller drug laws, which mandated a prison sentence of fifteen years to life for anyone possessing four ounces or more of any illegal drug. In the mayoral election of 1977, Ed Koch distinguished himself from his rivals by supporting the death penalty. Koch started a trend, and his successors, including Rudy Giuliani, embraced the "broken windows" theory of policing, which calls for strong penalties for even minor infractions, such as jumping subway turnstiles to avoid paying the fare. Harsher penalties naturally appealed to citizens of a city where criminals seemed to be in control.

Between 1980 and 2000, the number of inmates in the U.S. criminal system—in prison, in jail, on probation, or on parole—increased from 1.8 million to 6.4 million. Jails don't reform criminals, but they do stop crime through deterrence and, more important, by keeping criminals off the streets. There is extensive research examining the impact of incarceration on crime levels, and typically when sentence lengths double, crime rates decline by somewhere between 10 and 40 percent. Steven Levitt argues that the incapacitation effect of jails is usually more important than deterrence. One classic study of his used ACLU lawsuits against overcrowding that pushed prisons to let criminals out. After the releases, crime rates rose nearby, and he estimates that as prison populations drop by 10 percent, violent crime increases by 4 percent. Using this estimate, the increase in prison population can explain almost 40 percent of the drop in violent crime during the 1990s.

Millions of young men have been brought into the prison system for non-violent drug crimes. Some of these men would have done worse things if they had been free, and their incarceration helped reduce crime rates. But many of them would have led perfectly productive lives. The loss of their freedom and future prospects is the terrible price of reducing crime rates by increasing incarceration rates. I cannot say whether the costs to those prisoners and their communities is outweighed by the benefits of increased public safety, but I fervently hope that we can find less painful means of reducing crime in the future.

As Becker's logic suggests, another way to reduce crime levels is just to hire more cops. During the 1990s, the number of police in New York City increased by 45 percent. The number of police increased by 15 percent nationwide. Steven Levitt estimates that as the number of police increases by 10 percent, crime drops by 5 percent. If one accepts that number, then more cops can explain about one seventh of the national drop in crime and perhaps a quarter of New York's particularly sharp drop in violence. More cops aren't free, but they do seem to be at least as cost-effective as longer prison stays.

Is there a free lunch—a way to reduce crime without spending more on police or imprisoning millions of young men? Two strategies have gotten a lot of publicity over the past two decades, both of which aim to improve the flow of information in the police force. One of those strategies uses technology; the other relies on urban interactions. Both seem to be effective, even if we can't say that with the same confidence as we can about the impact of longer sentences or more police.

Police forces have long embraced new technologies like fingerprinting, automobiles, lie detectors, two-way radios, and the 911 system. The latest high-tech wave washed over law enforcement in the 1990s in places like New York, where an innovative data-driven system helped target police resources toward troubled areas. The idea seems to have started with a transit cop, Jack Maple, who marked a map of the New York Transit System so that he could see where robberies were most common. He used the map to determine where to assign his cops, following John Snow's lead in both mapmaking and self-protecting urban innovation.

Gradually, the system got more sophisticated, and a large contingent of officers would quickly descend on a subway station following a crime there. The number of subway robberies dropped dramatically, and Maple's idea was borrowed by his new boss, Police Chief William Bratton. Bratton and Maple then created CompStat, a computerized statistical system that allows precinct captains and their superiors to see exactly where crime is taking place and act accordingly. CompStat made the city safer by pinpointing where resources were needed most and making cops more accountable for crimes that occurred on their watch.

While CompStat relied on snazzy new technology to improve enforcement, "community policing" relied on personal contact. At its heart, community policing simply means that police should maintain good relations with a neighborhood and use face-to-face interactions to glean information that can help prevent crimes. Criminals, especially those in gangs, are often protected by their neighborhoods, both out of fear and because even the deadliest gangs often take care of their neighbors. But while the idea of community policing may be simple, the execution can be quite difficult.

Cops are often outsiders because they come from a different place or race than those in the communities they patrol. Also, earlier attempts at police professionalization had often worked to break the link between cop and community. Many cities adopted police rotation—periodically moving cops to new neighborhoods—because they thought it would reduce corruption by weakening the links between crooked cops like "Clubber" Williams and residents who would pay them off. But the riots of the 1960s, which often started with local groups attacking cops, pushed police departments to invest more in community relations in an attempt to improve their relationship with hostile neighborhoods.

In 1992, violence came to Boston's Morning Star Baptist Church when a funeral became a fight between rival gangs. A coalition of community leaders, drawn mostly from the clergy, came together and created the Ten Point Coalition, a league of religious leaders that is working to reduce violence in the city's poorer neighborhoods. The support of these leaders gave Boston's police better ties to troubled areas and made them considerably more effective. Crime rates fell dramatically.

Today, the Boston Police Department has a number of community policing initiatives, including "safe streets teams" and a bevy of neighborhood advisory councils. The officers who work these beats say that women are often their key contacts, and minority, female police officers can be particularly effective in building these bridges.

While it's hard to see the downside in policing strategies that leverage the urban ability to spread knowledge across space, there's little hard data to support the view that either community policing or CompStat-like programs have driven down crime rates dramatically. The introductions of these methods are rarely controlled experiments. But numerous case studies do suggest that they can help make city streets safe.

Neither CompStat nor community policing could protect the 2,794 New Yorkers who died when two Boeing 767 airplanes destroyed the World Trade Center on September 11, 2001. Despite the courage of so many New Yorkers, like the dead hero whose picture still shines from the firehouse on my mother's street, many doubted the city's ability to recover. They feared that urban concentration would present an irresistible target to terrorists who wanted to strike at the very core of our civilization. But there is little evidence to suggest that cities can't survive the threat of terrorism. Across countries, historically, terrorism does not deter either urbanization or the construction of tall buildings. Both Jerusalem and London have faced ongoing terrorist activity, but neither city's population growth seems to have declined as a result. Cities have powerful resources—large police forces, observant citizens, strong infrastructure—that have so far enabled them to protect themselves against even the most terrifying threats.

Health Benefits

A mass of people living on a small amount of land creates enormous health risks, but as of 2007, a child born in New York City could, if current death rates continue, expect to live one-and-a-half years longer than a child born in the United States as a whole. Los Angeles, Boston, Minneapolis, San Francisco, and many other cities can also boast age-adjusted death rates lower than the national average. The average life expectancy in counties with more than five hundred people per square mile is nine months longer than in counties with fewer than a hundred people per square mile. Between 1980 and 2000, life expectancies increased six months more in counties with more than five hundred people per square mile than in counties with less than that density.

New Yorkers' good health didn't just happen. It took massive public investment to bring in potable water. It took a tough, quasi-military leader who drastically increased his department's expenses to make Manhattan's streets clean. Lots of cops and higher rates of imprisonment made New York City safe. Every battle was won by accountable and empowered public leaders who spent huge amounts of money and enlarged the public sector. The troubled cities of the developing world must go through a similarly difficult process if they are to become safe and clean.

But these investments can only explain why large cities are no longer killing fields. The decline in urban infectious diseases and homicides can't explain why many cities like New York are healthier than the nation as a whole. It is easiest to understand why the death rate for Manhattanites between the ages of twenty-five and thirty-four is 60 percent lower than the comparable rate for the country. Accidents and suicides are the two leading causes of death for these younger people, and these are both rarer in big cities. New Yorkers in this age group are more than 75 percent less likely to die in a motor vehicle accident than their counterparts nationwide. Driving drunk is far more deadly than taking the bus while intoxicated.

The suicide rate for younger New Yorkers is about 56 percent of the national average, which reflects the fact that suicides are more common in rural areas. The death rates from suicide in Alaska, Montana, and Wyoming are more than 2.5 times higher than those in Massachusetts, New Jersey, and New York. While some of this effect may reflect the loneliness that can come from geographical isolation, my work with David Cutler and Karen Norberg on youth suicide also points to the fact that gun ownership is about four times as high in small towns as in big cities.

The majority of suicides among younger people involve firearms, and many studies find that suicides are more common when firearms are more common, a fact that is a little odd because guns are hardly the only means of killing oneself. Hunting is the strongest predictor of gun ownership in the United States, which explains why youth suicides rise significantly with the number of hunting licenses in a county.

While the low mortality rates of younger urbanites reflect a surfeit of buses and a dearth of firearms, lower mortality rates among older people are more of a puzzle. Death rates are 5.5 percent higher nationwide than in New York for people fifty-five to sixty-four years old, 17 percent higher for those sixty-five to seventy-four, and more than 24 percent higher for those seventy-five to eighty-four. Differences in education, employment, or income don't seem able to explain the disparity.

Mayor Bloomberg waged war against smoking by dramatically increasing cigarette taxes and limiting where one could smoke legally, but New York had become healthier than the nation as a whole before he took office. Perhaps all that walking makes New Yorkers healthier, but can that explain why they die less often from cancer? Los Angeles is also significantly healthier than the nation, and walking is far less common there. I'd like to think that the health of older New Yorkers reflects the vigorous nature of city life, but I can't rule out the possibility that selection may also be playing a role. Poor health increases the likelihood of retirement, and retirement increases the likelihood of leaving the city and moving someplace warmer.

The health of cities like New York, Los Angeles, and San Francisco represents an astonishing turnaround from the past, when density too often meant death. Throughout most of human history, proximity enabled the spread of infectious diseases that struck down those humans who had the temerity to risk living near one another. Huge investments in massive waterworks were needed to curb the spread of cholera and yellow fever, just as huge investments in policing were needed to reduce crime in the 1990s. The massing of millions in small land areas requires a vigorous public sector to combat crime and illness, which perhaps explains why people in New York are so much fonder of big government than people in rural Kansas.

Epidemics will continue. Long after the Croton Aqueduct brought clean water to Manhattan, the 1918 influenza pandemic and AIDS both managed to kill millions. But today the spread of disease in cities is limited by investments in public health, and self-protecting urban innovation is as important as ever. The AIDS virus was discovered because a Parisian clinician who was treating sick patients connected with retrovirus researchers at Paris's Pasteur Institute. The health of cities depends on the health-creating aspects of urban life—good hospitals, faster information flows, fewer cars and guns—dominating the disease-spreading consequence of density.

Calhoun's warning remains relevant: Urban density may create marvels, but it also comes with costs. The world lost much when plague ravaged Athens 2,400 years ago and when AIDS struck New York in the 1980s. Crime and congestion are still with us; their costs are most terrible in the growing cities of the developing world. But these problems are not insurmountable obstacles to urban success. Cities create their own champions, like Dr. John Snow or Colonel Waring or William Vickrey, who fight to make cities livable. They have often succeeded, and when they do, urban areas become not only habitable but delightful, for concentrated talent doesn't just make cities productive, it also makes them fun.

CHAPTER 5

Is London a Luxury Resort?

Winston Churchill and Franklin Delano Roosevelt are typically seen as firm, fearless men of destiny, but on Bond Street, their bronze statues sit chatting and smoking, looking for all the world as if they had just finished eating an expensive French feast and were now waiting for Eleanor and Clementine to finish shopping. The two men, whose friendship helped save London during its darkest hour, seem to be enjoying the city's latest incarnation as a place of pleasure. Nowhere are London's extravagances more evident than on Bond Street, whose shops are elegant echoes of London's past, filled with pricey baubles: oversize Graff diamonds, Patek Philippe watches, Chanel suits, Louboutin shoes, and whatever Sotheby's is auctioning right now.

Bond Street is at the center of one of the world's great urban playgrounds, a city filled with things to see and buy and taste and learn. If price is no object, you can enjoy Art Deco luxury staying at Claridge's, right off Bond, and eat Gordon Ramsay's cooking. If you walk down the Burlington Arcade, an elegant pre-Victorian cluster of shops that runs parallel to Bond Street, and cross over Piccadilly to have a look at the ornate waistcoats being sold in the Piccadilly Arcade, you can then reach, in quick succession, Churchill's shirt maker, New & Lingwood; his cigar merchant, JJ Fox; his shoemaker, John Lobb; and his wine merchant, Berry Brothers and Rudd. They are all still selling their wares to the world's elite.

London, of course, has other, more high-minded pleasures. Some of the city's intellectual adornments—the Linnean Society, the Royal Astronomical Society, and the Royal Academy of Arts—are housed right next to the Burlington Arcade in a splendid Palladian mansion. It's only a few minutes by London cab to the theaters of the West End or the treasures of the National Gallery. Samuel Johnson's words still resonate: "When a man is tired of London, he is tired of life; for there is in London all that life can afford."

Pleasure is powerful, and London's delights are more than just the stuff of glossy travel magazines. Urban enjoyments help determine a city's success. Talent is mobile, and it seeks out good places to consume as well as produce. London's amenities have helped the city attract thirty-two billionaires, according to *Forbes*, an impressive share of the world's wealthiest people. About half of those megarich Londoners are not English, like Lakshmi Mittal, who earns his fortune in India but lives in a mansion on Kensington Palace Gardens that he bought for $100 million in 2004. Some of those billionaires may come to England for the country's tax benefits, but within England they choose London because it is a good place to enjoy being rich.

Whereas the typical nineteenth-century city was located in a place where factories had an edge in production, the typical twenty-first-century city is more likely to be a place where workers have an edge in consumption. A century ago, firms were tied to spots like Liverpool or Pittsburgh because of natural attributes like harbors and coal mines. The global decline in transport costs means that companies are now footloose, free to locate where people want to live. In some cases, that freedom has led to suburbia or the Sunbelt, but increasingly, attractive cities like London also entice enterprises and entrepreneurs by their quality of life.

When I was a child in Manhattan in the 1970s, people fled New York because its crime and grime made it, for many, an unpleasant place to live. Housing wasn't particularly expensive, because New York wasn't that desirable. Certainly few were mad enough to live *in* Manhattan and commute *out* to suburban workplaces. While the New York depicted in the Scorsese classics of the 1970s was a place of harrowing crime, twenty-first-century New York is a playground for the prosperous. Until the bust started in 2006, real estate prices shot up far more quickly than income, which reflects the fact that people are willing to pay a lot just to live in New York.

One reason that London and New York and Paris are so pleasant is that they contain centuries' worth of investment in buildings and museums and parks, but they also benefit from the urban ability to magnify human creativity, which makes cities enjoyable as well as industrious. Urban innovation doesn't mean just new types of factories or financial instruments; it also means new cuisines and plays. Above all, the abundance of human talent in a place like London offers an opportunity to interact with people who interest you. One reason why billionaires favor places like London and New York is that they get to hang out with other billionaires, who presumably can empathize with their special trials and tribulations.

As humankind becomes wealthier, more people will choose their locations on the basis of pleasure as well as productivity. To understand why cities are succeeding and whether they will continue to thrive in the future, we must understand how urban amenities work and how consumer cities succeed.

Scale Economies and the Globe Theatre

In 2003, Oscar winner Kevin Spacey, who is certainly clever and entrepreneurial, moved to London to become the director of the Old Vic Theatre Company. Many Americans found this decision just as inscrutable as everything else about the ingenious actor. Spacey is a New Jersey native who grew up in California. Surely, Hollywood should be able to hold on to such a major movie star. If he was so hell-bent on live theater, then there was always Broadway, where he had enjoyed repeated success. What would draw an entertainer of his popularity to a London theater on the wrong side of the Thames?

The appeal of London's theaters to Kevin Spacey, and much of the rest of the world, reflects enduring urban advantages. First of all, live theaters involve substantial fixed costs. Any five-year-old can put on a play, but a modern West End experience includes a large stage, sophisticated lighting and sound equipment, and often ornate interior spaces. The fixed costs of plays also involve the time required for actors to learn their lines and perfect their roles, something most five-year-old performers skip. Drama is affordable to ordinary people, as the Old Vic was to its poorer audiences in Lambeth, because those fixed costs are spread across thousands of viewers.

The fixed costs involved in theaters, opera houses, and museums explain their connection with cities. Large urban areas have large audiences that can jointly share the costs of a sophisticated drama. Today Broadway is sustained by thousands of tourists, but fifty years ago, the Great White Way catered to the vast numbers of New Yorkers who attended the theater regularly.

The first significant public theater in the English-speaking world was built by James Burbage in 1576 and called, appropriately, the Theatre. London had grown dramatically during the sixteenth century, and its burgeoning population was eager for entertainment. Burbage built his playhouse close to the city but outside its walls, in a sort of regulation-free zone where places of ill repute, such as brothels, taverns, and theaters, could operate.

Medieval theater was primarily religious, and much of it took place in churches, which had infrastructure ready-made for performing. In the wake of the Renaissance and the Reformation, the English developed an interest in secular plays. English comedy made its first appearance in the 1550s with plays like *Ralph Roister Doister* and *Gammer Gurton's Needle,* which are rarely performed now, except by pre-Elizabethan extremists. By the 1560s, raised stages became common; there is a hot scholarly debate about whether court plays had such stages before then. The nobility provided some demand for theatrical productions, but because even the most dramatically precocious peer didn't want to see the same play night after night, acting troupes began catering to a wider audience.

Burbage belonged to a troupe of players supported by the Queen's favorite, the Earl of Leicester. Even though the earl was a generous patron, the troupe toured regularly to increase its earnings. By traveling, actors could get access to a large enough audience to support themselves, but the need to move inevitably meant that productions were sparse. But just as temporary medieval fairs evolved into sedentary commercial cities, traveling drama troupes morphed into sedentary theater companies. The growth of urban London made it possible to move to a more permanent system in which the actors stayed put and the audience came to them, which is how Broadway still works today. Burbage's Theatre was the start of this tradition, and it was followed by a succession of Elizabethan theaters like the Curtain, the Rose, and the Globe.

In the early days of London theater, there were no drama schools, so actors learned from each other, as James Burbage's more famous son, Richard, did from his father. Even more impressively, a series of great playwrights—

Marlowe, Jonson, Shakespeare—connected with each other in the city's the-atrical community and produced the first great works of English drama. The first written reference to Shakespeare in London's dramatic circles was in 1592, when he was disparaged by Robert Greene, a somewhat dissolute playwright who may have been the model for Shakespeare's Falstaff. Greene, Thomas Kyd, and Marlowe were all University Wits, well-educated, raffish writers who seem to have taught each other, and possibly Shakespeare as well, in London's dense streets and taverns.

We know only snippets about these interactions, but their plays certainly play off one another—the connections between the texts suggest a pattern of connected creativity. Greene may have attacked Shakespeare, but that didn't prevent the younger playwright from borrowing the structure of Greene's novel *Pandosto* for *The Winter's Tale*. Thomas Kyd is widely thought to have written the ur-*Hamlet*, performed in 1589. Kyd is also one of the possible au-thors (along with Greene) of *King Leir*, another precursor of Shakespeare. Kyd shared a room with the wild man of English drama, Christopher Marlowe, who was accused of being a spy, an atheist, a secret Catholic, a heavy tobacco user, and plenty of other apparently awful things.

Shakespeare's plays, such as *Hamlet* and *As You Like It*, have direct refer-ences to Marlowe's work. The connections between *The Merchant of Venice* and Marlowe's earlier *The Jew of Malta* have been long studied. *Dido, Queen of Carthage* is thought to have influenced *Antony and Cleopatra*. The moral choices of Doctor Faustus and Macbeth seem quite similar. Some experts, such as Harvard's Stephen Greenblatt, are confident that they personally knew each other. Given the small size of London's theatrical community, how could this not be true?

The connections between Shakespeare and Marlowe take nothing away from Shakespeare's brilliance, but instead remind us that genius knows enough to borrow ideas from its neighbors. London has also long taught thespians, who learn by acting in plays and studying the more senior performers around them. Shakespeare surely learned his acting skills in this fashion, and so did Edmund Kean two centuries later. The twentieth-century giants of the Brit-ish stage—Laurence Olivier, John Gielgud, Peggy Ashcroft, and Ralph Richardson—acted together, directed each other, and helped train the stage's future stars person-to-person. When he began his tenure as director of the National Theatre Company at the Old Vic, Olivier directed the young Peter O'Toole in *Hamlet*. By moving to the Old Vic, Kevin Spacey was choosing the city at the center of English-speaking drama, which continues to educate and entertain like nowhere else.

London's large audiences enable the Old Vic to cover the fixed costs of its expensive productions, but city size also enables smaller, more experimental live theater to survive. The Second City began in 1959 in cheap Chicago space that had once been a Chinese laundry. Their smaller productions could survive with modest audiences, a hundred would do, but would they have found even that modest level of demand for cutting-edge comedy in small-town America in the 1950s? To this day, big cities like New York and Los Angeles remain known for experimental live comedy theaters, like the Upright Citizens Brigade.

Live performance is connected to the spread of innovation in cities because the first stirrings of a new artistic phenomenon are almost always performed live long before they are distributed electronically. Larger cities' larger audiences help cover the cost of paying live disc jockeys, like DJ Kool Herc, who started playing his turntables like musical instruments in the early 1970s, moving back and forth from one record to another. Would-be performers, like Grandmaster Flash, who heard Herc in the house parties of the West Bronx, then riffed on his idea. If records were instruments, then why not add vocals? Grandmaster Flash and MC Melle Mel are celebrated as the seminal, Bronx-based partnership that brought rapping and mixing records together. Def Jam Records, which began with the urban connections of a Bronx hip-hop DJ (Jazzy Jay), a rap promoter (Russell Simmons), and an NYU student (Rick Rubin) who played in a punk rock band, then brought hip-hop into the mainstream with acts like Run DMC, LL Cool J, and the Beastie Boys.

The Division of Labor and Lamb Vindaloo

Today an evening's entertainment in a big city is more likely to mean a dinner at a restaurant than a night at the theater, and since so many more people eat out than go to plays, great restaurants are a more important draw for most cities than great theaters. In the United States as a whole, as of 2008, there are

1.8 times as many people working in full-service restaurants than in grocery stores. But in New York, that ratio is more than doubled; in Manhattan there are 5.4 times more people working in restaurants than in groceries, and between 1998 and 2008, employment in Manhattan restaurants increased by 55 percent.

While theaters illustrate the urban edge in paying for fixed costs, restaurants show the benefits that come because cities allow for the division of labor and specialization. Adam Smith noted that the division of labor is limited by the extent of the market and wrote that "In the lone houses and very small villages which are scattered about in so desert a country as the Highlands of Scotland, every farmer must be butcher, baker and brewer for his own family." Isolation meant that each family had to produce its own food. In Smith's day, cities had butchers and brewers. Today, cities have a wide array of restaurants offering a dizzying cornucopia of culinary styles, price ranges, and atmospheres.

In a low-density exurb where it takes thirty minutes to get to a restaurant, families cook their own food, whether or not they are good cooks. The fact that I occasionally inflict my awful cooking on my family is in and of itself a searing indictment of suburbia. In cities, people find it easier to eat out and take advantage of trained cooks who have a proven talent at putting together a good meal. Urban eaters also take advantage of specialized infrastructure, like high-end kitchens and elegant dining rooms, the costs of which are spread over hundreds or thousands of customers.

The very existence of professional cooks is one level of specialization, but of course big cities go far beyond this coarse division of labor. In New York, San Francisco, Chicago, or London, there are hundreds of targeted restaurants making food from distant parts of the globe and fusing geographically diverse cooking styles, catering to diverse sets of rich and poor consumers.

While inns and taverns are ancient, restaurants—meaning places that actually attract people by their cooking—came into their own in Paris in the late eighteenth century. Mathurin Roze de Chantoiseau is today credited as the first restaurateur. The odd use of the word *restaurant* to describe an eating establishment arose because Roze was selling healthy soups that were meant to restore, or *restaurer*, Parisians to robustness. Urban density created a market for specialized products, and healthy soups were one of those products. Roze's establishment seated people separately, offered them a choice of foods, and charged them on the basis of what they ordered, not a fixed fee. He cleverly managed to avoid the catering guild's harsh rules against selling food by paying a substantial sum to become an official caterer to the crown.

The problem with Roze's restaurant is that the food doesn't appear to have been that good. Even in the best of circumstances, healthy soups aren't always tasty, and Roze was an entrepreneur, not a chef. But his eatery set in the dense confines of Paris began a wave of innovation. In 1782, La Grande Taverne de Londres opened in Paris. According to Jean Anthelme Brillat-Savarin, the greatest of all foodies, its chef was "the first to combine the four essentials of an elegant room, smart waiters, a choice cellar, and superior cooking."

Before large urban markets, luxury cuisine, like secular drama, was a pastime of the nobility, who were the only customers rich enough to pay for their own chefs and their own acting troupes. In both cases, urban entrepreneurs realized that they could dispense with princely patronage if they could draw a large enough clientele. Naturally, that clientele was only found in cities. As drama and cooking became public, rather than private, pleasures, knowledge of each innovation spread more readily. Good restaurants both trained chefs and inspired their customers to improve their cooking at home.

Restaurants, like pubs or coffeehouses, are also a way of adapting to the high price of urban space. City apartments often have tiny kitchens and no dining room. Eating or drinking out is a way to share common space so that the urbanite isn't confined by a compact flat. In a sense, then, cities pull people out of private space into public areas, which helps make them centers for socialization and conspicuous consumption. The newly rich of the nineteenth century could go to Grand Vefour or to Maxim's and show off their wealth without having to host their own grand galas.

Cities have been cross-continental conduits for culinary knowledge just as surely as they have helped spread mathematics and marketing know-how. Delmonico's of Manhattan may have had the first significant French chef working on American soil, serving Gilded Age feasts of Lobster Newburg and Baked Alaska to New York's glittering gourmands. The greatest importer of French ideas into London was Auguste Escoffier, who learned his trade in Paris and Nice, then went on to cook in London at the Savoy Grill and the Ritz in the 1890s. Escoffier created his own dishes, like Peaches Melba and Tournedos

Rossini, and trained his own students, who brought his ideas to the tables of New York.

Despite Escoffier, forty years ago, London cuisine was better known for dreadful pork products, like the Scotch Egg, than for creative cooking. Yet today London has some of the best restaurants in the world. By importing talent from abroad and then allowing smart people to learn from one another, London has evolved into a superb place for a billionaire, or pretty much anyone else, to eat. The Roux brothers came to London from France and produced the first London restaurant to get three stars from the Michelin Guide. They trained a new generation of celebrity English chefs, such as the ubiquitous Gordon Ramsay, and then those chefs trained others.

Some of the most exciting restaurants in London have imported ideas from farther away than France. India was the brightest jewel in Queen Victoria's crown, and since her time, enterprising Indians have been coming to London. Today there are more than two hundred thousand Londoners who were born in India, and more than 5 percent of the city is of Indian descent. Just as Romanians brought pastrami to New York and Italians brought pizza to Chicago, Indians brought lamb vindaloo to London. A great Indian meal in London provides a very pungent example of the benefits that immigrants often bring to cities. Large cities are varied enough so that there is plenty of demand for even the most specialized cooking, while small towns in the United States must cater to such a wide range of palates that they are stuck serving that strange mélange, "continental cuisine."

Today, of course, Indian restaurants in London are more than just curry shops. In 2001, the Michelin Guide broke with its French haute cuisine traditions and gave stars to two Indian restaurants in London. One of the chefs responsible for those stars has followed the path of urban entrepreneurship and opened his own restaurant, Rasoi Vineet Bhatia, which well deserves the 27 rating for food it received from Zagat in 2010, only one point below the heights reached by Gordon Ramsay. London's top Indian chefs were generally born in India, but they have also spent years in the competitive world of London cooking. Their food is experimental and presents Asian traditions with haute cuisine flair. A good argument can be made that this fusion of India and Europe beats anything cooked in Mumbai.

The abundance of city amenities explains why urbanites are so much more likely to partake of public pleasures. Holding income, education, marital status, and age constant, over a twelve-month period, city residents are 19 percent more likely to go to a rock or pop concert, 44 percent more likely to visit a museum, 98 percent more likely to go to a movie theater, and 26 percent more likely to have a drink at a bar than their country cousins. These higher-end entertainments, which feature live interactions instead of passive TV watching, also have a particular appeal to wealthier and more educated people. If the world continues to get richer and better educated, the urban entertainment advantage will become even more valuable.

Shoes and the City

Food and drama are two areas where cities have an edge. Fashion is another. Even in the eighteenth century, London was attracting the world's best tailors, many of whose modern counterparts still ply their trade on Savile Row, which runs parallel to Bond Street and the Burlington Arcade. Mass production and cheap distribution costs have made it possible to buy inexpensive clothes online or at Target whose high quality would have made our grandparents jealous. Yet cities remain places where people disproportionately wear and buy expensive clothes.

Between 1998 and 2007, the number of people in Manhattan working in clothing and accessories stores increased by more than 50 percent. While the recession has surely led to a drop in that figure, the long-run trend will certainly remain strongly positive. Despite the rise of Internet shopping, New York's trendy boutiques and vast department stores have increased in size because New York's richer citizens are willing to pay a premium for the experience of an elegant store. While most of America is a service economy that caters to the middle classes, Manhattan's salespeople serve the urban haute bourgeoisie and the suburbanites who drive into the city to buy their Jimmy Choos.

The success of Manhattan's boutiques reflects the increasing desire for clothes that do more than just protect us from the elements. The demand for expensive city-bought garments reflects a desire for works of art that delight us, tools to help us present ourselves to the world. In a diverse, complicated city, clothes indicate the interests and income of their wearer. Since cities have more social heterogeneity and more social interactions, clothing plays a somewhat more important role there than it does elsewhere. This might help explain why households in cities with more than a million people spend 42 percent more on women's clothing than nonurban households, as a share of total household expenditures.

There is even a statistical reality behind the passion for shoes of the urbanites in *Sex and the City*. Big-city households spend 25 percent more on footwear, again relative to their total budgets, than households outside of cities, presumably because they are buying fancier shoes, although it is possible that their shoe leather is wearing out faster pounding the city pavement. As in *Sex and the City*, the urban desire to present an attractive appearance also reflects the fact that big-city density serves to connect people romantically, creating a market for mates that is, in its way, as important as the labor market.

London as Marriage Market

London has its share of creative mixologists who produce new and sometimes startling cocktails, like the Lychee and Elderflower Collins served in the bar of the St. Martins Lane hotel. But for many single people, and for a few errant spouses, drinking well is only a minor part of the bar experience. Bars provide an opportunity for romantic encounters. Cities attract more single people than other areas, in part, because urban density increases the odds of meeting a prospective partner. The same logic that pulls workers and firms together in dense areas pulls men and women together in cities.

The role of the city as marriage market helps us to understand the unusual demographics of dense urban areas. In 2008, the island of Manhattan housed 1.4 million people over the age of fifteen. Out of that group, about a third (460,000) were married and living with their spouses. About half of the population had never been married and about another 139,000 people were divorced. In the United States as a whole, about one half of people over fifteen are married and living with their spouses. Manhattanites are much more likely than other Americans to be singles between the ages of twenty-five and thirty-four.

Dense cities attract younger, single people for many reasons. Cities are good places to work hard and acquire knowledge. Suburbs cater to young parents because of better schools and larger homes, but cities also attract young single people because they are fun places to be young and single. Density and the ability to walk from bar to bar or restaurant to restaurant make them ideal places to meet the thousands of other young, single people who have come to the city for exactly the same reason.

Cities are singles magnets, but they also attract the most economically successful couples because of the ability of both spouses to find suitable jobs within a big urban labor market. Researchers Dora Costa and Matthew Kahn have found that among couples, one of whom has a college degree, about 40 percent locate in large metropolitan areas, while among couples, both of whom have college degrees, 50 percent locate in such places.

At the start of the twentieth century, when well-off women rarely worked, a well-educated successful man could run his business deep in the resource-rich hinterland. It didn't much matter that his wife couldn't get a decent job there. Today, that budding magnate's spouse is more likely to be a high-powered lawyer herself, who probably won't want to live in the middle of nowhere. So big cities like Washington, D.C., and Los Angeles increasingly attract power couples, both of whom need good jobs.

The urban edge in bringing people together goes beyond romantic relations. People who live in cities can connect with a broader range of friends whose interests are well matched with their own. Paris is famous for its literary salons. New York had groups of like-minded souls such as the Algonquin Round Table. Nineteenth-century political movements like Italy's Risorgimento and the Generation of 1837 in Argentina were hashed out in intellectual conversations held in the cafés and bookstores of Milan and Buenos Aires. Less dense areas provide people with a smaller range of potential dinner companions, another nonwork cost of living outside of cities.

In 1892, Theodore Dreiser came to Chicago from small-town Indiana to write for the *Chicago Globe*. Over the next forty years, he became one of the great chroniclers of American urban life, who described, with equal insight, the hard life of the urban working class and the peccadilloes of the mighty. One of his greatest characters was Carrie Meeber, the heroine of his first novel, *Sister Carrie*.

The novel begins with Carrie taking the train from rural Wisconsin to industrial Chicago. Chicago gives Carrie economic opportunity, but even more significant, an escape from the stultifying boredom of rural life. In the process of enjoying the pleasures and temptations of a big city, she manages to "ruin" a few city slickers, but Dreiser leaves us in no doubt that her life was a whole lot more interesting and fun than it would have been if she had stayed on the farm and married the earnest plowman five miles down the road.

Sister Carrie's somewhat sordid life reflects the availability of urban pleasures, but also the fact that traditional social mores tend to break down in big cities. If Carrie had carried on with married men so freely in rural Wisconsin, she would have been ostracized. In Chicago, she may have been disreputable and banned from polite society, but she still had plenty of other disreputable types to play with. The same thing was true of Frank Cowperthwaite, a Dreiser antihero based on a real-life streetcar magnate, Charles Yerkes, who found plenty of urban associates despite his scandalous behavior. For good and ill, cities have long freed people from social convention. Villages find it easy to impose rules because people who break those rules can be cut off from social connection and suffer, like the wearer of Hawthorne's scarlet letter, the pain of solitude.

In a big city, however, there's always some new network to try, so no nongovernmental group can enforce harsh rules on behavior without resorting to extralegal violence. Some cities, such as Puritan Boston or Calvinist Geneva, managed to maintain social discipline for a while, but these strictures always eventually break down. The more natural outcome for a city is the less restricted world of Paris or Chicago.

When Are High Wages Bad?

An increasingly wealthy and well-educated population, eager to sample new delights, is naturally drawn to big cities, which specialize in innovative pleasure. Novelty itself is a luxury good. Only the rich have enough resources to get bored with having excellent, ordinary food every day. As the world has gotten richer and more unequal, more people are willing to pay for the constant stream of new, high-end experiences that are most easily had in big cities.

A vast array of publications and Web sites strive—and inevitably fail—to keep up with all the art openings, restaurant debuts, concerts, and other events that unfold every week in cities like Barcelona or Los Angeles or Tokyo. These experiences are so numerous and so evanescent that it might seem impossible to evaluate their effect on a city's overall quality of life. How do we sort through all of them and determine whether cities are becoming more or less pleasant places to live?

One of the bedrock principles of economics is that free lunches are rare and markets require trade-offs. Investors can choose assets with higher returns only if they also take on more risk; suburbanites can get a bigger lot at the cost of a longer commute. In comparing metropolitan areas, there is a three-way trade-off among wages, prices, and quality of life. Most of the time, high wages and high prices go together; high housing costs are the price of accessing high-wage cities. But even correcting for prices and an individual's skills, real wages vary from place to place. Some cities, like San Diego and Honolulu, have unusually low real incomes, while others, like Dallas, Texas, and Rochester, Minnesota, have unusually high real incomes.

Should everyone in Honolulu be rushing to Dallas? Of course not. High real wages are compensating for frigid winters in Rochester and broiling summers in Dallas. Low real wages are the cost of experiencing the pleasures of San Diego and Honolulu. The market works, more or less, and when a city has really high housing prices relative to incomes, you can bet that there is something nice about the place. If an extremely attractive area had high wages and low prices, it would attract thousands of new residents who would quickly bid up the cost of living.

I once estimated which American metropolitan areas were the most expensive, holding wages constant, and found that nine out of the top ten cities were in coastal California. Honolulu was the tenth city. When you look at which places have particularly low prices relative to incomes, you find spots that are too cold, like Anchorage, Alaska, and spots that are too hot, like Midland, Texas. Other places in that bottom-ten list, like Detroit or Trenton, have other problems, like crime and unemployment.

Real wages—incomes corrected for local prices—are an effective tool for assessing urban amenities. If places have unusually low real wages, then quality of life must be high. If places have unusually high real wages, then something is wrong with those places. Somewhat paradoxically, the decline in real wages in places like New York provides us with the best evidence that, all in all, big-city amenities have become more valuable.

In 1970, there was a strong positive relationship between city size and real wages. Real wages increased by 3 percent as area population doubled. The same relationship also held in 1980. In the 1970s, when New York was a battleground, workers had to be given combat pay to put up with the city's problems. Those high real wages were a sign of urban failure—the painful crime rate and disintegration of urban amenities—not urban success.

Since 1980, the relationship between area population and real wages first leveled off and is now negative. In the year 2000, people were willing to accept *lower* real wages to live in New York, which means that they were coming to New York despite the fact that higher prices more than erased higher wages. It's not that New York had become less productive; the city's nominal wages, which reflect productivity, were higher than ever. But housing prices, fueled by the robust demand to live and play in the city, had risen even more than nominal earnings. If housing prices rise enough relative to nominal incomes, as they do when cities become far more pleasant, then real incomes can actually fall during a period of great urban success. Manhattan had changed from a battlefield to an urban playground, and people were willing to pay, in the form of lower real wages, for the privilege of living there.

Because economic logic suggests that places with high housing prices relative to income must be pleasant, I've tried to capture the pleasures of a place by ranking America's counties based on how unusually high their housing prices were in 1980 relative to their median incomes. On average, counties with high levels of amenities, meaning that they were in the top quarter of areas based on this index, saw their populations grow by 40 percent. Counties in the bottom quarter of areas based on this index had no population growth, on average. The high-amenity counties also saw real median incomes grow by 28 percent, as opposed to 14 percent in the low-amenity counties. The consumer city is on the rise.

The increased demand for city living has also driven the rise in reverse commuting. People who live in one place and work somewhere else are showing their appreciation of the amenities, or low housing costs, of their hometown. We know that New York doesn't have low housing costs, but there is an increasingly large number of people who live in the city and work outside it. Nationwide, the share of the population that commutes from central city to suburb has increased from 2.4 percent in 1960 to 6.8 percent today. The fact that more people will pay high urban prices and work somewhere else is further evidence that big-city amenities have become increasingly valuable.

Other variables that indicate an attractive location, like an abundance of tourists, also predict urban success. The correlation seems to hold in England and France, as well as in the United States. People are increasingly choosing areas on the basis of quality of life, and the skilled people who come to attractive areas then provide the new ideas that fuel the local economy. Smart, entrepreneurial people are the ultimate source of a city's economic power, and as those people become more prosperous, they care more about quality of life.

What publicly provided amenities matter most for attracting the skilled? People, especially those with more education, will pay plenty for safe streets and good schools for their children. The growing importance of the consumer city should serve mainly to keep civic leaders focused on doing the basic jobs of local government: policing the streets and improving public schools. Restaurants and theaters are also attractions, but they are neither as critical as safety and schools nor as amenable to governmental intervention. Those amenities come naturally in a thriving city, at least as long as the city hasn't overregulated its pleasures.

The importance of consumer pleasures also offers a lesson for downturns. City governments must not react to fiscal distress by cutting municipal services, like policing. The easiest way to ensure that a city won't survive an economic crisis is to turn it into a dangerous no-man's-land. Unsafe streets will repel the skilled workers that are so vital for urban rebirth.

New York, London, and Paris may be the world's most elite consumer cities, but there are plenty of other places that succeed by being playgrounds. University towns, like Charlottesville, Virginia, have attracted many retirees. Las Vegas leveraged its casinos into becoming the fastest-growing large city in America. Indeed, the city's boosters got so excited about all those restaurants and casinos that it experienced one of the most dramatic of all housing bubbles. Once the pain of the overbuilding has subsided, Las Vegas can go back to being a more normal, midsize place that succeeds by promoting a certain kind of fun.

The problem that New York and London and Paris face is somewhat different. Robust economies and abundant pleasures have made these places highly desirable. People want to live there, and when there isn't enough housing to satisfy demand, prices can soar. If the most attractive metropolises don't build more homes, they risk becoming boutique cities, depriving all but the wealthiest of their pleasures and their practical advantages. The barriers that prevent construction in these successful areas are the topic of the next chapter.

CHAPTER 6

What's So Great About Skyscrapers?

A walk from the Arc de Triomphe to the Louvre along the Champs-Élysées in Paris can seem like a stroll through history. It begins under a two-hundred-year-old arch celebrating French imperial triumphs that was inspired by a far older imperial arch in Rome, the Arch of Titus. It proceeds along one of the most famous boulevards in the world, where Marie Antoinette rode and Hitler marched and countless tourists have eaten ice cream. It passes the Hôtel de Crillon, where Hemingway drank and Woodrow Wilson slept during the Versailles Peace Conference. It crosses the Jardin des Tuileries, that ancient royal playground. It ends in a museum that was begun as a twelfth-century fortress and now houses the masterpieces of many millennia. This walk, like Paris itself, feels timeless: an unchanging urban experience that is far from the ever altering streetscapes of dynamic cities like Hong Kong and Singapore.

But of course, Paris had its beginnings and its builders. Today the city seems like a perfect argument for the value of preserving the past, but with a bit more historical perspective, Paris also makes a case for the virtues of allowing enormous change. Much of the Paris that people love most is the handiwork of one man, Baron Georges-Eugène Haussmann, who rebuilt the city in a single generation.

What comes to mind when you think of Paris? Perhaps a café au lait at Sartre's old haunt, Les Deux Magots, after a walk along the Boulevard Saint-Germain. That thoroughfare, like the Boul'Mich (Boulevard Saint-Michel), was created by Haussmann, carved out of a mess of older streets. If you prefer the walk I described along the Champs-Élysées, enjoying the view of the Arc de Triomphe, you are again in Haussmann territory. The street and the arch predate the Baron, but he planned the square that provides such clear views. Do you enjoy the miraculous uniformity of all those five-story buildings that line Parisian streets? That's Haussmann too. The Opéra? Haussmann. Beneath all that French glamour, there is a sewer system that separates clean water from waste. Thanks again to the Baron. Between 1853 and 1870, Haussmann's work removed more than half of the buildings in Paris. Haussmann did, in fact, destroy a city to save it.

Paris is an ordered whole. We relish the great monuments of Paris because they are easy to see, not obscured by nearby buildings. It's obvious that Paris wasn't built through the gradual accretion of density recommended by grass-roots urbanists. No, Paris is unified because it was the planned product of a single master builder, whose imperial overlord gave him a free hand.

Shakespeare's line "What is the city but the people" is true, but people need buildings. Cities grow by building up, or out, and when a city doesn't build, people are prevented from experiencing the magic of urban proximity. Preserving a city can, in fact, require destroying a part of it. The modern desire to preserve Haussmann's Paris has helped turn the affordable Paris of the past into a boutique city that can today be enjoyed only by the wealthy. The history of Paris is replete with great artists who spent their impecunious formative years there, but what poor artists can afford to live in central Paris today? When places overrestrict construction, they risk stagnation and steadily rising prices.

There is great value in protecting the most beautiful parts of our urban past, but cities shouldn't be embalmed in amber. Too much preservation stops cities from providing newer, taller, better buildings for their inhabitants. Height restrictions, in Paris and New York and Mumbai, may seem like obscure arcana of interest only to planning professionals. Nothing could be more wrong. These rules are shaping the future of our cities and our world. If the cities' history becomes a straitjacket, then they lose one of their greatest assets: the ability to build up.

Inventing the Skyscraper

In the Book of Genesis, the builders of the Tower of Babel declared, "Go to, let us build us a city and a tower, whose top may reach unto heaven; and let us make us a name, lest we be scattered abroad upon the face of the whole earth." These proto-developers correctly understood that cities could connect humanity, but God punished them for monumentalizing terrestrial, rather than celestial, glory. For much of the past two thousand years, Western city builders have taken this story's warning to heart, and the tallest structures were typically church spires. The wool-making center of Bruges was one of the first places where a secular structure, the 354-foot belfry built to celebrate cloth making, towered over a religious structure, the nearby Cathedral of Saint Donatus.

In worldly Bruges, wool topped worship by the end of the fifteenth century, but elsewhere it took another four centuries for secular structures to surpass religious towers. Until 1890, the 284-foot spire of Trinity Church, where my great-grandmother knelt in prayer, one block away from the Stock Exchange on Wall Street, was the tallest structure in New York. Perhaps that date, when this religious edifice was eclipsed by a skyscraper built to house Joseph Pulitzer's *New York World*, should be seen as the true start of the irreligious twentieth century. At almost the same time, Paris celebrated its growing wealth by erecting the 1,000-foot Eiffel Tower, which was 700 feet taller than the Cathedral of Notre Dame.

Since that tower in Babel, height has been seen both as a way to provide more space on a fixed amount of land and as a symbol of power. The belfry of Trinity Church and Gustave Eiffel's icon did not provide usable space. They were massive monuments to God and French engineering respectively. Pulitzer's World Building was certainly a monument to Pulitzer, but it was also a relatively practical means of getting his increasingly large news empire into a single building where journalists and editors and Mr. Pulitzer himself could interact.

For centuries, ever taller buildings have made it possible to cram more and more people on an acre of land, without forcing those people to cram together in coffin-size rooms, like those offered in some infamous Tokyo hotels. Yet until the nineteenth century, the move upward was a moderate evolution by which two-story buildings were gradually replaced by four- and six-story buildings. Until the nineteenth century, heights were limited by the cost of building and the human tolerance for climbing stairs. Church spires and belfry towers could pierce the heavens, but only because those towers were narrow and because few people, other than the occasional bell ringer, had to climb them. Tall buildings became possible in the nineteenth century when American innovators solved the twin problems of crafting tall buildings without enormously thick lower walls and of safely moving up and down in them.

Elisha Otis didn't invent the elevator; Archimedes allegedly built one, possibly in Sicily, twenty-two hundred years ago. And Louis XV had his own personal lift in Versailles so that he could visit his mistress. Yet for the elevator to become mass transit, it needed a good source of power, and it needed to be safe. Messrs. Matthew Boulton and James Watt provided the early steam engines used to power industrial elevators, which were either pulled up by a rope or pushed up hydraulically. As engines improved, so did the speed and power of elevators, which could haul massive amounts of coal out of mines or grain from boats.

But humans were still pretty wary of traveling long distances upward in a machine that could easily break and send them hurtling downward. Otis, tinkering in a Yonkers, New York, sawmill, took the danger out of vertical transit. He crafted a safety brake, which could work for either elevators or trains, and presented his invention in 1854 at New York's Crystal Palace Exposition. He had himself hoisted on a platform pulled by a rope, and then, dramatically, an axman severed the rope. The platform dropped slightly, then came to a halt as the safety brake engaged. The Otis elevator was a sensation, and Otis's company remains one of the world's leading elevator makers.

The first two buildings to install powered safety elevators were both in New York City: a department store on Broadway and the Fifth Avenue Hotel. In the 1870s, the elevator enabled pathbreaking structures, like Richard Morris Hunt's New York Tribune building, to reach ten stories. Across the Atlantic, St. Pancras Station in London also reached ten stories, and at 269 feet it was far taller than Hunt's New York skyscraper.

But the fortresslike appearance of St. Pancras hints at the building's core problem. The station lacks the critical cost-reducing ingredient of the modern skyscraper: a load-bearing steel skeleton. Traditional buildings, like St. Pancras or the Tribune building, needed enormously strong lower walls to carry the weight of a tall building. To go further up, lower walls had to get thicker and thicker, and that made costs prohibitive unless you were building a really narrow spire.

The load-bearing steel skeleton, which pretty much defines a skyscraper, applies the same engineering principles used in earlier balloon-frame houses. In a balloon-frame house, a light skeleton made up of standardized boards—two-by-fours, two-by-eights, one-by-tens—supports the weight of the structure. The walls then are essentially a curtain hung on the frame. Balloon-frame houses reduced the costs of putting up homes throughout nineteenth-century rural America. Skyscrapers, like balloon-frame houses, rest their weight on a skeleton frame, but in this case the frame is made of steel, which became increasingly affordable in the late nineteenth century.

William Le Baron Jenney's 138-foot Home Insurance Building, built in Chicago in 1885, is often seen as the first true skyscraper, but there is a lively architectural debate about whether Jenney was really the inventor of the skyscraper. That debate reflects the fact that the development of the skyscraper, like most other gifts of the city, didn't occur in a social vacuum, and it didn't occur all at once. Jenney's "first skyscraper" didn't have a complete steel skeleton. It had just two iron-reinforced, fireproof walls. Previous tall buildings in Chicago, such as Daniel Burnham and John Root's Montauk Building, built two years earlier, had also used steel reinforcement. Industrial structures, like the McCullough Shot Tower in New York and the St. Ouen Docks Warehouse near Paris, had used iron frames decades before.

Jenney's proto-skyscraper was a patchwork, stitching together his own innovations and ideas that were in the air of architect-rich Chicago. Other builders, like Burnham and Root, their engineer George Fuller, and Louis Sullivan, a former Jenney apprentice, then further developed the idea. Sullivan's great breakthrough came in 1890, when he designed a skyscraper, St. Louis's Wainwright Building, free from massive amounts of ornamental masonry. Whereas Jenney's buildings look Victorian, the Wainwright Building points the way clearly toward the modernist towers that now define so many urban skylines.

Ayn Rand's novel *The Fountainhead* is loosely based on the early life of Louis Sullivan's apprentice Frank Lloyd Wright. Sullivan and Wright are depicted as lone eagles, Gary Cooper heroes, paragons of rugged individualism. They weren't. They were great architects deeply enmeshed in an urban chain of innovation; Wright riffed on Sullivan's idea of form following function, and Sullivan riffed on Jenney, and Jenney relied on the fireproofing innovations of Peter B. Wight.

Their collective creation—the skyscraper—enabled cities to add vast amounts of floor space using the same amount of ground area. Given the rising demand for center-city real estate, the skyscraper seemed like a godsend. The problem was that those central cities already had buildings on them. Except in places like Chicago, where fire had created a tabula rasa, those cities needed to tear down in order to build up.

The demand for space was even stronger in New York than in Chicago, and skyscrapers were soon springing up in Manhattan. In 1890, Pulitzer's World Building had some steel columns, but its weight was still supported by seven-foot-thick masonry walls. In 1899, the World's height was surpassed by the Park Row Building, which soared to 391 feet supported by a steel skeleton. Daniel Burnham traveled east to build his iconic Flatiron Building in 1902, and in 1909, Wight's National Academy of Design was torn down to build the 700-foot Metropolitan Life tower, then the tallest building in the world. In 1913, the Woolworth Building reached 792 feet, and it remained the world's tallest building until the boom of the late 1920s.

The Soaring Ambition of A. E. Lefcourt

Those tall buildings were not mere monuments. They enabled New York to grow and industries to expand. They gave factory owners and workers space that was both more humane and more efficient. Manhattan's master builders, such as A. E. Lefcourt, made that possible.

Like a proper Horatio Alger hero, A. E. Lefcourt was born poor and started work as a teenage newsboy and bootblack. When he began working full-time in retail, he kept selling papers in the morning and shining shoes in the evening. He saved enough cash to buy a $1,000 U.S. Treasury bond, which he kept pinned to his shirt. When he was twenty-five, his garment industry employer decided to retire; Lefcourt shocked the man by announcing that he wanted to buy the firm. For about a decade, Lefcourt built up his business to the point where it was doing $2 million a year in sales (more than $40 million in 2010 currency).

In 1910, New York City was hit by the Great Revolt, in which sixty thousand garment workers stayed on the picket lines for ten weeks. Lefcourt, still in his early thirties, led the management side of the battle as the chairman of the

Cloak, Suit and Skirt Manufacturers' Protective Association. Despite the fact that the courts seemed willing to back the manufacturers all the way, Lefcourt accepted the terms of the mediator, future Supreme Court justice Louis Brandeis, in what became known as the Protocol of Peace. While Pittsburgh's Henry Clay Frick earned a place in history for using overwhelming force against the Homestead Strike, Lefcourt deserves credit for finding a less bloody and likely more profitable middle ground.

In the summer of 1910, at the same time that he was bargaining with the labor unions, Lefcourt began a new career as a real estate developer. He sank all of his capital into a twelve-story loft building on West Twenty-fifth Street that would house his own firm. He built more such buildings and helped move his industry from the old sweatshops into the modern garment district. Whereas the old downtown garment district had been anchored by the value of proximity to the port, Lefcourt's new garment district lay between Pennsylvania and Grand Central stations, anchored by the rail lines, which continued to give New York a transportation advantage. Transportation technologies shape cities, and Midtown Manhattan was built around two great rail stations that could carry in oceans of people. (Bedrock may have also played a role, but its impact appears to have been modest.)

Lefcourt discovered that he liked building even more than he liked making clothes. Over the next twenty years, he erected thirty-one edifices, many of them skyscrapers. Lefcourt used those Otis elevators in soaring towers that covered 150 acres, encased 100 million cubic feet, and contained as many workers as Trenton. The *Wall Street Journal* wrote that "he demolished more historical structures in New York City than any other man dared to contemplate." In the early 1920s, the New York of slums, tenements, and Gilded Age mansions was transformed into a city of skyscrapers, as builders like Lefcourt erected a hundred thousand new units each year, enabling the city to grow and to stay reasonably affordable.

By 1928, Lefcourt's real estate wealth was estimated at $100 million; he would have been a billionaire in today's dollars. He celebrated by opening a national bank bearing his own name. Lefcourt's optimism was unfazed by the stock market crash, and he planned $50 million of construction for 1930, sure that it would be a "great building year." But Lefcourt was wrong. As New York's economy collapsed, so did his real estate empire, which was sold off piecemeal to pay his investors. He died in 1932 worth only $2,500, seemingly punished, like the builders of Babel, for his hubris.

I suspect that Lefcourt, like many developers, cared more about his structural legacy than cash. Those structures helped house the creative minds that still make New York special. Two economists tried to understand the impact of building height on economic productivity by comparing areas that had natural features like bedrock, which makes it cheaper to build up, with areas where building up was naturally more difficult. They found that labor productivity and wages were significantly higher in those places where density was easier to develop.

Lefcourt's most famous building, which doesn't even bear his name, came to symbolize an entire musical style: the Brill Building Sound. From 1958 to 1965, artists connected in the Brill Building produced a string of hits like "Twist and Shout," "You've Lost That Lovin' Feeling," and fittingly enough, "Up on the Roof." Cities are ultimately about the connections among people, but structures—like those built by A. E. Lefcourt—make those connections easier. By building up, Lefcourt made the lives of garment workers far more pleasant and created plenty of new space for creative minds in other fields.

Regulating New York

New York's upward trajectory was not without its detractors. In 1913, the distinguished chairman of the Fifth Avenue Commission, who was himself an architect, led a fight to "save Fifth Avenue from ruin." At that time, Fifth Avenue was still a street of stately mansions owned by Astors and Rockefellers. The antigrowth activists argued that unless heights were restricted to 125 feet or less, Fifth Avenue would become a canyon with ruinous results for property values, congestion, and the city as a whole. Similar arguments have been made by the enemies of change throughout history and into our time. The chair of the commission was a better architect than prognosticator: Density has suited Fifth Avenue quite nicely.

In 1915, on the corner of Broadway and Nassau Street, in the heart of downtown New York, the Equitable Life Assurance Society constructed a 538-foot-high monolith, which contains almost two million square feet of office space and cast a seven-acre shadow on the city. The building became a rallying cry for the enemies of height, who wanted to see a little more sun. A political alliance came together and passed the city's landmark 1916 zoning ordinance, which allowed buildings to rise only if they gave up girth. New York's many ziggurat-like structures, which get narrower as they get taller, were constructed to fulfill the setback requirements of the 1916 ordinance.

The code changed the shape of buildings, but it did little to stop the building boom of the 1920s. Really tall buildings provide something of an index of irrational exuberance. Five of New York City's ten tallest buildings in 2009, including the Empire State Building, were completed between 1930 and 1933. Development of all of the older sites started during the go-go years of the late 1920s, when the city's future seemed unlimited. Builders like A. E. Lefcourt were confident they could attract tenants, and their bankers were happy to lend.

In the late 1920s, the builders of the Chrysler Building, 40 Wall Street, and the Empire State Building had a great race to produce the tallest structure in New York and hence the world. It is an odd fact that two of New York's tallest and most iconic edifices, Chrysler and Empire State, were built with money made from selling the cars that would move America away from vertical cities to sprawling suburbs. As it turned out, the winning Empire State Building, nicknamed the "Empty State Building," was neither fully occupied nor profitable until after World War II. Luckily for its builders, the building's construction costs also came in way below budget because there was plenty of cheap steel available during the Great Depression.

In the years after 1933, New York slowed its construction of skyscrapers, and its regulations became ever more complex. Between 1916 and 1960, the original zoning code was amended more than twenty-five hundred times. In 1960, the City's Planning Commission passed a new zoning ordinance that significantly increased the limits on building. The resulting 420-page code replaced a simple classification of space—business, residential, and unrestricted—with a dizzying number of different districts, each of which permitted only a narrow range of activities. There were thirteen different types of residential districts, twelve different types of manufacturing districts, and no less than forty-one different types of commercial districts.

Each type of district narrowly classified the range of permissible activities. Commercial art galleries are forbidden in residential districts but allowed in manufacturing districts, while noncommercial art galleries are forbidden in manufacturing districts but allowed in residential districts. Art supply stores are forbidden in residential districts and some commercial districts. Parking space requirements also differed by district. In an R5 district, a hospital must have one off-street parking spot per every five beds, but in an R6 district, a hospital must have one space for every eight beds. The picayune detail of the code is exemplified by its control of signs: "For multiple dwellings, including apartment hotels, or for permitted non-residential buildings or other structures, one identification sign with an area not exceeding 12 square feet and indicating only the name of the permitting use, the name or address of the building, or the name of the management thereof, is permitted."

The code also removed the complex system of setbacks and replaced it with a complex system based on floor area ratios or FARs—a FAR is the ratio of interior square footage to ground area. A maximum FAR of two, for example, means that a developer can put a two-story building on his entire plot or a four-story building on half of the plot. In residential districts R1, R2, and R3, the maximum floor area ratio was 0.5. In R9 districts, the maximum FAR was about 7.5. The height restriction was eased for builders who created plazas or other public spaces at the front of the building. While the standard building created by the 1916 code was a wedding cake that started at the sidewalk, the standard building created by the 1961 code was a glass-and-steel slab with an open plaza in front.

Fear of Heights

New York's zoning codes were getting more rigorous, but so were other restrictions on new development. After World War II, New York made private development more difficult by overregulating construction and rents while building a bevy of immense publicly supported structures, such as Stuyvesant Town and Lincoln Center. But then, during the 1950s and 1960s, both public and private projects increasingly ran into resistance from grassroots organizers, like Jane Jacobs, who were becoming adept at mounting opposition to large-scale development.

Jane Jacobs hardly seemed cut out for big-city glory. She graduated from Scranton's Central High School in 1934 and left the next year for New York

City, because she thought it would be more fun than northeastern Pennsylvania. She took extension-school classes at Columbia University without ever getting a college degree. Later she would turn down abundant offers of honorary degrees. When we first met in 1993, I was struck by how much pleasure she took in her self-made status. She got started writing freelance articles about the city for the *Herald Tribune,* eventually rising to the position of associate editor at the *Architectural Forum,* a monthly magazine that focused on buildings. She married an architect, Robert Jacobs, and chose to raise a family on Hudson Street in the West Village.

Her remarkable intellect, which still sparkled well into her eighties, and her New York City experiences led her to many profound and prescient insights. In the 1950s, she saw clearly the folly of those efforts of urban renewal, which replaced well-functioning neighborhoods with immense towers that were isolated from the streets that surrounded them. She opposed the accepted wisdom of urban planning, with its penchant for single-use neighborhoods; she advocated diversity. In the 1960s, she grasped the role that cities play in spreading knowledge and ideas and creating economic growth. In the 1970s, she understood that cities were actually better for the environment than leafy suburbs. Her insights came from her enormous gifts as an observer living and working in New York. Her knowledge came from walking around with her eyes open, which is still the best way to learn how a city works.

Gradually Jacobs also started getting involved in fights over urban development. As a Greenwich Village resident, she opposed a plan to run a road through Washington Square Park. While zoning advocates were increasingly pushing for single-use zoning, Jacobs became an advocate of mixed-use zoning, opposing "segregating New York into economically independent islands with endless, dreadful consequences." She vehemently opposed retail-free public housing projects, deriding them for their single-purpose sterility. She criticized Lincoln Center as a "piece of built-in rigor mortis."

In 1961, the same year that the City Planning Commission's new zoning plan came into effect, the commission got into a fight with Jane Jacobs over demolishing sixteen blocks of Greenwich Village for urban renewal. Jacobs got a court order to stop the project. She assembled a broad range of supporters who rushed the podium at a commission planning meeting. She insinuated that there were corrupt deals between city officials and builders. Eventually, she created enough heat so that the mayor himself, once a strong supporter of the project, gave it up.

In that same year, a few months after beating City Hall, Jacobs published her masterpiece, *The Death and Life of Great American Cities*. It is a great book, which investigates and celebrates the pedestrian world of mid-twentieth-century New York. She grounds her case for mixed-use zoning by arguing that street life is the essence of city living and city safety. She argues against high-density dwellings by pointing out that they segregate residents from their streets. In a world of short buildings, residents can monitor the paths outside their home, and eyes on the street make pedestrians safer. In a world of high-rises, those residents become oblivious to the street life beneath them.

There is some truth to her assertion that streets can suffer from high-rise buildings, at least when they're poorly designed and discourage street life. People who live in high-rises are about 6 percent more likely to be victimized by street crime than people who live in single-family dwellings, even controlling extensively for individual attributes of each potential victim. The people who live in big buildings are actually less likely to have their homes burgled, but they're more likely to be robbed on the street. Among richer people, there is no link between height and crime. My own interpretation of these facts is that the taller towers, occupied by the poor, are often public housing projects, where poverty is concentrated and ground-floor retail is rare. These conditions mean that streets can become dominated by troublemakers.

In more mixed settings, there are more shoppers and workers. In wealthier areas, there are doormen. A modicum of good urban planning can ensure that high-rises have enough foot traffic to keep streets safe. Neither Midtown Manhattan nor Hong Kong is short on pedestrians, and crime is relatively rare.

Jane Jacobs's opposition to urban renewal led her to a more sweeping dislike for tall buildings in general. In *The Death and Life of Great American Cities,* she argued that urban neighborhoods can only thrive when they have between one and two hundred households per acre. She argued that cities need at least a hundred homes per acre to generate enough street traffic to support exciting restaurants and shops. She also argued that two hundred homes per acre was a "danger mark"; once neighborhoods crossed that point, they risked sterile standardization. A typical Manhattan apartment, like the one that I grew up in, has about 1,300 square feet of floor space. To accommodate two hundred households per acre, structures should be about six stories high, just about the standard height for apartment buildings constructed before the age of the elevator.

While Jacobs well understood the virtues of the shorter neighborhoods that she lived in, it is less clear that she grasped the strengths that are also present in places with loftier structures. There's nothing particularly sterile about high-rise Manhattan neighborhoods, as long as they have enough ground-floor action. Taller neighborhoods can also have plenty of interesting stores and restaurants. Densities of three hundred or more households per acre are surely not for everyone, but human diversity demands a variety of living arrangements, and some people do want tall buildings. Jacobs's own preference for Greenwich Village–like neighborhoods was quite reasonable—I like the Village too—but one's own tastes are rarely a sound basis for public policy. For the government to mandate a single style of urbanism is no more sensible than for the government to enforce a single style of literature.

Jacobs's belief in the value of moderate densities led her to fight against tall structures, such as a nine-story library for New York University, just as she fought against single-use zoning and new expressways. Her urban vision was very much grounded in the experience of her own Greenwich Village neighborhood, with its taverns and thinkers and low-rise townhouses. She liked old buildings and thought that new skyscrapers wouldn't permit the mixed uses that she loved.

Jane Jacobs liked protecting old buildings because of a confused piece of economic reasoning. She thought that preserving older, shorter structures would somehow keep prices affordable for budding entrepreneurs. That's not how supply and demand works. Preserving an older one-story building instead of replacing it with a forty-story building does not preserve affordability. Indeed, opposing new building is the surest way to make a popular area unaffordable. An increase in the supply of houses, or anything else, almost always drives prices down, while restricting the supply of real estate keeps prices high.

The relationship between housing supply and affordability isn't just a matter of economic theory. There is a great deal of evidence linking the supply of space with the cost of real estate. Simply put, the places that are expensive don't build a lot, and the places that build a lot aren't expensive. Several papers have shown that new construction is lower and prices are higher in places that restrict building. One of the cleverest papers in this genre uses natural barriers to building, such as the hilliness of an area, and shows that places with tough topography have less new construction and higher prices.

Perhaps a new forty-story building won't itself house any quirky, less profitable firms, but by providing new space, the building will ease pressure on the rest of the city's real estate. Price increases in gentrifying older areas will be muted because of new construction. Growth, not height restrictions and a fixed building stock, keeps space affordable and ensures that poorer people and less profitable firms can stay, which helps thriving cities remain successful and diverse. Height restrictions do increase light, and preservation does protect history, but we shouldn't pretend that these benefits come without a price.

The Perils of Preservation

In 1961, the same year that Jane Jacobs published her great book, the Pennsylvania Railroad was preparing to raze its old New York station. That railroad had built the station on Thirty-third Street as a temple to trains in 1908, the height of the rail era. The old Penn Station was a stunning structure, complete with Doric columns and a waiting room based on the Baths of Caracalla. The building's architect, like Jane Jacobs, saw height as inimical to urban life, so he insisted that the building be short.

The decision to go low would prove to be the station's undoing. While the structure was an acknowledged architectural masterpiece, it also made less sense as rail travel declined in the twentieth century. By the end of the 1950s, the Pennsylvania Railroad was determined to get more value out of their well-placed, central Manhattan property. They tore down the Beaux Arts structure and replaced it with today's far less loved station and a thirty-four-story office tower. The rents from the tower could make up for some of their declining rail revenues.

Everything the Pennsylvania Railroad did was entirely legal, but the old station had been loved by both cognoscenti and ordinary commuters. The demolition of the beautiful station became a rallying cry for a growing preservationist movement that aimed to protect New York's most beautiful older buildings from Penn Station's fate. In 1962, Mayor Robert Wagner established a Landmarks Preservation Commission. Just in case there was any confusion about the mayor's motivation, the subtitle of the *New York Times* article announcing the formation of that new agency was "Wagner Names 12 to New Agency—Architects Decry Razing of Penn Station."

In 1965, despite vigorous opposition from the real estate industry, the Landmarks Preservation Commission became permanent. It initially seemed like a small sop to the preservationists. The number of landmarked buildings, seven hundred, was modest, and the commission's power was checked by the mayor, who could and can veto any one of their decisions.

Yet, like entropy, the reach of governmental agencies often increases over time, so that a mild, almost symbolic, group can come to hold sway over vast swaths of a city. By the spring of 2010, the New York Landmarks Commission had jurisdiction over twenty-five thousand landmarked buildings and one hundred historic districts. More than 15 percent of Manhattan's nonpark land south of Ninety-sixth Street is now in a historic district, where every external change must be approved by the Landmarks Commission.

In 2006, the developer Aby Rosen proposed putting a twenty-two-story glass tower atop the old Sotheby-Parke-Bernet Building at 980 Madison Avenue, in the heart of the massive Upper East Side Historic District. The building itself was not landmarked, but Rosen and his Pritzker Prize–winning architect, Lord Norman Foster, proposed keeping the original building's facade intact. The tower would have risen above the old structure, much as the former Pan Am Building rises above Grand Central Terminal. Well-connected neighbors didn't like the idea of more height, and they took their complaints to the Landmarks Preservation Commission. Tom Wolfe, who has written brilliantly about both the foibles of New York and the real estate industry, penned a 3,500-word piece in the *New York Times* insinuating that if the Landmarks Commission gave approval to the project, it would betray its mission. Wolfe & Co. won.

In response to his critics in the 980 Madison Avenue case, of which I was one, Mr. Wolfe was quoted Glaeser's in the *Village Voice* saying "To take [Glaeser's] theory to its logical conclusion would be to develop Central Park. . . . When you consider the thousands and thousands of people who could be housed in Central Park if they would only allow them to build it up, boy, the problem is on the way to being solved!" But one of the advantages of building up in already dense neighborhoods is that you don't have to build in green areas, whether in Central Park or somewhere far from an urban center. From the preservationist perspective, building up in one area reduces the pressure to take down other older buildings. One could quite plausibly argue that if the Landmarks Commission has decided that a building can be razed, then they should demand that its replacement be as tall as possible.

The cost of restricting development is that protected areas become more expensive and more exclusive. On average, people who live in historic districts in Manhattan are almost 74 percent wealthier than people who live outside such areas. Almost three quarters of the adults living in historic districts have college degrees, as opposed to 54 percent outside them. People living in historic districts are 20 percent more likely to be white. The well-heeled denizens of historic districts convincing the Landmarks Preservation Commission to stop taller structures have become the urban equivalent of those restrictive suburbanites who want to mandate five-acre lot sizes in order to keep out the riffraff. It's not that poorer people could ever afford 980 Madison Avenue, but restricting new supply anywhere makes it more difficult for the city to accommodate demand, and that pushes up prices everywhere.

The basic economics of housing prices are pretty simple—supply and demand. New York and Mumbai and London all face increasing demand for their housing, but how that demand affects prices depends on supply. Building enough homes eases the impact of rising demand on prices and makes cities more affordable. That's the lesson of New York in the 1920s, when New York built hundreds of thousands of homes and the city stayed affordable, and of affordable pro-growth cities, like Chicago and Houston, today. In the postwar boom years between 1955 and 1964, Manhattan permitted more than 11,000 units each year. Between 1980 and 1999, when the city's prices were soaring, Manhattan permitted an average of 3,120 units per year. Fewer new homes meant higher prices, and between 1970 and 2000, the median price of a Manhattan housing unit increased by 284 percent in constant dollars.

In New York City, the price of building an additional square foot of living space on the top of a tall building is less than $400. Prices do rise substantially in ultratall buildings, say over fifty stories, but for ordinary skyscrapers, it doesn't cost more than $500,000 to put up a nice, new 1,200-square-foot apartment. The land costs something, but in a forty-story building, a 1,200-square-foot unit is only using 30 square feet of Manhattan, less than a thousandth of an acre. At those heights, the land costs become pretty small. If there were no rules restricting new construction, then prices would eventually come down to somewhere near construction costs, about a half million dollars for a new apartment. That's a lot more than the $200,000 that it costs to put up a nice 2,500-square-foot house in Houston but a lot less than the $1 million or more that such an apartment now costs in New York.

Land is also pretty limited in Chicago's Gold Coast, on the shores of Lake Michigan. Demand may not be the same as in Manhattan, but it's still pretty high. Yet you can buy a beautiful condominium with a lake view for roughly half the cost of a similar unit in Manhattan. The cost of building in Chicago is cheaper than in New York, but not half as cheap. The big difference is that Chicago's leadership has always encouraged new construction more than New York's, at least before the Bloomberg administration. The forest of cranes along Lake Michigan keeps Chicago affordable.

Most people who fight to stop a new development think of themselves as heroes, not villains. After all, putting up a new building on Madison Avenue clearly bugs a lot of famous people, and one building isn't going to make much difference to the city as a whole. The problem is that all those independent decisions to prevent construction add up. Zoning rules, air rights, height restrictions, and landmarks boards together form a web of regulation that has made it more and more difficult to build. The increasing wave of regulations was, until the Bloomberg administration, making New York shorter. In a sample of condominium buildings, I found that more than 80 percent of structures erected in the 1970s had more than twenty stories, while fewer than 40 percent of the buildings erected in the 1990s were that tall. The elevator and the steel-frame skyscraper made it possible to get vast amounts of living space out of tiny amounts of land, but New York's building rules were stopping that process.

The growth in housing supply determines not only prices but the number of people in a city. The statistical relationship between new building and population growth across areas is almost perfect, so that when an area increases its housing stock by 1 percent, its population rises by almost exactly that amount. As a result, when New York or Boston or Paris restricts new construction, those places' populations will be smaller. If the restrictions become strong enough, then places can even lose population, despite rising demand, as wealthier, smaller families replace poorer, larger ones.

Jane Jacobs's insights into the pleasures and strengths of older, lower urban neighborhoods were certainly correct, but she had too little faith in the strengths of higher density levels. I was born a year before Jacobs left New York for Toronto, and I lived in Manhattan for the next seventeen years. My neighborhood looked nothing like low-rise Greenwich Village. I grew up surrounded by white, glazed towers built after World War II to provide affordable housing for middle-income people like my parents. The neighborhood may not have been as charming as Greenwich Village, but it had plenty of reasonably fun restaurants and quirky stores and even quirkier pedestrians. The streets were reasonably safe. It was certainly a functioning, vibrant urban space, albeit one with plenty of skyscrapers. Hong Kong, which has embraced verticality and change, is an even more extreme case, where exciting street life is perfectly compatible with soaring structures.

Not everyone should live in a high-rise. Plenty of urbanites, like Jane Jacobs, prefer older, shorter neighborhoods. However, plenty of others enjoy living in urban aeries, and government shouldn't stop skyscrapers from fulfilling their dreams either. Limiting high-rise development doesn't guarantee interesting, heterogeneous neighborhoods. It just guarantees high prices.

People in an affluent society want and expect comfortable, spacious homes. Today America builds those homes in the suburbs of the Sunbelt, which pulls people out of cities and toward Texas. But spacious, affordable homes can also be built in our older cities. There *can be* an urban future where more people live in central cities, but to do that, the most desirable of those cities must reduce the regulatory barriers that limit the construction of taller buildings.

Rethinking Paris

A century ago, Paris and New York offered completely different visions of urban development. Paris was built from the top down. The emperor had his vision, and his bureaucrat-baron made it so. New York's skyline was made by thousands of relatively unregulated builders putting up whatever the market would bear. New York was a chaotic but splendid jam session in which superb musicians paid only the slightest attention to what was going on around them, but Paris was a carefully composed symphony. New York's chaos was more dynamic, but Parisian order produced safer buildings. In 1900, fires were far more common in American cities than they were in Europe. Today it's hard to argue that new skyscrapers would in any way change the essential glory of New York. But opponents of change in Paris have a better argument.

Paris wasn't always that orderly or that beautiful. Before 1850, hundreds of thousands of poor Parisians crowded into narrow streets and ancient buildings. Paris had had land-use regulations for centuries. When Henry IV established the Bourbon dynasty in 1589, he also established building codes and built the Place des Vosges, which may be Paris's most perfect piazza. But the city's few early attempts at planning were lost in an urban maze. Dense Parisian chaos provided protection both for criminals and for the revolutionaries who toppled three monarchs in sixty years, starting in 1789. Early nineteenth-century Paris might well have appealed to Jane Jacobs, but it didn't seem so ideal to Napoléon III, which is why he turned to Baron Haussmann.

Karl Marx described the reign of Napoléon III as a farcical repetition of the tragedy of his uncle, Napoléon I, but the Second Empire's urban-renewal policies were no laughing matter. The younger Bonaparte's place in the world of city-building is as robust as the first Napoléon's place as a military strategist. There are many explanations for Napoléon III's devotion to reconstructing Paris. He wanted to clear the city of the dense warren of streets that harbored revolutionaries and to create large boulevards for his cavalry to mow down urban rebels. Still, the emperor wasn't just building defensible space. He hoped his public works would bring him both popularity and a place in history.

The emperor was a busy man, with wars to fight and a beautiful empress to impress. He needed an ultracompetent bureaucrat who would be loyal to him and would share his willingness to spend and move to remake his capital. Baron Haussmann was his man. Born in Paris in 1809, a few months before the first Napoléon demolished the Austrians at Wagram, Haussmann came from a family of outsiders, Protestants from Germany, who rose in the rough meritocracy of Napoleonic France. Haussmann's grandfather was a general turned into a baron by the emperor. His father supplied Napoléon's army.

Haussmann was educated in the elite Lycée Henri-IV, which is still one of the world's great schools, and then studied law and music. In 1830, when revolution brought in the bourgeois king, Louis-Philippe, Haussmann entered the Civil Service and was sent to Nérac, a small town outside of Bordeaux. He toiled for years in the provinces, until the return of a Bonaparte brought him opportunity. When the previous prefect of the Seine was relieved of his post for trying to stymie Napoléon III's grandiose urban plans, the ambitious baron leaped at the chance to become his replacement.

If you want to rebuild a city, it helps to have an autocrat behind you, and Haussmann did things that would be unthinkable in a more democratic age. He evicted vast numbers of the poor, turning their homes into the wide boulevards that made Paris monumental. He lopped off a good chunk of the Luxembourg Gardens to create city streets. He tore down ancient landmarks, like the prison of the Abbey of Saint-Germain-des-Prés. He spent 2.5 billion francs on his efforts, which was forty-four times the total budget of Paris in 1851. All that spending and upheaval turned Paris from an ancient and somewhat dilapidated city of immense poverty into an urban resort for the growing haute bourgeoisie.

Some of Haussmann's innovations, like the Bois de Boulogne, were public spaces meant to make Paris both more beautiful and healthier. Other innovations were attempts to retrofit a pedestrian city for newer forms of transportation, like rail and omnibuses. Haussmann also made Paris a bit taller. In 1859, the city's height limit was increased from fifty-four feet to sixty-two feet. Still, relative to later cities built in the elevator-rich twentieth century, Haussmann's Paris stayed short because people needed to climb stairs. In those days, top floors went at a discount because of all those stairs, which is why starving artists dying of consumption in Parisian garrets had great views.

Haussmann built before the elevator, but after the omnibus and steam train. He was trying to accommodate those faster modes of travel by providing bigger, straighter streets. When Haussmann cut his boulevards, he was accommodating those new technologies, foreshadowing the expressways that Jane Jacobs opposed in lower Manhattan. Like later builders, Haussmann had his critics, who sought to discredit his projects by accusing him of corruption and fictitious accounting. There were many legitimate reasons to oppose Haussmannization, but the stolid Alsatian bureaucrat was nothing if not honest. His spending was prodigious but legal.

Gustave Caillebotte's famous 1877 picture of a Haussmann-built Parisian street in the rain, now in the Chicago Art Institute, depicts an excessively monumental, anonymous city where disconnected men lived aimless lives surrounded by sterile grandeur. This picture would have been an apt illustration for Jane Jacobs's description of the breakdown in street life that comes from standardization and overly long city blocks. Other critics disliked the monotonous gray of all those apartment buildings. Some spoke out against the suffering that came from displacing so many Parisian families. The anti-imperialists saw Napoléon III's many monuments as the silly self-aggrandizement of a puffed-up pretender.

Yet if the purpose of architecture is to bring joy to the people who experience it, then Haussmann's remake was a rousing success. Before him, observers would write of the ugliness of Paris. After him, Paris became widely synonymous with urban beauty. Millions of tourists come every year to look at Haussmann's legacy. Millions of Parisians spend a fortune to live in the city that he built. Not only did Haussmann solve technical problems, like how to get clean water and trains into Paris, but he also left behind a city cherished by much of humankind.

Haussmann brought more change to Paris than any other older city in the world had yet experienced, and the result is his unified urban masterpiece. But by the twentieth century, Haussmann's work became an architectural icon not subject to revision. He had gotten an extra floor added with the maximum height regulations in 1859, but in 1902, heights were limited to ninety-eight feet on large thoroughfares and less on narrower streets, a restriction that would remain in effect for over half a century.

The regulations of Paris didn't matter much during the four terrible decades that started with Archduke Franz Ferdinand's assassination in 1914. The population and prosperity of France were grievously damaged by the German invasion the same year, which came so close to conquering Paris. There was little interest in rebuilding the city during the demographically challenged 1920s or the Depression-wracked 1930s. The 1940s brought another war that again left France in poverty. Only in the 1950s did the French economy come back, and with it the desire to modernize the country's long-stagnant capital. In 1967, the Paris City Council lifted the city's height restrictions. Empowered technocrats wanted newer, taller buildings and also wanted to eliminate alleged eyesores like the old central market, Les Halles.

Under de Gaulle and Pompidou, Paris built a little bit. Paris in the 1960s was not like New York in the 1920s, but the city did finally erect a proper skyscraper. Construction of the 689-foot Maine-Montparnasse Tower started in 1969. Two years later, Les Halles was wiped away, and the futuristic Pompidou Centre museum was built in the same year. But this change rankled Parisians who had gotten used to a static city. The Montparnasse Tower was widely loathed, and the lesson drawn was that skyscrapers must never again mar central Paris. Les Halles was sorely missed, in much the same way that many New Yorkers mourned the demise of the old Penn Station. France is a far more regulatory country than America, and when its rulers decide they don't want change, change will not occur. A 1974 regulation imposed a height limit of 83 feet in central Paris, a restriction that remains in effect as of 2010.

While rules stopped height in old Paris, building was allowed on the periphery. Today, the majority of Paris's skyscrapers are in relatively dense but far-flung complexes like La Défense. Today, La Défense is as vertical as central Paris is flat. It has close to 40 million square feet of commercial space and the feel of an American office park. Except for the distant view of the Arc de Triomphe, administrative assistants drinking lattes in a La Défense Starbucks could easily be in a bigger version of Crystal City, Virginia.

La Défense addresses the need to balance preservation and growth by segregating skyscrapers. In some senses, it is an inspired solution. People working there can still get to old Paris in about twenty minutes by Métro or an hour by foot. That Métro ride also means that businesses in La Défense can connect with the all-important French bureaucracy that remains centered in the old city. La Défense is one of Europe's most concentrated commercial centers, and it seems to have all of the economic excitement that we would expect from such a mass of skilled workers. The sector makes it possible for Paris to grow, while keeping the old city pristine.

But building in La Défense is not a perfect substitute for new construction in the more desirable central areas of Paris, where short supply keeps prices astronomical. The natural thing is to have tall buildings in the center, where demand is greatest, not on the edge. The lack of new housing in central Paris means that small apartments sell for a million dollars or more. Hotel rooms often cost more than $500 per night. If you want to be in the center of the city, you'll have to pay for it. People are willing to pay those high prices because Paris is so charming, but they must pay those prices because the city's rulers have decided to limit the amount of housing that can be built in the area. Average people are barred from living in central Paris just as surely as if the city had put up a gate and said that no middle-income people can enter.

In the world's oldest, most beautiful cities, La Défense provides a viable model. Keep the core areas historic, but let millions of square feet be built nearby. As long as building in the high-rise district is sufficiently unfettered, then that area provides a safety valve for the region as a whole. The key issue with La Défense is whether it is too far away. Its distance from the old city keeps central Paris pristine but deprives too many people of the pleasures of strolling to a historic café for lunch.

Unfortunately, there's no easy way to balance the benefits of providing more desirable space with the desire to preserve a beautiful older city. My preferences lead me to wish that some developments like La Défense had been built closer to the center of Paris, perhaps where Pompidou wanted to build, right around the Gare Montparnasse. But I also understand those who think that Paris is so precious that there should be more space between them and Haussmann's boulevards. Still, Paris is an extreme case. In much of the rest of the world, the argument for restricting development is far weaker, and nowhere have limits on development done more harm than in the Indian megacity of Mumbai.

Mismanagement in Mumbai

It's a pity that too few ordinary people can afford to live in central Paris or Manhattan, but France and the United States will survive. The problems caused by arbitrarily restricting height in the developing world are far more serious, because they handicap the metropolises that help turn desperately poor nations into middle-income countries. The rules that keep India's cities too short and too expensive mean that too few Indians can connect with each other and with the outside world. Because poverty often means death in the developing world, and because restricting city growth ensures more poverty, it is not hyperbole to say that land-use planning in India can be a matter of life and death.

Mumbai is a city of astonishing human energy and entrepreneurship, from the high reaches of finance and film to the jam-packed spaces of the Dharavi slum. If all this private talent got the government it deserved, it would get a public sector that performed well the core tasks of city government, like providing sewers and safe water, without overreaching and overregulating. One curse of the developing world is that governments take on too much and fail at their core responsibilities. Countries that cannot provide clean water for their citizens should not be in the business of regulating currency exchanges.

The public failures in Mumbai are as obvious as the private successes. Western tourists can avoid the open defecation in Mumbai's slums, but they can't avoid the city's failed transportation network. It can easily take you ninety minutes to drive the fourteen miles from the airport to the city's old downtown, with its landmark Gateway to India arch. There is a train that could speed up your trip, but few Westerners have the courage to brave its crowds during rush hour. In 2008, more than three people each day were pushed out of that train to their death. Average commute times in Mumbai are about fifty minutes each way, which is about double the average American commute.

The city has tried to build its way out of traffic congestion. Its elevated highways make things a little better, but I've already mentioned the research that shows that the total number of miles traveled increases essentially one-for-one with highway miles built. Mumbai has so many potential drivers that new roads alone can never eliminate congestion. The most cost-effective means of opening up overcrowded city streets would be to follow Singapore and charge more for their use.

If you give something away for free, people will use too much of it. Mumbai's roads are just too valuable to be clogged by oxcarts at rush hour, and the easiest way to get flexible drivers off the road is to charge them for their use of public space. Congestion charges aren't just for rich cities; they are appropriate anywhere roads come to a standstill. After all, Singapore was not wealthy in 1975 when it started charging drivers for using downtown streets. Like Singapore then, Mumbai could just require people to buy paper day-licenses to drive downtown and require them to show those licenses in their windows. Politics, however, not technology, would make this strategy difficult. Despite the fact that the poor would benefit enormously from more open streets, I suspect the city would lack the political will to fine drivers who violate the rules.

Mumbai's traffic problems reflect not just poor transportation policy, but a deeper and more fundamental failure of urban planning. In 1991, Mumbai fixed a maximum floor area ratio of 1.33 in most of the city. In those years, India was enthusiastic about all sorts of regulation, and limiting building heights seemed to offer a way to limit urban growth that was in keeping with fashionable ideas of English urban planning.

But Mumbai's height restrictions meant that, in one of the most densely populated places on earth, buildings could have an average height of only one-and-a-third stories. People still came; Mumbai's economic energy drew them even when living conditions were awful. Limiting heights didn't stop urban growth; it just ensured that migrants had to squeeze into less space. Keeping Mumbai flat also ensures longer commutes, and that makes the congestion that comes with crowding more severe.

Singapore is another former outpost of the British East India Company, but unlike Mumbai, its government is among the most competent in the world. While Singapore does amazing things to provide clean water, it doesn't stop tall buildings, and as a result, Singapore's downtown functions well, because it's tall and connected. Businesspeople work close to one another and can easily trot to a meeting. Hong Kong is even more vertical and even friendlier to pedestrians, who can walk in air-conditioned comfort from skyscraper to skyscraper. It takes only a few minutes to get around Wall Street or Manhattan's Midtown area. Even vast Tokyo can be traversed largely on foot. These great cities function because their height enables a vast number of people to work, and sometimes live, on a tiny sliver of land. But Mumbai is short, so everyone sits in traffic and pays dearly for space.

A city of 12 million people occupying a tiny land mass could be housed by corridors of skyscrapers. An abundance of close and connected vertical real estate would decrease the pressure on roads, ease the connections that are the lifeblood of a twenty-first-century city, and reduce Mumbai's extraordinarily high cost of space. Yet instead of encouraging compact development, Mumbai is pushing people out. According to Emporis.com, three of the six buildings in Mumbai that rise above 490 feet are being built this year, and more are on the way, because some of the height restrictions have been slightly eased, especially outside of the traditional downtown.

Mumbai's floor-area-ratio requirements have eased recently, but the change has been modest. Their continuing power explains why many of the new skyscrapers are surrounded by swaths of green space. That space places tall buildings in splendid isolation, so that cars, rather than feet, are still needed to get around. If Mumbai was trying to promote affordability and ease congestion, it should make developers use their land to the fullest, requiring any new downtown development to have at least forty stories. By requiring developers to create more, not less, floor space, the government would encourage more housing, less sprawl, and lower prices.

As long as Mumbai remains an extraordinarily productive place to live and work, new residents will flock there. Height restrictions just force people to crowd into squalid, illegal slums rather than legal apartment buildings. One study estimates that Mumbai's homes have only about 30 square feet per person, as opposed to 140 square feet per person in urban China. People are forced into so little space in Mumbai because real estate is more expensive there than in far richer places, like Singapore. Singapore is cheaper than Mumbai not because demand for that prosperous place is low, but because Singapore allows builders to put more floor space on the same amount of land.

Historically, Mumbai's residents couldn't afford such height, but many can today, and they would live in taller buildings if those buildings were abundant and affordable. Canyons of glass and steel and concrete, such as those along New York's Fifth Avenue, aren't an urban problem; they are a perfectly reasonable way to fit a large amount of people and commerce on a small amount of land. Only poor policy prevents a long row of fifty-story buildings from lining Mumbai's seafront, much as high-rises adorn Chicago's lakefront.

The magic of cities comes from their people, but those people must be well served by the bricks and mortar that surround them. Cities need roads and buildings that enable people to live well and to connect easily with one another. Tall towers, like Henry Ford II's Renaissance Center in Detroit, make little sense in places with abundant space and slack demand. But in the most desirable cities, whether they're on the Hudson River or the Indian Ocean, height is the best way to keep prices affordable and living standards high.

Three Simple Rules

The success of our cities, the world's economic engines, increasingly depends on abstruse decisions made by zoning boards and preservation committees. It certainly makes sense to control construction in dense urban spaces, but I would replace the maze of regulations now limiting building with three simple rules.

First, cities should replace the current lengthy and uncertain permitting process with a simple system of fees. If tall heights create costs by blocking light or views, then form a reasonable estimate of those costs and charge the builder appropriately. If certain activities are noxious to neighbors, then we should estimate the social costs and charge builders for them, just as we should charge drivers for the costs of their congestion. Those taxes could then be given to the people who are suffering, such as the neighbors who lose light from a new construction project.

I don't mean to suggest that such a system would be easy to design. There is plenty of room for debate about the costs associated with buildings of different heights. People would certainly disagree about the size of the neighboring areas that would receive compensation. But reasonable rules could be developed that would then be universally applied. For example, the developer of every new building in New York would pay some number of dollars per square foot in compensation costs in exchange for a speedy permit. Some share of the money could go to the city treasury and the rest would go to people within a block of the new edifice.

A simple tax system would be far more transparent and targeted than the current regulatory maze. Today, many builders negotiate our current system by hiring expensive lawyers and lobbyists and purchasing political influence. It would be far better for them to just write a check to the rest of us. Allowing more building doesn't have to be a windfall for developers; sensible, straightforward regulations can make new development good for the neighborhood and the city as a whole.

Second, historic preservation should be limited and well defined. Landmarking a masterpiece like the Flatiron Building or the old Penn Station is sensible. Preserving vast numbers of postwar glazed-brick buildings is absurd. But where do you draw the line between those two extremes?

My own preference is that in a city like New York, the landmarks commission should have a fixed number of buildings, perhaps five thousand, that it may protect. The commission can change its chosen architectural gems, but it needs to do that slowly. It shouldn't be able to change its rules overnight to stop construction in some previously unprotected area. If the commission wants to preserve a whole district, then let it spread its five-thousand-building mandate across the area. Perhaps five thousand buildings are too few, but without some sort of limit, the scope of any regulatory agency will try to constantly increase, either because of bureaucratic empire building or in response to community pressure.

The problem gets thornier when practically an entire city, like Paris, is beloved worldwide. In such cases, the key is to find some sizable body of land, reasonably close to the city center, that can be used for ultradense development. Ideally, this space would be near enough to allow its residents to enjoy walking to the beautiful streets of the older city.

Finally, individual neighborhoods should have some clearly delineated power to protect their special character. People in some blocks might really want to exclude bars; people in others might want to encourage them. Rather than regulate neighborhoods entirely from the top down, it would make more sense to allow individual neighborhoods to craft their own, limited set of rules about building styles and uses that are adopted only with the approval of a very large share of residents. But communities should not have the power to completely prevent construction, by restricting heights or imposing excessive regulations, lest local communities become NIMBYist enclaves. Ordinary citizens, rather than the planners in City Hall, should have more say over what happens next to them, but community control must unfortunately be limited, because local communities often fail to consider the adverse citywide consequences of banning building.

Great cities are not static—they constantly change and take the world along with them. When New York and Chicago and Paris experienced great spurts of creativity and growth, the cities reshaped themselves to provide new structures that could house new talent and new ideas. Cities can't force change with new buildings; the experience of the Rust Belt refutes that view. But if change is happening, the right kind of new building can help that process.

Yet many of the world's cities, both old and new, have arrayed rules that prevent new construction at higher densities. Sometimes these rules have a good justification, such as preserving truly important works of architecture. However, sometimes these rules are mindless NIMBYism or a misguided attempt at stopping urban growth. In all cases, construction restrictions tie cities to their past and limit the possibilities for their future. If cities can't build up, then they will build out. If building in a city is frozen, then growth will happen somewhere else.

The failure of places like New York and San Francisco to build up has pushed Americans elsewhere, to places that embrace new construction. In such areas, like Houston and Phoenix, development is unfettered, and as a result, prices stay low. The lure—and consequences—of affordable sprawl is the topic of the next chapter.

CHAPTER 7

Why Has Sprawl Spread?

T he streets of downtown Houston feel eerily reminiscent of downtown Detroit. Neither city has the pedestrian life of New York, London, Boston, or San Francisco. You wouldn't know from strolling the streets that while Detroit practically defines decline, Houston remains a great boomtown. The Houston metropolitan area had a million more inhabitants in 2009 than it did in 2000, making it the third-fastest-growing metropolitan area in the country, after Atlanta and Dallas.

To see Houston's masses of people, you have to leave the downtown and go elsewhere, like the Galleria shopping mall on the city's western edge. Twenty-four million people visit this 2.4-million-square-foot complex each year, making it the city's most popular attraction. On any given Saturday, the mall is mobbed with shoppers, tourists, and people just enjoying its public spaces. Even in sprawling Houston, the desire to experience density doesn't disappear. The Galleria has citylike features—plenty of pedestrians, offices, apartments, an ice-skating rink. The mall was, after all, modeled on hallowed urban space: Milan's Galleria Vittorio Emanuele, diagonally across the main square from the Duomo, the Milan Cathedral. But unlike its Milanese predecessor, the Houston Galleria is comprehensively air-conditioned, walled off from the outside world, and surrounded by vast garages.

Almost all of Houston is built to accommodate heat and cars. Arguably, the defining characteristic of American cities built in the late twentieth century is their accommodation of the automobile. Just as the winding streets of Bruges or Boston were designed around pedestrian pathways, and New York's grid supported the omnibus, today's newer cities reflect the dominant form of transportation of our age: the car. Car-loathers may detest Houston, but millions of Americans who enjoy driving, warmth, and big, cheap homes find the place pretty attractive.

Many of our most "progressive" states and cities, supposedly the great champions of those with modest means, have become the least hospitable places for middle-income Americans. In the Northeast, large minimum lot sizes mean that the average single-family home in 2008 sat on more than an acre, more than twice the national average. By contrast, the deep red state of Texas is far more affordable, not because the state is pro-poor, but because it isn't anticonstruction. Sunbelt sprawl would attract millions even without benighted local housing policies, but it doesn't help that older cities are foolishly turning people away.

I lived in older urban areas—Manhattan, Chicago, Washington, D.C.—for thirty-two of my first thirty-seven years on this planet. My only nonurban experiences were in college towns, like Princeton and Palo Alto. I had walked to work almost every day of my life. But then I was blessed with three usually delightful children, and I did what millions of other Americans have done facing an expanding household. I moved to a suburb and started driving.

There is nothing unusual in a middle-aged man leaving the city. As we've seen, cities disproportionately attract the young. Almost one fifth of Manhattan's residents are between the ages of twenty-five and thirty-four, while only 13 percent of the nation is in that age category. Still, given my love of cities, my decision to suburbanize deserves a bit more explanation. What terrible bout of insanity induced me to choose deer ticks as neighbors instead of people?

I remain unsure about whether my suburbanization was a mistake, but there were logical reasons for the move: more living space, spongy lawns for toddlers to fall on, my desire for a less Harvard-dominated neighborhood, a reasonably fast commute, and a good school system. Leaving the city meant an end to excellent accessible restaurants, but with three small children, I wouldn't be eating out often no matter where I lived. Thanks to the Massachusetts Turnpike, it doesn't take me much longer to get to the things in Boston that I value most: cannoli in the North End, Flemish painting in the Museum of Fine Arts, and Logan Airport.

This chapter is about precisely that type of calculus—the appeals of car-based living in lower-density places, which have attracted so many people, including myself. Older cities must compete against car-oriented areas, and it always makes sense to know your enemy. Ranting about the philistinism of people who choose car-based living in Houston may be emotionally satisfying to some, but it does nothing to help older cities attract more people. For millions, the appeal of suburban, Sunbelt places is real, but better policies, both at the national and local level, could enable older cities to compete more effectively.

Whether you or I love or loathe the exurbs should be irrelevant for public policy. The government should not be in the business of enforcing lifestyles that we happen to find appealing. The government's job is to allow people to choose the life they want, as long as they are paying for the costs of that lifestyle. Yet today, public policies strongly encourage people, including me, to sprawl.

I doubt that I would be in the suburbs if it weren't for the antiurban public policy trifecta of the Massachusetts Turnpike, the home mortgage interest deduction, and the problems of urban schools. Eliminating pro-sprawl policies won't bring back every declining city, and it won't kill the suburbs, but it will create a healthier urban system whereby walking cities can compete more effectively against the car. The stakes are even higher in the developing world, where cities are more fluid and where a wholesale move to American-style sprawl would mean a massive rise in driving and energy use.

Sprawl Before Cars

Transportation technologies shape our communities, and modern sprawl is the child of the automobile. The connections that define cities have always entailed some form of transportation. Sprawl isn't the opposite of urban density; rural isolation has that distinction. The people who live in sprawling exurbs have access to neighbors, stores, employers, and restaurants. They just have to drive. Sprawl began many centuries ago, when people started using something other than their own feet to travel, and since then boats, horses, omnibuses, elevators, subways, and cars have all influenced how cities were laid out and how they grew. Many older neighborhoods, like New York's Washington Square and Barcelona's Eixample, which are now beloved by urbanists, were the sprawl of earlier eras.

Each successful new type of transportation generally goes through three phases. First, technological breakthroughs enable the large-scale production of a faster way to move, such as a steam-powered train or a car. Second, a new transportation network is built, if needed, to accommodate this new technology. Third, people and companies change their geographic locations to take advantage of this new mode of transport.

The first transport revolution was the domestication of pack animals ten millennia ago, which seems to have started in the Middle East. Pack animals didn't require a new road network, for horses, donkeys, mules, and llamas can go pretty much anywhere a human can. But the pack animals did change human geography. The urban historian Paul Bairoch argued that before them, moving food was so hard that people *had* to live near food sources. Pack animals made cities possible, by making it easier to transport enough food to feed concentrated urban masses.

Wheels seem to have originated in Mesopotamia around eight thousand years ago, but the oldest existing wheel is five thousand years old and Russian. Egyptians and Indians had the wheel by at least 2000 B.C. As anyone who has ever been on a dune buggy knows, wheels don't need paved roads. Still, roads really speed up wheeled transport, especially in places without flat, dry ground. The Incas never developed the wheel, quite possibly because pack animals functioned better in the mountainous terrain of the Inca Empire.

Building and maintaining roads requires strong and wealthy civilizations. Good transportation brought far more honor and wealth to Rome than the bloody pageantry of the Colosseum. The empire's large cities were sustained by the wheeled transport that distributed vast amounts of grain brought by ship from Spain and Egypt to feed the nonfarming urbanites. Inside cities, Roman grids accommodated wheeled carts. After Rome fell, the ability to maintain roads disappeared, and without roads, wheels lost their value. The pack animal came back. Paving returned with centralized political power in the High Middle Ages, when leaders like Philip Augustus, the great consolidator of France who pushed the English out of Normandy in the thirteenth century, started paving Paris for the first time since the Roman era.

Much ink has been spilled about medieval innovations in horse travel, such as the stirrup and the saddle, which increased the importance of earlier equine innovations, like the breeding and training that enabled humans to ride horses at least five millennia ago. But throughout most of history in the densely populated, non-nomadic parts of the world, horses have been an elite transport technology. Maintaining a large life form for personal transport was far beyond the means of most ordinary farmers or townsmen. Horses only began transporting large numbers of people when their costs could be shared, through mass transit.

In philosophical circles, Blaise Pascal is known for his reflections on Christianity, while mathematicians know him for his contributions to geometry and probability theory. Pascal's famous wager, which suggests that if there is any chance that God exists, then it makes sense to be good, is still the stuff of undergraduate bull sessions. Among urbanists, however, his glory comes from being a father of the bus. In 1662, Pascal organized the first public bus line, charging five sous for the privilege of being carried by horse across Paris.

Pascal's public buses were, appropriately enough, a gamble that required sufficient scale to be a good bet. Running a bus route along a fixed line only makes sense if there are enough customers. Seventeenth-century Paris had the paving and the population to make a bus line possible but not actually successful. The real era of bus transit began in the 1820s, when city populations had expanded dramatically, and horse-drawn buses started appearing in Paris, New York, and London.

The first public transit in New York City was a twelve-person omnibus that ran along Broadway in 1827. The poor quality of New York City's roads slowed the bus down, so its owner laid down rails. Over time, a rail network was built to carry those horse-drawn omnibuses. It was paid for by private operators, but it was also subsidized, as the city gave them right-of-way on previously open city streets.

A half-hour commute on foot can bring an average walker only about 1.5 miles; the omnibus easily doubled that range, which enabled the growth of uptown neighborhoods that catered to the well-off. An omnibus ride may have cost only five to seven cents, but ordinary laborers earned only a dollar a day, so they kept walking. Like the car, buses started off as transportation for the prosperous. By selectively speeding the rich, buses began the exodus of the wealthy from the urban core. When everyone walked in New York, the rich lived in Bowling Green, a central location with easy access to the wharves. After the omnibus, the prosperous were able to commute in from less dense quarters uptown, and the suburban pattern started.

There is a clear demarcation between the older areas of New York and Boston, with their chaotic, unplanned streets built during the pedestrian era, and the much more orderly city built around wheeled transport. The fifty-foot minimum street widths and straight lines of New York's 1811 grid were designed to accommodate masses of horse-drawn vehicles, even those, like the omnibus, that hadn't yet shown up in New York.

Before the bus, the land that is now the southern end of Fifth Avenue had been one of the poorest parts of the city, an early African-American district and cemetery. In 1826, the city bought a big plot of land in the area, Washington Square, and turned it into a marching ground. With the omnibus, this once almost rural outpost became a quite plausible home base for well-to-do merchants to commute from. Wealthier New Yorkers built stout row houses that still stand, enjoying their views over the city's green acres. Washington Square, now an archetypal urban space, was then a proto-suburb, a place that grew because a faster form of transportation enabled the rich to travel farther and buy bigger homes with more land. In the 1950s, when Jane Jacobs fought against running a road through Washington Square Park, she was fighting to save nineteenth-century sprawl from twentieth-century sprawl.

The next step after the omnibus was to power carriages with something other than equine muscle. Matthew Boulton understood that the steam engine could move wheels, and Richard Trevithick built the first functioning train in 1804. As steam engines became more reliable and coaches more comfortable, entrepreneurs started laying down rail networks. Intra-urban systems were built on existing roads, in tunnels, and on elevated rails. Building at street level was cheap but used valuable city real estate and created lots of noise and smoke. London, the world's largest city, with the greatest demand for faster transport, pioneered the underground rail system in 1863. More than twenty-five thousand people started using it almost immediately.

Running steam engines in tunnels may be better for pedestrians, but it isn't great for the riders sitting in smoky cars. New York City, which also had plenty of demand for its streets, went for elevation rather than tunnels. The city's subways didn't appear until 1904, more than thirty years after steam trains traveled above Manhattan. Tens of millions of dollars were invested in elevated rail networks, which were run by some of the most infamous figures of the Gilded Age, like Jay Gould and Charles Yerkes.

Those rail networks enabled New York City to sprawl farther. The northern stops on the Manhattan elevated train lines initially attracted tourists eager to see the island's relatively uninhabited upper reaches. The elevated railroad made it possible to live in neighborhoods like Harlem and commute at the rapid rate of 12 miles per hour to jobs downtown. My grandfather grew up in one of those northern Manhattan neighborhoods made accessible by the El. From one perspective, the steam train–enabled growth of the nineteenth-century city looks like a great burst of urban expansion.

But those steam trains were also creating early suburbs. If Washington Square is the sprawl of the omnibus era, then the Philadelphia Main Line provides the quintessential examples of suburbs built on steam. In the 1860s, the Pennsylvania Railroad acquired 283 acres in Lower Merion Township, on which it created the town of Bryn Mawr. At first, the new homes were weekend houses, but as trains got faster, a new form of suburban living came into being. Just as Washington Square housed the elite New Yorkers described by Henry James and Edith Wharton, the Main Line provided homes for the wealthy Philadelphians played by Cary Grant and Katharine Hepburn in *The Philadelphia Story.*

Werner von Siemens took the next step by powering an urban train with electricity in Berlin in 1881. No horses. No steam. Just gliding trains powered either with an overhead cable or with a third rail underneath. Electricity proved a perfect fit for mass transportation in densely populated cities, but electric streetcars and trains required two networks, one to ride on and one to provide power. Frank Sprague was, like Henry Ford, a brilliant mind collected by Thomas Edison. Also like Ford, Sprague left Edison and transformed city life with his transportation innovations. He invented the trolley pole, which brought electricity to cars throughout the city via a network of overhead wires. By the late 1890s, urban landscapes were full of trolleys. Siemens and Sprague helped cities move up as well as out. Siemens invented the electric elevator; Sprague co-invented the Sprague-Pratt elevator, which ran more swiftly and safely. Even though trains and streetcars lowered the price of traveling into the city center from far away, the late nineteenth century saw cities stretch up as well as out.

Electric streetcars, like the earlier omnibuses, shifted population within cities worldwide. The Passeig de Gràcia, in Barcelona, is one of the most architecturally important streets in the world, with masterpieces by Antonio Gaudí, Josep Puig, and the other greats of Catalan architecture. The Passeig, a broad, beautiful thoroughfare, runs outward from the Plaça de Catalunya, on the edge of the old city, through the Eixample, a nineteenth-century district made possible by streetcars. The Eixample was outside the old city's walls, but when those walls were torn down in the 1850s, the city held a competition to create a plan for a new district. The competition was won by Ildefons Cerdà, a civil engineer, who planned the area's octagonal blocks. While New York City's grid is detested by many urban planners for its plodding uniformity, Cerdà's plan is celebrated for its quirky creativity. He designed it to accommodate transportation innovations: Those octagons were meant to enable the turning of large, steam-powered vehicles.

The Eixample was first reached with horse-drawn carriages, but in 1900, the streetcars that ran down the Passeig de Gràcia were electrified. The new transportation made the area a magnet for prosperous Catalans who paid the city's best architects to design their homes. The Casa Milà, an undulating masterpiece by Gaudí, was built for a developer who was known for dressing and marrying well. Another architectural icon, the Casa Amatller, was built for a chocolate magnate.

While the nineteenth century saw several transit innovations, the twentieth-century city was dominated by one: the internal combustion engine. Germans Nikolaus Otto, Gottfried Daimler, and Wilhelm Maybach, connected by the city of Cologne, produced the four-stroke internal combustion engine and used it to power the world's first gas-powered motorcycle in 1885. In Mannheim, 120 miles away, Karl Benz developed his own gas-powered two-stroke engine, and in 1886 he patented his Motorwagen. While Germans were responsible for the key innovations in producing the automobile, Americans, especially Henry Ford, deserve the credit for mass-producing cars. By the end of the 1920s, Americans had 23 million cars on the road. Cars, unlike trains, functioned reasonably well on the existing roads, which were already being converted to asphalt in the nineteenth century. Henry Ford's Model T's were sturdy vehicles, simple enough to be repaired by ordinary people, and they traveled easily at modest speeds even on dirt.

But drivers soon realized that cars could run much more quickly on limited-access highways with smooth asphalt paving. America began building a highway network to accommodate the new form of transportation. New York State opened the first part of its parkway system in 1908. That system was meant to give drivers easy access to the city at the soaring speed of 25 miles per hour. By the 1920s, the federal government started organizing and funding a system of paved roads throughout the nation. The Federal Highway Act of 1921 provided $75 million of matching funds ($765 million in 2007 dollars) for state highway projects, such as the parkways built on Long Island by Robert Moses, New York's master builder (and Jane Jacobs's bête noire), who was also one of the world's great experts on and advocates of limited-access highways. During the Great Depression, the New Deal put people to work paving highways, such as Route 66, immortalized in song by Bobby Troup and Nat King Cole, and in prose by John Steinbeck. The Okies in *The Grapes of Wrath* traveled to California along the "Mother Road."

President Eisenhower dramatically deepened the federal government's commitment to highways—a commitment that lives on to this day. Mobility is often crucial to military success, which may explain why generals are often keen on improving transportation. General Washington was passionate about canals, and General Eisenhower loved highways. With some cause, the Eisenhower Interstate Highway system has been called the largest public works project in history. Today, the system includes forty-six thousand miles of roads, built and maintained with tens of billions of dollars of federal and state spending. The vast scale of federal support for the highway system has led some to see a devilish conspiracy of automakers who used public funding to destroy the streetcar. Certainly automobile manufacturers, like most other firms, wanted to defeat their competitors, who happened to run buses and streetcars. But if there was a conspiracy, then it operated in full view and with abundant popular support. Americans loved their cars and were happy to spend billions creating a fast network of highways.

If Henry Ford's assembly lines were the first phase of the car era, and the highway system was phase two, then mass suburbanization and the rise of car-oriented cities has been phase three—the population's response to the new transport technology. Income and population growth have been significantly higher in those metropolitan areas that were included in the highway system. Suburbs grew more quickly in areas with more roads, and cities emptied. Nathaniel Baum-Snow, a Brown University economist, has calculated that each "new highway passing through a central city reduces its population by about 18 percent." One potential problem with such calculations is that more highways may have been built in areas that expected more suburbanization, but Baum-Snow handles this problem by focusing on the highways that were planned in 1947 for military purposes. Like omnibuses and streetcars, the automobile reshaped urban America.

America had begun to reorganize its cities in response to the car in the 1920s, but in those years, car-based living in the suburbs was still expensive for ordinary Americans. Even Fitzgerald's Nick Carraway, a poor man relative to Jay Gatsby but much richer than most, took the train in from Long Island, at least when he wasn't being driven by beautiful, feckless golfers. The process of mass suburbanization was stalled by the Great Depression and World War II, but it began in earnest when veterans started coming back from the war.

William Levitt and Mass-Produced Housing

One of those veterans was a lieutenant in the Seabees named William Levitt. Levitt, the son of a British-born lawyer, was born in New York in 1907. He dropped out of New York University to get into construction with his brother Alfred, who became the designer while Bill took care of the business side of the operation. Together they built two thousand homes in the 1930s, mostly for rich clients on Long Island. Levitt began experimenting with large-scale housing for middle-income Americans, but his early efforts produced decidedly mixed results. His sixteen-hundred-shack project in Norfolk, Virginia, built before World War II, still had unsold units in 1950.

After the war, Levitt was determined to become the Henry Ford of the building business, creating an inexpensive product on a vast scale. Together with his father and brother, he assembled almost twenty square miles of land near Hempstead, Long Island. Potato farmers got rich as Levitt pushed prices from $300 to $3,000 an acre. Levitt wasn't going to bottom-fish, as he had in Norfolk. He was building a high-quality product, at least for its time. The homes had modern appliances and sturdy construction. He master-planned the community. It had, and has, parks and schools and plenty of green space.

Although the result—Levittown—drove highbrow critics like the *New Yorker*'s Lewis Mumford to fits of literary condescension, the town's low prices and relative opulence made it wildly popular with ordinary folks. The critics may have been right in decrying the endless monotony of similarly styled ranch and colonial buildings, but tenements were hardly architectural masterpieces either. More important, as the sociologist Herbert Gans wrote in his description of Levittown life, critics write from a "tourist perspective" that prizes "visual interest, cultural diversity, entertainment, esthetic pleasure, variety (preferably exotic), and emotional stimulation." A typical resident who bought in Levittown wanted "a comfortable, convenient, and socially satisfying place to live—esthetically pleasing, to be sure, but first and foremost functional for his daily needs." Architectural experts do tend to value stylistic sophistication much more than most home buyers. Appreciating art is, after all, the experts' job. But home buyers, unless they are very rich, tend to put more weight on floor space, lot size, modern conveniences, good schools, and access to jobs.

Like Ford, Levitt fought ferociously to cut costs. He shut the unions out, which brought on the picket lines. One possibly apocryphal story told of a picketer who liked Levitt's houses so much that he bought one. Avoiding unions made it possible for Levitt to use the latest building technologies, like spray painting, which violated make-work rules. He bypassed middlemen and bought everything from lumber to televisions directly from the manufacturers. He set up his own nail-making plant. Home production was broken down into twenty-six separate steps and farmed out to scores of subcontractors. To this day, mass production remains a key reason why new homes in growing suburban areas are much less expensive than bespoke houses built in older places. By building thousands and thousands of homes quickly in one area, Levitt was able to sell a comfortable modern house for less than $8,000 in 1950, less than $65,000 in 2009 currency.

Levitt's average home buyer earned about half that amount per year. Few of them would have had eight grand to put down for a new Levitt house, but the federal government was splurging on housing subsidies. The GI Bill offered no-down-payment housing loans for veterans, and the Federal Housing Administration (FHA) guaranteed up to 95 percent of mortgages for middle-income buyers. With a government-guaranteed loan, Levitt's buyers only needed to come up with $400 to buy a home packed with modern appliances and surrounded by leafy space. Levitt's eight-hundred-square-foot ranch houses now seem tiny and quaint, but to New Yorkers who had grown up in crowded tenements, they were the McMansions of their day.

Neither federal housing policies nor interstate highway spending were designed to be antiurban, but they certainly hurt cities. The highway program was meant to connect the country, but subsidizing highways ended up encouraging people to commute by car. Encouraging home buying through the home mortgage interest deduction and government-guaranteed mortgages was meant to correct alleged imperfections in the mortgage market and create property-owning citizens with a stake in their country. The biggest public home-ownership subsidy of all ended up being the tax deductibility of mortgage interest, which began not as a housing policy but as a by-product of the general deductibility of interest expenses—an almost accidental part of the income tax code that has ended up having a huge impact on the way we live. Subsidizing the purchase of big houses ended up encouraging people to leave the cities. FHA loans went disproportionately to middle-class enclaves in the suburbs, perhaps because those areas seemed like good bets to FHA administrators or perhaps because this was where new homes were being built. The government wanted to reward veterans with bigger homes, but those bigger homes tended to be suburban. Owner-occupied houses are overwhelmingly single-family houses, and they tend to be in suburbs. When public policy promotes home ownership, it also pushes people to leave cities.

When Levittown was built, in the 1940s, access to public transportation was still important to residents. The town had a train station, and many Levittowners rode the rails to their Manhattan jobs. But American suburbs were coming to depend on the car far more than older, higher-density areas like Barcelona's Eixample. In Levittown, residents still needed a car to get to the train station or to run errands around town. Moreover, plenty of early residents carpooled to get to work, still a common practice, albeit one now used largely by the less wealthy. Still, Levittown was a hybrid: a town that required a car for local driving but that still connected with trains for longer-distance travel.

Rebuilding America Around the Car

As master-planned suburban communities followed the path of William Levitt, they increasingly dropped the connection with public transit altogether. In the growing areas of Sunbelt sprawl, businesses are dispersed throughout the area rather than centralized in a single downtown. Almost half of the jobs in America's ninety-eight largest metropolitan areas are more than ten miles away from the city center. People do their shopping in malls built around the car, rather than in conventional downtowns. Cheap trucks and highways freed firms from ports, railway depots, and the Great Lakes system.

Car-based suburbs are the latest installment in the move to sprawl that started in Washington Square and Eixample, but car-based communities feel very different from every older area. All of the previous transport innovations still required some walking. You had to get by foot from the bus stop or train station to your job or home. The presence of foot traffic kept the older communities fairly dense. But the car changed all that. By eliminating the need for walking, the car supported a quantum leap in the size of land areas that people could occupy. As a result, the inverse connection between density and car usage is extremely strong—across a broad range of cities, as density doubles, the share of the population that takes a car to work typically drops by 6.6 percent.

Cars also need much more space than omnibuses or elevated rail lines or walking. Nine square feet of road space is plenty for a pedestrian walking down Fifth Avenue, and on a busy day, walkers will put up with much less. The Honda Accord, a modest-size car, takes up about a hundred square feet on its own. If that car is going to have a couple of feet around it and several car lengths ahead of it, its space needs can easily increase to three or four hundred square feet on a highway. The fortyfold increase in space that accompanies the shift from walking to cars explains why so much of the land in car-based cities is given over to highways.

And cars don't use up space only when they're hurtling down the asphalt.

They also require space when they're standing still. A typical parking space can often be more than 120 square feet—about the size of a standard work cubicle. Bringing a car to work essentially doubles the amount of space that someone needs on the job. In older, dense cities, that space requires structured parking, which can cost more than $50,000 per space to build.

The mismatch between the car and the world's dense older cities explains why cars have led to the construction of vast new low-density living spaces, sometimes on the edge of older cities and sometimes out on their own in the middle of the Sunbelt. Even the shifts in the late nineteenth century, when skyscrapers rose higher and streetcar suburbs were built, seem small relative to the massive creation of spaces built around the automobile.

Some have suggested that American sprawl represents an English cultural heritage that puts an outsize value on single-family detached houses and back-yards, but there are obvious reasons why Europeans have remained more urban than Americans. Many European cities are old and enjoy the architectural legacy of centuries of genius. Living in central Paris is fundamentally different from living in most American central cities. European governments slowed the advance of the automobile by taxing gas more heavily and spending less on highways. The average gas tax in France over the past thirty years has been about eight times higher than average gas taxes in the United States. In the mid-1990s, when the average price for a gallon of gas in the U.S. was close to $1, the average price per gallon in Italy or France was close to $5.

Comparing seventy cities worldwide, Matthew Kahn and I found that when countries move from having low gas taxes to high gas taxes, the density of development increases by more than 40 percent. Vehicle ownership, unsurprisingly, falls as well. Despite higher gas taxes, as Europeans have gotten wealthier, they've started driving more like Americans. Today, 84 percent of passenger transport, by mile, in France is done by car. In Italy there are about 6 cars for every 10 people; the comparable numbers for France and Germany are 5 and 5.66. The United States still has more cars—there are 7.76 cars for every 10 Americans—but the gap is narrowing considerably.

As European car ownership has increased, Europeans have also moved to the suburbs. Cars, not culture, are the root of sprawl. A report from the European Environment Agency notes that since the 1950s, more than 90 percent of the new construction in cities like Vienna, Marseilles, Brussels, and Copenha-

Cities are so monumental that we easily forget how fast they can fall—and rise. In the 1970s, New York verged on bankruptcy; President Ford refused to bail it out (left), and President Carter toured the grim ruins of the South Bronx (above). Three decades before these iconic images, Gotham had been an urban paragon, and three decades after them, it is again.

[Art 1:] *New York Daily News* Archive / Getty Images
[Art 2:] *Teresa Zabala* / The New York Times / *Redux Pictures*

The MindTree campus in Bangalore is a pristine and elegant flat-world phenomenon that thrives by connecting smart people from India and around the world. *MindTree Ltd.*

A market in Bangalore is neither pristine nor elegant, but it is an exciting explosion of human energy.

Copyright Ruban Phukan

East meets West during Europe's largely rural Dark Ages and the urban heyday of Islam. Here emissaries from Hārūn al-Rashīd, leader of the Arab world, present a sophisticated water clock to Charlemagne, whose empire had no such technology.

The Homage of Caliph Hārūn al-Rashīd to Charlemagne by J. Jordaens (1593–1678) & A. Utrecht (1599–1652) / Phillips, The International Fine Art Auctioneers, UK / Photo © Bonhams, London, UK / Bridgeman Art Library

Japanese contact with the Dutch through the city of Nagasaki gave them a considerable edge over their Asian neighbors. The Japanese navy used this ship, given by the Dutch in the nineteenth century, to develop skills that would allow it to hold its own against European naval powers.

Collection Maritime Museum Rotterdam

Detroit's 1967 riot destroyed more than two thousand buildings and came to symbolize the decline of that once-great city. *Rolls Press / Popperfoto / Getty Images*

Detroit tried to reverse its decline with foolish investments like its People Mover, which here glides over essentially empty streets.

Dennis MacDonald / World of Stock

From his experience on Wall Street, New York's Mayor Michael Bloomberg learned the value of face-to-face connection, and he turned City Hall into a wall-less bullpen that enables the speedy flow of information.

Copyright City of New York, Used by Permission of the Office of the Mayor, City of New York

Most North Americans would consider the Rocinha favela (foreground) in Rio to be a sign of blight, but it actually indicates urban vitality. The people who settle there have more opportunities and better services than in Brazil's hinterland. *Ivo Gonzalez / Agência O Globo*

A man transports children through the bustle—and fetid streets—of Mumbai's Dharavi slum. Conditions like this are similar to those that faced many residents of Paris, London, New York, and other large cities in the nineteenth century. *Prashanth Vishwanathan / Bloomberg / Getty Images*

John Snow's famous 1854 cholera map helped him to determine that a pump well was the source of London's epidemic.

Wikimedia Commons (Published by C.F. Cheffins, Lith, Southhampton Buildings, London, England, 1854 in Snow, John. On the Mode of Communication of Cholera, 2nd Ed. John Churchill, New Burlington Street, London, England, 1855.)

George Waring and other pioneers of sanitation transformed the motley crew of New York street cleaners (left, in 1868) into a well-organized and effective force (right, in 1920).

[Art 13 and 14:] Picture Collection, The New York Public Library, Astor, Lenox and Tilden Foundations

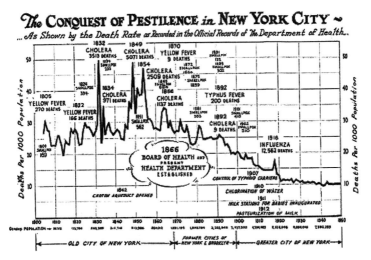

New York City's Department of Health shows the timeline of the city's mortality rate, which sharply dropped with the provision of clean water in the nineteenth century.

New York City Department of Health and Mental Hygiene

The stately order of Parisian boulevards is the product of a massive urban renewal project that dramatically altered that city during the second half of the nineteenth century. Now stringent rules prevent any significant alteration of this cityscape.

Library of Congress Prints and Photographs Division (Detroit Publishing Company, 1905)

The Chicago Home Insurance Building, built in 1885, is widely considered the world's first metal-framed skyscraper. This technology would come to dictate the shape of most cities in the twentieth century and beyond.

Chicago History Museum / Getty Images

Until nearby commercial structures began to dwarf it in 1890, Trinity Church had been New York's tallest building for forty years. The two buildings to the church's left held that honor for thirty years until they were destroyed in a terrible attack that ultimately illustrated the resilience of a great city.

Jeff Greenberg / World of Stock

The great urbanist Jane Jacobs looks none too happy with the tall buildings surrounding her. She argued vigorously against such high-rises and in favor of a low-slung cityscape like that of New York's Greenwich Village. Her arguments have not all proven correct.

Bob Gomel / Time & Life Pictures / Getty Images

Levittown, New York, provided thousands of mass-produced homes that helped America rebuild itself around the car.

Hulton Archive / Getty Images

The Woodlands, outside Houston, shows how much more luxurious and sylvan large-scale suburban development has become since Levittown. Unfortunately, the expansion of the exurbs has lead to more carbon intensive lifestyles. All that greenery is really pretty brown.

© *Ted Washington*

Mumbai grew large as a trading post of the British East India Company, and it is still a gateway between India and the rest of the world. Unfortunately, it also adopted some of the worst aspects of British urban policy, such as severely restricted building heights, that have made it too flat, too congested, and too expensive. Some skyscrapers have gone up recently, but Mumbai's entrepreneurial people remain cursed by a dearth of good buildings and good transport options.

Scott Eels / Bloomberg / Getty Images

Singapore is another legacy of the British East India Company, but it is now a model of superb urban management. It has a world-class water system, plenty of tall buildings, and a congestion-pricing system that electronically charges drivers for the social costs of their motoring. The result is a hyper-dense city-state with traffic that moves more fluidly than in many small U.S. towns.

Land Transport Authority of Singapore

Hong Kong is still another Asian city that bears the imprint of British management and continues to play its historic role as a prime link between East and West. It has combined good management with economic freedom, including the freedom to rebuild and build up. The result is a churning cauldron of activity that's a lot messier than Singapore but no less productive.

DAJ / Amana Images / Getty Images

gen has taken place in "low density residential areas." No country has a more venerable urban culture than Italy. Most tourists to Milan take away a strong memory of the spectacular Duomo and the nearby Galleria Vittorio Emanuele. But just like Detroit and St. Louis, the central city of Milan has lost hundreds of thousands of people, many of whom have moved to more car-intensive suburbs. The people fighting to save Leipzig are also battling a strong surge of suburbanization there.

It would be great for older cities if people just stopped liking cars, but that won't happen. For individual commuters in developed countries, cars save a lot of time. As mentioned in the introduction, in the United States, in 2006, the average car commute lasted twenty-four minutes; the average commute by mass transit took forty-eight minutes. The problem with public transportation is the time involved in getting to the bus or subway stop, waiting to be picked up and then getting from the final stop to one's ultimate destination. That time cost, which is independent of the distance of the journey, averages about twenty minutes for buses and subways. Even before the bus has traveled a stop, the commuter has used up as much time as many car commuters spend on their entire trip.

Some urbanists hope that rising gas prices will put an end to car-based living, and certainly higher gas prices make density more attractive. Yet unfortunately for cities, automotive ingenuity favors the suburbs. If current gas prices doubled, the gas costs of a family that drives twenty-five thousand miles a year in 25-mile-per-gallon cars increases by $3,000. But that family could completely undo this increased cost by switching to a Prius. Given the already vast investment in suburban infrastructure, I wouldn't bet on Americans giving up their cars even if gas prices rise enormously. Higher gas prices are more likely to reduce sprawl in the developing world, where infrastructure isn't yet in place and poorer people will be more responsive to higher costs.

Older cities can't count on either higher gas prices or a sudden disgust with the automobile to bring more Americans back to downtown living. But they can make city life more attractive by speeding the trips of their own residents. Urban bus commutes can be improved, as they have been in London and Singapore, by charging congestion fees that reduce the numbers of drivers on city streets. Even more important, new compact high-rise development can provide the one commute that is even faster than a twenty-four-minute drive: a fifteen-minute walk. In many cities, like New York, once-poor neighborhoods, like Tribeca, that can offer fast commutes on foot to core business districts have come back, spurred by the same increasing value of time that pushed Americans out of public transit into cars. Cities can compete, but they need radical new designs that offer affordable housing and quicker commutes. Yet today, the most creative developments are in the suburbs.

Welcome to The Woodlands

Today, cities aren't competing against the relatively spartan suburbs built by the Levitts. They're fighting against far more attractive developments built in Sunbelt exurbs that manage to provide affordability and space and a wealth of amenities. About thirty miles north of Houston, on twenty-eight thousand sylvan acres, over ninety-two thousand people live in The Woodlands. Levittown, which today has four homes for every acre, is more than three times as dense as this Texas suburb. About 28 percent of The Woodlands land is given over to parks and other protected green space.

The Woodlands is the brainchild of natural gas mogul George Phydias Mitchell, who is, like Levitt, the son of an immigrant. Mitchell's father, born Savvas Paraskevopoulos, left a mountainous quarter acre of land in Greece to come to America and lay railroad track. He eventually ended up running a shoeshine and dry cleaning business in Galveston, Texas. His son George grew up catching fish and selling them to Houston tourists who would then proudly parade them as their own catches. George went to Texas A&M to study geology and petroleum engineering. He graduated first in his class and then spent World War II in the Army Corps of Engineers. After the war, he started wildcatting for natural gas, which was in great demand because cities were creating regulations that stopped private homes from burning coal for heating and cooking. The foes of this regulation argued that its costs would be enormous, but they underestimated the power of human creativity. Mitchell was a leader in the natural gas industry, which has provided a far greener way to heat America's cities than coal or oil.

So maybe it's no surprise that George Mitchell is something of an environmentalist. Apart from some nasty allegations about polluting a Texas aquifer, Mitchell has managed to cultivate a reputation for being a green energy man, which is not the stereotype of the Texas wildcatter. In the 1960s, he decided to diversify into real estate, and he envisioned a vast city in a forest thirty miles north of Houston. Building a large new community in the middle of nowhere takes deep pockets, and Mitchell had to borrow millions to make his place-making bet. The Department of Housing and Urban Development gave The Woodlands a $50 million loan guarantee. But that guarantee came with conditions, one of which was the need for environmental sensitivity.

Mitchell then hired Ian McHarg, a Glaswegian based in Philadelphia, as his environmental consultant, and told him, "I have named my project The Woodlands and there had better be some woodlands when we get done." Mitchell's green sensibilities had been intrigued by McHarg's *Design with Nature,* a tract on urban planning that emphasizes an area's natural ecology. Together Mitchell and McHarg built The Woodlands. The community grew slowly. It didn't even acquire its first mall, the sine qua non of a true suburban development, until 1994. But as Houston expanded, The Woodlands exploded. Its population more than doubled in the 1990s, and it grew by over 40 percent between 2000 and 2008.

More than half of the adults in The Woodlands have a college degree, and the median household income is over $100,000. The residents are also spending remarkably little on housing, given their income levels. According to the Census Bureau, the average home value there is about $200,000, although it is certainly possible to spend more. I went to an open-house for a pretty impressive three-thousand-square-foot home that cost well under $300,000.

One of the most interesting, and almost urban, aspects of The Woodlands' management is its focus on social capital. The Woodlands works precisely because it is not a collection of isolated individuals; its social infrastructure has been designed to foster interpersonal connections. In 1975, Mitchell hired a Wharton-trained Lutheran minister to run The Woodlands Religious Community Incorporated, now called Interfaith, which was meant to "plan the religious community and all the human services in this new town." The minister bought a motor scooter and followed moving vans, meeting new residents as they arrived. Interfaith made sure that The Woodlands provided appropriate space for social, particularly religious, activities. Because nothing sours an area like religiously motivated hatred, Interfaith makes sure that religious messages are kept positive. In the aftermath of the 9/11 attacks, Interfaith managed to get rabbis to pray for Palestinians and Islamic leaders to pray for Jews.

Almost half of The Woodlands' households have children under eighteen, and The Woodlands specializes in schools. There are two highly rated traditional public high schools and an Academy of Science and Technology. There are four private high schools, two religious and two secular. The Woodlands knows that its well-educated residents care about their children's education. Only recently have big cities shown the same level of concern for providing the high-quality schools that will attract more educated residents.

Apparently The Woodlands' customers also care about golf. The development has seven golf courses. The Woodlands also has the Houston Symphony's summer home, a large and shiny shopping mall, and over 150 restaurants. The developers have even created a walking town area, where people can stroll and shop, but the Texas climate isn't always ideal for strolling, and far more people shop at the mall. Of course, most people drive to The Woodlands mall and its walking downtown. While there is a bus service that connects the area to Houston, fewer than 3 percent of commuters in the area use public transit. One of the great ironies of Mitchell and McHarg's environmentalism is that they tried to build a green community with plenty of trees and energy-efficient homes, but home owners drive so much that they undo most of those environmental benefits. Moreover, as I'll discuss in the next chapter, Texas has such a hot, humid climate that cooling those homes and restaurants inevitably generates a big carbon footprint.

Because The Woodlands is thirty miles from Houston's downtown towers, you might think that its residents face horrendous commutes. MapQuest gives the driving time from The Woodlands to Houston as thirty-seven minutes, and that optimistic estimate is based on light traffic, not a normal rush hour. Yet for 2006–2008, the Census Bureau gave the average commute time in The Woodlands as 28.5 minutes because so many people there aren't commuting into Houston at all. According to The Woodlands' management, about a third of its residents work in The Woodlands itself. The community has its own research park, which houses the corporate towers of a number of energy companies. If companies had remained rooted in city centers, then suburbanization would have been limited by lengthy commutes, but America's highways enabled the suburbanization of companies as well as families. Fifty-six percent of the jobs in Houston are more than ten miles from the city center. Businesses have naturally relocated to be close to the vast number of potential employees living in Houston's northern suburbs.

According to Woodlands' management, a lot of their residents are also commuting to the airport, which is only fifteen minutes away. Many suburban communities have grown up around airports, like Chicago's O'Hare. This pattern is, in a way, no different from the earlier tendency of people and companies to locate near wharves and rail yards.

To all but the most ardent urbanist, The Woodlands is an attractive place. It has won numerous awards, and it attracts plenty of residents. The community offers a combination of high-quality construction, pleasant amenities, and costs that are far lower than those in suburban New York or coastal California. The Woodlands' success helps explain why so many people are moving to Houston and places like it.

Accounting for Tastes: Why a Million People Moved to Houston

Houston generates strong emotions. Its boosters, Texan to the core, love the place. Many coastal and European urbanists seem to view the city as Satan's earthly home. The anti-Texans hate the politics, the cars, the weather, the culture (or alleged lack thereof), the hunting, the oil industry, and pretty much anything else that goes on in America's fourth-largest city. Obviously, these people should not move to Houston.

But more than a million other people have moved to the area since the 2000 Census. Houston has much in common with other Sunbelt cities like Atlanta, Dallas, and Phoenix, the other fastest-growing metropolitan areas in the United States. If the advocates of older cities want to actually help their cities, they should try to understand Houston rather than criticizing it.

What is Houston giving its millions of inhabitants that older places, like New York or Detroit, are not? Houston's chief advantage over the Rust Belt is earnings. In Wayne County, Michigan, which surrounds Detroit, the median household in 2008 earned $53,000 a year; median household income in Harris County, Texas, which surrounds Houston, is $60,000. In June 2010, the unemployment rate in Texas was 8.2 percent; the unemployment rate in Michigan was 13.2 percent. For the Rust Belt to compete more effectively against Texas, it would need to find its way to a more robust economy. As the cross-city statistics suggest, that would involve more skill accumulation.

But New York is better educated than Houston, and its wages are higher, yet Houston is attracting many more people. Houston is not luring people who could choose to live in San Francisco or New York because its economy is stronger or its climate is better than those cities. After all, Houston averages ninety-eight days each year when the temperature rises above 90 degrees. Yet its scorching summers aside, Houston succeeds by providing an affordable, attractive lifestyle for middle-class people.

It's hard to imagine anywhere better to be a Master of the Universe than New York. Manhattan is a great place to get rich and a great place to spend your wealth. With enough cash, you can live in a spacious aerie overlooking Central Park, shop at Barney's, eat at Le Bernardin, and send your children to some of the best private schools in the world. New York is also a pretty good place for poorer people, like the immigrants who cram into small apartments in the outer boroughs. Mass transit means that they don't need cars. The city has reasonable social services, and there are plenty of entry-level service-sector jobs with wages that beat those in Ghana or Guatemala.

But what if you are neither a partner at Goldman Sachs nor a poor immigrant? What if you're an average American family with two children, skills that put you in the middle of the U.S. income distribution, and aspirations toward a middle-class lifestyle? It's telling to work through the economic facts of life for a middle-income family deciding between New York and Houston, so that's what we'll do for the next couple of pages.

The average American family earned about $60,000 in 2006. Both members of the family were likely to work, although one spouse often works only part-time. Most middle-income people are in the service sector, working as nurses or sales representatives or store managers. In the 2000 Census, the average registered nurse earned $40,000 in Houston and $50,000 in New York. The average retail manager earned $27,800 in Houston and $28,000 in New York. People working in less idea-intensive industries don't get the same economic kick from Manhattan as financiers and publishers. To reflect the higher incomes in New York, I'll assume that our middle-income family earns $60,000 in Houston and $70,000 in New York.

What kind of housing will that money buy in the two areas? According to the U.S. Census, the average owner-occupied housing unit in the Houston area was worth about $120,000 in 2007. More than three quarters of the homes in the city were valued by their residents at less than $200,000. The National Association of Realtors gives $161,000 as the median price of a Houston home sold in the third quarter of 2009. When I did some Internet shopping for homes in the spring of 2007, I found that there were plenty of homes in Houston selling for less than $200,000 that are relatively new and often have four bedrooms or more. Some have more than three thousand square feet of living space, and others have pools. Some of them are in gated communities, and almost all of them seem to be in pleasant neighborhoods.

For the first thirty-seven years of my generally East Coast life, I lived in homes that are much less luxurious than what you get for $160,000 in Houston, even when I paid many times that cost. When I insured my first house in Cambridge, the agent, a Texan, laughed at the absurdly high price I'd paid for such a modest residence. When I sold the home, *Boston* magazine ran a photo of it to illustrate how even mediocre housing had become expensive. In 2006, the Census gave the average home price in Los Angeles as $614,000 and the average home price in New York City as $496,000.

These average homes are way out of reach for a family earning $70,000 in New York. Unless the family wins the housing lottery and gets a subsidized unit, Manhattan is pretty much out of the question. They could buy a perfectly pleasant home with three bedrooms and two baths on Staten Island for about $340,000. For example, New Brighton, the hometown of Tess McGill, Melanie Griffith's character in *Working Girl,* offers a number of older homes for about $375,000. These houses don't have the amenities of the new Houston houses, but they do offer about two thousand square feet of living space. Or a middle-income family could buy a condominium with two or three bedrooms in Queens, say in Howard Beach or Far Rockaway.

If the family can muster about $35,000 as a down payment, the basic annual housing costs, like interest payments, will run about $24,000 in New York (for a $340,000 home) and about $9,700 in Houston (for a $160,000 home). You get much more house in Houston, and you pay a lot less for it. This gap would be just as big if I compared Houston with coastal California. More than anything else, cheap housing explains why Houston looks so good to so many middle-income Americans.

The Texas State Constitution of 1876, written as a renunciation of big government during Reconstruction, creates a number of roadblocks against any state income tax. As a result, Texas has no state or city income taxes. Houston residents will have to pay property taxes, which would come to around $4,800 for a $160,000 home. In New York City, this family would have to pay local property taxes, probably around $3,400, plus maybe another $3,400 in state income and city income taxes. The state and local tax difference therefore adds about $2,000 more to the burden of living in New York rather than Texas. These tax differences are real, but for middle-income Americans, housing costs are far more important. After paying for housing and federal and local taxes, the Houston family is left with about $37,000. The New York family, which started with $10,000 more, is left with closer to $30,000.

Now the Texans do need a car for each adult; there's no other way to get around. On average, American families earning $60,000 spent up to $8,500 per year on transportation. That amount could, barely, cover the payments on two relatively cheap cars, gas, and insurance in Texas. The New Yorkers could save by giving up on cars altogether, but in Staten Island or outlying Queens, they would likely want one car to buy groceries and move kids around, even if they took mass transit to work. It's likely that the New Yorkers will end up spending at least $3,000 less per year than the Texans on transportation.

The New Yorkers would spend less to get around, but they'd offset this financial gain in lost time. In the most recent Census data (2008), the average Houston commute is 26.4 minutes. In Queens, the average commute is 42.7 minutes. In Staten Island, the average commute is 42.1 minutes, and it is something of a multimode marathon. First, you've got to get from your home to the ferry, either walking or taking a bus. The ferry ride itself is only 25 minutes, but then you've got to get to your final Manhattan destination. A commute to Wall Street might be only 45 minutes; a commute to Midtown could be easily over an hour. All told, each adult working in Manhattan is spending between 125 and 250 extra hours per year riding on mass transit. This time loss is the equivalent of losing between three and seven weeks of work in travel.

Public-transit aficionados will argue that it's a lot more pleasant than driving. This is sometimes true, but a packed Manhattan subway can be a lot closer to hell than heaven. In a car, the driver can control the temperature and listen to CDs of Saul Bellow or Bruce Springsteen with less background noise than in a subway. Research on commuters' tastes shows that people dislike time spent on mass transit more than time spent driving.

After cars and houses and taxes, the Texans have $28,500 left, and the New Yorkers have $24,500 left, but those dollars will go further in Houston. The American Chamber of Commerce Research Association (ACCRA) produces local price indices for different areas of the country, including Houston and Queens (but not Staten Island). Apart from housing, the biggest price gaps are in groceries, which are, according to ACCRA, about 50 percent more expensive in Queens than in Houston. A T-bone steak costs over $3 more in Queens; chicken is 50 percent more expensive in New York. Correcting for these price differences, the after-tax, after-housing, after-transport real income of the Queens residents is a little less than $19,750. The same figure for Houston residents, who start off earning $10,000 less, is $31,250. In real dollars, the Houston family is 58 percent richer.

What about public services, like education? Ordinary public schools would be pretty comparable for a family in Houston and in Staten Island. If the New York family's kids got into one of the city's superstar public schools, like Stuyvesant, they would be getting a superb education for free. But even without a brilliant child, the Houston resident has the option of paying a little bit more and moving into a slightly more expensive school district, like Spring Branch, where SAT scores averaged 1058, in 2008, which is higher than in many New York suburbs. The New Yorkers could also get better schools by moving to the suburbs, but the price and commuting costs are going to be a lot more than the $225,000 it costs to buy a decent home in Spring Branch.

All told, the Houston residents are solidly in the middle class, with plenty of money for eating first-rate Tex-Mex at Pappasito's and shopping at the Galleria. They have decent options for schools, and relatively fast, comfortable commutes. The family in Staten Island or Queens is straining to make ends meet, constantly reminded that life is a struggle. For millions of Americans, the decision to move to Houston makes clear economic sense. If the expensive cities on America's coasts want to compete more effectively with Texas, then they must figure out how to become more accessible to ordinary people. For middle-income people, the biggest economic advantage of Texas is not lower taxes or higher earnings, but affordable housing.

Why Is Housing So Cheap in the Sunbelt?

Why are Houston, and Atlanta and Dallas and Phoenix, so much cheaper than the cities on America's coasts? During brief periods of irrational exuberance, housing prices can become almost unfathomable. The bizarre doubling of home prices in Las Vegas between 2002 and 2006, which was followed by an equally severe price collapse, is beyond this economist's ken. But over longer time periods, housing prices generally conform to the laws of conventional economics. These laws may bend briefly, as they did in Las Vegas, but they then furiously reassert themselves.

Prices reflect the interaction of demand and supply. High prices, for housing or anything else, can only persist when demand is high and supply is limited. Low prices can result from either weak demand or abundant supply. The demand for water is vast, but glasses of it are often given away for free because there's so much of it. My dreadful sketches of bears, drawn for the captive audience of my children, could never command a high price, no matter how short their supply. Poor quality ensures low demand and low prices.

The demand for housing in a particular metropolitan area reflects the wages that can be earned in that area and the other pleasures the place offers. Almost two thirds of the variation in metropolitan prices can be explained by per capita income and two temperature variables. On average, if an area has family incomes that are 1 percent higher, its housing prices increase by 1.35 percent. If an area has January temperatures that are 5 degrees warmer, its prices go up by 3 percent. For every $1.00 that a metropolitan area's income rose between 1980 and 2000, housing prices increased by $1.20.

In the expensive areas on America's coasts, demand is robust, because of high incomes and pleasures like those discussed in chapter 5. California's Santa Clara County, Silicon Valley, has a splendid Mediterranean climate and incomes that are 60 percent above the U.S. average. Unsurprisingly, people will pay plenty to live there. Between 2005 and 2007, average housing prices in the county were close to $800,000, more than four times the U.S. average. Prices have dropped since then, but according to recent sales data, the San Jose metropolitan area, which includes Santa Clara County, remained the most expensive place in the continental United States in the second quarter of 2009.

Yet Santa Clara's high prices reflect more than just good weather and high incomes. During the eight years between 2001 and 2008, Santa Clara permitted only about sixteen thousand new single-family homes, or one new home for every fifty acres of land. Despite booming demand, the area's stock of single-family homes increased by less than 5 percent, less than one third of the U.S. average building rate over that time period. If Silicon Valley had built two hundred thousand more homes over those eight years, then standard housing statistics suggests that housing prices would be about 40 percent lower, despite the good weather and high incomes.

Between 2001 and 2008, Harris County, Texas, which includes Houston, did permit more than two hundred thousand new single-family homes, or almost one new home for every five acres. That abundance of construction helps explain why Houston is so affordable. Certainly, a Houston home will never be as expensive as a home in Silicon Valley, at least as long as Californians earn more and enjoy nicer summers. Yet Houston's economy is much stronger than most of the Rust Belt's economies, and many Americans do seem to prefer a hot, humid climate to the cold of the Midwest. A lot of people want to live in Houston, but prices stay low because building is so easy.

Not every place with low prices is kept cheap through abundant new construction. The combination of economic collapse and cold weather limits the demand for living in Detroit, and that's why prices there are so low. Average household income in Detroit is 48 percent below the U.S. norm, and an average home is valued at $90,000, half the U.S. average. Detroit's freezing winters make the city's prices even lower than the area's incomes would predict. Indeed, Detroit's housing prices are below the cost of building new homes, which ensures that there will continue to be almost no private development and consequently continued population loss. When prices aren't high enough to support new construction, there will be no new homes and no new people. In places like Detroit, we can tell that prices are held down because of low demand because there is also little construction in the city. In places like Houston, we can tell that prices are held down by abundant supply, not low demand, because there is so much new construction in the city.

Plentiful housing doesn't just make prices lower, it also reduces price swings, such as those that have recently rocked the American economy. Between May 2002 and May 2006, the peak of the recent bubble, American housing prices rose by 64 percent, according to Case-Shiller housing price data, which covers twenty large metropolitan areas and which, by looking at repeated sales of the same homes, tries to eliminate the impact of changes in housing quality. That data excludes Houston but includes Dallas, which has a similar housing market. In Dallas, prices rose by only 8 percent over those four boom years, less than the rate of inflation. During the three years that followed the bubble's peak, prices in general dropped by an average of 32 percent, but prices in Dallas fell by only 5.5 percent. As prices in much of America dropped off a cliff, National Association of Realtors data shows that prices in Houston have stayed remarkably constant. The average sale price was $152,500 in 2007, $151,600 in 2008, and $153,100 in 2009.

Prices in Houston remained flat, despite the extreme volatility of housing markets worldwide, because construction responded to changing demand. In 2006, during the height of the boom, Harris County permitted more than thirty thousand units, and that building helped keep prices low. By 2008, building had dropped in half, and that fall in construction cushioned the drop.

Elastic housing supply usually limits price bubbles. From 1996 to 2006, on average, real prices rose by 94 percent in twenty-six of America's cities where building is most difficult, but only by 28 percent in America's twenty-eight least supply-constrained cities. In the boom of the 1980s, real estate prices went up by 29 percent in the supply-restricted areas, but only by 3 percent in the elastic places. Flexible housing supply isn't a perfect antidote to homebuyer madness; there are few barriers to building in Las Vegas and Phoenix, yet these places experienced extremely large and painful price swings. But elastic supply does make such episodes less likely.

Texas builders can supply so many new, inexpensive homes because the physical cost of building a standard house in Houston is about $75 a square foot. Why should housing in Texas, or anyplace with abundant land, cost much more than the cost of building a home? Texas and California together have so much space that if the *whole world* lived in those two states, each person would have more than 1,600 square feet of land. America's abundance of land has meant that in much of the country, homes typically cost no more than 25 percent more than the physical costs of construction.

Yet in much of coastal America, home prices are dramatically higher than construction costs. In Los Angeles, construction costs are 25 percent higher than in Houston, but housing is over 350 percent more expensive in Los Angeles. It's harder to compare Houston with Manhattan because it's so much more expensive to build up than it is to build out. Yet in recent years, the prices of new Manhattan condominiums have been more than twice the physical cost of building up. Something other than building costs is responsible for high prices in coastal America.

The most straightforward explanation for high prices in coastal America is that land is scarce and therefore expensive. There certainly isn't much land in Manhattan, which is why people go to the expense of building up. But it doesn't take more land to add an extra story to a high-rise, so the lack of land can't explain why Manhattan prices are so much higher than the costs of adding an extra story. Moreover, in expensive suburban areas, like Santa Clara County and Westchester County, New York, there is actually more land per household than in Houston. In Harris County, Texas, there are 3.6 people per acre. The comparable figures for Westchester and Santa Clara counties are 3.44 and 2 people per acre respectively. In those places, there's plenty of land; it just isn't available for construction.

All land isn't equal. Flat land is easy to build on; hills are a problem. Wharton economist Albert Saiz's work on local topography has found that natural barriers to building, including mountains and water, help explain the differences in housing supply across metropolitan areas. Houston is flat, and so is most of Westchester County, but much of Silicon Valley is far more vertical. Yet even if 60 percent of Santa Clara County is too hilly to be built upon, there are only five people and two homes on every acre of remaining land, which hardly seems like overcrowding.

There is a land shortage in Santa Clara County and throughout much of coastal America, but that shortage is the handiwork of regulation, not nature. Together with Bryce Ward and Jenny Schuetz, I've tried to measure the effect of land-use regulations throughout greater Boston. Out of 187 cities and towns, the majority had average minimum lot sizes that were greater than one third of an acre. Most of these places had 10 percent or less of their land that could be used to build multiunit developments.

Over the past thirty years, Massachusetts towns have imposed stricter and stricter rules preventing new development and subdivisions. One municipality forbids building anyplace where there's a "wicked big puddle." Protecting wetlands is important, but taken to this extreme, environmentalism becomes mere NIMBYism, the reflexive opposition to any new building nearby.

In Massachusetts, the more land-use restrictions there are, the less new building there will be. Each extra type of rule is associated with about 10 percent less building. Across areas, a ten-thousand-square-foot, or quarter-acre, increase in minimum lot size is associated with a 10 percent drop in construction between 1980 and 2002. This shouldn't be a surprise. The amount of land is fixed. If you require more land per home, you get fewer homes and higher prices. That ten-thousand-square-foot increase in minimum lot size comes with a 4 percent increase in prices. California's growth controls have similarly reduced the amount of new construction and pushed prices up. Indeed, the same pattern applies to the nation as a whole. In America's expensive coastal regions, housing supply is restricted not by lack of land but because public policies make it hard to build.

By contrast, Houston has always been prodevelopment. The city was founded by two real estate developers from upstate New York who promised prospective settlers fresh water and invigorating ocean breezes. Over the next 150 years, local business interests led by the Houston Chamber of Commerce have coaxed and prodded Houston into becoming an urban giant. Above all, the city's leaders have made sure that nothing stands in the way of new building. Houston is unique among all American cities in that it lacks a zoning code. More than in any other place, Houston's developers have successfully argued that restrictions on development will make the city less affordable to the less successful. These arguments are patently self-interested, but they are also correct. Houston's freewheeling growth machine has actually done a better job of providing affordable housing than all of the progressive reformers on America's East and West coasts.

In the early 1920s, New York was also a builders' paradise, and as a result, housing stayed affordable. In the postwar years, New York increasingly restricted development and tried to make up for the lack of private supply with rent control and public housing. This strategy failed miserably, as it has throughout Europe. The only way to provide cheap housing on a mass scale is to unleash the developers.

Levittown, The Woodlands, and hundreds of other large developments can be built so cheaply because they are built on a large scale. Mass production has made clothing and cars affordable for everyone; it has the same effect in the housing market. Places like New York and San Francisco, which claim to care about providing low-cost housing for the poor, are generally unafford- able. Texas, which has never shown any commitment to social housing, leads the country in building inexpensive homes. If older cities with high prices are going to compete, then they must act more like Houston and allow more building.

What's Wrong with Sprawl?

In the nineteenth century, economics drove the growth of America's cities. People moved to places, like Chicago, that were economic engines. In the twentieth century, an increasingly affluent population started making choices based on quality of life as well as wages. Los Angeles' early growth came from its oil wells and its port, but also from the allure that its climate had for retir- ing Midwestern farmers or footloose authors, like L. Frank Baum and Edgar Rice Burroughs. When people move to places that are more productive, the country as a whole becomes more economically vibrant. When people move to pleasant places, they enjoy life more, and when they move to more temper- ate climates, they use less energy.

But in the late twentieth century, public policies, both national and local, started playing an outsize role in urban change. As we've seen, the fastest growing places in the United States—Atlanta, Dallas, Houston, and Phoenix— are growing not because of high wages and temperate climates but because their governments are friendlier to new development than older communities in California and the Northeast. The path of America's future is being deter- mined by the whims of local zoning boards that don't want more people living in their highly productive, pleasant communities.

A different set of policies has played an equally important but largely hid- den role, pushing people to suburbanize. I am sufficiently unusual that I'm always cautious about using my own life to infer anything about anyone else's, but my decision to suburbanize was a conventional one, driven for the most part by common factors. At the start of this chapter, I listed the forces that brought me to a suburb: living space, soft grass for spill-prone toddlers, a desire to diversify my life with greater distance from my employer, a fast commute, and good schools. Of these five factors, only two—the grass and distance from Harvard—are independent of public policies.

My wife and I were pretty sure that we wanted to live someplace where we could eat out anonymously, but that didn't necessarily imply living in a suburb. We could have moved to Boston, which is a charming and pleasant city. One of the factors that pushed against Boston is that a five-mile commute from an urban apartment across the Charles River would have been no quicker than a fifteen-mile drive in from the suburbs. If I leave early enough, that drive takes me less than twenty-five minutes, thanks to the interstate highway system, which was generously subsidized by the federal government. My commute itself is on a highway that was funded by tolls, but when I drive to the airport, I rely on a recent expensive extension largely funded by state and federal largesse. As a matter of public policy, I remain skeptical of the $15 billion Big Dig, but I'd be foolish not to use it when I drive to Logan. My commute is also cheap because American governments have, unlike their European counterparts, decided not to heavily tax gasoline.

Another factor that pushed us to the suburbs was the cost of living space. Cambridge strongly restricts new construction, and that keeps prices up, but my suburb is also artificially expensive because of its draconian limitations on new development. The big difference between city and suburb in this case is that the federal government heavily subsidizes home ownership by allowing me to deduct interest on my home mortgage. That subsidy makes owning cheaper than renting, and being pro-home-ownership means being anticity.

The long, passionate love affair between American politicians and home ownership is a curse to the cities that power the American economy. More than 85 percent of people living in multifamily dwellings rent their living quarters. More than 85 percent of people in single-family detached dwellings own them. This connection isn't a random statistical artifact. It makes sense to have one roof, one owner. When people rent single-family homes, they often take bad care of them. Homes depreciate by 1.5 percent more per year if they are inhabited by renters rather than owners, who work hard to take care of their important asset. By contrast, in multifamily dwellings, dispersed ownership is a big headache. Think of the battles that roil co-op boards. Because dense cities are filled with multiunit buildings, they're also filled with renters. In Manhattan, 76 percent of housing units are rentals. When the federal government encourages people to own, it is implicitly encouraging people to leave dense cities.

Perhaps the most important factor encouraging suburbanization is our school system. Big cities attract poor people for many good reasons, but educating the children of poorer parents creates stresses for urban school systems. Big-city schools tend to have much lower test scores despite spending per student as much as or more than many suburban school districts. There's no reason why big cities can't have great schools. Paris has some of the finest high schools in the world, and many American cities boast superb private and magnet schools. The same forces of competition and density that make big cities havens for excellent restaurants could also make them great places for education.

However, the American public school system essentially puts a public quasi-monopoly in charge of central-city schools. A public monopoly that must struggle to provide the basics to hundreds of thousands of less fortunate children will naturally have trouble providing first-rate education for upper-middle-class parents, at least relative to a homogeneous suburb filled with upper-middle-class people. The American public school system, which forces people to move in order to find better public schools, has been another unnecessary curse on cities.

As noted earlier, this problem could be eased by a move either to the left or the right. If the United States emulated France and embraced nationwide quality schooling funded by the state, there would be less reason to flee urban areas. If the United States adopted a large-scale voucher program under which parents could send their children to school anywhere, urban competition would ensure that cities developed better schools, and city dwellers could always send their kids to suburban schools. The current system has its virtues: Local control over small school districts *can* give the kids in those schools a great education. But for our cities, it has been a disaster.

Suburbs aren't intrinsically bad, and there's a lot to like in Houston. For many people, Sunbelt sprawl makes sense. But sprawl of the sort that Houston embodies has been encouraged by mistaken public policies. The fault with Houston's growth doesn't lie in the area itself, but elsewhere, in more temperate and economically productive places that have used regulations to stymie development and make housing unaffordable. There's no sense in blaming the suburbs or the suburbanites. The fault lies in our policies and regulations, which have created incentives that force too many Americans to leave our cities.

The fact that suburbia continues to be artificially boosted by mistaken policies should offer some hope to the anxious urbanist. These policies need not be permanent. In 2005, a tax-reform panel, appointed by a Texan Republican president who repeatedly lauded the ownership society, advocated a major decrease in the size of the home mortgage interest deduction. If federal housing policies become less antiurban, then our big cities will become more appealing.

Moreover, many of the benefits of suburbia may become less important if America continues to grow. The ability to commute to work quickly on vast, uncluttered highways is a plus for many, but as sprawl continues, those highways will become more and more congested. Already we have seen people who highly value their time return to once downtrodden downtown areas like Tribeca to reap the advantages of walking to work.

Today suburban schools are, on average, better than their big-city counterparts. But no immutable law makes this so. Well-run city schools that harness the power of urban human capital and competition can, and sometimes do, beat the suburbs. It once seemed that big cities would always be synonymous with crime, but that's no longer the case. There could certainly come a time when cities are widely seen as the best places to educate our children.

Eliminating the mistaken policies that hurt our cities makes sense, because sprawl has costs as well as benefits. Like most other growing places, sprawling suburbs must struggle with water issues, sanitation, and congestion. Perhaps the biggest economic question is whether suburban office enclaves can generate the same degree of intellectual excitement as traditional downtowns. These areas involve far fewer random interactions, and they often concentrate in a particular industry, which reduces the chances of cross-field leaps in innovation.

Most worrisome of all is the prospect that the developing world will adopt the car-based lifestyle that reigns in much of America. Few cities feel as immense as São Paulo, with its scores of separate high-rise centers stretching out from the inner city. The urban region goes on for miles and miles. Many of São Paulo's suburbs are the traditional poor settlements of the developing world, whose people ride public transit to work and live in small homes that would be substandard in the United States or Europe. But there are also plenty of wealthier enclaves that look like Houston's suburbs. You can find similar places around Bangalore, Mumbai, Cairo, Mexico City, and pretty much any growing city throughout the world.

If the entire world starts looking like Houston, the planet's carbon footprint will skyrocket. Houston residents, for all the sensible suburban logic of their lives, are some of the biggest carbon emitters in the country. All those 90-degree days and all that humidity mean that Houston is a ravenous consumer of electricity. All that driving gobbles up plenty of gas. Urbanization will continue in India and China, and that's a good thing—there is no future in rural poverty. But it would be a lot better for the planet if their urbanized population lives in dense cities built around the elevator, rather than in sprawling areas built around the car.

CHAPTER 8

Is There Anything Greener Than Blacktop?

On a pleasant April day in 1844, two young men went out for a walk in the woods along the Concord River. Since there hadn't been much rain lately, the water was low, and they could "fitly procure our food from the stream, Indian-like." Using a match they had gotten from a shoemaker, they built a fire in a pine stump near Fair Haven Pond. The two intrepid explorers were hungry and looking to cook some chowder.

The same dearth of rain that made for easy fishing made the grass around their cooking area dry and flammable. Wind spread their fire to the grass and "as every thing around them was as combustible almost as a fireship, the flames spread with rapidity, and hours elapsed before it could be subdued." One of the men rushed to town to raise the alarm, but the fire could not be stopped. Over three hundred acres of prime woodland were razed by a careless fire lit by these two young pleasure seekers.

Smokey the Bear could use this story to teach children the dangers of forest fires, but at least one of the culprits steadfastly denied any guilt. He wrote: "I have set fire to the forest, but I have done no wrong therein, and now it is as if the lightning had done it." The other residents of Concord were less forgiving, taking an understandably dim view of even inadvertent arson. They called the young incendiary a "dammed rascal" and a "flibbertigibbet." The *Concord Freeman*'s text sounds like a stuffy nineteenth-century New Englander channeling Smokey: "It is to be hoped that this unfortunate result of sheer carelessness, will be borne in mind by those who may visit the woods for recreation."

The unrepentant forest burner was Henry David Thoreau, a somewhat underemployed Harvard graduate who has since become the secular saint of environmentalism. Thoreau's *Walden* is one of those rare books whose influence seems only to grow over time. During his lifetime, his journal, describing two years of isolated living, received little attention. But in the twentieth century, it became a global bestseller, read by millions and taught by environmentally conscious high school teachers around the world.

Thoreau loved the woods, but he was also part of an urban chain of intellectuals. He had been educated in the intellectual hothouse of early nineteenth-century Harvard. More important, he was one of a remarkable concentration of minds brought together by Ralph Waldo Emerson in Concord, a town filled with creative thinkers. Emerson assembled, and occasionally funded, brilliant minds, including Herman Melville, Nathanial Hawthorne, Margaret Fuller, Bronson Alcott, Louisa May Alcott, and Thoreau.

Thoreau was part of Emerson's Transcendentalist salon, but he extolled the virtues of rural isolation rather than urban interaction. In his introduction to *Walden,* Emerson described Thoreau thus: "An iconoclast in literature, he seldom thanked colleagues for their services to him, holding them in small esteem, whilst yet his debt to them was important." Would Thoreau have been able to write so well about living alone if he hadn't also connected with so many smart people in towns? Yet the eloquent cadences of *Walden* preach the virtues of sylvan solitude. Just as Thoreau and his disciples have rarely seen the virtues of cities, they have also had little empathy for the *Concord Freeman*'s warnings against rural recreation.

Thoreau's walk in the woods did much more for his soul than for the woods themselves, and my move into the countryside has done nothing but harm the environment. I've gone from being a relatively parsimonious urban energy user to emitting massive amounts of carbon. While my compact urban living space could be easily warmed, it takes hundreds of gallons of fuel oil to heat my drafty home over a New England winter. My modest attempts to reduce energy use have led my mother to accuse me of trying to freeze my children. I call it building character. What with lights and air conditioning and appliances, my electricity bill has tripled. Of course, like most of nonurban America, I've also become dependent on the car, burning roughly a gallon of gas every time I go to a full-size grocery store. It all seems pretty absurd to someone who, city-born, didn't learn how to drive until he was in graduate school.

My story, like Thoreau's, makes a fundamental point: Cities are much better for the environment than leafy living. Residing in a forest might seem to be a good way of showing one's love of nature, but living in a concrete jungle is actually far more ecologically friendly. We humans are a destructive species, even when, like Thoreau, we're not trying to be. We burn forests and oil and inevitably hurt the landscape that surrounds us. If you love nature, stay away from it.

In the 1970s, Jane Jacobs argued that we could minimize our damage to the environment by clustering together in high-rises and walking to work, and this point has been eloquently argued by David Owen in his book *Green Metropolis*. We maximize our damage when we insist on living surrounded by greensward. Lower densities inevitably mean more travel, and that requires energy. While larger living spaces certainly do have their advantages, large suburban homes also consume much more energy.

There is still much debate about the relationship between greenhouse gases and global warming, and there is plenty of uncertainty about the effects global warming will have on the planet. I am no climatologist, and I have little to add to these contentious discussions. However, even those who doubt that humans are responsible for much of the recent rise in global temperature should still recognize that there are environmental risks associated with massively increasing the amount of carbon we emit.

Anyone who believes that global warming is a real danger should see dense urban living as part of the solution. Over the next fifty years, China and India will cease to be poor rural nations, and that's a good thing. They—like the United States and Europe before them—will move from farms to urban living. If billions of Chinese and Indians insist on leafy suburbs and the large homes and cars those suburbs entail, then the world's carbon emissions will soar. Some environmentalists seem to wish that these countries would just stay rural. Thank goodness that isn't a real option. Remaining rural means poverty and its attendant curses. The critical question is whether, as Asia develops, it will become a continent of suburban drivers or urban public-transit users.

Environmentalists can make the case for greener living in dense cities, but to do this they must give up their antipathy to concrete. Today ecofriendly households raise their children on Dr. Seuss's fable *The Lorax*, which depicts a callous city destroying a once beautiful landscape. True environmentalists should toss their copies of this book into the recycling bin and denounce the

Lorax fallacy—that cities are bad for the environment. High-rise pioneers like William Le Baron Jenney and A. E. Lefcourt are better guides to a greener future than Henry David Thoreau.

The Dream of Garden Living

It is, of course, unfair to single Thoreau out for touting low-density living. For millennia, writers have praised the virtues of going back to nature, which actually made some sense before cities got clean water. The classical poet Horace, who left his father's farm to be educated in Athens and Rome, wrote, "The chorus of writers, one and entire, detests the town and yearns for the sacred grove." At the start of the nineteenth century, the age-old pleasures of English country living acquired one of the greatest public relations teams ever. Wordsworth, Coleridge, Keats, Shelley, and their fellow Romantic poets all extolled the magnificence of the countryside.

These poets were reacting to the first explosion of industrial urbanization. They understandably saw more poetry in autumn or the west wind than in a textile mill. Byron was one of the Luddites' few defenders in the House of Lords. In a sense, Thoreau's years in Walden were just a more extreme version of Wordsworth's life in the Lake District. Indeed, neither one was crazy to flee the disease and disorder of nineteenth-century cities, where life was too often nasty, brutish, and short.

The Romantics' love of nature spread to the more practical arts of architecture and urban planning. John Ruskin was raised in early nineteenth-century London, but as an art critic, he urged painters to "go to nature in all singleness of heart . . . rejecting nothing and selecting nothing." He loathed the standardization that marked both industrialization and classical art forms. He favored the vagaries of nature and Gothic structures. Ruskin was also an early advocate of town planning. He urged that "from any part of the city perfectly fresh air and grass and the sight of far horizon might be reachable in a few minutes walk." He had in mind a compact, walled town, girded by a "belt of beautiful garden and orchard round the walls." Ruskin's message underwent a slight metamorphosis when it crossed the Atlantic, for Peter B. Wight, who helped make urban skyscrapers possible in the United States, started off as one of Ruskin's most fervent American apostles.

Enjoying nature is something of a luxury good, which may explain why environmentalism has grown stronger as mankind has gotten richer. Hungry people can be skittish about giving up a decent meal for a "sight of far horizon." The poor farmers who came to Manchester's mills were willingly abandoning nature in order to put bread on their tables. But as the world grew wealthier over the nineteenth century, an increasingly large segment of the population came to want a little green mixed in with the urban density. Open spaces offered a bit of relief from the foul air and water of the early industrial cities.

Historically, the wealthy managed to combine city and country by having two homes. Winter months were spent in the city. In the hot summers, when disease spread most virulently, the prosperous fled cities for their country estates. Yet this two-home model has remained relatively rare, because building two houses is such an expensive way for city dwellers to get access to the countryside. Out of America's total housing stock of 128 million units, only a little more than 3 million are recreational second homes.

A more affordable alternative is bringing the countryside into the city, which city planners have long strived to do. Ruskin offered one variant of this ideal: the small town surrounded by a greenbelt. Ebenezer Howard, a towering figure in urban planning, wrote his classic *Garden Cities of Tomorrow* in 1898 and made Ruskin's vision concrete both intellectually and literally. Howard's garden cities were to be surrounded by abundant land, which would provide food, clean air, and recreational space for the urbanites. During the twentieth century, greenbelts became a regular feature of English town planning. Today London's Green Belt covers more than two thousand square miles, Toronto's is even larger, and these rings of nature have also become popular in America's Pacific Northwest.

London's Green Belt does, however, show the limitations of this strategy. If you're in central London, the Green Belt is hardly within walking distance; it can easily take an hour on mass transit to get outside of London's city limits. Greenbelts may serve to check urban growth—which may or may not be desirable—but they certainly don't bring trees into the daily life of big-city residents.

To make up for this shortfall, nineteenth-century urban planners built parks. In the United States, Frederick Law Olmsted specialized in bringing bucolic vistas to the heart of a city. Olmsted's Central Park in New York remains a remarkable example of a man-made sylvan wonderland in the heart of an extremely dense place. Olmsted also gave Boston an emerald necklace, built Jackson Park in Chicago, and provided Detroit with Belle Isle. He built green spaces in Buffalo, Louisville, Milwaukee, Montreal, and Washington, D.C., and helped plan the campuses of both Berkeley and Stanford. While some might debate the merits of each individual project, most city dwellers blessed with an Olmsted creation have been grateful that he leavened their dense cities with a touch of leaf.

But neither greenbelts nor central parks became the dominant way of merging city and country. Instead, millions of people adopted a far more extreme approach—following Thoreau and Wordsworth far more completely. Starting in the late nineteenth century, suburban developments made quasi-country estates more affordable to ordinary people. From Bryn Mawr to Houston's Woodlands, developers have built homes on generous wooded plots. Why put up with the inconvenience of shared parks or long trips to the countryside when you could live, like Thoreau, with your own trees right outside your door?

The emergence of faster, cheaper transportation made it possible to live with trees and work in the city. Streetcars enabled towns like Brookline, Massachusetts, to grow as they offered green spaces and access to urban density simultaneously. As an 1841 description notes, "The whole of this neighborhood of Brookline is a kind of landscape garden, and there is nothing in America of the sort, so inexpressibly charming as the lanes which lead from one cottage, or villa, to another." Who wouldn't want that, at least if you can afford it?

Olmsted himself got into the suburb-building business in 1869 by designing Riverside, on the edge of Chicago, which may be America's first "planned" suburban community. Together with his partner, Calvert Vaux, he eschewed the regularity of a grid in favor of curving roads laid out along natural pathways. Lots were large and trees were abundant. The modern suburb was born.

Still, as late as the 1920s, many urban analysts missed the trend toward tree-lined suburban living. Architects like Raymond Hood (who later built Rockefeller Center), Hugh Ferriss, and others saw an urban future that looked like Batman's Gotham City. Indeed, Ferriss's drawings would be an inspiration for the comic book. They envisioned a vertical world of taller and taller buildings connected by multilevel highways with embedded airplane hangars. Le Corbusier's city of the future included a lot more greenery, but it was still a world of vast towers, and Fritz Lang's 1927 film *Metropolis* provides the ultimate dark vision of this urban future.

As it turned out, the 1920s were the high-water mark for vertical America. Between 1930 and 1933, five new buildings opened that soared above 849 feet, the height of the tallest skyscraper in Western Europe today. America would not build another tower that tall for another thirty-six years. The move upward was overshadowed by the growth of places that looked more like Brookline and Riverside than like Rockefeller Center. Streetcars had made leafy living close to the city available for a moderate number of prosperous urban burghers, and cars made suburbs available to anyone in the middle class. As the car finally bested the elevator, the majority of Americans came to live in suburban places that combined city and nature.

While the car enabled people to suburbanize, environmentalists meanwhile protected millions of acres of land within urban areas so that people could experience the countryside constantly. In the beautiful landscape of the San Francisco region there are endless miles of open mountain ranges and protected seascape. The computer magnates of Silicon Valley live in a region blessed not only by an extraordinary climate, but also by a beautiful setting protected from development by some of the world's most restrictive land-use controls.

America seemed on a path to widespread Walden living, where everyone could be surrounded by greenery, but somewhere along that road, something went environmentally wrong. The dream of garden living envisioned by Ruskin and Wordsworth and designed by Howard and Olmsted turned out to be an ecological nightmare. Just as Thoreau's forest fire suggests, living within nature can have terrible consequences for the environment. The move to low-density living ended up being far less sensitive to nature than Ferriss's vision of a towering metropolis.

We've all heard the dire warnings from an Nobel Prize–winning former vice president and climatologists alike about how carbon dioxide emissions are causing the earth to warm. Global temperatures have been rising continuously for close to sixty years. At the same time, carbon dioxide in the atmosphere continues to grow. Higher levels of carbon dioxide are thought to create higher temperatures through the greenhouse effect, whereby gases in the atmosphere absorb infrared radiation and warm the land below. The basic intuition of the mainstream hypothesis on climate change is that more greenhouse gases mean more infrared absorption and higher surface temperatures.

For those of us who endure New England or Midwestern winters, a few extra degrees in February sounds swell, but unfortunately the side effects from rising global temperatures are potentially terrible for almost everybody. The poorest people in the world tend to live near the equator, and more heat is particularly problematic for them. The polar ice caps appear to be melting quickly and threatening seaside cities from New York to Hong Kong with the prospect of severe flooding. And higher ocean temperatures may create more volatile, stormier weather worldwide.

Temperatures do fluctuate for many reasons, but that doesn't change the fact that a colossal increase in carbon emissions could still radically affect the weather. Humanity has spent millennia adjusting to our current environment. If our carbon emissions radically alter that environment, the costs may well be enormous. The potential risks from a different climate make it reasonable for the world to take significant action to reduce the growth of carbon dioxide emissions. Among other things, that means favoring construction in areas that are greener and reducing building in areas that are more brown.

Dirty Footprints: Comparing Carbon Emissions

Matthew Kahn and I have put together a carbon inventory of new housing throughout America. We wanted to determine the amount of carbon emissions that come from building a typical new home in different parts of the country, so we based our estimates primarily on homes built over the last two decades.

In 2006, the United States produced about 6 billion metric tons of carbon dioxide, which doesn't include the emissions related to the goods we import from elsewhere on the planet. That figure represents about one fifth of total world carbon dioxide emissions, more than any other country except China and more than the amount emitted by Europe and Latin America. Together, homes and cars account for about 40 percent of an average household's output and also about 40 percent of America's and 8 percent of the world's carbon footprint. About 20 percent of America's carbon dioxide emissions are related to residential energy use, and almost another 20 percent is associated with our motor vehicles.

Using a gallon of gas produces about twenty-two pounds of carbon dioxide, if you factor in the carbon used in refining and distributing gasoline. An average family in the United States buys about a thousand gallons of gas a year, which is associated with about ten tons of carbon dioxide. It may be easier to imagine American families buying more fuel-efficient cars than giving up on car-based living altogether, but historically the bulk of variation in gas usage among various people over various periods of time comes from total miles traveled, not from fuel efficiency. Cars now get, on average, about 22 miles per gallon, and the big difference is whether you drive three hundred miles per year or thirty thousand, which depends on whether you live in a city or a suburb.

Kahn and I found that area density and distance to the city center are both strongly associated with gasoline usage. The average household living in a census tract with more than ten thousand people per square mile uses 687 gallons of gas per year, while the average household living in an area with fewer than one thousand people per square mile (about one household per acre) uses 1,164 gallons of gas per year. The density of one's home neighborhood matters because most car trips aren't commutes downtown. People drive millions of miles to buy groceries, to go out to eat, and to pick their children up at school. The density of stores and schools in an area determines the average distance of those trips. In a city, you often walk to a restaurant. In a low-density area, eating out might entail a twenty-five-minute drive each way.

Holding family income and size constant, gas consumption per family per year declines by 106 gallons as the number of residents per square mile doubles. These estimates suggest that if the average Northeastern household moved from living at one family per acre to five families per acre, then that family would consume 350 fewer gallons. These facts remind us that mass transit isn't the only way to lower gas consumption. If people lived in denser areas, they'd travel far fewer miles and burn much less gas, even if they still drove to work.

Public transportation emits carbon too, but most forms of public transit are a lot more energy efficient than driving vast distances in our own personal gas burners. For example, the New York City Transit system uses 42 million gallons of diesel fuel and 14.8 billion megawatts of electricity each year to deliver 2.6 billion trips to its riders. That works out to an average of 0.9 pounds of carbon dioxide per trip—a tenth as much as the nine pounds of carbon dioxide emitted in an average car trip.

Kahn and I predicted the amount of gas that an average family with about $60,000 of income would consume in every census tract and every metropolitan area in the country. While every other area in our sample was associated with more than 1,000 gallons of gas per year, the average household in the New York metropolitan area was connected with fewer than 850 gallons of gas per year. While people in the United States as a whole are more than fifteen times as likely to drive themselves to work as to use public transportation, New York City residents are more than twice as likely to take mass transit as to drive to work.

Throughout the country, big cities mean less driving. On average, when population doubles, per-household carbon dioxide emissions due to driving decline by almost a ton per year. Southern cities have particularly high driving levels, and over 75 percent more gasoline usage than New York. Sunbelt cities like Greenville, South Carolina, Nashville, Tennessee, and Oklahoma City were built at low densities and have widely dispersed employment, and their residents use the most gas.

In almost every metropolitan area, city dwellers consume a lot less gas than suburbanites. Predictably, some of the biggest city-suburb gaps are in older areas, like New York, where the average urban family consumes more than three hundred fewer gallons of gas per year than its suburban counterpart. But some of the largest gaps between cities and suburbs also occur in places like Atlanta and Nashville. It isn't that central Nashville or Atlanta has so little driving, but that people drive so much in their suburbs. These facts suggest that city density reduces carbon emissions in the older areas of the Northeast, but also in the newer areas that are growing fastest.

Cities are also greener than suburbs because urbanites use less electricity. Electrical appliances account for two thirds of residential energy use. The main factor that explains the difference in energy use among various metropolitan areas is summer heat. Everybody runs refrigerators and appliances, but air conditioning really drives the differences from place to place. The rise of the American Sunbelt in the postwar period owes much to the availability of cheap, cool air. Who would want to put up with Houston's ninety-nine 90-degree days a year without air conditioning?

America's lowest electricity-using metropolitan areas are in coastal California and the Northeast. San Francisco and San Jose have the coolest summers in our sample of metropolitan areas, and they're two of the places that use the least electricity. By contrast, the hot, humid cities of Houston, New Orleans, and Memphis lead the pack in electricity consumption. In these places, the summer months are almost unbearable without an artificial climate.

Warm Julys aren't the only force driving up electricity usage. Bigger, denser cities, where people own smaller homes, use less electricity. The average single-family detached home consumes 88 percent more electricity than the average apartment in a five-or-more-unit building. The average suburban household consumes 27 percent more electricity than the average urban household. When we standardize for income and family size, we find that central-city residents use less electricity in forty-four out of the forty-eight metropolitan areas that we analyzed. More centralized metropolitan areas, such as New York, Boston, and even Las Vegas, use less electricity than more sprawling places, like Dallas or Phoenix.

In warmer areas of the country, electricity is sometimes used for heating, but natural gas is America's primary source of warmth, and it is responsible for almost a fifth of residential carbon emissions. Home heating has actually gotten a lot greener over time. We started off burning wood, which emits plenty of carbon, and then moved on to coal, which darkened the skies of American cities until after World War II. Gradually cities started forcing people to switch away from coal, and luckily, just as coal was being phased out, natural gas from the American West became far more available (and George Mitchell made his fortune). Fuel oil, an older source of heat, still accounts for almost a tenth of residential carbon emissions, despite the fact that it is rarely used, because fuel oil emits much more carbon than natural gas.

Home heating emissions make the Snow Belt look less green than temperate California. Detroit and Grand Rapids, Michigan, lead our sample of metropolitan areas in natural gas consumption. Buffalo, Chicago, and Minneapolis are close behind. By contrast, Florida consumes hardly any natural gas. Miami is still pretty warm in January, even at night.

To form a total estimate of household carbon emissions, we just add together the emissions from driving, electricity, and heating, and add public transit. By now, it should be no surprise that cities are greener than suburbs.

But the differences between metropolitan areas are even larger than the differences between individual cities and their suburbs. Coastal California is by far the greenest part of the country. The Deep South is by far the brownest. The five greenest metropolitan areas in the country are San Diego, San Francisco, Los Angeles, San Jose, and Sacramento. The five places with the highest carbon emissions per home are Houston, Birmingham, Nashville, Memphis, and Oklahoma City. The gap between these two extremes is dramatic. A household in San Francisco emits 60 percent less carbon than its equivalent in Memphis.

Older places in the Northeast and Midwest lie at various points between these extremes. They use more electricity than California but less than Houston, and they use plenty of energy for heating. New York is one of the greener cities, because of its density. Detroit, being the Motor City, has much higher emissions.

The Unintended Consequences of Environmentalism

So how should we interpret all this data? Simply put, if we wanted to reduce emissions by changing our land-development policies, more Americans should live in denser, more urban environments. More Americans should move to coastal California and fewer should live in Texas. California is blessed with a splendid natural climate that doesn't require much cooling in the summer or heat in the winter. Living in Houston or Atlanta requires a lot more energy for habitability, so then why aren't more Americans living in California?

The answer certainly isn't overcrowding. California's coastal areas are remarkably open. The drive along Route 280 through the heart of Silicon Valley is like a drive through an open Eden. There are about 2 people living on each acre in Santa Clara County. Marin County, just north of the bay, has more than one-and-a-quarter acres per person. By contrast, Montgomery County in Maryland has about 3 people per acre. Cook County, Illinois, has almost 9 people per acre. Manhattan has 111 people per acre, and that isn't counting the vast crowd of workers that comes and goes each day.

Coastal California could house many millions more than it already does, but the growth in these coastal regions has fallen dramatically from its postwar heyday. Between 1950 and 1970, the population of Santa Clara County more than tripled, from fewer than three hundred thousand to more than one million. But between 1990 and 2008, Santa Clara County grew by only 17.8 percent, less than the national average, from 1.5 million to 1.76 million. Over the last seventeen years, Silicon Valley has been one of the most productive places on the planet, but its population growth has lagged behind the rest of the nation's.

Coastal California hasn't grown because it hasn't built much housing. Any area that doesn't build much won't grow much. Coastal California's construction declines don't reflect a lack of demand. In 2007, the National Association of Realtors median sales price passed $800,000 in both San Francisco and San Jose. Even after the crash, these places remain the two most expensive areas in the continental United States, with average housing prices around $600,000 in the second quarter of 2010. Prices in California are kept high by draconian limits on new construction, like the sixty-acre minimum lot sizes that can be found in Marin County. These rules are joined with a policy of pulling more and more land off the market as protected parks and wildlife areas. By 2000, one quarter of the land in the Bay Area has become permanently protected, that is, off limits to building.

Many environmentalists see the reduction of development in the San Francisco Bay region as a great triumph. The pioneers of the Save the Bay movement, which formed to block development around the water, have become iconic figures in American environmentalism. The *Friends of Mammoth* case, which imposed environmental reviews on all new California projects, is seen as a watershed victory. The advocates of California's growth limitations are often put forward as ecological heroes. But they're not.

The enemies of development in California are quick to point out that restricting construction is necessary because of the state's sparse water supplies. Yet California would have more than enough water for its citizens if it didn't use so much of it irrigating naturally dry farmland. California's cities and suburbs use about 8.7 million acre-feet of water each year. California agriculture gets subsidized water and uses 34 million acre-feet of water each year for irrigation. America is filled with wet regions that can raise crops. By redirecting water from farm areas to cities, California could easily provide enough water to sustain much higher density levels, which would reduce America's carbon footprint.

While limits on California's growth may make that state seem greener, they're making the country as a whole browner and increasing carbon emissions worldwide. Houston's developers should thank California's antigrowth movement. If they hadn't stopped building in coastal California, where incomes are high and the climate is sublime, then there wouldn't have been nearly as much demand for living in the less pleasant parts of the Sunbelt.

People who fight development don't get to choose the amount of new construction throughout the country; they only get to make sure it doesn't occur in their backyard. At the national level, a principle that could be called the law of conservation of construction appears to hold. When environmentalists stop development in green places, it will occur in brown places. By using ecological arguments to oppose growth, California environmentalists are actually ensuring that America's carbon footprint will rise, by pushing new housing to less temperate climates.

The 1970 California Environmental Quality Act was a pioneering piece of legislation, which mandated that any local government project have an environmental impact review before it went forward. In 1973, an environmentally activist California Supreme Court interpreted this act to mean not only projects undertaken by local governments, but also projects permitted by local government, which means pretty much any large construction in the state. In 2008, California's regulations generated 583 environmental impact reviews, considerably more than the 522 impact reviews that occurred nationwide in response to federal guidelines. These impact reviews add costs and delays to new construction, which ultimately make it even more expensive.

The great flaw of environmental impact reviews is their incompleteness. Each review only evaluates the impact of the project if it's approved, not the impact if it's denied and construction begins somewhere else, outside the jurisdiction of the California Supreme Court. The incompleteness of these reviews stacks the environmental deck against California construction and makes it seem as though it's always greener to stop new building. The full impact would note that permitting building in California would reduce construction somewhere else, such as the once pristine desert outside of Las Vegas. Assessing the full environmental cost of preventing construction in California would make that state's environmental policies look more brown than green.

Two Green Visions: The Prince and the Mayor

Environmentalism is hardly a tidy, well-ordered movement. In the United States, it includes the bird watchers of the Audubon Society and the activists of Greenpeace, the hikers of the Appalachian Trail and the drivers of Toyota hybrids. In Europe, the movement is even more successful and even broader. Any movement that diverse and that successful will inevitably attract individuals with wildly different worldviews, such as His Royal Highness, the Prince of Wales, and "Red" Ken Livingstone, the erstwhile Labour Party politician, who led London, first as head of the Greater London Council between 1981 and 1986 and then as London's first citywide mayor from 2000 to 2008. Livingstone has said that "climate change caused by CO_2 emissions" is "the single biggest problem facing humanity"; Prince Charles has declared climate change to be the "greatest threat to mankind." They're both doing their best to help the planet, but they share little else besides their views about mankind's "biggest threat."

The prince was born in 1948 in Buckingham Palace and promptly baptized by the archbishop of Canterbury. Livingstone was born three years earlier in Lambeth, the traditionally poor area of London that surrounds the Archbishop's Palace. Prince Charles received more formal education than any British king, going to elite private schools and Cambridge. Livingstone's education was spotty, and while still a teenager, he went to work as a lab technician, eventually, as the London *Sunday Times* reported, "cultivating tumors in the smaller rodents," before he was elected to the Lambeth City Council in 1971.

While Livingstone spent the 1970s rising in the London-Lambeth Labour Party, Prince Charles was being a dutiful royal, serving in the Royal Navy, flying jets and helicopters, and eventually commanding his own boat, HMS *Bronington*. A media explosion surrounded the young prince's Cinderella wedding in 1981 to Lady Diana Spencer. In the same year, Livingstone became head of the Greater London Council, which caused a tabloid known more for its Page Three pictures than for trenchant political analysis to blare the headline "Red Ken Crowned King of London." Half the world was desperate to see the Prince and Diana's marriage, but Ken Livingstone refused to attend.

In the 1980s, both men increased their involvement with urban planning. As "King of London," Livingstone's nascent environmentalism appeared in some areas but not others. Livingstone argued loud and long that low public-transit fares would keep people out of cars and reduce both congestion and pollution. He fought for more housing, but he opposed skyscrapers, especially Richard Rogers's plans for a "Berlin Wall" of high-rise buildings on the south side of the Thames. At the same time, Prince Charles began to establish his public persona as a patron of sustainable agriculture and a foe of modernism. The Prince of Wales is also Duke of Cornwall, and his Cornish estates provided an opportunity to push for organic farming and reject the high yields of genetically modified food. Just as Prince Charles likes more traditional farming, he likes traditional buildings. In 1984, he made headlines with a tough attack on modernist architecture he delivered in what was expected to be a perfunctory address to the Royal Institute of British Architects.

Prince Charles offered a nostalgic vision that "London before the last war must have had one of the most beautiful skylines of any great city." By contrast, a proposed modernist extension to the national gallery was "a monstrous carbuncle on the face of a much-loved and elegant friend." The prince wanted to know "Why has everything got to be vertical, straight, unbending, only at right angles—and functional?" He joined the fight against a proposed Mies van der Rohe–designed modernist tower next to London's magnificent eighteenth-century Mansion House. Prince Charles called the tower "a giant glass stump better suited to downtown Chicago." Richard Rogers was one of the many architects supporting the tower (so was my father), but the prince won, sort of. There would be no Miesian tower in London.

Prince Charles's fight for traditional British architecture continues unabated, as does his fight for his "model community" of Poundbury. In his agricultural estates in Cornwall, the prince is building his vision of an ideal English town, which has been described as looking like "an early Victorian market town, as if architecture stopped in 1830." His royal patronage has given a great boost to Leon Krier, Poundbury's planner, who is also one of the intellectual forces behind the New Urbanist movement. The New Urbanism "stand[s] for the restoration of existing urban centers and towns within coherent metropolitan regions, the reconfiguration of sprawling suburbs into communities of real neighborhoods and diverse districts, the conservation of natural environments, and the preservation of our built legacy."

Poundbury is considerably more conservationist than the New Urbanist communities of America, such as Seaside, Florida; Kentlands, Maryland; Breakaway, North Carolina; and the Disney Corporation's town of Celebration, Florida. These places do try to reduce car dependence, but their objectives seem as much social as they are environmental. In Celebration, 91 percent of people who leave their homes to work take cars. More people (64.5 percent) drive to work in Poundbury than in neighboring areas. Three quarters of Poundbury's residents drive on their shopping trips. These areas appeal not to the diehard urbanites of Livingstone's London, but to people who like the idea of a more traditional small town, with plenty of cars.

The houses in these areas are not small; hence they use plenty of energy. About 70 percent of the homes in Celebration are single-family, and only 17 percent of Poundbury's homes are apartments. The New Urbanist communities do have a higher concentration of condominiums than America as a whole, but they are still mostly full of traditional large homes that use lots of energy. For example, a quick look at Seaside, Florida, real estate for sale found houses between 2,000 and 3,800 square feet, a far cry from a 1,000-square-foot urban apartment. Kentlands, Maryland, another New Urbanist model, was similarly full of four- and five-bedroom homes that need plenty of air conditioning during humid Maryland summers.

While Prince Charles seems to long for a simpler, more agrarian world, Ken Livingstone's green vision combines sustainability and dynamic urban growth. When he became London's mayor, Livingstone took a dramatic step against driving. He initially required all drivers to pay £5 each time they entered an inner corridor of London; the charge later rose to £8. For forty years since William Vickrey introduced the idea, congestion charging has appealed to economists who think that people should pay for the social costs of their actions. One person's driving creates congestion for everyone, so a tax on driving is a good way to use roads more wisely. Ken Livingstone was fearless, as usual, and congestion charges appealed to him for reasons beyond the economists' customary love of efficiency. Livingstone saw congestion charging as a means of helping the environment by moving people out of cars and into subways. He also saw it as progressive legislation, as drivers tend to be rich and bus riders tend to be poor. By taxing drivers and spending the proceeds on public transit, Livingstone was playing to less wealthy supporters.

The congestion charge immediately had a dramatic impact on London's streets. There was a greater than 20 percent reduction in driving in the first two weeks. Overall, congestion dropped by 30 percent over the next two years, and public-transit usage boomed. Livingstone's pet policy helped make London more urban by favoring the trains and buses that are the modes of old urbanism, and he helped the environment in the process.

As mayor, Livingstone also came to see the virtues of high-rise construction in London. Despite the prince's opposition, London was starting to grow upward. The postmodernist Number 1 Poultry Building, which Prince Charles likened to a "1930s wireless set," rose on what would have been the site of the Mies tower. More significant, a Canadian development company was putting high-rises on the site of an old wharf. Their Canary Wharf development provided modern digs for London's financial services industry.

Livingstone's conversion from antigrowth advocate to supporter of scale reflected the broader perspective that came from leading a big city. Livingstone, like almost every other big-city mayor, wanted a larger tax base. Even if he didn't much like London's financiers, he recognized that their earnings would help him improve the lives of his poorer constituents. The fact that cities must compete in a globalized world can turn even the most antibusiness politician into an advocate of glossy high-rises, because those high-rises house the people whose taxes will pay for social programs. Livingstone also recognized that concentrating people in London would be good for the environment because they'd end up living in smaller homes and driving less often.

Prince Charles and Mayor Livingstone are both diehard greens. Ken Livingstone won the Climate Group's Low Carbon Champions Award. Prince Charles has also received environmental awards. Indeed, he created something of a furor when he flew his entourage of twenty across the ocean to pick up a Global Environmental Citizen Award from Harvard Medical School's Center for Health and the Global Environment.

But their visions of environmentalism are starkly different. The prince's is rural and traditional. He looks backward and hopes for a return to old ways of living and traditional structures. Livingstone's environmentalism is urban and radical. He imagines a bold future full of tall structures and mass transit. The modernist architect Richard Rogers chaired Livingstone's Architecture and Urbanism Unit. In the foreword to that committee's report, "Housing for a Compact City," Livingstone embraced higher-density building to protect London's Green Belt and other community open spaces. By contrast, Charles has condemned skyscrapers as "overblown phallic sculptures and depressingly predictable antennae that say more about an architectural ego than any kind of craftsmanship."

Which environmentalism will be more effective—Livingstone's big-city modernism or Prince Charles's agrarian utopianism? In principle, traditional rural communities are pretty green. If people don't heat their homes much, or travel much, and stick to traditional rural pursuits, then they'll use little carbon. On the other hand, you just can't make a city run without a certain amount of electricity for elevators and public transportation. If people really could be counted upon to act like fifteenth-century rural peasants, then rural ecotowns could be extremely green.

But people don't want to live like medieval serfs. If they end up living in a low-density area, they'll drive a lot, and they'll want big houses that are comfortably cooled and heated. In cities, however, people end up sharing common public spaces, like restaurants, bars, and museums. The urban model is green when used by real people. The data shows that, and we know why: High costs of land restrict private space, and density makes car usage far less attractive. Urban living is sustainable sustainability. Rural ecotowns are not.

The Biggest Battle: Greening India and China

Higher-density construction in the United States and Europe will reduce carbon emissions, but the most important battles over urban development in the coming years will be waged in India and China. About half of America's homes in 2000 were built between 1970 and 2000, so let's assume that about half of America's housing stock thirty years from now will also be new. If every prodensity effort is wildly successful in the United States, emissions from driving and powering these new houses might fall by 50 percent. That would be a great achievement, reducing America's household carbon emissions by 25 percent and America's total emissions by 10 percent. Yet from this momentous shift, world carbon emissions would fall by only 2 percent. That calculation is not meant to excuse inaction, but rather to make the point that America is something of a sideshow in the long-run battle against climate change. America has trillions of dollars of infrastructure built around the car, and any developed country changes slowly.

India and China are changing fast, and they have a lot more people than America does. If carbon emissions in India and China rose to American per capita levels, the world's carbon consumption would increase by 139 percent, even if their population stayed the same. The biggest environmental benefits from supporting higher-density development in the United States may well be in helping persuade the Chinese and Indians to build up rather than out.

Today, the United States is the world's second biggest carbon emitter; on average, Americans emit about 20 metric tons of carbon dioxide per person per year. Canadians, who also drive a lot, emit almost the same amount per person. Western Europeans are a lot greener. The English emit a little less than 10 tons of carbon dioxide per year; Italians are responsible for about 8 tons; and the French, with all their nuclear energy, produce only about 7 tons of carbon dioxide per person annually.

The Chinese are producing almost 5 tons of carbon dioxide per person per year; the Indians, 1 ton. If the Chinese per capita carbon emissions rise to American levels, this would lead to an extra 20 billion tons of carbon emitted every year, increasing world carbon emissions by 69 percent. But if energy consumption in India and China levels off at the output of France, world emissions would rise by about 30 percent—an increase that could conceivably be offset by carbon cutbacks in the United States and elsewhere. So it's essential that we encourage these countries to keep their carbon emissions at the more modest European levels rather than emulating current American energy use and development patterns.

Today China's carbon emissions are largely industrial. Like the black smoke that once surrounded Pittsburgh or Manchester, they're the by-product of a great industrial power on the rise. So far, China's households are remarkably parsimonious energy users. Matthew Kahn, Rui Wang, Siqi Zheng, and I did a city-by-city analysis of China's household carbon emissions, similar to the one that we did for the United States. While the typical household in the Washington, D.C., area generates 43 tons of carbon dioxide per year, the typical Beijing household emits only 3.997 tons—and Beijing is one of the brownest places in China. In more than 60 percent of the Chinese cities we examined, carbon dioxide emissions per household ran at 2 tons a year or less. Household emissions in Daqing, China's oil capital and brownest city, are one fifth of emissions in San Diego, America's greenest city.

Chinese household emissions are driven by home heating and electricity. As countries develop, warmth comes first, long before air conditioning. The heaviest carbon-emitting places in the United States are hot and humid, but the heaviest emitters in China today are cold places, because China heats but it doesn't yet cool. While half of U.S. household emissions reflect personal transportation, only a tenth of Chinese emissions currently come from cars. The relative paucity of driving and air conditioning in China keeps current emission levels low, but we can hardly expect an increasingly prosperous Chinese population to forgo the luxuries that Americans take for granted. If anything, the case for air conditioning in India seems even stronger.

A generation ago, both China and India were solidly rural. They did little environmental damage because, like all poor places, they used little energy. Over a fifty-year period, however, they're achieving the same industrial and urban transformation that took centuries in the West. The result is an inevitable explosion in energy consumption, which is today helping to drive up oil prices and in the future could produce extraordinary increases in carbon emissions.

It may be tempting to wish that China and India would just stay committed to traditional agriculture, but subjecting 2.4 billion people to the deprivations of permanent poverty is no solution for climate change. The agricultural past of China and India meant endemic infant mortality and starvation. Permanent poverty means that billions will be subject to every plague that humankind can carry without the help of high-tech medicine. Poverty is a breeding ground for dictatorship, so if India and China stay poor, the rest of us will face the military risks associated with powerful, dictatorial neighbors. There is, however, a middle way that combines prosperity and growth with fewer environmental risks. That path involves high-density urban living, not the cars of American exurbs.

Growth patterns in India and China offer both hopeful and disturbing signs. On the plus side, the great cities of both nations are enormously dense.

Mumbai has more than fifty thousand people per square mile, about double the density of New York City. Kolkata and Bangalore are above twenty thousand per square mile. Shenzhen, the rapidly growing metropolis in mainland China across the water from Hong Kong, has more than fifteen thousand people per square mile. These densities fit well with buses and trains and elevators but make car usage practically impossible. The world will be safer if China's future involves hyperdense places made more comfortable with better public transportation and high-rise residences.

But there are also warning signs. Shanghai and Beijing, with their 20 million and 17 million inhabitants respectively, are vast places about one tenth as dense as New York City and less than half as dense (about 2,600 people per square mile) as Los Angeles. Car usage in both India and China is soaring. Chinese car ownership hit 60 million vehicles in 2009, with an annual rate of increase of over 30 percent. A few more 30 percent years, and China could have 500 million cars by 2020. Meanwhile, India's Tata Group made headlines by producing a $2,500 car, and Tata's cars could put a billion Indians behind a wheel, if they can handle the traffic jams. A billion Indian drivers will emit a lot of carbon.

Seeking Smarter Environmentalism

There is a powerful whiff of hypocrisy associated with energy-mad Americans—and I'm part of this group—trying to convince Asians to conserve more. One distinguished economist likened it to a "nation of SUV drivers trying to tell a nation of bicyclists not to drive mopeds." My awkward suburban life is certainly no model of green living. The only way the West can earn any moral authority on global warming is to first get its own house in order. As long as America leads the developed world in per capita carbon emissions, we'll never be able to convince China and India and the rest of the developing world to do anything other than emulate our own energy-intensive lifestyles.

The West also needs to embrace a smarter form of environmentalism. In the first phase of environmentalism, when the objective was just to make people care about nature, the exact policy prescription was less important than raising public consciousness. Today the stakes are higher. We cannot endorse every land conservation plan no matter how misguided or counterproductive. We need instead to focus on those proposals that will have a meaningful impact on climate change.

Smart environmentalism requires thinking through the inadvertent side effects of different environmental policies and recognizing those that actually do more harm than good. The conservationists who keep the Bay Area free from new construction are preventing development in the greenest part of America. The law of conservation of construction then means that building will consequently increase in America's browner areas. The alleged environmentalists who suffer from the Lorax fallacy and fight high-density development close to urban cores in order to preserve local green spaces are ensuring that development will move to the exurban fringe and that people will drive more.

Smart environmentalism needs to embrace incentives. Ken Livingstone's congestion charge showed the power of using prices to get people out of their cars. This can be done in other cities. Throughout the world, we can adopt a global emissions tax that charges people for the damage done by their carbon emissions. The actual size of the tax needs to be worked out by the experts who can best gauge the true cost of carbon emissions, but the basic principle is one we should all embrace: Unless we charge people for the carbon they emit, they won't emit less. Opponents of big government understandably worry that this type of policy will just turn into an added source of revenue for the government, but this worry can be reduced with a public commitment to rebating the tax to citizens as an energy dividend, much as the state of Alaska pays each of its citizens an annual dividend from oil revenues.

Richer countries must also offer incentives for poorer countries to use less energy. We can lecture the Chinese about being more French in their energy usage, but our lectures will fall on deaf ears unless we put some of our own resources on the table. The political hurdles facing this type of transfer—you might call it "cash for no oil"—are enormous. I can already hear the isolationists screaming. But the stakes are also large. If the developed world can subsidize more fuel-efficient technology in the developing world, or better yet, subsidize the development of new fuel-efficient technologies that would then be given away free to developing countries, those countries may be able to live better lives with a more moderate increase in energy use. Yet fuel efficiency is unlikely to be the only answer, because Jevons's paradox reminds us that as engines and appliances get more efficient, they will also be used more.

If the future is going to be greener, then it must be more urban. Dense cities offer a means of living that involves less driving and smaller homes to heat and cool. Maybe someday we'll be able to drive and cool our homes with almost no carbon emissions, but until then, there is nothing greener than blacktop.

For the sake of humanity and our planet, cities are—and must be—the wave of the future. There are several models of urban success that will carry us into that future. The next chapter discusses the types of cities that will thrive in this century and beyond.

CHAPTER 9

How Do Cities Succeed?

T olstoy may have been right that "Happy families are all alike; every unhappy family is unhappy in its own way," but among cities, failures seem similar while successes feel unique. Someone wandering through Leipzig's boarded-up neighborhoods could very well think she was in Detroit. Empty houses give off a similarly depressing feeling whether they're in England or Ohio. But no one could ever confuse Bangalore with Boston or Tokyo with Chicago. Successful cities always have a wealth of human energy that expresses itself in different ways and defines its own idiosyncratic space.

The air-conditioned skyways that connect the shimmering towers of downtown Hong Kong are full of the kinds of chain stores that can be found on several continents, and yet few people would think they were anyplace other than Hong Kong. Tokyo and Singapore also boast tall towers and chain stores, but they bear no resemblance to either Hong Kong or each other. While Hong Kong is decidedly multicultural, Tokyo is profoundly Japanese, with special sensibilities that are so hard for outsiders to understand. Singapore is, if anything, even more open to Westerners than Hong Kong, but its streets are less crowded, and its rules are far stricter. All three cities have great food, but the cuisines are also quite different. No one would confuse raw tuna with Cantonese duck or the multiethnic mixture that makes eating in Singapore such a delight.

But all successful cities do have something in common. To thrive, cities must attract smart people and enable them to work collaboratively. There is no such thing as a successful city without human capital. Today, especially in the developed world, skilled people have usually been well educated in traditional schools—although their most important knowledge is usually acquired after graduation. At other times, and in poorer places today, human capital is more likely to come in the form of intelligent, energetic entrepreneurs who, like Henry Ford or James Watt, received little formal education. The best cities have a mix of skills and provide pathways for those who start with less to end with more.

But different cities have found different ways to attract talent. In some cases, either raw political power or sensible probusiness policies attract skilled people. Tokyo became one of the largest cities in the world in the seventeenth century when the Tokugawa shogunate made it Japan's de facto capital. Three hundred years later, it continues to attract that country's best and brightest. Hong Kong and Singapore have thrived by establishing themselves as bastions of economic freedom and the rule of law in an often disorderly part of the world.

In other cities, like Boston, a long tradition of higher education continues to bear rewards. In Minneapolis and Atlanta, local universities also serve as anchors for their urban economies. In other areas, skilled people come for the quality of life—the pleasures that define Paris and that a sheikh hopes will boost Dubai. Finally, a city with enough other attractions can, as Chicago has, gain an advantage by lowering barriers to new construction so that it becomes a cheaper place to live than its competition.

In this chapter, I review the paths that different cities have taken to success. Not only is there no one formula toward urban eminence, but also the sources of success are often highly nation specific. Certainly Detroit could do very well if it—like Tokyo—became the capital of a highly centralized country with an abundance of nationally funded universities, but how exactly can that unsurprising piece of information help Mayor Bing? The Rust Belt can benefit more by a nuanced understanding of the idiosyncratic sources of Tokyo's or Singapore's strength, so as to guard against blind imitation and draw the locally appropriate lessons from far-flung urban success stories.

The Imperial City: Tokyo

In 1590, the warlord Hideyoshi unified Japan. When he died, his ally Tokugawa Ieyasu replaced him as master of Japan, and his new castle home, Edo, became the country's effective capital. The powerless emperor continued to live amid the cherry blossoms of Kyoto, but the real business of government went on in the city that came to surround the Tokugawa shoguns.

The shoguns' power over Japan was much greater than that wielded by contemporary European monarchs in their own countries. As much as half of Japan's rice revenue ran through the shoguns' hands. The more centralized a nation's government, the larger its capital city, because people are attracted to power as ants are to picnics. Well-functioning democracies manage to provide political rights even to people who live far away from the corridors of power; dictatorships generally do not. As a result, the largest cities in dictatorships, which are almost invariably the capitals, contain, on average, 35 percent of their countries' urban population. The largest cities in stable democracies contain only about 23 percent of their countries' urban population. By the end of the eighteenth century, Edo had a million people, making it one of the two or three largest cities in the world.

The Tokugawa shoguns were ousted in 1868 as the Meiji Restoration reestablished imperial power, but that did little to reduce Edo's size. The Meiji emperor moved his court from Kyoto to Edo, renaming it Tokyo, or Eastern Capital. The ancient shogun's castle became the imperial palace, as it remains today. From 1868 onward, Tokyo has been the political center of a successful, politically centralized country, and that ensures the city's success.

After the restoration, Japan grew as it opened itself to trade with the West. Even before Meiji, Japan seems to have been well educated, and that helped make its transition to industrialization fast and effective. Since 1945, Japan has been one of the world's great economic success stories, even when taking into account its "lost decade" of economic stagnation in the 1990s.

Even in 1960, when Japan was still poor, its people were remarkably well educated. At that time, the average income in Japan was lower than in Argentina or Chile and about half the average income in France. But the average Japanese male had 7.4 years of schooling, substantially more than in France, the Netherlands, or Spain. That education was the springboard for the country's economic takeoff, and it ensured that Tokyo would be a skilled city. The powerful capital was bound to attract more than its share of Japan's stars.

In the 1980s, when Japan seemed endowed with perpetual economic growth, experts attributed its success to any and all of its idiosyncrasies, including the government's aggressive support for particular companies and entire industries, like electronics and automobiles. Japan's Ministry of International Trade and Industry (MITI) had long financed and otherwise supported many firms. But despite the fact that MITI employed far more experts than any city or state economic development agency could hope to hire, it usually picked losers rather than winners. Industrial policy is not always a mistake—I'll discuss Singapore's success later—but MITI's failures stand as a warning to urban leaders who want to play venture capitalist. Japan's economic strength reflects the skill of its workers and entrepreneurs, not the expertise of its government's economic planners.

However, the power of the government's Tokyo-centered bureaucracies helps explain why the nation's capital became so large. It was useful for firms to be physically close to MITI if they wanted the agency's support. It's still valuable to be near the Japanese Diet and the vast bureaucracy. As in other highly centralized nations, like France, the most talented young Japanese often start their careers working for a government agency like MITI, gaining contacts that serve them well throughout their lives. Talent clusters around power, and Tokyo became a vast agglomeration of politics, business, and pleasure.

Tokyo's physical structure reflects this reality. At the very center of the city lies the emperor's palace, which is surrounded by acres of land inaccessible to lesser mortals for all but one day each year. Outside the palace grounds are vast governmental buildings—the brains of the nation's sizable public sector. The business districts and Tokyo's urban playgrounds, like the Ginza shopping sector, are a little farther out. The city is Washington and New York rolled into one.

But Tokyo's size is manageable, and in many ways it provides a model for many of Asia's growing megacities. Japan's bureaucrats may not be able to beat private venture capitalists, but they wisely allowed Tokyo to grow tall, and they built a superb public transit system. The streets are clean and safe. The silk curtain of Japan's insular culture remains relatively difficult for outsiders to part, which ensures that the city will never rival New York or London as a mecca for worldwide talent, but Japan has an abundance of smart, well-educated people. As long as they keep coming to Tokyo for proximity to each other and the nation's government, Tokyo will remain one model of a successful city.

The Well-Managed City: Singapore and Gaborone

Much of the world suffers under awful governments, and that provides an edge for those cities that are administered well. Some of the most prominent examples of that fact are the former outposts of the British East India Company, Hong Kong and Singapore. While Tokyo grew great because it was the center of a growing country, Hong Kong and Singapore have been successful because they were places apart, politically separate from the large nations next to them. They succeeded by offering businesses a better government than nearby states, with fairly applied rules that favored investment. Their political institutions attracted the human capital that made them great.

The success of the British East India Company also owed much to its ability to attract and empower talent, like Thomas Stamford Raffles. Raffles was the son of a slave trader who was born at sea off the coast of Jamaica. His father died bankrupt when Raffles was fourteen, and Raffles joined the East India Company as a clerk. Ten years later, he went to Malaysia as assistant secretary to the company's local governor, and he immersed himself in all things Malay. After helping lead the British conquest of Java during the Napoleonic wars, Raffles was given authority in Indonesia, where he displayed an odd but quintessentially English combination of impressive amateur scholarship, moral mission, and buccaneering ambition.

Raffles's *History of Java*, written in 1817, still reads well. He was passionate about flora and fauna, keeping a sun bear cub as a pet. He later became the first president of the London Zoo. Despite his father's occupation, Raffles banned trading slaves, as well as opium. Most important, he negotiated the deal that gave his employer the right to build a trading post on an island named Singapore, or Lion City, off the tip of the Malay Peninsula.

Over the next 140 years, except for its occupation by the Japanese during World War II, Singapore was a shiny sapphire in Great Britain's crown. The island's location, in the straits between Malaysia and Sumatra, made it an ideal port at the center of Asia's sea lanes. That port and the rule of law enforced by England attracted tradesmen of the Chinese diaspora who had fled their own country's chaos.

In 1850, China's Guangdong province exploded in rebellion, and 25 million people may have died in the bloody conflagration that followed. Twelve years later, while the war was still ongoing, Lee Bok Boon left Guangdong for the safety of the British-managed Straits Settlements, which included Singapore. His family prospered, and his great grandson Lee Kuan Yew was educated at Raffles College in Singapore and then Cambridge. When the Japanese occupied Singapore, Lee became a teenage entrepreneur selling tapioca-based glue. After World War II, he worked as a lawyer and became a leader in the fight for independence from Britain. Initially, Singapore separated from England to become part of Malaysia, but in 1965, irreconcilable differences between the puritanical, intellectually ferocious Lee and the pleasure-loving, aristocratic leader of Malaysia led Singapore to become an independent city-state.

As the island's first prime minister, Lee faced vast challenges. His 217-square-mile domain had a population of 1.9 million but no natural sources of food or water, and it was surrounded by two hostile giants: Malaysia and Indonesia. If Raffles himself had been betting on the success of the tiny city, he would have demanded long odds. But it turns out that a city on its own without any rural hinterland can not only survive but thrive.

In 1965, incomes in Singapore were about one fifth of those in the United States. Yet over the next forty years, the city-state's economy averaged more than 8 percent growth per year, among the highest rates in the world. In the 1960s, Singapore was a poor shantytown where indoor toilets were a rarity. Today, Singapore is a glistening First World city with one of the highest per capita gross domestic products on earth.

Singapore's success reflects the remarkable ability of a dense agglomeration of smart people to innovate and thrive when blessed with a remarkably competent public sector. Lee followed an incongruous but extremely successful combination of free-market capitalism and state-led industrialization. He inherited Raffles's penchant for paternalism, subsidizing savings, fining people for misbehavior like spitting, and heavily taxing alcohol. Singapore is happy to profit by attracting foreign gamblers to a massive new casino complex, but it doesn't encourage its own citizens to bet. They must pay more than $70 just to enter the casino.

Singapore—like Japan—invested in education. In 1960, the average adult in Singapore had only three years of schooling, less than the average adult in

Lesotho or Paraguay and less than half the Japanese figure. By 1995, Singapore's thirteen-year-olds led the world in the Test of International Math and Science, and Singapore has routinely been a top performer since then. Those test scores reflect a national commitment to home-grown human capital, but Singapore's skills also reflect an influx of foreign talent drawn by sensible policies and reliable legal institutions.

Singapore's industrial policy seems to have been more successful than that of Japan, probably because Lee Kwan Yew was playing educator more than venture capitalist. By moving his population into garment manufacturing, then electronics, and then biomedical production, Lee pushed them to acquire new skills.

In places like Ireland and Israel, factions have wasted decades fighting over land. Singapore's success illustrates the irrelevance of acreage. The city-state grew wealthy not just despite its lack of land, but probably even because it had so little space. Precisely because Singapore had so few natural resources, Lee had to adopt sensible policies that would attract international capital. A large literature now documents the perverse tendency of natural resource windfalls to harm countries by allowing corrupt, inept, or destructive politicians and policies to endure.

Much of the Third World has long been mired in corruption. Lee understood that First World investors wanted rule of law, not backroom bribery, and he lifted Singapore out of the Third World by giving them just that. Lee protected judicial independence. To keep his bureaucrats honest, he gave them high salaries and even higher penalties for malfeasance. Inspector Clouseau in *The Pink Panther* implausibly explains his larcenous wife's expensive furs by saying that she is very frugal with the housekeeping. In Singapore, Madame Clouseau's spending would be enough to convict the inspector, for an extravagant lifestyle is sufficient to prove a public official's guilt. "Clubber" Williams, the New York police officer with the yacht and country home, would never have been able to get off by claiming to be a successful speculator in Japanese real estate.

Singapore's rule of law has long been complemented by excellent infrastructure, particularly its port. The World Bank rates Singapore as having the world's best logistics for trade and transport. Good infrastructure and the rule of law helped lure foreigners who brought their skills to the island, and Singapore makes it especially easy for them to come by maintaining a superb airport and national airline.

Singapore attracts expatriates, in part, with a quality of life that is remarkably high, given its minute land area, absence of natural resources, and sweltering location right on the equator. While New York City could readily import water from upstate via the Croton Aqueduct, Singapore has no hinterland and inherently lacks water. Until recently, it had to import much of its water from Malaysia, but it has overcome this problem by building desalination plants and a $3.65 billion Deep Tunnel Sewerage System, which was named Water Project of the Year in 2009 because of its "contribution to water technology and environmental protection." The system runs for thirty miles, sixty-six feet or more below ground, removing sewage and then recycling the wastewater.

You might expect traffic jams in the world's second most densely populated nation, but Singapore's streets are fluid because it adopted congestion pricing in 1975. Lee Kwan Yew's initially simple system has constantly evolved, and today toll-collecting arches electronically charge cars throughout the city. Every car must have a transponder attached to a source of funds, and as a result, driving around this dense Asian city is easy. Buses move quickly on the uncongested roads. For longer distances, the city's rail network is safe and fast. Commute times run around thirty-five minutes, despite the fact that housing is often far away from the city center.

Singapore's streets are safe, clean, and often tree lined. Lee Kwan Yew understood that the Lion City could keep its green space only by building up, and as of 2009, forty-two of its buildings rise above 490 feet, more than triple the number in either London or Paris. Americans visiting Singapore can be forgiven for wistfully wondering why our own cities don't seem so well managed.

The success of Botswana's capital, Gaborone, in southern Africa, is less extreme than Singapore's, but it may be even more remarkable, given the troubles that have afflicted so many of its neighbors. The two cities have both relied upon rigorous management to rise above the squalor and corruption that typify so many cities in the developing world. When Botswana became independent from Great Britain in 1966, it was one of the poorest places on earth. Over the next thirty-five years, it may have experienced the second-fastest GDP growth of any country, and it is now one of the two or three most prosperous nations in sub-Saharan Africa. Gaborone was founded in 1965, but it now has around two hundred thousand people, about a tenth of the country's population.

Botswana's success rests on good governance and natural resources. The country's first president, Seretse Khama, who led the country for fourteen years, was a traditional tribal chief and an Oxford-trained lawyer. Like Lee Kwan Yew, Khama fought corruption, kept taxes low, and protected property rights. In much of Africa, gifts of nature like Botswana's diamonds have led to civil war, but Botswana has used its natural resources to fund investments in physical and human capital. Between 1965 and 2000, the average years of schooling in Botswana increased from 1.34 to 5.4 years, which makes it one of the best-educated places in sub-Saharan Africa.

Gaborone's growth has paralleled Botswana's, increasing more than tenfold between 1971 and 2001. Its modest, modernist skyline was built at the country's edge, next to the railway line that leads to Pretoria. Its public transportation functions well, and it is well linked to the outside world. And Gaborone is home to two of the campuses of the University of Botswana, the country's primary source of higher education.

Like much of Africa, Gaborone has suffered terribly from AIDS, but the government's response to the plague—delivering free antiretroviral drugs to everyone—has been humane and moderately effective, raising the life expectancy substantially for those with HIV. No one is going to confuse Gaborone with Paris, but it is a striking success among African cities, primarily because its government is effective. In the world's poorest places, success above all reflects decent political institutions and investment in education, and that's what has made Gaborone a well-functioning city.

The Smart City: Boston, Minneapolis, and Milan

Singapore and Gaborone are imperfect models for cities that are neither independent states nor national capitals. They also can't serve as examples for places in regions where decent economic policies are the norm. Singapore succeeded, in part, by investing in education and by choosing economic policies that would positively differentiate itself from its neighbors. No American, European, Indian, or Chinese city has that much control. In larger countries, economic policies are determined mostly at the national level, not the municipal level. Generally speaking, America and Europe have a relatively well-established rule of law, so no one place is going to stand out too much in that arena. The ability of any city within a large country to determine its education level is also more limited, for migrants will generally be educated elsewhere.

Indeed, historical accident plays a large role in determining which American cities are the best educated, and in many cases, the most successful. Most of the differences in college achievement in 2000 can be explained, in a statistical sense, by education levels in 1940. If less than 5 percent of an area's adult population had a college degree in 1940, then, on average, less than 19 percent of that area's population had a college degree in 2000. If more than 5 percent of an area's population had a college degree in 1940, then, on average, 29 percent had a college degree in 2000. We can see such effects even if we look much further back into history. Boston, like New York, has staged a remarkable comeback since the 1970s, a rebirth that owes as much to decisions made in the 1630s as to any recent policies.

Boston was founded by John Winthrop and his friends for largely religious motives. Winthrop came to the New World because "It will be a service to the Church of great consequence to carry the Gospell into those parts of the world, to helpe on the coming of the fullness of the Gentiles, & to raise a Bulwork against the kingdom of AntiChrist which the Jesuits labour to rear up in those parts." The anti-Jesuit hysteria of Winthrop and his companions does them no credit, but their fear-filled competition with Rome was the starting point for Boston's success in education.

Like many Protestants, the early Bostonians believed that reading the Bible was the surest means of knowing God's will. They saw education as a key brick in that "Bulwork against the kingdom of AntiChrist" and founded the Boston Latin School in 1635. The next year, they allocated £400, more than half of the colony's tax revenues in 1635, for a college. Another £375 and four hundred books came from the estate of John Harvard, a Cambridge-educated Puritan minister. These investments made Massachusetts "a federation of parishes made up of laity who were devotees of the religion of the book: possibly the most literate society then existing in the world."

Boston's human capital mattered because the city and its region had little worth exporting. New England's climate is very similar to that of old England, so Boston couldn't send much overseas that the English couldn't get more cheaply closer to home. Yet Bostonians wanted to buy European manufactured goods, like guns and Bibles. In its early years, Boston operated as a sort of colonial-era Ponzi scheme: the first wave of immigrants sold basic survival items, like food and clothing, to the next wave of immigrants, who, like John Harvard himself, came over with money.

The problem with Ponzi schemes is that they require eternal exponential growth, and Boston's growth stalled when the English Civil War established a Protestant commonwealth in the old country. Boston's citizenry then tried a lot of different moneymaking experiments, like ironworks and printing presses, but its first reinvention owes more to luck than skill. In 1647, a famine hit the rich sugar colonies of the West Indies. The planters sent boats north looking for food, and one found its way into Boston harbor. It started the triangle trade that made Boston's fortune during the Colonial era. The city exported basic commodities south to the cash colonies, where land and slaves were too valuable to waste on producing food and wood. Those colonies exported sugar and tobacco to the Old World. Manufactured goods were exported to Boston, which could buy them with the money made from selling food and wood to the Caribbean.

Boston's first-mover advantage in this triangle trade didn't last forever. New York had a better river and was closer to the South; Philadelphia was surrounded by richer farmland. Boston faltered again, and then reinvented itself again in the early nineteenth century. The same improvements in ship technology that established New York as the hub of transatlantic travel made it possible for Bostonian mariners to create a global trade network. Faster trips and longer journeys decreased the relative cost of starting in Boston and increased the value of the city's oceangoing human capital, built up over centuries of seafaring. The city had top-notch sailors and merchants, who set up trading networks in places as far away as China and South Africa.

But all that sail-specific human capital lost its value with the rise of steamships, and in the midnineteenth century, Boston had to reinvent itself yet again, this time around manufacturing. A Harvard-educated scion of a shipping family, Francis Cabot Lowell, had traveled to England in 1810 and brought an understanding of Manchester's power looms back to the Boston area. Lowell's mills were powered by rivers outside the city, but as engines got smaller, factories moved within city limits.

In the nineteenth century, the area's intellectual establishment flourished alongside its resurgent economy, and various elements in Boston's vibrant religious mosaic founded new colleges: Tufts by Universalists in 1852, Boston College by Jesuits in 1863, Boston University by Methodists in 1871, and Wellesley by a lawyer-turned-lay-preacher in 1875. Even more portentous, new institutions like the Lawrence Scientific School, at Harvard, and MIT, a land-grant college, were being formed to transmit technical knowledge.

In the twentieth century, the advantages of rail and urban factories evaporated in many cities, and by the 1970s, Boston was a hollowed-out hull. Real estate was priced far below construction costs. Ethnic strife, epitomized by an epic battle over school busing, tore the city apart. Yet Boston, like New York, managed to reinvent itself again, and this time the reinvention relied heavily on educational institutions built up over centuries.

Boston's postindustrial success has been built on engineering, computers, financial services, management consulting, and biotechnology—all education-oriented industries. A young MIT engineer, Vannevar Bush, partnered with his college roommate to create the American Appliance Company, which became Raytheon, which has spent the last eighty-five years working on the commercial applications of cutting-edge science, especially missiles. Raytheon's current headquarters in the old watch town of Waltham looks across the Cambridge Reservoir to Route 128, a technology corridor that once rivaled Silicon Valley as a computer hub. In the 1950s and 1960s, engineers from MIT and Harvard created companies like Wang Laboratories and Digital Equipment Corporation (DEC), which located throughout greater Boston and competed with IBM for a share of the growing computer industry. At their height, Wang had 30,000 employees and DEC had over 120,000. Even before Wang and DEC went out of business, economist AnnaLee Saxenian at Berkeley foretold the decline of Boston's computer industry, arguing that its firms in their isolated office parks had lost the edge that comes from urban density.

Luckily, Boston was generating plenty of new technologies to offset the demise of the computer industry. Like New York, Boston has long been an innovator in financial services, establishing the first business trusts in 1827 and the first investment trusts, or closed-end mutual funds, as early as the 1890s. The most successful of all the Boston funds, Fidelity Investments, was long led by Edward C. Johnson II, a bow-tied product of Exeter, Harvard College, and Harvard Law School. His vision for Fidelity included risky investments, selling funds to a mass market, and above all, making a fetish out of serious stock research, all of which have become hallmarks of America's finance industry.

Boston also saw the birth of management consulting in 1886 when an MIT chemist, Arthur D. Little, started his own firm to do freelance scientific research. Over the past 120 years, the firm can boast of many innovations, from high-altitude oxygen masks to computerized technologies for inventory control and American Airlines' pioneering SABRE reservation system. Even more important, Arthur D. Little was a training ground for smart people like Jack Treynor and Fischer Black, and it created spin-offs, like the Boston Consulting Group, which then spawned its own spin-offs like Bain and Company.

The Boston region has long been a hotbed of biomedical research. Harvard Medical School teachers were performing autopsies in a small chapel in Harvard Yard, where I often teach, before America had a constitution. But treating a city's own citizens generally can't generate enough revenue to fund future innovations, so for medical knowledge to create urban success, the city had to figure out ways to "export" health. Boston exports its skills by drawing non-Bostonians to its hospitals for treatment, just as non-Bostonians flock to the region's universities. Boston also exports its biomedical expertise more directly, by creating and selling new health technologies.

Boston Scientific, which started in Watertown, was an early pioneer in tiny medical devices, and the region has since spawned a slew of biomedical research companies, like Biogen and Genzyme, which take advantage of the area's human capital. Foreign firms, like Novartis, have also come to Cambridge for its skilled workers. Novartis's Cambridge office is located in the former home of the New England Confectionary Company, maker of Necco Wafers. There was a time when urban economists thought that Cambridge could never survive the decline of its candy industry. They underestimated the ability of skilled cities to reinvent themselves.

Many might also have written off Minneapolis, which lost 30 percent of its population between 1950 and 1980 and hardly seemed like a natural candidate for urban renaissance. The city's winters make Boston seem balmy, and the advantages that once came from its riverside location became largely irrelevant after World War II. But Minneapolis, like Boston and New York, has come back. In 2009, per capita personal income in the Minneapolis metropolitan area was $45,750, making it the highest-earning metropolitan area in the Midwest and the twenty-fifth highest in the country.

The secret of the city's success is education: 47.4 percent of the city's adults have a college degree, and 37.5 percent of the Minneapolis area's adults have a college degree, making it the seventh-best-educated metropolitan area with more than a million people in America. The Scandinavian Lutherans who originally settled the region brought with them a belief in learning, but most of all, Minneapolis's highly educated population reflects its land-grant college, the University of Minnesota. The city's most striking economic success stories have some link to that school.

Medtronic, which earns $14.6 billion in annual revenues and has thirty-eight thousand employees, was formed in 1949 when a graduate student in electrical engineering at the University of Minnesota partnered with his brother-in-law to make medical devices in a garage. The company's early success reflected, in part, connections with people like Walt Lillehei, a University of Minnesota professor and a pioneer in open-heart surgery, who saw the need for a small, battery-powered pacemaker and turned to Medtronic to whip one up. Minneapolis's megaretailer, Target, owes much of its success to Bob Ulrich, another University of Minnesota graduate, who helped create the chain's blend of logistics and style. Target's slightly more highbrow alternative to big-box competitors like Walmart and Kmart seems natural for the sophisticated Ulrich, a collector of African art who has spent a fortune endowing a Museum of Musical Instruments.

Milan is another former manufacturing giant that has come roaring back in the postindustrial age, and education has been part of its success. In the eighteenth century, Empress Maria Theresa initiated a series of school reforms (paid for with confiscated Jesuit wealth) that reinvigorated education around Milan and the nearby University of Pavia, which then trained two mathematicians who went on to lead education in Italy at the time of reunification. They then founded advanced schools, such as Milan's Polytechnic Institute, or Politecnico, and the academy that would later become the University of Milan. The Politecnico was worldly, modeled on German industrial schools, and became an incubator for entrepreneurs, like the rubber baron Giovanni Battista Pirelli.

Pirelli was among the first graduates of the Politecnico. His stellar performance won him a 3,000 lire prize, which paid for a tour of Europe to learn about a "new or scarcely diffused industry in Italy"—the use of rubber. Pirelli visited European factories, inspecting machinery and learning modern management practices, using his education to import ideas into Italy. Today Pirelli may be best known for its tires, but the company was also an information technology pioneer. Before it made its first tire, Pirelli was making telegraph cables insulated with rubber, starting in 1879. This high-tech business induced Pirelli to set up its own research team, populated with engineers hired from the Politecnico.

While Michelin linked itself with good food, Pirelli established a link between its products and design. Lots of tire companies give away cheesecake calendars, but Pirelli's pulchritudinous calendar aspires to be art. Goodyear's corporate headquarters in Akron is a nondescript office building. Pirelli's Milan headquarters is an architectural icon, built in the 1950s by Gio Ponti, another graduate of the Politecnico. Ponti founded and edited two design magazines, one of which (*Domus*) is still in print. He was a professor at the Politecnico who designed ceramics, bottles, and chairs, including the featherweight modernist classic, the Super Leggera. Ponti reminds us that education occasionally improves aesthetics, which proved to be another element in Milanese endurance.

Industry enabled Italy and Milan to come back after World War II, but the same forces of globalization and technological change that caused manufacturing to decline in the American Rust Belt also made Milan's population plummet after 1970. Yet as in Boston and Minneapolis, human capital enabled Milan to reinvent itself for our age, when ideas are more valuable than machinery. The city's population increased between 2000 and 2008, and as of 2008, Milan's per capita productivity is the highest of any geographic area in Italy, a solid 54 percent above the nation as a whole. Today, three quarters of Milan's workers are in services, and finance is a major occupation, just as it is in New York and London. Also like those cities, Milan is a hub of fashion.

Miuccia Prada and Patrizio Bertelli are a well-educated couple. She holds a PhD from the University of Milan; her husband studied engineering at the University of Bologna, two hours away from Milan. Bertelli brings an engineer's rigor to the management and marketing of the brand. Prada's fabrics, like the waterproofed nylon called Pocone, are often cutting-edge, and Prada stores were early adopters of radio frequency identification, which provides instantaneous inventory information. When a handbag is scanned by a high-tech wand, images of the bag start streaming from abundant screens. While Prada and Bertelli surely learned more from doing than from studying, their success and style still bear the imprint of formal education.

The Versaces represent the opposite side of human capital in Milanese fashion. While Gianni Versace did study architecture, he left school at twenty-one, and much of his learning seems to have come from working in his mother's dress shop. His style was not the international cool of Prada and Armani, but a local lushness, borrowed heavily from Italy's Baroque past. The head of Medusa, which adorns so many Versace products, was also used by the Milanese armorer Filippo Negroli for his emperor's parade shield. European human capital reflects millennia of culture, and that can also provide the education that creates comparative advantage for both a company and a city. In Milan's case, all that designing talent does more than make the city a dynamic exporter of clothes and handbags; it also makes the city more fun and exciting to inhabit, a place to consume as well as produce, and that is another road to urban success.

The Consumer City: Vancouver

Vancouver also attracts talent by being one of the world's more pleasant places to live. A quarter of the Vancouver area's residents over the age of fifteen have at least a college degree, as opposed to 18 percent in Canada as a whole. It regularly lands at the very top of global quality-of-life rankings, and that helps it attract thousands of talented migrants each year.

Of course, Vancouver enjoys natural advantages that are denied to Boston or Minneapolis or, for that matter, Singapore. Its Januaries average 37 degrees, far warmer than Boston or Minneapolis, and its Julys average 63 degrees, which is cooler than the other two cities. Add in Vancouver's abundant coastline, beautiful mountains, and lovely countryside, and nobody could deny that the city has been extravagantly blessed by nature. But Vancouver has taken canny advantage of those blessings.

Vancouver was a logging town with a natural harbor that became important as the western terminus of the Canadian Pacific Railway's intercontinental line in 1886. A fire that wiped away the town's older structures that year gave Vancouver, and its largest property owner, the Canadian Pacific Railway, the opportunity to start fresh with good sewers, trolley cars, and sturdy, safer new buildings. The City Council requested that a thousand acres, then part of a military base, be set aside as a park, which remains one of the city's many pleasant green spaces. In 1915, the University of British Columbia was founded there, giving the city a source of well-educated citizens.

Vancouver's trajectory during the twentieth century followed a familiar pattern. Its population stagnated during the Great Depression and then fell during the heyday of suburbanization between the 1960s and the early 1980s. But since then, the city has expanded from 415,000 to 610,000 people, an increase of almost 50 percent. Vancouver's boom has been fueled by a passionate attention to quality of life, a willingness to build up, and a flow of talented Asian immigrants.

In many areas, Vancouver is typical of prosperous non-American cities, with clean streets, a generous safety net, and high taxes. Vancouver's more distinctive features are its physical bones and the remarkably diverse set of people who make its structures come alive. There is even an urban planning philosophy, called Vancouverism, which is defined by open spaces, tall slender skyscrapers that afford ample views, and plenty of public transportation.

Arthur Erickson is often called the father of Vancouverism. He was born in Vancouver but left to fight with the British army in World War II. After the war, inspired by Frank Lloyd Wright, he studied architecture at McGill University in Montreal and earned a fellowship to study buildings around the world. After his wanderings, he returned to Vancouver, started teaching at the University of British Columbia, and began an architectural partnership with the well-connected Geoffrey Massey, whose father, Raymond, was a famous Canadian actor and whose uncle was Canada's governor general.

As early as 1955, when Vancouver was still a modest town on Canada's edge, Erickson had a vision of a soaring skyline. His Plan 56 remains a stunning vision of a high-rise city, where buildings are not massed together as in New York, but elegantly arranged in an undulating cascade that complements the city's natural beauty. Erickson did more than just dream. In 1963, he won the competition to build British Columbia's Simon Fraser University—now one of Canada's best. Two years later, Erickson got the chance to actually change Vancouver's skyline when he was picked by forestry giant MacMillan Bloedel to build its new office building, a twenty-seven-story, half-million-square-foot "concrete waffle," which has since become an architectural icon. In the 1970s, Erickson designed Robson Square, the 1.3-million-square-foot civic center that brought together law courts, UBC's downtown campus, and plenty of open space.

Erickson became a national icon, described by the Toronto *Globe and Mail* in his obituary as "the greatest architect we ever produced." Following his vision, Vancouver has built up and generally built well. A Chinese immigrant, James Cheng, who came to Vancouver to learn from Erickson, has designed more than twenty structures with more than twenty stories in Vancouver since 1995. Cheng is known for his combination of green glass and concrete, which has helped give Vancouver its distinctive look. Good planning has meant that many of these structures, like Cheng's Living Shangri-La, Vancouver's tallest building, are mixed-use, which helps to cut commutes and ensure that the city's downtown doesn't become deserted at night. Good planning also places these buildings far enough apart to let in light and views and provide plenty of open spaces.

And good urban planning, along with Canada's eminently sensible immigration policy, has helped Vancouver attract human capital. A full 40 percent of the city's population is foreign-born, and a quarter of its citizens were born in Asia. Moreover, its immigrants are disproportionately skilled, like those in Canada as a whole. More than half of the people who came to the country in 2006 have a college degree, making them far better educated than native Canadians. Also, nearly half of the Canadians with a PhD were born somewhere else.

Canada has an abundance of land, and fertility levels among its native-born people are well below replacement rates. The more than two hundred thousand immigrants who arrive during a typical year help keep the country growing. Like the United States, Canada gives some preference to relatives of the native-born, but the bulk of visas are granted to so-called independent immigrants, who are admitted based on a points system that, according to the Canadian government, rewards "education, language ability, employment experience, age, arranged employment, and adaptability." Canada has proven particularly attractive to Asians, like the many Hong Kong residents who fled that city before it became part of the People's Republic of China. Vancouver has drawn those immigrants because it is a tolerant city on the Pacific Ocean with well-established Asian communities. A fifth of its residents are ethnic Chinese—only slightly less than the 26 percent who describe themselves as being of English extraction.

Those immigrants have helped make the city culturally interesting and economically vital. James Cheng is responsible for much of the city's skyline. Members of the Chan family, also from Hong Kong, rank among Vancouver's most generous philanthropists. From restaurants to skyscrapers to investment houses, Vancouver's immigrants have helped turn a picturesque logging town into a global city.

The Growing City: Chicago and Atlanta

One of the morals of chapter 2 of this book, on urban failure, was that building in declining cities with little housing demand does no good and that it was a fallacy to think that soaring skylines could bring back declining cities. One of the morals of chapter 7, on sprawl, was that Houston has attracted so many Americans with the abundance of affordable housing that results from unrestricted building in places with sufficient demand. Building can allow a place to expand and attract exciting people not just in the Sunbelt sprawl, but also in older cities, if they have enough else going for them.

When I moved to the South Side of Chicago in 1988, the city was splendid but grim. Great stone structures, like the Beaux Arts–style Museum of Science and Industry, which greets drivers on their way to the University of Chicago's campus, served as reminders of a more glorious urban past. Neighborhoods near the university had grand mansions, like those that once housed Chicago's beef magnates and Muhammad Ali, but they were selling for a fraction of construction cost because of the area's high crime rate.

Chicago lost almost 18 percent of its population between 1970 and 1990, a lot less than Cleveland or Detroit but far more than New York or Boston. In the twelve years after the death of longtime mayor Richard J. Daley in 1976, Chicago had five mayors, none of whom was able to consolidate power or reduce the crime rate. But since 1990, Chicago has been one of the few large Midwestern cities that has grown, despite the facts that its population is not as well educated as that of Minneapolis or Boston and that its weather can be brutal.

Chicago succeeds by offering the benefits of density while still remaining affordable and pleasant. The city's economy depends on information-intensive industries, like finance and business services, that seem to particularly value density. Financial entrepreneurs, like the billionaire hedge-fund manager Kenneth Griffin, choose Chicago because it has the size and the well-educated workforce to provide the professionals and services that their organizations need, while still maintaining a strong quality of life and a family-friendly, wholesome Midwestern feel, as compared with Manhattan.

The city's longtime mayor, Richard M. Daley (son of the other longtime Mayor Daley), has proven himself to be one of America's most effective urban leaders. He knows that the city can succeed only by providing a business-friendly environment and a decent quality of life. When he took office, he made a fetish of tree planting. He built the city's Millennium Park by generating substantial private donations. He took over and improved the public schools. He has also fervently supported construction. Numerous new buildings have made Chicago a far more affordable alternative to New York or San Francisco.

Chicago's construction has given it plenty of high-quality, attractive real estate that appeals to the type of people who work for Ken Griffin. Between 2002 and 2008, Chicago issued 68,000 housing permits, equal to about 6 percent of its year-2000 housing stock. In the same period, Boston issued 8,500 housing permits, equal to only 3.3 percent of its 2000 housing stock. Chicago issued more than three times as many housing permits as San Jose, California, a city that is almost as large and far less dense. Among Chicagoans, 10.8 percent live in housing built since 1990, which is significantly higher than the 7.6 percent figure for New Yorkers or the 8.3 percent figure for Bostonians. Moreover, Chicago has allowed plenty of building along its long, beautiful lakefront, while New York has decided to "preserve" almost all of the best blocks facing Central Park.

Chicago's real estate is both newer and cheaper than either Boston's or New York's. Census data shows that median rents are 30 percent higher in Boston than in Chicago, and housing prices are about 39 percent higher. According to the National Association of Realtors, the median sales price of a condominium in the Chicago metropolitan area in the second quarter of 2010 was $186,000, as opposed to $290,000 in the Boston area and $405,000 in the San Francisco area. In downtown Chicago, $650,000 can get you a three-bedroom condominium with 1,650 square feet in a new glassy tower. An equivalent unit in New York City would cost at least twice as much.

Chicago also builds plenty of offices—almost 40 million new square feet of office space was built in the metropolitan area between 1990 and 2009. That new space keeps the cost of doing business down. Office rents in Chicago have, for many years, been about 30 percent cheaper than rents in Boston or San Francisco.

In other cities, like Boston and San Jose, preservationists and fans of lower density have pushed city leaders to restrict new construction, but Daley lets them build. Why? All those cranes create structures that house highly skilled workers. Lower housing costs allow employers to pay lower wages, which helps keep Chicago economically competitive. The mayor knows that and also knows that Chicago won't survive unless its costs are lower than those in coastal America. Building can't save places like Buffalo or Detroit, where demand is just too low, but in places that are more attractive, reducing the barriers to new construction can provide a major comparative advantage.

Unfettered construction has also been a critical part of the success of many Sunbelt cities, like Houston and Miami, but only one of those cities has managed to both expand rapidly and become highly educated. The Atlanta metropolitan area added 1.12 million people between 2000 and 2008, more than any area in the United States except Dallas. All that growth would have been impossible without plenty of construction, both in the sprawling suburbs and in glossy downtown skyscrapers that house offices and condominiums. Atlanta's office space has grown by more than 50 percent since 1990, and as a result, its business space is typically 20 percent cheaper than even Chicago's.

As Atlanta has grown, it has also become remarkably well educated. The central city has about the same share of adults with college degrees as Minneapolis and more than Boston, the self-proclaimed Athens of America. More than 47 percent of Fulton County's adults have a bachelor's degree, making them better educated than those in Westchester County, New York, or Fairfield County, Connecticut, or Santa Clara County, California, and almost as well educated as adults in Middlesex County, Massachusetts. Atlanta's education reflects history, proeducation policies, and also housing.

Atlanta has a wealth of older colleges and universities. It was a center for the Union Army after the Civil War, and its remarkable roster of historically black colleges generally formed during that era. Emory and Georgia Tech, the latter explicitly modeled on Massachusetts schools, also opened their doors in the decades after the Civil War.

More recently, Georgia decided to use its state lottery earnings to fund the Hope Scholarship program, which provides generous financial aid to any academically successful student who attends college in state. As a means of righting social inequities, the policy is a flop, for its largesse flows disproportionately to the prosperous. But as a means of attracting talented parents who care about educating their children, and as a tool for keeping talented scholars in state, the program is clearly a success.

Atlanta, like Houston, has a powerful business community that has long pushed the region's growth. That community sees the value of education and the value of building up. As a result, Atlanta offers educated people remarkably cheap housing, which has helped attract more educated people to an already highly educated metropolis. Between 2000 and 2008, Fulton County's share of college graduates has grown two thirds faster than that of the country at large.

Too Much of a Good Thing in Dubai

Dubai never had the chance to be an imperial city, but it seems to have tried almost every other strategy we've discussed here. Historically, Dubai succeeded, like Hong Kong or Singapore, by having a good location and good economic institutions. Dubai came under British protection in 1892, and early in the twentieth century, the city's proximity to India made it a natural connector between the subcontinent and the Middle East. Dubai has some oil itself, but the city's real growth is due to its port, which is a conduit for the vast flow of black gold from other countries, like Saudi Arabia.

Dubai's ports, however, handle more than just oil. The city competes effectively for international trade by offering good, modern infrastructure and business-friendly institutions. Just as Hong Kong thrived by being an oasis of economic freedom next to once highly restrictive Communist China, Dubai succeeds by offering better economic institutions than its neighbors. The Jebel Ali Free Zone attracts businesses by giving them freedom from both taxes and regulations. Dubai isn't just more business-friendly than its Middle Eastern neighbors; its good legal institutions and excellent infrastructure also make it an easier place to do business than overregulated India, making it a natural commercial hub for the entire region. In Mumbai, you can meet plenty of businesspeople who work in Dubai but come back home on weekends.

While those Indians see Dubai as a place to work, not play, Dubai's leadership has decided to transform it from an oil-shipping port into a consumer city, which attracts financiers and entrepreneurs. The two urban functions are intimately linked. Dubai can succeed as a business center if it convinces people throughout the Middle East that they'd rather be there than somewhere else, like Kuwait or Cairo. If Dubai becomes the most exciting place to live in the Middle East, the thinking goes, it will also attract businessmen who'll make sure that the city is more than a mere tourist destination.

Just as Las Vegas grew by offering pleasures outlawed in more restrictive states, Dubai could grow because it's relatively free from the religious restrictions that bind so much of the region. Sheikh Mohammed's personal faith doesn't seem to prevent him from building a city that is almost as free-spirited as any wandering businessperson might want.

Dubai could have easily succeeded as a midsize center of fun and commerce, but Sheikh Mohammed's ambitions go far beyond that. In 2008, Dubai was one of the largest construction sites on earth. The Burj Al Arab, built on an artificial island, was the tallest hotel in the world when it was built, at 1,027 feet. It has only 202 oversize suites—the smallest of which is eighteen hundred square feet.

A 2,684-foot mixed-use building opened in 2010; it is now the tallest man-made structure in the world. The Dubai Mall contains 5.9 million square feet of internal space, 12 million in all, making it one of the biggest in the world. Sheikh Mohammed had envisioned an artificial three-hundred-island archipelago, modestly called the World, and a 230-building central business district called Business Bay, and an entertainment complex, Dubailand, to be larger than Disney World.

In principle, the combination of construction and quality of life is sensible, but the extraordinary extent of the sheikh's building far exceeds the level needed to satisfy current demand for his city. Mayor Daley is only allowing private developers to build; construction in Chicago reflects their independent assessments that prices there will cover their costs. Sheikh Mohammed is investing huge amounts of public funds, so Dubai's construction reflects to a large extent his own judgment that a vastly larger city will thrive. But the market seems to have found his exuberance somewhat irrational, and Dubai defaulted on its loans in 2009. Only with the financial help of neighboring Abu Dhabi was Dubai spared the pain of an even more dramatic failure.

The sheikh's general vision of history is correct. Cities like Dubai must move beyond a purely economic model of success by embracing quality of life. Cities must build to succeed. But that doesn't mean that any place can become New York or Shanghai. City builders must be visionaries, but also realists.

Flat World, Tall City

T here is little that you own or use or know that wasn't created by someone else. Humans are an intensely social species that excels, like ants or gibbons, in producing things together. Just as ant colonies do things that are far beyond the abilities of isolated insects, cities achieve much more than isolated humans. Cities enable collaboration, especially the joint production of knowledge that is mankind's most important creation. Ideas flow readily from person to person in the dense corridors of Bangalore and London, and people are willing to put up with high urban prices just to be around talented people, some of whose knowledge will rub off.

Rousseau famously wrote, "Cities are the abyss of the human species," but he had things completely backward. Cities enable the collaboration that makes humanity shine most brightly. Because humans learn so much from other humans, we learn more when there are more people around us. Urban density creates a constant flow of new information that comes from observing others' successes and failures. In a big city, people can choose peers who share their interests, just as Monet and Cézanne found each other in nineteenth-century Paris, or Belushi and Aykroyd found each other in twentieth-century Chicago. Cities make it easier to watch and listen and learn. Because the essential characteristic of humanity is our ability to learn from each other, cities make us more human.

No matter how mundane a city's origins, urban concentrations can have magical consequences. Roman soldiers settled on an island in the Seine because it was a good spot to defend themselves against unfriendly Gauls. From that humble start, over the past two thousand years, Parisians have produced vast amounts of cultural, economic, and political innovation. The Netherlands' medieval cities were built on the wool trade, but urban density enabled their burghers to foment the modern world's first successful republican revolution. Chicago's location made it the ideal place for Midwestern hogs to be slaughtered on their journey east, but the city attracted a remarkable cluster of architects—Jenney, Burnham, Sullivan, Wright—who collectively invented the skyscraper. Shanghai began as a cotton town, but in the 1920s, its density helped create a wave of innovation in music, movies, and animation.

Artistic movements tend to develop in one place—like fifteenth-century Florence or nineteenth-century Paris. In eighteenth-century Vienna, Haydn passed his symphonic ideas to his friend Mozart and his student Beethoven. The great chains of artistic innovation forged by painters or composers who live together in dense cities bear a striking resemblance to the far more prosaic chain of urban innovations that gave us junk bonds, leveraged buyouts, and mortgage-backed securities.

Pundits and critics have long argued that improvements in information technology will make urban advantages obsolete. Once you can learn from Wikipedia in Anchorage, why pay New York prices? But a few decades of high technology can't trump millions of years of evolution. Connecting in cyberspace will never be the same as sharing a meal or a smile or a kiss. Our species learns primarily from the aural, visual, and olfactory clues given off by our fellow humans. The Internet is a wonderful tool, but it works best when combined with knowledge gained face-to-face, as the concentrations of Internet entrepreneurs in Bangalore and Silicon Valley would attest. Every one of Harvard's economics students uses technology constantly, but they also get plenty out of face-to-face meetings with their peers and professors. The most important communications still take place in person, and electronic access is no substitute for being at the geographic center of an intellectual movement.

The declining cost of connecting over long distances has only increased the returns to clustering close together. Fifty years ago, most innovators played on a local stage. High transport costs limited one's ability to make money quickly from selling a good idea worldwide. Today, traders in London or New York or Tokyo can instantly exploit a mispriced asset halfway around the world. The death of distance may have been hell on the goods producers in Detroit, who lost out to Japanese competitors, but it has been heaven for the idea producers of New York and San Francisco and Los Angeles, who have made billions on innovations in technology and entertainment and finance. Even when the financial world flails in one of its recurring downturns, we should be confident that its collective intelligence will eventually produce another boom.

Countries still make wars, and governments slaughter their own citizens. Much of the world is still poor, while many in richer countries are less happy than they could be, and everyone's environment is at risk. To face these challenges, humanity needs all the strength it can muster, and that strength resides in the connecting corridors of dense urban areas. The fact that we need our cities so much makes me optimistic about their future. The world recognizes the value of new ideas. People still flock to cities to get the skills they need to succeed. As those skills are acquired, new ideas multiply, and innovations emerge.

Ahead of us lies a new emerald-green age of cities, if we choose our policies wisely. Car-based living on the urban edge will surely continue, but it will be accompanied by denser development close to the urban core. We can build taller towers that give people plenty of space in the heart of downtown, but build them in a way that guarantees environmental sustainability and good sight lines and plenty of street life. We can make sure that everybody, not just the privileged few, can enjoy the pleasures of Manhattan or Paris or Hong Kong. But to achieve all this, we must encourage cities instead of sprawl. We must embrace the changes that drive great cities forward, instead of clinging to a stultifying status quo.

No matter what we do, some people will never want an urban lifestyle. They will want, like Thoreau, to be surrounded by open space and green trees. No one who can afford such a bucolic life should be forced to live in a city. But far too many people live outside cities because of mistakes that our societies have made. We should not force urban growth, but we must eliminate the barriers that artificially constrain the blossoming of city life.

Give Cities a Level Playing Field

The central theme of this book is that cities magnify humanity's strengths. Our social species' greatest talent is the ability to learn from each other, and we learn more deeply and thoroughly when we're face-to-face. I have also tried to show that the achievements of cities—whether in Brunelleschi's Florence or Ford's Detroit—benefit the entire world. Democracy and printing and mass production are only a few of the gifts of the city. The ideas that emerge in cities eventually spread beyond their borders and enrich the rest of the world. Massachusetts rises or falls with Boston just as Maharashtra rises or falls with Mumbai.

Too many countries have stacked the deck against urban areas, despite the fact that those areas are a—if not *the*—source of national strength. Cities don't need handouts, but they need a level playing field.

Economists often advise individual businesses on how to better their bottom lines while they simultaneously decry industrial policies that would favor one firm over another. This may seem hypocritical, but it's quite logical. Indeed, at the heart of economics is the belief that businesses work best by competing furiously in a market that the government oversees as impartial umpire. The same is true for cities. Competition among local governments for people and firms is healthy. Competition drives cities to deliver better services and keep down costs. The national government does no good by favoring particular places, just as it does no good by propping up particular firms or industries. It's far better for companies to compete, and it's also far better for cities to find their own competitive advantages.

This belief in the market may seem hard-hearted, but it isn't. I'm not against protecting the people who suffer as a result of this competition, and I certainly think society should do more for the least advantaged. Of course, my belief in reducing poverty is a personal opinion, not a matter of economic insight. Economics has much to say about income redistribution—Do taxes reduce efforts? Does inequality hurt growth?—but economists have no special wisdom about the biggest question: Is it right to take money away from richer people to give it to poorer people? That's a matter for philosophers, politicians, and the hearts of voters. Economists can, however, point out that throwing resources at troubled firms or troubled cities is usually a terribly inefficient means of taking care of troubled people. Helping poor people is an appropriate task for government, but helping poor places and poorly run businesses is not.

Cities can compete on a level playing field, but over the past sixty years,

America's policies have slanted the field steeply against them. In the areas of housing, social services, education, transportation, the environment, and even income taxes, American policies have worked against urban areas. Cities have managed to survive despite these disadvantages because they have so much to offer. Yet precisely because cities play such a critical role in the economy and society, we must eliminate the artificial barriers that hold them back. The world would be more productive and more just if our policies were more spatially neutral. I'll return to spatial neutrality when I discuss policies toward declining cities and sprawl, beginning on page 255 below.

Urbanization Through Globalization

During the millennia since Athens attracted the finest minds of the Mediterranean world, cities have grown by attracting people from diverse cultures. The most successful cities today—London, Bangalore, Singapore, New York—still connect continents. Such cities attract multinational enterprises and international expatriates. Immigrants are often a vital part of their economic model, both at the top and the bottom ends of the pay scale, and the success of global cities depends on national policies toward trade and immigration.

An open city can't exist in a closed nation. At the start of the twentieth century, when Argentina was one of the world's most open countries, Buenos Aires was a vibrant, international city full of English and Spanish and Italian and even Swedish entrepreneurs. Over the course of the century, Argentina closed its borders, and Buenos Aires became an insular place, whose beautiful older buildings reminded visitors of a more dynamic, cosmopolitan past. In every decade but one between 1790 and 1970, America's urban population increased by more than 19.5 percent. It was only during the 1930s, when the economy faltered and tariffs effectively closed borders, that America's urban growth slowed dramatically.

My father was born in Berlin in 1930, when Germany and almost all of its neighbors were reasonably democratic. The 1930s were a terrible economic period for the world, made worse by policies like America's Smoot-Hawley tariff, which shut down international trade. As economies faltered, countries like Germany, Austria, and Spain moved from democracy to dictatorship.

Eventually, Europe descended into the madness of war. The world devolved from an urban ideal of commerce and intellectual exchange to a battlefield where dictators glorified a feudal, agricultural past.

The free flow of goods and services among nations is good for cities and good for the world. Restrictions on free trade will make it more expensive for Americans to buy everyday goods and will harm our major trading partners. We're far better off allowing our consumers to take advantage of inexpensive foreign products and forcing our producers to adapt than we would be hiding behind tariff walls.

Industrial policies like massive aid to declining industries threaten global trade and growing cities. For years, America has—to its credit—loudly denounced such policies. We have done our nation and the world much good by championing the principle that companies should compete on a level playing field without subsidy or protection. If America gives up on its principles and targets aid to domestic producers but not to foreign companies with plants in the United States, then we are implicitly discouraging foreign direct investment in our country. We're also encouraging other countries to favor their own producers against Americans. It would be far better to stick to a policy that enables free trade and international investment everywhere.

Immigration is also essential to urban success. The growth of New York and Chicago over the past two decades is largely due to the hundreds of thousands of immigrants who have come to those cities. Cities are good for immigrants and immigrants are good for cities.

While the biggest beneficiaries of immigration into prosperous countries are the immigrants themselves, the United States has benefited enormously from all the talented people who have settled here. Cities especially benefit from an influx of talent, because foreigners help urban areas play their crucial role of connecting countries. A diversity of cultures also helps make a city more fun, as the proliferation of good Indian restaurants in London suggests. Cities, and the country as a whole, will benefit even more if we work, as Canada and New Zealand do, to admit more skilled immigrants.

Over the past ten years, the dangerous specter of nativism has returned to America and parts of Europe. This sentiment is not new. In the 1840s, the American, or Know-Nothing, Party rose to oppose the increasing numbers of Catholic Irish and German immigrants. In the 1920s, the Ku Klux Klan appeared in Northern cities buoyed on a wave of anti-immigrant hysteria. I believe strongly that America became a great nation because of the stream of human talents that flowed to its shores before 1921 and that shutting down that flow after World War I was one of the greatest mistakes that the nation has ever made. Immigration from a poor country to a rich country may well be the best way to turn a poor person into a rich one, and over the course of history, immigrants from Alexander Hamilton to Google cofounder Sergey Brin have done extraordinary things in and for America. So far, opponents of immigration have failed to capture either party, and an immigrant's son occupies the White House, but neonativism remains a threat. Developed countries would gain much by increasing the flow of immigrants into America, especially by increasing the number of H-1B visas, which allow skilled workers to settle here.

Lend a Hand to Human Capital

Education is, after January temperature, the most reliable predictor of urban growth, especially among older cities. Per capita productivity rises sharply with metropolitan area size if the city is well educated, but not if it isn't. Cities and schools complement each other, and for that reason, education policy is a vital ingredient in urban success.

In the United States in 2007, college graduates earned about $57,000 per year, and people with only a high school diploma earned about $31,000 per year. In other words, going to college is associated with an over 80 percent increase in earnings. The impact of education seems even larger when we look at entire cities or countries. As the number of college graduates in a metropolitan area increases by 10 percent, individuals' earnings increase by 7.7 percent, no matter how educated they are. Among nations, an extra average year of schooling is associated with a 37 percent increase in output per capita, which is pretty remarkable, because an extra year of schooling typically raises individual wages by less than 20 percent. Some of the massive correlation between schooling and national productivity may reflect other, unmeasured national attributes, but I believe that the country-level returns from schooling are also high because they include all of the extra benefits that come from having well-educated neighbors, including a more reliable, less corrupt government.

Thomas Jefferson wrote that "If a nation expects to be ignorant and free, in a state of civilization, it expects what never was and never will be." The link between education and democracy is strong because education creates democracy, not because democracies invest more in education. For example, the post-1990 political history of the better-educated members of the Warsaw Pact, like the Czech Republic or Poland, has been much brighter than the path of less educated areas, like Kazakhstan. A study of compulsory-schooling laws across states found that people who got more education because of these laws become more civically engaged. Education doesn't just improve a region's economic prospects; it also helps create a more just society. Giving poor children a good education may be the single best way to help them become prosperous adults.

While it's easy to cheer for education, it's hard to improve school systems. Thirty years of research suggests that just throwing money at the problem achieves very little. Smaller class sizes improve students' test scores, but only slightly. Bigger results are achieved with early interventions, such as Head Start, but to really improve education, we need systemic reform, not just more cash.

Recent research on charter schools in Boston and New York has shown spectacular gains for lower-income students who attend such schools. These results dovetail nicely with earlier research that showed the effectiveness of parochial schools in disadvantaged areas. Large state monopolies can provide good school systems, as shown by many European countries like France, but competition is even better. Even socialist Sweden has switched to a system that gives its children more choice.

Cities succeed by encouraging competition and diverse innovations. Public school monopolies destroy both of those advantages. With enough money and competent administration, we might be able to create universal access to excellent purely public education, but that seems pretty implausible in the American context. Better schools seem more likely to come from policies that allow more competition and diversity in schooling, such as charter schools or choice within public school systems.

The largest ingredient in school quality, just like in urban success, is human capital—the talents of the teachers. Research has uncovered huge gaps in effectiveness between the good ones and the bad ones. Charter schools often produce better results than public schools, in part, because they can select better educators. Teachers' unions are right to argue that higher wages will attract better teachers, but they're wrong to fight against tying teachers' pay to performance. Any union that fights to protect poorly performing teachers is putting its membership ahead of our children.

Other research shows that a school's curriculum also matters. The move to increased math and science training, which began in the 1980s, seems to have improved the performance of students, especially the poorer ones. Our schools must focus on getting—and keeping—teachers of those skills, like numeracy, that are increasingly critical for success.

For cities, investing in schooling yields two payoffs. Students acquire more skills, which eventually makes the place more productive. Better schools also attract better-educated parents, who make the place more productive right away. The single best way to create a smart city is to create schools that attract and train able people.

Help Poor People, Not Poor Places

The dearth of education in many postindustrial cities helps explain why these places have had such trouble reinventing themselves. They've also suffered because their model of having vast firms in a single industry stunts entrepreneurship and innovation. Throughout American history, older areas have always been supplanted by upstart cities. In 1800, six of the twenty largest cities in the United States were in Massachusetts (Boston, Salem, Newburyport, Nantucket, Gloucester, and Marblehead). Only one of these places remained a major metropolis by the end of the nineteenth century, as the population moved west and built great cities along America's inland waterways. The relative decline of the Massachusetts towns troubled their residents, but it was good for the country.

Today, urban distress troubles the late-nineteenth-century cities that formed as those Massachusetts towns declined. The second half of the twentieth century hit these industrial cities hard, and the recent recession dealt them another blow. The people suffering in those cities deserve our support, but we should not freeze urban change or artificially forestall urban decline. People moved to the Sunbelt for good reasons, and there's no reason why the country as a whole should try to restore Detroit's peak population of 1.85 million.

National government should try to reduce human misery, but it shouldn't try to stop the great course of urban change. Those currents are just too strong to hold back, and there's no reason to even try.

For decades, the federal government has subsidized inane attempts at urban renewal, such as Buffalo's light rail system, and acted as if this balanced antiurban policies like the highway system and the home mortgage interest deduction. But these policies make little economic sense, and they don't help the poor people who live in such cities.

Helping poor people is simple justice; helping poor places is far more difficult to justify. Why should the government effectively bribe people to live in declining areas? Why should growing areas be handicapped simply to keep people in older places? Moreover, investments in places don't always benefit the people living there. How were the residents of Poletown helped when the city of Detroit helped General Motors evict them? Renters who lived near the Guggenheim Museum in Bilbao may well have been hurt by the art gallery, at least if they had little taste for contemporary art or architecture, because their rents rose significantly.

The conflict between people and place got national attention in 2005 when Hurricane Katrina destroyed a great swath of New Orleans. President Bush got into the urban-renewal business and declared that "the great city of New Orleans will rise again." He shouldn't have committed the federal government to an expensive goal that was unlikely to do much good. New Orleans reached its economic apogee in 1840 when it was the great port of the antebellum South. The city has been losing population since 1960 because, like Detroit, changing patterns of technology meant that firms no longer needed access to its port, and, as in Liverpool, containerization meant that its port employs fewer workers.

Hurricane Katrina was a great human tragedy, and common decency pushes us to help the people who were hurt by the storm. But again, helping poor people doesn't mean helping poor places. Indeed, new research on the human diaspora created by the storm shows that the children who left New Orleans have learned more since leaving than comparable children who stayed. Dartmouth economist Bruce Sacerdote found that children displaced from New Orleans by Katrina had a significant improvement in their test scores. He found that the biggest beneficiaries of the exodus were children from poorly performing schools who left the New Orleans area altogether.

Well-meaning urban advocates, motivated by the real suffering in the Crescent City, proposed spending up to $200 billion rebuilding New Orleans. That's more than $400,000 for every man, woman, and child living in the city before the hurricane, or more than $200,000 for every household in the much larger New Orleans metropolitan area. Surely the people of New Orleans would have been better off just getting that money directly, in the form of checks or housing and school vouchers, than for great gobs of cash to go to contractors. If it wasn't for the durability of its homes, the city would have been much smaller a long time ago. No matter how much we all love New Orleans jazz, it never made sense to spend more than $100 billion putting infrastructure in a place that lost its economic rationale long ago. By wrapping policy discussions up in misty dreams of urban comeback, absurdly expensive projects suddenly seem reasonable.

The government shouldn't be indifferent to the problems of New Orleans or Detroit or Buffalo. Cities house many of America's poorest people, and a humane society must help them. However, national policy should be aimed at giving those people the skills they need to compete, wherever they choose to live, rather than encouraging them to stay in one particular locale. Above all else, every child should have access to good schools and safety, and the federal government has every reason to invest in America's children, whether they're in Houston, New York, or Detroit.

The Challenge of Urban Poverty

Cities can be places of great inequality; they attract some of the world's richest and poorest people. Although poverty can accompany urban decline, poverty often shows that a city is functioning well. Cities attract poor people because they're good places for poor people to live. But whenever people crowd together, it's more likely that disease will spread and water will become contaminated. When those crowded people are disproportionately poor, then the risks increase, because they have fewer resources to handle such problems on their own. At the local level, high concentrations of population and poverty demand strong policies that will combat the costs of density. Clean water and safe streets did not come easily to the cities of the West, and they won't appear automatically in the developing world today. In the West, creating healthy, attractive cities required huge financial investments and often heavy-handed governmental intervention. George Waring never could have cleaned Manhattan's streets if he had worried about offending every citizen who was inconvenienced by his street cleaners. Singapore has been so effective at providing a clean and safe city because its government operates with fewer constraints than governments in many other places.

But even the strongest cities can't—and shouldn't have to—handle the costs of urban poverty by themselves. In the 1960s and 1970s, rich and middle-class city dwellers fled to the suburbs in part to escape having to pay the costs of addressing urban inequality. Rich enclaves have often formed right outside of urban political boundaries, where the prosperous can be close to the city without having to pay its taxes or attend its schools. A level playing field means that people should be choosing where to live based on their desires for neighborhood or opportunity, not based on where they can avoid paying for the poor.

A nation's poor are every citizen's responsibility, not just the people who happen to live in the same political jurisdiction. It is fairer, both to the poor and to cities, if social services are funded at the national rather than the local level. We remedy some of this problem when states and the federal government provide aid to poorer areas, but middle-class people still have too much incentive to flee cities and avoid paying for the poor.

One downside of America's education system that I have already discussed is that too many children end up with too little learning. A second problem is that our localized school system creates strong incentives for people to suburbanize in order to get better schools. There is no innate reason why suburbs should have better schools than cities. Paris has some of the best public high schools in the world, and some of the finest schools in America are big-city private schools. Yet the combination of inner-city poverty and locally funded schooling means that urban public schools are often a disaster. In some cases, this represents mismanagement, but even in the best-run school systems, urban poverty creates enormous challenges for educators.

Poor children are more likely to have behavioral problems and less training at home. Holding spending constant, schools filled with well-off children have much higher test scores than schools for the poor. That doesn't mean that the poor can't thrive—many of them do—but it does mean that poverty makes education more difficult. Because public schools bring together all the children in a school district, the presence of poverty in big cities pushes the prosperous to flee to form their own enclaves.

There are less-antiurban alternatives to the current system. Regional voucher programs could break the link between where a family lives and where its children go to school. If big-city schools can harness the forces of competition and variety that thrive in dense metropolises, then urban schools will start improving. More aid to big-city schools is also an effective, if expensive, means of leveling the playing field. Grouping students together by skill level, whether in separate classrooms or in magnet schools, also makes urban public education more attractive to parents of bright children. The opponents of tracking argue that it deprives less-fortunate children of good peers, and they are right. But if poorer students are going to be deprived of those peers anyway, because of flight to the suburbs, then it's better for wealthier families to stay in the city.

When the neighbors of poor people are forced to carry single-handedly the financial and social burdens of poverty, then those neighbors will leave, impoverishing cities further and isolating the poor. A far better and more practical approach would be for higher levels of government to distribute funds in a way that offsets the added costs of poverty. In many states, including Massachusetts, state aid to localities increases with the poverty of the locale, and that makes sense. Providing more support for cities that must address the problems of poverty reduces the incentive for richer people to leave those cities.

The Rise of the Consumer City

Of course, successful cities attract rich people as well as poor people. As cities have become safer and healthier, they have become increasingly attractive to the well-heeled. Today, New York residents are actually willing to pay a premium to enjoy its pleasures. The success of London and New York and Paris today reflects, in part, their strengths as consumer cities. There is every reason to think that an increasingly prosperous world will continue to place more value on the innovative enjoyments that cities can provide. The bottom-up nature of urban innovation suggests that the best economic development strategy may be to attract smart people and get out of their way.

But how can places become consumer cities and attract skilled residents? One vision, espoused by urbanist Richard Florida, emphasizes the arts, toleration for alternative lifestyles, and a fun, happening downtown. A second vision focuses on better providing the core public services that have always been the province of cities: safe streets, fast commutes, good schools. City leaders typically have scarce resources; they can't do everything for everybody. Even if one believes, as I do, that every city should subscribe to a bit of each vision, there will always be the question of where to invest the revenues of city government and the energy of its leaders.

In a sense, the relative appeal of the two visions depends on whom you think of when you imagine an ideal citizen. The first vision, with its fondness for coffeehouses and public sculpture, seems aimed at a twenty-eight-year-old wearing a black turtleneck and reading Proust. The second vision, with its focus on core urban services, seems to address the needs of a forty-two-year old biotech researcher concerned about whether her family will be as comfortable in Boston as it is in Charlotte. There are roughly three times as many people in their thirties, forties, and fifties as there are in their twenties, so it would be a mistake for cities to think that they can survive solely as magnets for the young and hip.

As much as I appreciate urban culture, aesthetic interventions can never substitute for the urban basics. A sexier public space won't bring many jobs if it isn't safe. All the cafés in Paris won't entice parents to put their kids in a bad public school system. If commuting into a city is a lengthy torment, then companies will head for the suburbs, no matter how many cool museums the city has.

The Curse of NIMBYism

In cities and suburban enclaves alike, opposition to change means blocking new development and stopping new infrastructure projects. Residents are in effect saying "not in my backyard." In older cities like New York, NIMBYism hides under the cover of preservationism, perverting the worthy cause of preserving the most beautiful reminders of our past into an attempt to freeze vast neighborhoods filled with undistinguished architecture. In highly attractive cities, the worst aspects of this opposition to change are that it ensures that building heights will be low, new homes will be few, prices will be high, and the city will be off-limits to all but rich people.

Unfortunately, it is all too easy to understand why people oppose change:

- You've bought a house in a leafy suburb. Right now, there aren't a lot of homes there, and you like that. After all, that's why you bought. A neighboring landowner wants to put up twenty townhouses on her five acres of land. You're furious. That's not why you came to this town. You don't want the bother of the nearby construction or the extra traffic once the new neighbors move in. You want things as they were.
- You've bought an apartment on Manhattan's Upper East Side with lovely views. A developer wants to put up a high-rise across the street. You'd be able to see it from your apartment, and you don't want to lose your views. Also, you're not sure you'd like the new people who'd move into that building. You want the neighborhood to stay the way it was when you moved in. You want things as they were.
- You've lived in a Boston triple-decker for twenty years. A university wants to build a contemporary art museum on its land a few blocks away. You'll be able to see it from your apartment. You expect that the museum will attract many outsiders into your area. You don't much like contemporary art anyhow. You want things as they were.

These are real-world examples of NIMBYism. Case by case, they couldn't be more comprehensible. Someone else is changing your neighborhood. You don't want to live in a denser, or taller, or artsier place. You just want the status quo. What could be more reasonable than that?

But NIMBYism that seems reasonable can often have terrible consequences. Stopping new construction may seem like a good idea to you, but it imposes costs on everyone who would have liked to live in a new subdivision or apartment building. Stopping a new, privately funded museum deprives the city of an amenity that would have appealed to many residents and brought in tourists who would have contributed to the local economy. The interests of people who oppose change are certainly comprehensible, but their interests usually don't match the public interest.

Moreover, in each of these cases, the angry neighbor doesn't even own the property that he wants to control. The property owner with five acres owns her land, as does the urban developer and the university. The enemies of change essentially want to control somebody else's property. From that vantage point, stopping growth isn't so much maintaining the status quo as it is taking someone else's rights and reducing the value of someone else's property.

There are two powerful, interlocking psychological biases that lie behind the popularity of NIMBYism. The first is called status quo bias, which is an overly strong attachment to the current state of affairs. One set of famous experiments illustrating this bias shows that people will forgo far more money to keep a mug that they have been given than they will pay to buy the exact same mug. The second bias is impact bias, which causes people to significantly overestimate the impact that a negative shock will have on their happiness. The enemies of a new high-rise may think that the tower will make them miserable, but in reality, they will quickly adapt to the new situation.

Over the past forty years, we've experienced a little-remarked revolution in property rights in America. We have gone from a system wherein people could essentially do what they wanted with their own property to a system wherein neighbors have enormous powers to restrict growth and change. Some of this revolution in rights is for the better, but much of it is for the worse.

Not all change is good, but much change is necessary if the world is to become more productive, affordable, exciting, innovative, and environmentally friendly. At the national level, we mistakenly oppose change when federal policies try to preserve older places at the expense of growing regions. At a local level, activists oppose change by fighting growth in their own communities. Their actions are understandable, but their local focus equips them poorly to consider the global consequences of their actions. Stopping new development in attractive areas makes housing more expensive for people who don't currently live in those areas. Those higher housing costs in turn make it more expensive for companies to open businesses. In naturally low-carbon-emissions areas, like California, preventing development means pushing it to less environmentally friendly places, like noncoastal California and suburban Phoenix. Local environmentalism is often bad environmentalism.

In older cities, preservationists can be the great enemies of change. They couch their arguments in terms of beauty and history. I respect their values enormously, but also believe their power must be checked. Many buildings must be protected, but cities also must grow to thrive. Striking the right balance between protecting architectural treasures and allowing change will never be easy. It's hard enough in San Francisco and New York, and it becomes even more complicated in places like Paris and Rome, where humanity's history is written in stone. The key is to make the most use of the space that is allowed to change. In no way do I favor running roughshod over the most important and beautiful structures in older cities, but in those areas where rebuilding is permitted, it makes sense to allow as much new development as possible. Smarter preservationism would push new buildings to be taller, not shorter. Building taller, newer structures would reduce the pressure to tear down other, older monuments.

The importance of allowing change becomes particularly clear when America or anyplace else considers building new infrastructure. The same forces that have slowed private development of homes and apartment buildings have also made it far more difficult to construct urban megaprojects that could benefit cities and society as a whole. In France, Germany, and Japan, high-speed rail service has connected major cities for decades. In 1994, Amtrak tried to bring such rail service to the United States with its Acela line. The Acela can reach speeds of 150 miles per hour, which would bring New York–to–Boston train service down to less than ninety minutes, making trains a speedy, eco-friendly alternative to plane service. However, NIMBYist politics keeps Amtrak from laying the straight track that would enable the Acela to reach those speeds. Its current, circuitous route keeps speeds down to an average of 86 miles per hour, and travel times between New York and Boston exceed three hours. In today's political climate, community opposition makes it impossible to straighten a route, even if the economic and environmental advantages of faster rail service outweigh the costs.

I return every once in a while to the neighborhood where I grew up, on Sixty-ninth Street between First and Second avenues. Brownstones still line the street across from my old apartment building, as does a Magyar church that recalls the area's erstwhile ethnic identity. Would I be sad if those brownstones and that church were replaced by high-rise apartment buildings? Perhaps. But those buildings would make it possible for many other children to experience, as I did, the wonders of growing up in New York City. I'll take the side of people over buildings any day.

In developing countries, the case against overregulation is even stronger. In rapidly growing places like Mumbai, height restrictions cause enormous damage by forcing people to spread themselves horizontally rather than vertically, which helps to create massive congestion. The last thing that Mumbai or any developing megacity needs is regulation that prevents the construction of good, usable real estate. Cities are the path out of poverty, and preventing urban growth makes developing countries artificially poor.

The Bias Toward Sprawl

Over the past century, tens of millions of people have left cities for suburbs. As much as I love cities, I can't fault their choice. I suburbanized too. But I can fault a system that stacks the deck against cities and creates artificial inducements to leave urban areas. I've already discussed the problems that come from expecting cities' richer residents to pay for the needs of the poorer ones. An antiurban bias is even more obvious in housing and transportation policy, which seems almost intentionally designed to hurt the cities that enrich their countries and the entire world.

The centerpiece of federal housing policy is the home mortgage interest deduction, which allows home owners to deduct from their taxes the interest on up to a million dollars of mortgage debt. Because more than 60 percent of Americans are home owners, this policy has become politically inviolate, but it is deeply flawed. The home mortgage interest deduction is a sacred cow in need of a good stockyard. It encourages Americans to leverage themselves to the hilt to bet on housing, which looks particularly foolish in the wake of the great housing bust of 2006–2008. Subsidizing home ownership actually pushes up housing prices by encouraging people to spend more. And the deduction's benefits accrue overwhelmingly to the richest Americans. The average deduction for American families earning more than $250,000 is more than ten times higher than the average deduction for American families earning between $40,000 and $70,000.

Environmental concerns should push toward a tax policy that encourages thrifty living in modest residences. The home mortgage interest deduction pushes us in the opposite direction, encouraging people to buy bigger homes, which are often suburban. The post–World War II move to enclaves like Levittown and The Woodlands was fueled by pro-home-ownership tax policies. I'm happy for people to enjoy the pleasures of large houses on large lots, but there is little reason why federal tax policy should subsidize those who buy big. A simple way to ease this problem without harming middle-class Americans would be lowering the upper limit on the home mortgage interest deduction to some more modest figure, like $300,000.

The home mortgage interest deduction is part of a seventy-year-old federal push toward home ownership. Government-sponsored enterprises like Fannie Mae and Freddie Mac long received implicit and now receive overt federal funding to encourage the mortgage market. The Federal Housing Administration and the Veterans Administration have long encouraged Americans to buy their own homes. While there are some social benefits of home ownership, subsidizing ownership hurts cities. Home owners do vote more and get involved solving local problems—and they own more guns. Maybe these things are worth subsidizing, but surely it makes more sense to subsidize any desirable activities directly rather than encouraging people to borrow as much as possible to bet on housing markets. The great housing crash of 2006–2008 well illustrates the folly of pushing people to wager all they have and more on the vicissitudes of property markets.

The high price of urban land leads naturally toward multiunit dwellings, and 85 percent of such dwellings are renter-occupied. It is possible to have owner-occupied cooperatives and condominiums, but those complex ownership structures create their own difficulties, which is why they remain relatively rare. As long as owner-occupied housing remains disproportionately nonurban, then subsidizing ownership will hurt cities.

President Obama is the first urban president since Teddy Roosevelt, but the infrastructure component of the 2009 stimulus bill was as stacked against urban America as most of America's previous infrastructure spending. Per capita stimulus spending from March to December 2009 was twice as high in America's five least densely populated states as in the rest of the country. Perhaps this fact shouldn't surprise us, for those five states control 10 percent of the Senate with only 1.2 percent of the population. But that doesn't make the disproportionate flow of resources to less dense areas any more sensible, especially as this was supposed to be antirecessionary spending and the five least dense states managed to sit out the recession with an average unemployment rate of 6.4 percent, as of December 2009.

Over the last twenty years, transportation funding for the ten most densely populated states has been half as much, on a per capita basis, as funding for the ten least dense states. In the stimulus package, which uses the old formula, the ratio is the same. We're using our infrastructure money more to make rural America accessible than to speed the flows of people within dense urban areas. Yet slow commutes are far more likely in big crowded cities than in low-density areas. The average commute in the ten largest metropolitan areas takes 20 percent longer than in the country as a whole.

As the White House Office of Management and Budget writes of the federal highway program, "funding is not based on need or performance and the program has been heavily earmarked." In the 1950s, the interstate highway program made it much easier for people to flee cities. By continuing to subsidize low-density areas, transportation spending continues to entice people away from urban America.

Granted, transportation spending in urban areas is difficult. Large urban projects are extremely expensive. As the famed battle over the Lower Manhattan Expressway between Jane Jacobs and master builder Robert Moses reminds us, building where people already live invariably involves far more community opposition than building in green fields. Moreover, far too many urban transportation projects have gone into declining cities that don't need more infrastructure. After all, the defining feature of such cities is that they have lots of structure relative to people. We need to build in ways that make increasingly crowded cities more functional. The difference between good projects and follies like Detroit's People Mover is that good projects create tangible benefits for large numbers of users. Bad projects just create patronage opportunities and rewards for developers.

People who support the disproportionate flow of transportation money into less dense areas argue that these areas deserve the largesse because they're paying more in gas taxes, the chief source of federal funds for transportation. If that's the case, then more dense areas should be better compensated for paying more income taxes. Over half of American income is earned in twenty-two metropolitan areas. If the federal government apportioned money based on tax revenues, big cities would be getting a lot more federal money.

But unlike the argument for giving cities back more of the money they pay in income taxes, the argument for giving gas-guzzling states more transportation dollars is faulty on its face. One of the primary reasons for the gas tax is to make drivers bear some of the social costs of their road use. Basic economics tells us that if drivers increase pollution and congestion, they should be charged for those costs. But if the gas taxes they pay are then plowed back into highways, thereby subsidizing more driving, then the benefits of the gas tax largely vanish. To give cities a level playing field, drivers should be charged for the pollution their gas usage causes, and they shouldn't get that money back in the form of more roads.

To create the right externality-relieving gas tax, we need to know exactly how much damage drivers inflict on other people through pollution, traffic fatalities, and congestion. One recent article added together all of these costs and came up with a figure of $2.30 a gallon, which suggests that current U.S. gas taxes are too low, but European gas taxes may be too high. If America moved toward the European model, certainly more of sprawl's denizens would start thinking that compact living made more sense. Ending the antiurban bias of federal policies also means charging suburban drivers for the environmental costs of their actions.

Even the income tax can be seen as a tax on big-city life. Earnings are higher in big cities because people are more productive there. By taxing higher earnings, we make the simple life of nonmetropolitan areas more attractive. Income taxes essentially make it less attractive to earn more, and people earn more in cities. I am not suggesting that we should do away with the income tax, but it does make sense to limit the antiurban effects of the tax. More tax revenues should flow back to the areas that paid those taxes. Taxing cities to build up rural America is a foolish policy that hurts our urban engines of prosperity.

Green Cities

One of the costs of subsidizing sprawl is that America's carbon emissions are higher than they should be. Cities are green. Living at high densities and walking is a lot more environmentally friendly than living in a low-density suburb and driving everywhere. America's failure to have a sensible environmental policy that charges people for the environmental costs of their actions also creates a dangerous antiurban bias.

People who like suburbs should be able to live there, but their choice should be based on the true costs and benefits of suburbanization. Suburbanites use much more energy and emit much more carbon than urbanites. The need to price carbon emissions appropriately is particularly important in places like India and China, whose lifestyle decisions will determine the world's future carbon emissions.

The most straightforward way to address climate change is a simple carbon tax. If energy users are taxed for the social costs of their actions, then they'll use more fuel-efficient cars and live in more energy-efficient houses. They'll also find energy-conserving big-city life more appealing. By not taxing energy use properly, we are implicitly subsidizing energy-intensive suburban lifestyles and pushing people out of cities.

Over the next forty years, India and China will continue to urbanize rapidly. Their decisions about land use will have a huge impact on energy consumption and carbon emissions. If they live at high densities and use public transit, then the whole world will benefit. If they sprawl, then we will all suffer from higher energy costs and higher carbon emissions. One important reason the West must shrink its own carbon footprint is to reduce the hypocrisy of telling India and China to be greener while driving our SUVs to the mall.

Gifts of the City

Our cities' gleaming spires point to the greatness that mankind can achieve, but also to our hubris. The recent recession reminds us painfully that urban innovation can destroy value as well as create it. Any downturn challenges the world and its cities. As trade and financial markets contract, urban areas suffer. As tax revenues decline, cities must struggle to provide basic services. Rising unemployment levels burden those services further, especially in the cities that are already poor.

Yet our urban future remains bright. Even the Great Depression failed to dim big-city lights. The enduring strength of cities reflects the profoundly social nature of humanity. Our ability to connect with one another is the defining characteristic of our species. We grew as a species because we hunted in packs and shared our kills. Psychologist Steven Pinker argues that group living, the primitive version of city life, "set the stage for the evolution of humanlike intelligence." We built civilizations and culture together, constantly learning from one another and from the past. New technologies from the book to Google have failed to change our fundamentally social nature. They've made it easier to learn some things without meeting face-to-face, but that hasn't eliminated the extra edge that comes from interacting in person. Indeed, since new technologies have increased the returns from new ideas, they have also increased the returns from face-to-face collaboration.

During the late twentieth century, declining transportation costs eliminated the former production advantages of the great industrial cities. The car moved Americans to suburbs and to car-based cities in the Sunbelt. These events traumatized many older urban areas, yet they did not sound the city's death knell. The advantages of being close to other humans are just too great.

China's leaders seem to understand that high densities will enable their once poor country to become rich. They seem to get the fact that tall towers enhance productivity and reduce environmental costs. If China embraces height rather than sprawl, the world's carbon emissions will be lower, the planet will be safer from global warming, and China will be less dependent on the oil-producing nations of the Middle East.

India's future will also be urban, but the shape of its urban areas is harder to predict. Indian cities have so far embraced the worst aspects of English land-use planning, leading to short buildings and dispersed populations. The costs that this model imposes on India are so enormous that the subcontinent may well be forced to abandon its antipathy toward high-density construction. If India and China both become highly urban civilizations, then American suburbs will begin to look like an exception rather than a prognosis of the world's future.

I suspect that in the long run, the twentieth-century fling with suburban living will look, just like the brief age of the industrial city, more like an aberration than a trend. Building cities is difficult, and density creates costs as well as benefits. But those costs are well worth bearing, because whether in London's ornate arcades or Rio's fractious favelas, whether in the high-rises of Hong Kong or the dusty workspaces of Dharavi, our culture, our prosperity, and our freedom are all ultimately gifts of people living, working, and thinking together—the ultimate triumph of the city.

ACKNOWLEDGMENTS

This book was a collaborative effort, and I am enormously grateful to the many people who helped make it happen. My agents, Suzanne Gluck and Eric Lupfer of William Morris Endeavor, not only encouraged me to write a popular book but also contributed constantly and constructively from start to finish. Several of my favorite phrases in the book are their creation.

Eamon Dolan of The Penguin Press was a superb editor, who not only polished my prose, but helped sculpt the entire book. He is patient, thoughtful, and wise. If my thoughts have in any way cohered into a unified volume, much of the credit is due to him.

I also received tremendous institutional support from the Manhattan Institute; its president, Lawrence Mone; and its research director, Howard Husock. With generous and patient support from the Smith Richardson Foundation, they provided financial and intellectual help throughout this project. Several of the ideas in this book were first explored in articles in *City Journal*, and I am grateful for the guidance provided by its editor, Brian Anderson, and its managing editor, Ben Plotinsky.

I also received significant institutional and financial support from the Taubman Center and the Rappaport Institute at the Harvard Kennedy School, both of which I have been fortunate enough to direct during the writing of this book. Erin Dea and Heather Marie Vitale provided helpful assistance throughout the project. David Luberoff and Sandra Garron have been good friends and supporters. My dean, David Ellwood, has been a support and inspirational leader.

Within the Taubman Center, I am particularly grateful to Kristina Tobio, the assistant director, who went over and above any reasonable call of duty and spent hundreds of hours doing research support for the book. She deserves credit for assembling the footnotes and for pruning many of my incorrect excesses. She also led the team of research assistants who worked on this book at various stages, including Elizabeth Cook-Stuntz, Nathan Hipsman, and Sarah Moshary.

I am also indebted to the many people who helped me to travel through India,

Hong Kong, Singapore, and elsewhere to better understand their cities. Above all, I am grateful to M. K. Singh of Mumbai, who was unstintingly generous with his time and wisdom. I am also grateful for the wise guidance of Jyotish Saha in Kolkata, Mahika Shishodia and Guninder Kaur Gill in Delhi, Sabroto Bagchi, K. Kuman, Ruban Phukan, Eric Savage, G. Srinivasan, Murali Vullaganti, and especially K. R. Srikrishna in Bangalore, and Tripty Arya and Sunil Handa in Mumbai. My experience of Singapore was greatly assisted by Peter Ho, Donald Low, and Koh Tsin Yen, and I am grateful to them as well. Tim Welbes took me around The Woodlands in Texas and shared his insights. Emily Beam gave me a superb walking tour of inner-city Detroit. Many others were also enormously patient as I tried to get a feel of the world's cities by walking their streets, and I apologize to those whom I have failed to thank by name.

I am particularly grateful to those people who read the book and provided helpful comments: Joshua Gottlieb, Jesse Shapiro, Andrei Shleifer, Lawrence Summers, and Mitchell Weiss. Neil Levine helped me on the architectural history in the book. Stephen Greenblatt read the section on Shakespeare; his wisdom has been most helpful.

The broader intellectual debts of this book are enormous. I have been profoundly influenced by my teachers, my colleagues, my coauthors, my students, and the many great urbanists whose work I have long admired. This book's core thesis—that ideas spread easily in dense environments—was taught to me at the University of Chicago, and I very much saw the process in action, as I learned from Gary Becker, Edward Lazear, Sherwin Rosen, and George Tolley. The ideas in this book are particularly indebted to the early influence of Jose Scheinkman and Robert Lucas.

I have been blessed by wonderful colleagues at Harvard who have taught me much about cities, including Alan Altshuler, John Campbell, David Cutler, Benjamin Friedman, Roland Fryer, Claudia Goldin, Tony Gomez-Ibanez, Lawrence Katz, and Andrei Shleifer. I am particularly indebted to John Kain and John Meyer, two great figures in the economics of cities who are sadly gone.

Many of the ideas in this book were first expressed in academic articles that were coauthored with David Cutler, Denise DiPasquale, Glenn Ellison, Jess Gaspar, Joseph Gyourko, Matthew Kahn, Hedi Kallal, William Kerr, Janet Kohlhase, Jose Scheinkman, and Andrei Shleifer. Many of those articles have also been written with students and former students, including Alberto Ades, Guy Dumais, Joshua Gottlieb, Jed Kolko, David Mare, Matthew Resseger, Bruce Sacerdote, Albert Saiz, Jesse Shapiro, and Jacob Vigdor.

It would take a long and tedious bibliographic essay to mention all the distinguished urbanists who have moved my thinking, but it should be obvious that much of the book bears the imprint of Jane Jacobs, who bestrides the world of cities like a colossus.

Following common practices, Wikipedia is not listed in the bibliography or citations, because any Wikipedia fact was verified with a more standard source. But I still have a great debt to the anonymous toilers of Wikipedia who made my research much easier at many points in time. I apologize if any phrases from that, or any other source, crept into my prose—one research assistant was assigned the explicit task of purging such inadvertent borrowing—but mistakes do sometimes get through.

Finally, I would like to express my particular gratitude to my family for their support of forty years of thinking about cities. My late father, Ludwig Glaeser, started me thinking about urban design when I was a child. My mother, Elizabeth Glaeser, first taught me about economics, and has been a bulwark throughout everything. My stepfather, Edmund Chaitman, has also greatly shaped my understanding of people and the world. My children, Theodore, Elizabeth, and Nicholas, have been remarkably patient as I dragged them from Houston to Ravenna. They have been a constant source of inspiration and joy.

Above all, though, I am grateful to my wife, Nancy Schwartz Glaeser, to whom this book is dedicated. She has been a wonderful partner in this project, as she is in life. She has helped edit the volume and given constant feedback. She also led the book's image selection and assembly. Her love and support mean everything.

NOTES

Most of the notes are given in abbreviated form. Full citations for these can be found in the bibliography, alphabetized by the first word in the note reference. In the case of the U.S. Census Bureau and a few other government entities, however, most citations are given in full in the notes without a separate bibliography entry.

INTRODUCTION: OUR URBAN SPECIES

1 *Two hundred forty-three million Americans . . . is urban:* The population of the United States in July of 2009 was 307,006,550, and 79 percent of the population lives on urban land. Thus, the urban population is 242,535,175. U.S. Department of Agriculture, Economic Research Services, *Major Uses of Land in the United States 2002*, "Urban and Rural Residential Uses." http://www.ers.usda.gov/publications/EIB14/eib14g.pdf and U.S. Census Bureau, Annual Estimates of the Resident Population for the United States, Regions, States, and Puerto Rico: April 1, 2000, to July 1, 2009 (NST-EST2009-01), http://www.census.gov/popest/states/NST-ann-est.html.

1 *Thirty-six million people live . . . in the world:* PricewaterhouseCoopers, "Which Are the Largest City Economies?"

1 *Twelve million people reside . . . almost as large:* United Nations, Department of Economic and Social Affairs, Population Division, *World Urbanization Prospects: 2009*, File 12, "Population of Urban Agglomerations with 750,000 Inhabitants or More in 2009, by Country, 1950–2025," http://esa.un.org/unpd/wup/CD-ROM_2009/WUP2009-F12-Cities_Over_750K.xls.

1 *all of humanity could fit . . . townhouse:* Texas has 261,797 square miles of land, or 7.3 trillion square feet of land. According to the U.S. Census, the world population is approximately 6.9 billion as of July 12, 2010. If we divide 7.3 trillion square feet by 6.9 billion people, we get 1,034 square feet per capita, which is more than enough ground area for a modest townhouse per person. If we wanted to allocate for roads, commerce, and so on, we might have to assume that there were an average of two people living in each townhouse. U.S. Census 2000, GCT-PH1: Population, Housing Units, Area, and Density 2000, Summary File 1, 100-Percent Data, generated using American FactFinder; and U.S. Census Bureau, International Database, World Population Summary, www.census.gov/ipc/www/idb/worldpopinfo.php.

1 *Five million more people . . . is urban:* United Nations Habitat, *State of the World's Cities 2010/2011—Cities for All: Bridging the Urban Divide*, 2010. http://www.unhabitat.org/pmss/listItemDetails.aspx?publicationID=2917.

3 *Grand Central Terminal, which has more platforms:* "Largest Railroad Station" (by number of platforms), *Guinness World Records 2008* (New York: Bantam Dell, 2007), 374–75.

3 *Forty-seventh Street . . . gems:* 47th Street Business Improvement District, The Diamond District, www.diamonddistrict.org/home.html.

3 *Under the leadership of . . . taxes in the nation:* Henig, "New York City: Paying the Tab."

3 *New York, or more properly . . . (now Wall Street):* Burrows and Wallace, *Gotham*.

3 *In the eighteenth century . . . sugar and tobacco colonies:* Glaeser, "Urban Colossus," 9, 11.

3 *During the first half . . . urban colossus:* Gibson, "Population of the 100 Largest Cities."

3 *At the start . . . the natural hub:* Albion, *Rise of New York Port*, 38–54; and Glaeser, "Urban Colossus," 12.

4 *Shipping was the city's . . . around the harbor:* Glaeser, "Urban Colossus," 14.

4 *Sugar producers . . . English novels:* Burrows and Wallace, *Gotham*, ch. 27.

4 *The Harper brothers:* Mott, *Golden Multitudes*, 68.

4 *In the twentieth century . . . mammoth:* Glaeser and Kohlhase, "Decline of Transport Costs."

5 *Today, the five zip codes . . . Oregon or Nevada:* The five zip codes are 10017, 10019, 10020, 10022, and 10036. According to County Business Patterns, the combined payroll in these areas in 2007 was over $80 billion, and total employment was 617,984. When we divide total payroll by total employment, we calculate average earnings of approximately $130,000 per worker. In the County Business Patterns, 2007 payroll in Oregon was $56 billion and in Nevada was $44.4 billion, and 2007 employment in New Hampshire was 573,209 and in Maine was 503,789. U.S. Census Bureau, County Business Patterns 2007, www.census.gov/econ/cbp.

5 *Academic knowledge about . . . assets:* Bernstein, *Against the Gods*, 300–302.

5 *Michael Milken's high-yield (junk) bonds:* Lewis, *Liar's Poker*, 111.

5 *Henry Kravis to use those . . . leveraged buyouts:* "The Team," KKR, Kohlberg Kravis Roberts & Co., 2010, www .kkr.com/team/theteam.cfm.

5 *mortgage-backed security magnate . . . mailroom:* Lewis, *Liar's Poker*, 96.

5 *Today, 40 percent . . . still-thriving city:* Because New York County is equal to Manhattan, we are able to add up the total payroll of all industries in New York County in 2007, which is nearly $210 billion. Payroll in the financial services industry—North American Industry Classification System (NAICS) codes 521, 522, 523, and 525—is nearly $84 billion; $84 billion divided by $210 billion equals 39.88 percent. U.S. Census Bureau, County Business Patterns 2007, www.census.gov/econ/cbp.

5 *Between 2009 and 2010, as the American economy . . . outside of Greater New York.* Bureau of Labor Statistics, Economic News Releases, *County Employment and Wages*, "Table 1. Covered establishments, employment, and wages in the 327 largest counties, first quarter 2010," http://www.bls.gov/news.release/cewqtr.t01.htm. (Last modified date: October 19, 2010.)

6 *Within the United States . . . higher costs of living:* Using the 2000 U.S. Census Integrated Public Use Microdata Series, we keep the observations for men aged 25–55. We drop any observations where a person is not in the labor force or works less than full-time (defined as at least 35 hours per week and at least 40 weeks per year). We also drop any observations where a person earns a salary less than the salary earned by a worker earning minimum wage and working less than half-time (that is, less than one half times 1,400 hours per year, which is 35 hours per week times 40 weeks per year). Finally, we drop any outliers (those earning less than the 1st percentile, or more than the 99th percentile). We compare the average of those living in nonmetropolitan areas ($58,665.72 per year, in 2000 dollars) with those living in large (populations of 1 million or more) metropolitan areas ($77,086.05 per year, in 2000 dollars). The difference between these two numbers is $18,420.33, which is 31 percent higher than the average salary of those living in nonmetropolitan areas. Ruggles et al., *Microdata Series.*

6 *Americans who live . . . stronger in poorer nations:* Using 2008 GDP for Metropolitan Statistical Areas (MSAs) from the Bureau of Economic Analysis and MSA population from the U.S. Census Bureau, we determine the GDP per capita for each MSA by dividing GDP by population. We then find the average GDP per capita for MSAs with more than 1 million people in 2008, which is $52,546.85 per capita. We find the average GDP per capita for MSAs with less than 1 million people in 2008, which is $38,090.70, or 38 percent less than $52,546.85. Bureau of Economic Analysis, Gross Domestic Product by Metropolitan Area, www.bea.gov/regional/ gdpmetro; U.S. Census Bureau, Population Division, Table 5, Estimates of Population Change for Metropolitan Statistical Areas and Rankings: July 1, 2007, to July 1, 2008 (CBSA-EST2008-05), March 19, 2009, www.census .gov/popest/metro/tables/2008/CBSA-EST2008-05.xls.

7 *Bangalore, India's fifth-largest city:* United Nations, Department of Economic and Social Affairs, Population Division, *World Urbanization Prospects: 2009*, File 12, Population of Urban Agglomerations with 750,000 Inhabitants or More in 2009, by Country, 1950–2025, http://esa.un.org/unpd/wup/CD-ROM_2009/WUP2009 -F12-Cities_Over_750K.xls.

7 *Echoing antiurbanites . . . "700,000 villages":* Kumar, "The Whole Truth of a Home Economy," 135.

7 *"the growth . . . its villages":* Gandhi, *Essential Writings*, 120.

7 *near-perfect correlation:* Author's calculations using Maddison, "Statistics on World Population"; and United Nations, Population by Sex and Urban/Rural Residence, http://data.un.org.

7 *On average . . . 30 percent:* Ibid.

8 *An explosion . . . of that process:* White, *Birth and Rebirth of Pictorial Space.*

8 *Eight of the ten . . . since then:* In 2008, Detroit's population was 777,493. This is 42 percent of the 1950 population of 1,849,568. The ten largest cities in America in 1950 were (in descending order) New York, Chicago, Philadelphia, Los Angeles, Detroit, Baltimore, Cleveland, St. Louis, Washington, D.C, and Boston. All but New York and Los Angeles have lost population by 2008. American Community Survey, 2008 Data Profile for the United States and the City of Detroit, generated using American FactFinder; and Gibson, "Population of the 100 Largest Cities." See Glaeser, "Can Buffalo Ever Come Back?" for further discussion of that particular declining city.

9 *if $200 billion:* $200 billion divided by the population of New Orleans before Katrina (437,186) is about

$457,471 per person. American Community Survey, 2005 Data Profile for the City of New Orleans, generated using American FactFinder.

10 *More than a quarter... five years ago:* In 2000, the population of Manhattan age five or older was 1,462,015. The population of those who had lived in another county in 1995 was 381,919, or 26 percent. U.S. Census Bureau, Census 2000 Summary File 3, Sample Data, Table P4; residence in 1995 for the population five and older, county and state level, generated using American FactFinder.

10 *poverty rates in Rio... rural northeast:* This is discussed in further detail in chapter 3. Rio de Janeiro has a poverty rate of about 9 percent, while the rural northeast has a rate of 55 percent. Skoufias and Katayama, "Sources of Welfare Disparities."

10 *they were spending... postal service:* Cutler and Miller, "Water, Water Everywhere," 183–86.

10 *New York City... as a whole:* Life expectancy for a male born in 1901 in New York was 40.6. Life expectancy for an American male at birth in 1901 was 47.6. New York City Department of Health and Mental Hygiene, *Summary of Vital Statistics 1961,* table 6; and Arias, "United States Life Tables, 2006," table 12.

11 *Because she saw... ensure affordability:* Jacobs, *Death and Life,* 187–99.

12 *sight lines... preservation first:* Le Plan Local d'Urbanisme, www.paris.fr/portail/pratique/Portal.lut?page _id=6576&document_type_id=5&document_id=753&portlet_id=14938, with an objective to "préserver le patrimoine architectural et urbain" (preserve the architectural and urban heritage). The texts related to the plan are listed at www.paris.fr/portail/pratique/Portal.lut?page_id=7042&document_type_id=4&document _id=21439&portlet_id=16186.

12 *The Prince... Cathedral:* Many newspaper articles discuss various stands or complaints of the prince's regarding this issue. For example, see Alan Hamilton, "You're Scraping Wrong Part of the Sky."

12 *Mumbai's... one-and-a-third stories:* Bertaud, "Mumbai FSI Conundrum," 4.

12 *Shanghai remains far more affordable:* Gómez-Ibáñez and Ruiz Nuñez, "Inefficient Cities."

13 *average commute... twenty-four minutes:* Glaeser and Kahn, "Sprawl," 2499–2500.

14 *At Walden Pond... "insignificant":* Thoreau, *Walden,* Routledge, 117.

14 *"parklike setting" of suburbs:* Mumford, *City in History,* 492.

14 *"deterioration of the environment":* Ibid., 461.

14 *Fewer than a third... New York City:* Author's calculations from the American Community Survey, 2008 Data Profile for the City of New York and the United States, generated using American FactFinder.

15 *Carbon emissions... Chinese metropolitan area:* Zheng et al., "Greenness of China."

15 *If per capita... only 30 percent:* In 2006, per capita emissions in the United States were 19.78 metric tons. In France, they were 6.60 metric tons; in China, 4.58 metric tons; and in India, 1.16 metric tons. Total emissions in 2006 were 29.195 billion metric tons. If we subtract from this total China's 2006 emissions (1.314 billion people times 4.58 metric tons per capita for a total of 6.018 billion tons) as well as India's (1.112 billion people times 1.16 metric tons per capita for a total of 1.293 billion tons), and then add China's total emissions if they were at the U.S. per capita level (1.314 billion people times 19.78 metric tons for a total of 25.998 billion tons) as well as India's (1.112 billion people times 19.78 metric tons per capita for a total of 21.988 billion tons), the new world total would be 69.8601 billion tons, an increase of 139 percent. If, instead, we used France's 6.60 metric tons per capita figure, China's revised emissions would be 8.668 billion (1.314 billion people times 6.60 metric tons per capita) and India's would be 7.334 billion (1.112 billion people times 6.60 metric tons per capita), for a revised world total of 37.887 billion tons, or an increase of about 30 percent. U.S. Energy Information Administration, *International Energy Annual 2006,* table H.1cco2, "World Per Capita Carbon Dioxide Emissions from the Consumption and Flaring of Fossil Fuels, 1980–2006," www.eia.doe.gov/pub/international/ iealf/tableh1cco2.xls.

CHAPTER 1: WHAT DO THEY MAKE IN BANGALORE?

18 *India's powerful labor unions:* Besley and Burgess, "Can Labor Regulation Hinder Economic Performance?" 92.

18 *sold it to MIH Holdings:* See, for example, Ranjan, "Bixee, Pixrat Acquired."

18 *One ranking agency... 2010:* Real Website Worth, "bixee.com," realwebsiteworth.com, http://208.87.241.248/ traffic_report/bixee.com.

18 *He has since left MIH:* The Web site is Educrest.com, though the site is currently under construction. Jacob, "Now, Social Networking Gets a Voice."

19 *Athens was hardly the intellectual center:* Hall, *Cities in Civilization,* 26.

19 *The most exciting Greek thinkers... older civilizations of the Near East:* Ibid.

19 *Miletus... Thales:* McNeill, *Western Civilization,* 58.

19 *Hippodamus, whose gridlike plans:* Cartledge, *Ancient Greece,* 54.

19 *Athens grew by trading wine, olive oil, spices, and papyrus:* Hall, *Cities in Civilization,* 49–50.

19 *The city cemented its power... places like Miletus:* Cartledge, *Ancient Greece,* 98.

19 *Just as rich, ebullient... battle-scarred Asia Minor:* Ibid., 104.

19 *Hippodamus came from Miletus to plan the city's harbor:* Ibid., 54, 91.
19 *This remarkable period . . . freedom to share their ideas:* Ibid., 104.
20 *Theodoric, saw the advantage of cities like Ravenna:* "Theodoric (King of Italy)" *Encyclopædia Britannica.*
20 *But while the Goths and Huns . . . deliver food and water:* McNeill, *Western Civilization*, 207.
20 *Charlemagne . . . sophisticated civilization:* Pagden, *Worlds at War.*
20 *A thousand years ago . . . Constantinople:* Chandler, *Four Thousand Years of Urban Growth*, 538.
20 *The other three . . . were all Islamic:* Bairoch, *Cities and Economic Development.*
20 *The Islamic caliphates . . . powerful emirs and caliphs:* Lyons, *House of Wisdom.*
21 *The Abbasid caliphs . . . physical and human marvels:* Ibid., 59, 62.
21 *They collected scholars . . . translate it into Arabic:* Ibid., 63.
21 *The scholars there translated . . . mathematical knowledge:* Durant, *Age of Faith*, 240–41.
21 *from the Sindhind to develop algebra:* Lyons, *House of Wisdom*, 72–73.
21 *Indian numerals . . . compatible with Islamic theology:* Ibid., 73, 175; and Gari, "Arabic Treatises."
21 *Medical knowledge came to Baghdad from the Persians:* Lyons, *House of Wisdom*, 86.
21 *paper-making came there by Chinese prisoners of war:* Ibid., 57.
21 *Venice . . . ideas, as well as spices, throughout the Middle Ages:* McNeill, *Venice: The Hinge of Europe.*
21 *When the Spanish retook Toledo . . . its classics into Latin:* Bakhit, *History of Humanity*, 115.
21 *crusaders captured Antioch . . . Arabic medical and science texts:* Lyons, *House of Wisdom*, 104.
21 *In the Islamic cities of Spain . . . transferred to Christendom:* Ibid., 142.
22 *Those texts came to the new universities . . . built on Greek and Islamic philosophy:* Knowles, "The Evolution of Medieval Thought."
22 *In monasteries, Benedictine monks . . . like the waterwheel:* Lucas, "Role of the Monasteries"; Baumol, "Entrepreneurship: Productive, Unproductive, and Destructive."
22 *Merchants congregated in trade fairs . . . vulnerable infrastructure:* Milgrom et al., "The Role of Institutions in the Revival of Trade."
22 *Eventually urban powerhouses . . . armed artisans or mercenaries:* Pirenne, *Medieval Cities* and Murray, *Bruges: Cradle of Capitalism.*
22 *The growth of cities run by merchants . . . princes and monarchs:* de Long and Shleifer, "Princes and Merchants."
22 *These dense places . . . knowledge of the East:* McNeill, *Western Civilization*, 331.
22 *The commercial cities developed the legal rules:* Ibid., 327–28.
22 *the Great Revolt . . . first modern republic:* Geyl, *Revolt of the Netherlands.*
23 *When American ships . . . on the world stage:* Goodman, *Japan and the Dutch*, 9.
23 *Between 1894 . . . Korea:* Iriye, "Japan's Drive to Great-Power Status."
23 *By the middle of the twentieth century . . . American counterparts:* Meyer, *Japan*, 261.
23 *The first contacts . . . nearby island of Tanegashima:* McClain, *Japan*, 2.
23 *Over the next three hundred years . . . Western learning:* Goodman, *Japan and the Dutch*, 107–8.
23 *In 1590, Portuguese Jesuits . . . printing press in Nagasaki:* Boorstin, *Discoverers*, 508.
23 *Forty-six years later . . . profitable trading opportunity:* Goodman, *Japan and the Dutch*, 16.
23 *Western medicine entered Japan . . . East India Company's resident physician:* Ibid., 37–38, 40.
23 *Soon Japanese students . . . medical techniques to Japan:* Ibid., 38.
23 *By the start of the nineteenth century . . . Eastern herbs to produce unconsciousness:* Stevens, "Anaesthesia in Japan."
23 *In addition to Western medicine . . . sunglassess through Nagasaki:* Sugita, *Western Science in Japan*, 17.
24 *In 1720, an inquisitive shogun started allowing Western books in Japan:* Goodman, *Japan and the Dutch*, 51.
24 *When the American gunboats . . . trained in the "Dutch Studies":* Morris-Suzuki, *Technological Transformation*, 62.
24 *In 1855, the Dutch gave . . . Nagasaki Naval Training Station:* Murdoch, *Tokugawa Epoch*, 616.
25 *Bangalore does have . . . Delhi:* India, Government of, "Climatological Data of Important Cities."
25 *Infosys was founded . . . consulting:* "Who We Are," Infosys, www.infosys.com/about/who-we-are/pages/history .aspx.
25 *educating thousands . . . Ivy League school:* Schlosser, "Harder than Harvard."
27 *A 10 percent increase . . . between 1980 and 2000:* Author's calculations using data from U. S. Census Bureau, 1980 Census and 2000 Census.
27 *As the share . . . 22 percent:* Author's calculations using data from U.S. Census Bureau, American Community Survey, 2008, Bureau of Economic Analysis, Regional Economic Accounts, Gross Domestic Product by Metropolitan Area, 2008.
28 *Between 1970 and 2000 . . . by 37 percent:* Author's calculations using county-level census data from Haines, "Historical, Demographic, Economic, and Social Data: The United States, 1790–2002."
28 *For each worker . . . 8 percent higher earnings:* Card, "Estimating the Return to Schooling."

28 *extra year of schooling ... gross domestic product:* Barro and Lee, "International Data on Educational Attainment"; and Maddison, "Statistics on World Population."

28 *The connection ... since the 1970s:* Goldin and Katz, *Race Between Education and Technology.*

28 *In 1980, men with four years of college ... nearly 70 percent:* Economic Report of the President 1997, United States Government Printing Office, Washington, DC, Feb. 1997, www.gpoaccess.gov/usbudget/fy98/pdf/erp.pdf.

28 *One school of thought ... need for unskilled labor:* Acemoğlu, "Why Do New Technologies Complement Skills?" 1055–58; Doms et al., "Workers, Wages, and Technology," 253–54.

29 *Many studies have shown ... corn and computers:* Nelson and Phelps, "Investment in Humans," 70; Schultz, "Ability to Deal with Disequilibria," 834; and Krueger, "How Computers Have Changed the Wage Structure."

29 *A second school ... less-skilled workers:* Sachs and Shatz, "U.S. Trade with Developing Countries."

29 *A century ago, when New York ... horse farm:* "Birth of the University," *History of Stanford.*

29 *"life is ... useful career":* Elliott, *Stanford University,* 88–89.

30 *Stanford University's first ... wasn't even eighteen:* Aitken, *Continuous Wave,* 103.

30 *But his backers ... reliable wireless service:* Ibid., 104–5.

30 *But instead of giving up ... Federal Telegraph Corporation:* Sturgeon, "How Silicon Valley Came to Be," 19.

30 *Lee De Forest ... first vacuum tube:* Ibid., 24.

30 *another product ... transistor:* Ibid., 17.

30 *Even after ... talented students:* Ibid., 20–23.

30 *Stanford's first ... at FTC:* Ibid., note 15; and "Electrical Engineering Timeline," Stanford Engineering, http://ee.stanford.edu/timeline.php.

30 *Two Danes ... Magnavox:* Sturgeon, "How Silicon Valley Came to Be," 30.

30 *Another FTC employee ... Fisher Research Laboratories:* Ibid., 32.

30 *Litton Industries ... FTC offspring:* Ibid., 32-34.

31 *But no FTC employee ... come to the valley:* Gillmor, *Fred Terman at Stanford.* The Nobel citation credits the two men with the "discovery of the transistor effect," but there is some controversy over this (see R. G. Arns, "The other transistor: early history of the metal-oxide semiconductor field-effect transistor").

31 *William Shockley ... shared the Nobel Prize in Physics:* Shurkin, *Broken Genius.*

31 *In one notorious incident ... hand on a pin:* Ibid., 176.

32 *eight of his best young scientists ... to form Intel:* "Fairchild Semiconductor Corporation," *Encyclopædia Britannica.*

32 *Another left ... next wave of innovators:* "'Fairchildren' Who Came to Dominate the World of Technology," *Financial Times* (London), Oct. 31, 2007, Business Life.

32 *Two former Hewlett-Packard ... Apple Computer:* "Apple Inc." *Encyclopædia Britannica.*

32 *A former Apple employee started eBay:* "Who We Are: History," eBay, www.ebayinc.com/milestones; and Viegas, *Pierre Omidyar,* 34.

32 *Both Yahoo! and Google:* "The History of Yahoo!—How It All Started . . ." Yahoo! Media Relations (Yahoo! 2005), http://docs.yahoo.com/info/misc/history.html; and "Google Milestones," Corporate Information, Google, 2010, www.google.com/corporate/history.html.

32 *A few companies ... Santa Clara County:* U.S. Census Bureau, American Community Survey, 2008 Data Profile for County of Santa Clara, generated using American FactFinder.

33 *Even after the housing bust ... buy a home:* National Association of Realtors, Median Sales Price of Existing Single-Family Homes for Metropolitan Areas for First Quarter 2010, www.realtor.org/research/research/metro price.

33 *Only 22.2 percent ... college degree:* U.S. Census Bureau, American Community Survey, 2008 Data Profile for City of Palo Alto, generated using American FactFinder.

33 *The Valley's other major drawback:* U.S. Census Bureau, County Business Patterns 2008, www.census.gov/econ/cbp.

33 *single-industry cities ... new ideas and companies:* Glaeser et al., "Growth in Cities," 1132, 1150–51.

33 *Jane Jacobs ... old ideas:* Jacobs, *Economy of Cities,* 47–53.

33 *Michael Bloomberg ... could help them:* "Biography," Office of the Mayor, New York City, 2010, www.nyc.gov/portal/site/nycgov/menuitem.e985cf5219821bc3f7393cd401c789a0.

33 *Facebook started ... wanted to share:* Nguyen, "Online Network Created by Harvard Students Flourishes."

33 *When eBay ... American public:* "Meet Meg Whitman," Meg 2010: A New California (Meg Whitman for Governor of California, 2010), www.megwhitman.acemof/aboutMeg.php.

34 *One experiment ... any other sort of interaction:* Rocco, "Trust Breaks Down."

35 *The very first ... bicyclist:* Strube, "What Did Triplett Really Find?" 271.

35 *He noted that ... another child:* Triplett, "Pacemaking and Competition," 510

35 *Modern statistical evidence ... occupational niche:* Rosenthal, et al., "Agglomeration, Labor Supply, and the Urban Rat Race."

35 *In one major chain ... productive peers.*: Mas and Moretti, "Peers at Work."

35 *Telephone calls ... over the phone:* Gaspar and Glaeser, "Information Technology."

35 more *electronic communications:* Ibid., 152.

35 *In the average county ... 30.6 percent of adults have college degrees:* Author's calculations, taking the average of the share of the population with bachelor's degrees for counties with a population density of less than one person per acre and those with more than two people per acre. County-level Census data from Haines, "Historical, Demographic, Economic, and Social Data: The United States, 1790–2002."

36 *Innovations cluster ... continents and seas:* Paraphrase of Glaeser et al., "Growth in Cities," 1127.

36 *In 1993 ... geographically close:* Jaffe et al., "Geographic Localization of Knowledge Spillovers."

36 *More recent ... geographically close:* Maurseth and Verspagen, "Knowledge Spillovers in Europe," 542.

36 *Recent research ... in their industry:* Lychagin et al., "Spillovers in Space."

36 *For over a century ... face-to-face meetings:* Gaspar and Glaeser, "Information Technology," 136–37.

37 *business travel has soared:* Ibid., 149.

37 *Facebook is another ... effective:* http://onlinelibrary.wiley.com/doi/10.1111/j.1083-6101.2007.00367.x/full.

37 *Studies find that Facebook ... real-life conversation:* http://web.ebscohost.com.ezpprod1.hul.harvard.edu/ehost/pdfviewer/pdfviewer?vid=8&hid=107&sid=8532ef3f-5e9d-48f8-98ec-d2a5e260d6e8%40sessionmgr111.

37 *Moreover, the initial idea ... Harvard students:* Mezrich, *The Accidental Billionaires.*

38 *Gutenberg ... world center of printing:* Howard, *The Book.*

39 *The city's rich ... for its presses:* Ibid.

39 *In later centuries ... into its port:* Burrows and Wallace, *Gotham,* 441.

39 *Martin Luther ... "act of grace":* Couch et al., *Information Technologies,* 124.

39 *"Between 1517 ... significance of the Press":* A. G. Dickens, quoted in Philip M. Taylor, *Munitions of the Mind,* 97.

39 *Protestantism has an inherent superiority ... global commerce:* Glaeser and Scheinkman, "Neither a Borrower."

39 *The great Dutch revolt ... local Catholic church:* Geyl, *Revolt of the Netherlands,* 93.

40 *In 1581 ... the island of Manhattan:* "Netherlands," *Encyclopædia Britannica.*

40 *Act of Abjuration:* Zagorín, *Rebels and Rulers,* vol. 2, 118.

CHAPTER 2: WHY DO CITIES DECLINE?

41 *The corner of ... fourth-largest city:* I was inspired to visit this block by a superb article: McWhirter, "Homes Give Way to Urban Prairie."

41 *Between 1950 and 2008 ... half the U.S. average:* In 2008, Detroit's population was 777,493, which is 42 percent of the 1950 population of 1,849,568 and a loss of over 1 million people. Gibson, "Population of the 100 Largest Cities"; and U.S. Census Bureau, American Community Survey, 2008 Data Profile for City of Detroit, generated using American FactFinder. According to the same American Community Survey, 33.3 percent of people who live in Detroit have incomes that for the last twelve months have been below poverty level; and median family income in Detroit is $32,798, which is 52 percent of the nation's median family income of $63,366. U.S. Census Bureau; American Community Survey, 2008 Data Profile for City of Detroit and for the United States, generated using American FactFinder. In 2009, Detroit's city's average unemployment rate was 25 percent, 2.7 times the U.S. average 2009 rate of 9.3 percent. Bureau of Labor Statistics, *Local Area Unemployment Statistics,* "Unemployment Rates for the 50 Largest Cities, 2009," www.bls.gov/lau/lacilg09.htm, and *Statistics from the Current Population Survey,* "Employment Status of the Civilian Noninstitutional Population, 1940 to Date," www.bls.gov/cps/cpsaat1.pdf.

41 *In 2009, the city's unemployment rate:* Bureau of Labor Statistics, *Local Area Unemployment Statistics,* "Unemployment Rates for the 50 Largest Cities, 2009," www.bls.gov/lau/lacilg09.htm.

41 *In 2008 ... New York City's:* Federal Bureau of Investigation, *Crime in the United States 2008,* Sept. 2009, www.fbi.gov/ucr/cius2008/data/table_08.html.

41 *Detroit was unique ... since the bust:* Case-Shiller Home Price Indices, July 21, 2010.

42 *Six of the sixteen ... since that year:* Gibson, "Population of the 100 Largest Cities," table 1, "Annual Estimates of the Resident Population for Incorporated Places Over 100,000, Ranked by July 1, 2009 Population," April 1, 2000, to July 1, 2009 (SUB-EST2009-01), www.census.gov/popest/cities/SUB-EST2009.html.

42 *Skilled cities have been more successful:* Glaeser and Saiz, "Skilled City," 47.

42 *only 11 percent of Detroit's adults:* U.S. Census Bureau; American Community Survey, 2008 Data Profile for City of Detroit, generated using American FactFinder.

42 *People and firms ... comprise the Rust Belt:* Glaeser and Tobio, "Rise of the Sunbelt."

43 *New York's garment industry:* U.S. Bureau of the Census, Census 1950, www.census.gov/prod/www/abs/decennial/1950.html.

43 *In 1900, all twenty:* Gibson, "Population of the 100 Largest Cities." Here are the twenty largest cities and one of their associated waterways: New York, NY, Eastern seaboard; Chicago, IL, Lake Michigan; Philadelphia, PA,

Eastern seaboard; St. Louis, MO, Mississippi River; Boston, MA, Eastern seaboard; Baltimore, MD, Chesapeake Bay; Cleveland, OH, Lake Erie; Buffalo, NY, Erie Canal; San Francisco, CA, San Francisco Bay; Cincinnati, OH, Ohio River; Pittsburgh, PA, Allegheny, Monongahela, Ohio Rivers; New Orleans, LA, Mississippi Delta; Detroit, MI, Detroit River; Milwaukee, WI, Lake Michigan; Washington, DC, Potomac River; Newark, NJ, Newark Bay; Jersey City, NJ, Hudson River; Louisville, KY, Ohio River; Minneapolis, MN, Mississippi River; and Providence, RI, Eastern seaboard.

43 *Detroit was founded . . . and the United States:* Hudgins, "Evolution of Metropolitan Detroit."

44 *In 1816, it cost as much:* George Rogers Taylor, *Transportation Revolution,* 132–33.

44 *cannons than with canals:* Bernstein, *Wedding of the Waters,* 22–23.

44 *Before he became the president . . . Potowmack Canal Company:* Achenbach, *The Grand Idea.*

44 *The great liquid highway . . . east-west transport:* George Rogers Taylor, *Transportation Revolution,* 33–34, 197.

44 *Cities soon sprang up . . . plied the canal:* Bernstein, *Wedding of the Waters,* 359–61.

45 *The need to lift . . . transform cities:* Ibid., 362.

45 *From 1850 until 1970 . . . along that route:* Data from 1900–1980: Gibson, "Population of the 100 Largest Cities." In 1860, the cities that shared this distinction were, in order of population, New York, NY; Brooklyn, NY; New Orleans, LA; St. Louis, MO; Chicago, IL; and Buffalo, NY. In 1960, they were New York, NY; Chicago, IL; Detroit, MI; Cleveland, OH; and St. Louis, MO.

45 *the city's land market exploded:* Hoyt, *One Hundred Years of Land Values in Chicago.*

45 *Between 1850 . . . 1.5 million inhabitants:* According to the 2008 American Community Survey, 10.8 percent of Detroit's population over twenty-five has a college degree. U.S. Census Bureau, American Community Survey, 2008 Data Profile for City of Detroit, generated using American FactFinder.

45 *In 1889, Iowa corn yields:* United States Department of Agriculture—National Agricultural Statistics Service, Crops by State (95111), cn186629.csv, http://usda.mannlib.cornell.edu/MannUsda/viewDocumentInfo.do?documentID=1269.

45 *Cities like America's Porkopolis . . . by nearby farmers:* Cronon, *Nature's Metropolis.*

45 *Chicago's stockyards . . . kept them cool:* Williams, *Food in the United States,* 87.

46 *from 21,000 to 206,000 people:* U.S. Census Bureau, Population Division, Release Date June 2010; and Gibson, "Population of the 100 Largest Cities."

46 *By 1907 . . . New York or London:* Nolan, "How the Detroit River Shaped Lives and History."

46 *Liverpool and Manchester were tied together:* David Elystan Owen, *Canals to Manchester.*

46 *Canal building during the Georgian era:* Minchinton, "Bristol."

46 *rail would complement waterways:* Lay, *Ways of the World,* 138.

46 *Detroit Dry Dock . . . sophisticated engine production:* Nevins and Hill, *Ford,* vol. 1, 84–85.

47 *ready access to wood . . . place to build cars:* Ibid., 515.

47 *Both carriages . . . nearby Flint:* Pelfrey, *Billy, Alfred, and General Motors,* 28–29, covers carriages and Durant's involvement therein.

47 *The basic science of the automobile . . . mass scale:* Nevins and Hill, *Ford,* vol. 1, 125–35.

47 *In general, there's . . . growth of a region:* Glaeser et al., "Clusters of Entrepreneurship."

47 *After Ford left . . . experimenting with engines:* Nevins and Hill, *Ford,* vol. 1, 87.

47 *neighbor's Westinghouse threshing machine:* Ibid.

47 *working on Westinghouse engines:* Ibid.

47 *a proto-tractor:* Ibid., 112.

47 *joined Westinghouse's archrival:* Ibid., 117.

47 *In 1893, he was promoted to chief engineer in the Detroit plant:* Ibid., 135.

47 *"Young man, that's the thing!":* Brinkley, *Wheels,* 26.

47 *In 1896 . . . top speed:* Nevins and Hill, *Ford,* vol. 1, 154–55.

47 *fast enough . . . 1899:* Ibid., 174–75.

47 *expensive and of low quality:* Ibid., 190–92.

48 *lumber baron didn't give up:* Weiss, *Chrysler, Ford, Durant, and Sloan,* 11.

48 *Ford, Ransom Olds . . . in the Motor City:* Nevins and Hill, *Ford,* vol. 1, passim.

48 *Ford was able to open . . . financing and parts:* Ibid., 231.

48 *In 1906, Ford produced . . . front ranks of the automotive industry:* Brinkley, *Wheels,* 87.

48 *In 1908 . . . (about $19,000 in 2010 currency):* Nevins and Hill, *Ford,* vol. 1, 388.

48 *Five years later . . . meshed perfectly:* Ibid., 447–80. For Adam Smith's observations regarding the pin factory, see Smith, *Wealth of Nations,* Cosimo, 10–11.

49 *In 1917, he began . . . southwest of Detroit:* Nevins and Hill, *Ford,* vol. 2, 201–2.

49 *At River Rouge . . . workspace:* Ibid., 293.

49 *River Rouge had its own . . . single facility:* Ibid., 212–16.

50 *By the 1950s, both New York and Detroit started shrinking:* U.S. Census Bureau, Population Division, Release Date June 2010; and Gibson, "Population of the 100 Largest Cities."

50 *Between 1890 and today ... twenty cents to two:* Glaeser and Kohlhase, "Decline of Transport Costs."

50 *Samuel Gompers, the founder:* Harvey, *Samuel Gompers,* 40–44.

50 *was a cigar maker from New York City:* Ibid., 6.

50 *Great Revolt of 1910:* Tyler, *Look for the Union Label,* 63.

50 *On a May afternoon ... beating women up:* Nevins and Hill, *Ford,* vol. 3, 139–41.

50 *It would take ... United Auto Workers:* Nevins and Hill, *Ford,* vol. 3.

50 *National Labor Relations Act:* Russell A. Smith, "Taft-Hartley Act."

51 *Taft-Hartley Act ... closed shops:* Ibid.

51 *right-to-work states:* Vedder, "Right-to-Work Laws," 172.

51 *One classic paper ... anti-union side:* Thomas J. Holmes, "Effect of State Policies on the Location of Manufacturing," 693.

51 *UAW whipsawed ... began to decline:* June Manning Thomas, "Planning and Industrial Decline."

51 *Boston's maritime industries ... steam-powered ships:* Glaeser, "Reinventing Boston," 131–32.

51 *New York's garment industry imploded:* Glaeser and Kahn, "From John Lindsay."

51 *and the city lost ... between 1967 and 1977:* Author's calculations using U.S. Census Bureau, County Business Patterns 1967 and 1977.

52 *three years before John Lennon was born:* BBC News, "Liverpool Hails Population Rise," http://news.bbc.co.uk/2/hi/uk_news/england/merseyside/3644164.stm.

52 *But since 1937 ... its population:* McElroy, *Key Statistic Bulletin.*

52 *containerization put thousands of stevedores out of work:* Levinson, *The Box.*

52 *In 1959, Franco belatedly empowered:* "Spain," *Encyclopædia Britannica.*

52 *its GDP grew faster than that of any:* Maddison, "Statistics on World Population."

52 *Low wages ... competing with its industries:* "Bilbao," *Encyclopædia Britannica.*

52 *Bilbao's population fell:* Instituto Nacional Estadistica (Spain), www.ine.es, De Facto Population Figures from 1900 Until 1991 and De Jure Population Figures from 1986 Until 1995.

54 *New York's murder rate ... disturbing trend:* Monkkonen, *Homicides in New York City.*

54 *This is the site ... Detroit was ablaze:* Sugrue, *Origins of the Urban Crisis,* 259.

54 *failed to control the thousands of rioters:* Rucker and Upton, *Race Riots,* vol. 1, 167.

54 *The riot didn't end until after Tuesday:* Thompson, *Whose Detroit?*

54 *By the time ... seven thousand arrests:* Rucker and Upton, *Race Riots,* vol. 1, 165.

55 *riots were most common ... had smaller riots:* DiPasquale and Glaeser, "Los Angeles Riot," 56.

55 *"repression works":* Charles Tilly, Louise Tilly, and Richard Tilly, *The Rebellious Century.*

56 *In 1977, workers in ... in Manhattan:* Using County Business Patterns for 1977, we extracted data for Wayne County, Michigan, and New York County (Manhattan), New York. For Wayne County, total wages paid were $12,231,051,000 and total employees were 797,342, for an average yearly wage of $15,340. For Manhattan County, total wages paid were $26,342,663,000 and total employees were 1,765,942, for an average yearly wage of $14,917, about 3 percent less than the wage in Wayne County. U.S. Census Bureau, 1986-04-28, County Business Patterns, 1977: U.S. Summary, State, and County Data, http://hdl.handle.net/1902.2/8464, Interuniversity Consortium for Political and Social Research, version 1.

56 *In 1975, New York State ... nation's highest taxes:* Cannato, *Ungovernable City.*

56 *Hipper urbanists look to Andy Warhol and the arts:* Currid, *Warhol Economy.*

56 *In 2008, more than $78.6 billion:* U.S. Census Bureau, County Business Patterns 2008, www.census.gov/econ/cbp.

56 *Benjamin Chinitz ... kids to take risks:* Chinitz, "Contrasts in Agglomeration," 281, 284–85.

56 *Certainly, financial billionaire ... someone else:* Langley, *Tearing Down the Walls,* 8.

56 *The growth of finance ... leveraged buyouts:* Bernstein, *Against the Gods,* 300–302.

57 *RJR/Nabisco:* Burrough and Helyar, *Barbarians at the Gate,* 5.

57 *In the 1970s, Bloomberg ... with him to City Hall:* Bloomberg and Winkler, *Bloomberg.*

58 *In metropolitan areas ... how big the cities are:* Glaeser et al., "Clusters of Entrepreneurship."

58 *Coleman Young's family had moved:* Young and Wheeler, *Hard Stuff,* 16.

58 *He got a job working for Henry Ford:* Ibid., 40–41.

58 *but was ultimately blacklisted ... civil rights issues:* Coleman A. Young Foundation, biography, www.cayf.org/about_person.php.

59 *In World War II ... had been outside Detroit:* Young and Wheeler, *Hard Stuff,* 59.

59 *seventeen blacks and no whites:* Ibid., 84–85.

59 *The federal government ... Fort Knox:* Ibid., 65–78.

59 *founded the National Negro Labor Council:* Ibid., 113.

59 *whose radicalism ... "stool pigeon":* "Coleman A. Young, 79, Mayor of Detroit and Political Symbol for Blacks, Is Dead," *New York Times,* Nov. 30, 1997.

59 *Finally, in 1963 . . . state senate:* Young and Wheeler, *Hard Stuff,* 165.

59 *Three years later, he became the senate minority leader:* Ibid., 169.

59 *He pushed through open-housing laws:* Ibid., 166.

59 *Detroit's first income tax:* Rich, *Coleman Young,* 86.

59 *Research by four economists . . . higher tax rates:* Haughwout, et al., "Local Revenue Hills: Evidence from Four U.S. Cities."

60 *in 1973 . . . elected mayor:* Ibid., 105.

60 *win his next four mayoral elections easily:* Ibid., 112, 115, and 118 cover the 1977, 1981, and 1985 elections; Steven A. Holmes, "The 1989 Elections."

60 *was 11.1 percent white in 2008:* U.S. Census Bureau, American Community Survey, 2008 Data Profile for Detroit, generated using American FactFinder; and Gibson and Jung, "Historical Census Statistics on Population Totals by Race," Working Paper No. 76, detailed tables, Michigan.

60 *"properly used curse words":* Young, *Quotations of Mayor Coleman A. Young,* 6.

60 *"The victim of racism":* Ibid., 1–2.

60 *"hit the eight-mile road":* Ibid., 35.

60 *the Curley Effect:* Glaeser and Shleifer, "Curley Effect," 2.

60 *Curley cast himself . . . right old wrongs:* Beatty, *Rascal King,* 3.

61 *calling Anglo-Saxons "a strange and stupid race":* Ibid., 170.

61 *He was elected mayor . . . term as governor:* Ibid., 3.

61 *Curley spent two terms in jail:* Ibid., 443, 465, 473, 481.

61 *"Take every damn one of them":* Ibid., 5.

61 *Vespasian . . . the Colosseum:* Levick, *Vespasian,* 127–28 (Colosseum), 129 (building in general).

61 *Potemkin . . . Catherine the Great:* "Grigory Aleksandrovich Potemkin," *Encyclopædia Britannica,* www.britan nica.com/EBchecked/topic/472610/Grigory-Aleksandrovich-Potemkin-Prince-Tavrichesky-Imperial-Prince.

62 *building the Joe Louis Arena:* Ankeny and Snavely, "Renovate Joe or Build Rink?"

62 *the People Mover:* Wilkerson, "Detroit's Monorail Opens."

62 *The three-mile system . . . to operate:* Henion, "People Mover Grows Up."

62 *tax breaks . . . private rather than public folly:* Nicholson and Jones, "Detroit's New Towers of Hope."

62 *Unfortunately . . . $100 million in 1996:* Meredith, "G.M. Buys a Landmark."

62 *Poletown:* Wylie, *Poletown,* ix, 52.

62 *Activists protested . . . the city limits:* Wylie, *Poletown.*

62 *The plant still functions . . . within city borders:* Whitford, "Factory Gets a Second Chance"; and Wylie, *Poletown,* ix.

63 *Detroit's per capita income was $14,976:* U.S. Census Bureau; American Community Survey, 2008 Data Profile for City of Detroit and for the United States, generated using American FactFinder.

63 *unemployment rate was 13.7 percent:* Bureau of Labor Statistics, *Local Area Unemployment Statistics,* 2010, "Unemployment Rates for Metropolitan Areas," www.bls.gov/web/metro/laummtrk.htm; "Unemployment Rates for the 50 Largest Cities, 2006," www.bls.gov/lau/lacilg06.htm.

63 *temperatures average 24.7 degrees:* U.S. Census Bureau, County and City Data Book 2000, table C–7, "Cities—Government Finances and Climate," www.census.gov/prod/2002pubs/00ccdb/cc00_tabC7.pdf.

63 *why 777,000 people remain:* U.S. Census Bureau, American Community Survey, 2008 Data Profile for City of Detroit, generated using American FactFinder.

63 *Any area's population . . . disappear overnight:* Glaeser et al., "Urban Growth and Housing Supply."

64 *far below the cost of new construction:* U.S. Census Bureau, American Community Survey, 2008 Data Profile for City of Detroit, generated using American FactFinder; and Glaeser and Gyourko, "Urban Decline and Durable Housing."

64 *Spain has turned to transportation:* Catan, "Spain's Bullet Train."

64 *Liverpool had a flurry of new construction:* "Liverpool, Capital Of Culture 2008: City on the up—It's All in the Facades," *Guardian Magazine* (London), Jan. 5, 2008.

64 *The high-speed . . . the rail connection:* Catan, "Spain's Bullet Train."

65 *Research has found . . . just one job:* Busso and Kline, "Do Local Economic Development Programs Work?"

65 *from 1.4 million visitors in 1994 to 3.8 million in 2005:* Plöger, "Bilbao City Report," 30.

65 *attracts a million visitors:* "Guggenheim Bilbao Receives 5% Fewer Visits," *El Mundo,* www.elmundo.es/ elmundo/2009/01/12/cultura/1231778022.html.

66 *nine hundred new jobs:* Plaza, "Guggenheim Museum Bilbao," 459.

66 *cost the Basque treasury $240 million:* Ibid., 461.

66 *the National Centre . . . closed the same year:* "Debts Rock Pop Museum," *BBC News,* Oct. 18, 1999, http://news .bbc.co.uk/2/hi/entertainment/478616.stm.

66 *a total of 62,500 units:* Plöger, "Leipzig City Report."

66 *lost more than half of its 1970 population:* U.S. Census Bureau, American Community Survey, 2008 Data Profile for City of Youngstown, generated using American FactFinder; and Gibson, "Population of the 100 Largest Cities."

66 *Many of these homes are being destroyed:* City of Youngstown, Ohio, *Youngstown 2010: The Plan,* www.cityof youngstownoh.com/about_youngstown/youngstown_2010/plan/plan.aspx.

66 *more reasonable use of space:* Saulney, "Detroit Is Razing Itself"; Davey, "Detroit Mayor's Tough Love."

CHAPTER 3: WHAT'S GOOD ABOUT SLUMS?

69 *Plato noted . . . "the other of the rich":* Plato, *Republic,* 111.

70 *is 17.7 percent within cities and 9.8:* DeNavas-Walt et al., "People and Families in Poverty," 14.

70 *The poverty rate among . . . long-term residents:* Glaeser et al., "Why Do the Poor Live in Cities?" 4.

71 *When American cities . . . near those stops:* Ibid., 16.

72 *In the 1870s and 1880s . . . still legal:* Burns, *History of Brazil,* 126, 177; Levine, *History of Brazil,* 77.

72 *By the middle . . . were slaves:* Hugh Thomas, *Slave Trade,* 742.

72 *Runaway slaves . . . ancestors of favelas:* Burns, *History of Brazil,* 46.

72 *Emperor Pedro II . . . rest of the country:* Barman, Roderick J. *Citizen Emperor: Pedro II and the Making of Brazil,* 233.

72 *Finally, in 1888 . . . emancipation proclamation:* Chasteen, *Born in Blood and Fire,* 173.

72 *making it the last country in the Americas to end slavery:* Ibid.

72 *In the next year . . . Braganza dynasty:* Ibid., 173–74.

73 *The first true favela . . . a tax rebellion:* Burns, *History of Brazil,* 248–50.

73 *Canudos had grown . . . whiskey rebellion:* Levine, *Vale of Tears,* 16.

73 *In 1896 . . . take the town:* Burns, *History of Brazil,* 251–52.

73 *about fifteen thousand people were killed:* Levine, *Vale of Tears,* 185.

73 *While the Brazilian army won . . . came to Rio:* O'Hare and Barke, "Favelas of Rio," 232.

73 *One recent study reported . . . above that poverty line:* Ferreira et al., "Robust Poverty Profile for Brazil," 83.

73 *the extreme-poverty rate in rural Nigeria:* Canagarajan et al., "Evolution of Poverty and Welfare in Nigeria," 18.

73 *About three quarters . . . less than 30 percent:* World Bank, "Nigeria," 12.

74 *Kolkata is also . . . 24 percent:* India, Planning Commission of, "Poverty Estimates for 2004–05," 5.

74 *In recent years . . . less than 1 percent:* "Bengal Leads Hunger List."

74 *went for centuries without . . . human capital:* In 1999, average total schooling for Brazilians twenty-five years and older was 4.6 years. For comparison, the United States averaged 12.24 years, most of Western Europe averaged above 8, and many other South American countries ranked higher. For example, Argentina averaged 8.487, and Chile averaged 7.89. Barro and Lee, "Educational Attainment."

74 *Leila Velez . . . customers as employees:* Gergen and Vanourek, *Life Entrepreneurs,* 85–86.

74 *$30 million a year of beauty products:* McConnell, "Next Silicon Valley."

75 *Madam C. J. Walker . . . of her time:* Bundles, *On Her Own Ground,* 88, 277.

75 *suffer from poor soil quality:* Hartemink, "Soil Map Density and a Nation's Wealth and Income," 53–54; and Sachs, "Breaking the Poverty Trap."

76 *Rio was the nation's capital until 1960:* "Rio de Janeiro," *Encyclopædia Britannica.*

76 *campaign to make Rio's favelas healthier:* Meade, "'Civilizing Rio,'" 301.

76 *The "City of God" . . . for favela dwellers:* Portes, "Housing Policy," 5–6 (Cidade de Deus on p. 8).

76 *The ironic result . . . to the favelas:* Meade, "'Civilizing Rio,'" 304.

76 *Irish immigrants who fled starvation . . . sought-after neighborhood:* Berger, "Hell's Kitchen."

76 *Upper East Side . . . nineteenth century:* Plunz, *History of Housing in New York City,* 54–56.

76 *The Upper East Side Armory . . . unruly immigrants:* Burrows and Wallace, *Gotham,* 1037–38.

77 *New York actually received . . . from Eastern Europe:* Glaeser, "Reinventing Boston," 131–32.

77 *Boston received . . . through New York:* Ibid.

77 *Patrick Kennedy . . . hit the Kennedys' meager farm hard:* Maier, *The Kennedys,* 18–23, 334–39.

77 *a cooper in East Boston:* Ibid., 32.

78 *buy a saloon:* Koskoff, *Joseph P. Kennedy,* 6.

78 *He was first elected . . . "Honey Fitz":* Ibid., 7, 17.

78 *Joe Kennedy started out . . . substantial holdings:* Derbyshire, *Six Tycoons,* 207.

78 *made a fortune on Wall Street:* Ibid., 209.

78 *as of 2008, 36 percent of New Yorkers are foreign-born:* American Community Survey, 2008 Data Profile for the United States, generated using American FactFinder.

78 *foreign-born music directors:* New York Philharmonic, List of Directors, http://nyphil.org/about/musicDirec tors.cfm.

79 *Robert Cain . . . House of Lords:* Routledge, *Cains.*

79 *Carlos Slim . . . dry goods store:* Mehta, "Carlos Slim"; Carlos Slim Helú, biography of, www.carlosslim.com/biografia_ing.html.

79 *"in a regime of ignorance":* Stigler, *Organization of Industry,* 206.

80 *The great African-American writer . . . economic opportunity:* Rowley, *Richard Wright,* 4 (birth), 40 (final move to Memphis—he had lived there briefly earlier), 48–49 (move to Chicago).

80 *"I headed north . . . beneath the stars":* Wright, *Black Boy,* 285.

80 *In Chicago . . . to do some writing:* Rowley, *Richard Wright,* 55–60.

80 *Even more important . . . "help you to write":* Wright, "I Tried to Be a Communist."

80 *Wright was laid off . . . Louis Wirth:* Rowley, *Richard Wright,* 62–68.

80 *She also got him work . . . Works Progress Administration:* Ibid., 108–9.

81 *He moved to New York . . . big-city living:* Ibid., 124 (move), 144 (*Panorama*).

81 *In 1938 . . . Harper and Company:* Ibid., 138.

81 *Guggenheim Fellowship to write* Native Son: Ibid., 164.

81 *A Southern sharecropper . . . $445 a year:* Braunhut, "Farm Labor Wage Rates in the South," 193.

81 *A black worker . . . $5 a day:* Raff and Summers, "Did Henry Ford Pay Efficiency Wages?" S59.

81 *Only 2 percent of New York's . . . in 1900:* Gibson and Jung, "Historical Census Statistics on Population Totals by Race," Working Paper No. 76, detailed tables, Illinois and New York.

82 *McMechen . . . "the best friends that the colored people have":* "Baltimore Tries Drastic Plan." Information that he went to Morgan College and Yale is from Morgan State University's official Web site, www.morgan.edu/About_MSU/University_History.html.

82 *Similar measures . . . Southern cities:* C. Johnson quoted in Power, "Apartheid Baltimore Style," 289.

82 *"unconstitutional, unjust":* "Baltimore Tries Drastic Plan."

82 *Hawkins took Baltimore . . . in state court:* Power, "Apartheid Baltimore Style," 305–6 (first case), 311 (second case background), 314 (second case decision).

83 *greatest courtroom victory for black America up to that time:* Power, "Apartheid Baltimore Style," 312–14; and *Buchanan v. Warley,* 245 US 60, Supreme Court 1917.

83 *terrorized blacks who ventured into white areas:* Godshalk, *Veiled Visions;* and "Race Riots," *Encylopedia of Chicago,* http://encyclopedia.chicagohistory.org/pages/1032.html.

83 *Restrictive covenants . . . the world wars:* Stephen Grant Meyer, *As Long as They Don't Move Next Door,* 10.

83 *Almost forty years ago . . . housing in St. Louis:* Kain and Quigley, "Housing Market Discrimination," 272–73.

83 *African-American "residents . . . on the Lakeside drive":* Groner and Helfeld, "Race Discrimination in Housing," 432.

83 *Throughout the country . . . were more segregated:* Cutler et al., "Rise and Decline of the American Ghetto," 482.

83 *Two Baltimore attorneys . . . restrictive covenants:* Ware, "Invisible Walls," 759 (Perlman), 765 (Marshall).

83 *Swayed by their arguments . . . ending their usefulness:* Ibid., 770–71.

83 *Ten years later . . . New York's lead:* Collins, "Political Economy of State Fair-Housing Laws," 3–4.

83 *Between 1970 and 2000 . . . well-off African Americans:* Cutler et al., "Rise and Decline of the American Ghetto," 496 and passim.

84 *Between 1970 and 1990 . . . less than 10 percent:* Ibid., 467.

84 *The nature of segregation . . . half a century ago:* Ibid., 457–58.

84 *By 1990 . . . out of work:* Cutler and Glaeser, "Are Ghettos Good or Bad?"

84 *Young black women . . . single mothers in more segregated cities:* Ibid.

84 *William Julius Wilson argued that . . . communities became rudderless:* Wilson, *Declining Significance of Race.*

85 *a single transportation mode . . . horrendous commutes:* Glaeser et al., "Why Do the Poor Live in Cities?"

85 *The U.S. poverty line:* "The 2009 HHS Poverty Guidelines," U.S. Department of Health and Human Services, Assistant Secretary for Planning and Evaluation, http://aspe.hhs.gov/poverty/09poverty.shtml.

85 *$9,000 on car-related transportation:* Bureau of Labor Statistics, *Consumer Expenditure Survey, 2008,* www.bls.gov/cex, table 2400: "Population Size of Area of Residence: Average Annual Expenditures and Characteristics."

87 *alternative view . . . suffering of segregation:* Kain and Persky, "Alternatives to the Gilded Ghetto."

87 *Moving to Opportunity:* Kling et al., "Experimental Analysis of Neighborhood Effects," 84.

87 *The results were strikingly mixed:* Ibid., 103–5.

87 *For almost forty years . . . outcomes and reducing crime:* Harlem Children's Zone, "History," www.hcz.org/about-us/history.

88 *In 2004, as New York began . . . in its first year:* Dobbie and Fryer, "High Quality Schools," 6–7.

88 *Entrance into the school is determined by lottery:* Ibid., 3.

88 *Roland Fryer . . . gap in mathematics:* Ibid., 15–16.

88 *particular success with boys:* Ibid., 51.

88 *"when I'm President":* Obama, "Changing the Odds."

89 *In 1989, the ... than in Missouri:* According to a publication by the U.S. Department of Health and Human Services, annual AFDC benefit levels for a mother and two children with no earnings was $5,209 in Illinois, 20 percent higher than the $4,341 aid in Missouri. "Eligibility, Benefits and Disposable Income," *Aid to Families with Dependent Children: The Baseline,* Human Services Policy, Office of the Assistant Secretary for Planning & Evaluation, June 1998, p. 91, http://aspe.hhs.gov/hsp/afdc/afdcbase98.htm.

89 *If you were out of work ... any other declining Rust Belt city:* U.S. Census Bureau, Census 1990, Summary Tape File 3, Sample data, Detailed Tables, generated using American FactFinder.

89 *Since welfare reform in 1996 ... narrowed considerably:* U.S. Census Bureau, American Community Survey, 2006–2008 Data Profile for City of St. Louis and City of East St. Louis, generated using American FactFinder.

89 *prosperous Parisian parents ... Louis le Grand:* Lycée Henri-IV, http://lyc-henri4.scola.ac-paris.fr/index.html, and Lycée Louis le Grand, www.louis-le-grand.org/albedo/index.php.

89 *the 1964 Civil Rights Act ... opportunity for African Americans:* Pride, "End of Busing," 207–8.

89 *Enemies of busing ... travel long distances:* Gary Orfield, *Must We Bus? Segregated Schools and National Policy* (Washington, DC: Brookings Institution, 1978), 117.

89 *Milliken v. Bradley:* Amaker, "*Milliken v. Bradley,*" 349.

CHAPTER 4: HOW WERE THE TENEMENTS TAMED?

93 *The Dharavi neighborhood ... on around 530 acres:* Saunders, "Slumming It Is Better."

93 *a thousand inhabitants for every working toilet:* Watkins, "Beyond Scarcity," 37.

93 *tuberculosis ... seven years lower:* Mumbai, *Mumbai Human Development Report 2009.*

94 *Dharavi is pretty safe:* Patel, "Dharavi," 47.

95 *"works unmitigated mischief":* Theodore Roosevelt, *Rough Riders,* 2004, p. 426.

96 *Kinshasa had bad beginnings:* "Kinshasa: History," *Encyclopædia Britannica.*

96 *mass killings as a management tool:* "Congo Free State," *Encyclopædia Britannica.*

96 *government improved ... corruption continued unabated:* Edgerton, *Troubled Heart of Africa;* and Gondola, *The History of Congo.*

96 *from 446,000 to 10.4 million people:* According to the World Bank, the 1960 population of Kinshasa (then Léopoldville) was 446,013. In 2007, population in the urban agglomeration was 10,449,998. World Bank, World Development Indicators, Population in the Largest City.

96 *more than 30 percent larger than capital cities in stable democracies:* Ades and Glaeser, "Trade and Circuses."

96 *study of corruption in Indonesia:* Fisman, "Estimating the Value of Political Connections."

96 *one third of children ... are infected with the malaria parasite:* Kazadi et al., "Malaria in Primary School Children and Infants in Kinshasa."

96 *typhoid fever outbreak in 2004–2005:* World Health Organization, "Typhoid Fever."

97 *earliest HIV-positive blood samples:* Moore, "Puzzling Origins of AIDS."

97 *found that 5 percent of the population was infected:* Quinn et al., "AIDS in Africa."

97 *one of the world's ten most dangerous cities ... "criminal activity:"* CNN, www.cnn.com/2010/WORLD/americas/04/10/dangerous.cities.world/index.html; U.S. Department of State, http://travel.state.gov/travel/cis_pa_tw/cis/cis_1104.html.

97 *to the relative safety of Congo's capital:* "Kinshasa: History," *Encyclopædia Britannica.*

97 *Seventy-three out of every thousand children:* Congo, *Enquête Démographique,* p. 189, table 12.2, "Taux de mortalité des enfants selon certaines caractéristiques sociodémographiques."

97 *ten times the U.S. average ... rural Congo:* Ibid.; and Xu et al., "Deaths: Final Data for 2007."

97 *more than 10 percent of the children ... exceed 30 percent:* Tollens, "Food Security."

97 *thirty minutes for potable water:* Congo, *Enquête Démographique,* p. 20, table 2.6, "Approvisionnement en eau potable."

97 *Plague came to Athens:* Durack et al., "Hellenic Holocaust."

97 *Plague came to Constantinople:* Russell, "That Earlier Plague."

97 *three centuries after 1350:* McNeill, *Plagues and Peoples,* 160–72.

97 *death rates were much higher in urban areas:* Wrigley and Schofield, *Population History,* 472.

98 *Plague vanished from Europe:* McNeill, *Plagues and Peoples,* 171–72.

98 *yellow fever invaded, and cholera:* Ibid., 271–75, 280.

98 *Nine years later, Snow walked:* Steven Johnson, *Ghost Map,* 60.

98 *map of the cholera outbreak:* Ibid., 172–73.

98 *a particular water pump:* Ibid., 193.

98 *"the above-mentioned pump well":* Brody et al., "Map-Making," 65.

99 *Philadelphia ... went the public route:* Warner, *Private City,* 103.

99 *New York followed a private path:* Reubens, "Burr, Hamilton," 592.

99 *cautioned against the "burthensome" taxes:* Reubens, "Burr, Hamilton."

99 *The charter's key provisions:* Ibid., 599.

99 *"monied transactions not inconsistent":* Ibid., 600.

100 *lose more than a half percent:* New York City Department of Health and Mental Hygiene, *Summary of Vital Statistics 2008,* Jan. 2010, cover.

100 *Croton Aqueduct . . . had an impact:* Jervis, *Description of the Croton Aqueduct.*

100 *remarkable sixty-year decline:* In 1832, New York City had 50 deaths per 1,000, a rate of 5 percent. New York City Department of Health and Mental Hygiene, *Summary of Vital Statistics 2008,* Jan. 2010, cover.

100 *almost 1,700 public water systems:* Cutler and Miller, "Water, Water Everywhere," p. 169, table 5.1.

100 *municipalities were spending as much on water:* Ibid., 183–86.

100 *Economic historian Werner Troesken:* For instance, Troesken, "Typhoid Rates."

101 *larger reductions in other diseases:* Ferrie and Troesken, "Water and Chicago's Mortality Transition."

101 *"introduction of pure water":* Ibid.

101 *seven years lower in New York:* New York City Department of Health and Mental Hygiene, *Summary of Vital Statistics 2008* and *1961,* table 6; and Arias, "United States Life Tables, 2006," table 12.

102 *"I bought real estate in Japan":* "'Czar Of Tenderloin' Left Only $14 Estate: Tax Appraiser Finds Inspector Williams's Property Almost Balanced by Debts," *New York Times,* January 30, 1918, p. 18, ProQuest Historical Newspapers, Document ID: 102663258.

102 *New York's 1894 election:* "Will Be Mayor Three Years: Lawyers Say Mr. Strong's Term Is Not Abridged," *New York Times,* Nov. 11, 1894, p. 9, ProQuest Historical Newspapers, Document ID: 106840521.

102 *"a far better man for his purpose":* Theodore Roosevelt, *Rough Riders,* 423.

102 *Waring had gotten his start in . . . street cleaning:* "No Platt Republicans: Mayor-Elect Strong Overlooks the Boss in Six Appointments; Col. Waring to Clean the Streets," *New York Times,* Dec. 30, 1894, p. 8, ProQuest Historical Newspapers, Document ID: 109722641 (accessed Aug. 18, 2010).

102 *became a lightning rod:* "To Keep Streets Clean: Col. Waring Allowed over $3,000,000 for His Department; Discussion over 'Final Disposition'; Bill Favored for Grading Salaries," *New York Times,* Dec. 28, 1895, p. 9, ProQuest Historical Newspapers, Document ID: 103379346.

102 *"a dammed lot of drunken bums":* "Reproved by the Assembly: The Lower House of the Legislature Stands by the Grand Army, *New York Times,* Apr. 23, 1895, p. 2, ProQuest Historical Newspapers, Document ID: 103365239.

102 *Waring . . . called for his removal:* "Attack on Col. Waring: Gen. Viele Charges Him with Crimes Nearly Forty Years Old; Revenge, the Commissioner Says," *New York Times,* Apr. 21, 1895, p. 9, ProQuest Historical Newspapers, Document ID: 103493165.

102 *He insisted on seizing vehicles left idle:* "A Battle for Col. Waring's Men: Seizing Trucks in Mott Street Last Night They Were Attacked by a Mob of Owners and Italians," *New York Times,* June 2, 1895, p. 1, ProQuest Historical Newspapers, Document ID: 102460052.

102 *"marvels have been done toward the sanitation of the city":* "Clean Streets at Last: Fruitless Search for Derelict Wagons and Stray Bits of Paper; a Drive with Colonel Waring," *New York Times,* July 28, 1895.

102 *a new technology—asphalt:* "The Life of a Pavement: Results of Many Costly Experiments in New York," *New York Times,* Feb. 8, 1883.

103 *paved with oblong granite blocks:* Ibid.

103 *New York's male life expectancy:* New York City Department of Health and Mental Hygiene, *Summary of Vital Statistics 2008* and *1961,* table 6; and Arias, "United States Life Tables, 2006," table 12.

103 *replaced by a Tammany man . . . ice monopoly:* "Robert A. Van Wyck Dies in Paris Home: First Mayor of Greater New York Had Lived Abroad for 12 Years; He Was Croker's 'Choice,' His Administration Marked by So-Called Ice Trust, Ramapo Water Steal, and Police Scandals," *New York Times,* Nov. 16, 1918, p. 13, ProQuest Historical Newspapers, Document ID: 97044205.

103 *corruption decreases as education levels rise:* Glaeser and Saks, "Corruption In America."

103 *The old model of machine politics . . . became the age of the bureaucrat:* Wallis et al., "Politics, Relief, and Reform."

104 *vehicle miles traveled increases:* Duranton and Turner, "Fundamental Law of Road Congestion."

104 *The best way to reduce traffic congestion:* Columbia University, "Practical Economic Solutions."

105 *"users of private cars . . . their use imposes":* Vickrey, "New York's Subway Fare Structure."

105 *congestion pricing . . . traffic-jam free:* Goh, "Congestion Management."

105 *London adopted its own congestion charge:* Leape, "London Congestion Charge."

106 *first modern police force:* Schivelbusch, "Policing of Street Lighting."

106 *filled with violent disorder:* In 1650, Paris was the fourth-largest city in the world and the largest in Europe. Chandler, *Four Thousand Years of Urban Growth,* 534.

106 *vast street-lighting project:* Schivelbusch, "Policing of Street Lighting."

106 *"where the money is"*: Federal Bureau of Investigation, *Famous Cases,* "Willie Sutton."
106 *more than 20 percent of people . . . people were victims*: Glaeser, "Are Cities Dying?" and Glaeser and Sacerdote, "Why Is There More Crime in Cities?"
106 *In 1986, murder rates*: Glaeser and Sacerdote, "Why Is There More Crime in Cities?"
107 *financial returns to an average crime*: Ibid.
107 *overall crime rate in Mumbai*: India, Government of, National Crime Records Bureau, *Crime in India 2008,* ch. 2, "Crime in Megacities," 44, 48.
107 *two hundred years of murders in New York*: Author's calculation using Monkkonen, *Homicides in New York City.*
107 *Murder fell from 1800 to 1830*: Ibid.
107 *between three and six murders per hundred thousand*: Ibid.
108 *a weak link between corruption and homicide*: Ibid., using personal judgment regarding the definition of a Tammany mayor.
108 *peaked during the Roaring Twenties*: Monkkonen, *Homicides in New York City.*
108 *national homicide rate fell by about 29 percent*: Ibid.
108 *cities became more lawless than ever*: Ibid.
108 *One might guess . . . one fifth of the rise in crime*: Levitt, "Changing Age Structure."
108 *The Crips*: Estimates are 30,000 to 35,000. U.S. Department of Justice, National Gang Intelligence Center, National Gang Threat Assessment, Jan. 2009, p. 25, www.justice.gov/ndic/pubs32/32146/32146p.pdf.
109 *New York was about as healthy as the rest*: New York City Department of Health and Mental Hygiene, *Summary of Vital Statistics 2008* and *1961,* table 6; and Arias, "United States Life Tables, 2006," table 12.
109 *a 2.7-year gap opened up*: Ibid.
109 *This gap didn't appear for women*: Ibid.
109 *"wond'rous toy"*: Hyland, *Richard Rogers,* 32.
109 *legalization of abortion played some role*: Donohue and Levitt, "Impact of Legalized Abortion on Crime."
109 *economics of crime and punishment*: Becker, "Crime and Punishment."
109 *makes sense of recidivism rates*: Needels, "Go Directly to Jail and Do Not Collect?"
110 *about 50 percent of murders lead to a conviction*: Glaeser and Sacerdote, "Why Is There More Crime in Cities?"
110 *In Bogotá and Rio, fewer than 10 percent*: Ungar, "Prisons and Politics," 920.
110 *Kerner Commission recommended*: National Advisory Commission on Civil Disorders, *Report of the,* 11.
110 *the Rockefeller Drug Laws*: Farrell, "D.A.'s Assail Rockefeller Drug Penalties."
111 *number of inmates in the U.S. criminal system*: U.S. Bureau of Justice Statistics, "U.S. Correctional Population Reaches 6.6 Million," Aug. 25, 2002, http://bjs.ojp.usdoj.gov/content/pub/press/ppus01pr.cfm; and Cahalan, "Historical Corrections Statistics," tables 4-1 and 7-9A.
111 *sentence lengths double, crime rates decline*: Spelman, *Criminal Incapacitation;* Donohue, "Fighting Crime," 48; and Levitt, "Prison Population Size."
111 *the incapacitation effect of jails*: Levitt, "Prison Population Size."
111 *number of police . . . nationwide*: Levitt, "Understanding Why Crime Fell."
111 *Steven Levitt estimates*: Ibid.
112 *Jack Maple, who marked a map*: Maple said he used crayons to mark the crimes; in Dussault, "Jack Maple."
112 *subway robberies dropped dramatically*: Interview with Maple; and Dussault, "Jack Maple."
112 *CompStat*: Dussault, "Jack Maple."
113 *the Ten Point Coalition*: Berrien and Winship, "Lessons Learned," 25
113 *a number of community policing initiatives*: Gelzinis, "Commissioner Connecting."
113 *Neither CompStat nor community policing*: http://www.nyc.gov/html/doh/downloads/pdf/vs/wtc-deaths.pdf.
113 *Across countries, historically, terrorism does not deter*: Glaeser and Shapiro, "Cities and Warfare."
114 *expect to live one-and-a-half years longer*: New York City Department of Health and Mental Hygiene, *Summary of Vital Statistics 2008,* table 6; and Xu et al., "Deaths: Final Data for 2007."
114 *death rates lower than the national average*: Age-adjusted death rate for the United States is 760.3 per 100,000 people: Xu et al., "Deaths: Final Data for 2007." Los Angeles—age-adjusted rate 624.4: California Department of Public Health, *Los Angeles County's Health Status Profile for 2010.* Boston—age-adjusted rate 729.1: Massachusetts Department of Public Health, Bureau of Health Information, Statistics, Research, and Evaluation, "Massachusetts Deaths 2007," Apr. 2009, www.mass.gov/Eeohhs2/docs/dph/research_epi/death_report_07.pdf. Minneapolis—age-adjusted rate 701.1: Minnesota Department of Health, Health Statistics Portal, https://pqc .health.state.mn.us/mhsq/frontPage.jsp. San Francisco—age-adjusted rate 601.2: California Department of Public Health, San Francisco County's Health Status Profile for 2010.
114 *average life expectancy in counties with more . . . than that density*: Author's calculations, using data from Murray et al., "Eight Americas," Dataset S1, and county density data from Haines, "Historical, Demographic, Economic, and Social Data: The United States, 1790–2002."

114 *death rate for Manhattanites:* New York City Department of Health and Mental Hygiene, Overall Mortality, 2007, by age group and borough, generated using New York City Vital Statistics Query, https://a816-healthpsi .nyc.gov/epiquery/EpiQuery/VS/index.html (July 28, 2010); and Xu et al., "Deaths: Final Data for 2007."

114 *Accidents and suicides . . . rarer in big cities:* National Center for Injury Prevention and Control, "10 Leading Causes of Death, United States," 2007, All Races, Both Sexes, data generated using WISQARS, http://webappa .cdc.gov/sasweb/ncipc/leadcaus10.html; and Xu et al., "Deaths: Final Data for 2007."

114 *than 75 percent less likely to die in a motor vehicle:* New York City Department of Health and Mental Hygiene, *Summary of Vital Statistics 2007*, tables 2 and 14; and Xu et al., "Deaths: Final Data for 2007."

115 *The suicide rate . . . more common in rural areas:* New York City Department of Health and Mental Hygiene, *Summary of Vital Statistics 2007*, tables 2 and 15; Xu et al., "Deaths: Final Data for 2007," table 11; and Cutler et al., "Explaining the Rise in Youth Suicide."

115 *death rates from suicide:* As of 2007, Alaska's rate is 22.09 deaths from suicide per 100,000 people; Montana's, 19.42; and Wyoming's, 19.73. Massachusetts's rate is 7.62; New Jersey's, 6.69; and New York's 6.9. National Center for Injury Prevention and Control, WISQARS Injury Mortality Reports, 1999–2007, All Races, Both Sexes, data generated using WISQARS, http://webappa.cdc.gov/sasweb/ncipc/mortrate10_sy.html.

115 *gun ownership is about four times as high in small towns:* Cutler et al., "Explaining the Rise in Youth Suicide"; and Kleck, *Point Blank*. Kleck reports that 42.8 percent of households in communities with fewer than five thousand people own a gun, but only 10.5 percent of people living in places with more than a million people own a gun.

115 *suicides are more common when firearms are more common:* For example, Miller et al., "Household Firearm Ownership and Suicide Rates"; and Kellermann et al., "Suicide in the Home."

115 *suicides rise significantly with the number of hunting licenses:* Glaeser and Glendon, "Who Owns Guns?"

115 *Death rates are 5.5 percent higher . . . seventy-five to eighty-four:* New York City Department of Health and Mental Hygiene, *Summary of Vital Statistics 2007*, tables 2 and 5; and Xu et al., "Deaths: Final Data for 2007," table 9.

116 *The AIDS virus was discovered . . . Paris's Pasteur Institut:* Institut Pasteur. HIV/AIDS research at the Institut Pasteur: The discovery of the AIDS virus in 1983. http://www.pasteur.fr/ip/easysite/go/03b-000027-00i/the -discovery-of-the-aids-virus-in-1983.

CHAPTER 5: IS LONDON A LUXURY RESORT?

117 *Nowhere are London's extravagances . . . Gordon Ramsay's cooking:* http://www.bondstreetassociation.com/.

117 *If you walk down the Burlington Arcade . . . the world's elite:* http://www.piccadilly-arcade.com/.

118 *"When a man is tired of London, he is tired of life":* Boswell, *Life of Samuel Johnson*, 160.

118 *thirty-two billionaires:* "Billionaires' Favorite Hangouts" and Bertoni et al., "Billionaires."

118 *Lakshmi Mittal:* Hessel, "Conspicuous Consumption."

118 *pay a lot just to live in New York:* Glaeser et al., "Consumer City."

119 *Kevin Spacey . . . moved to London:* Gussow, "Spacey's New Role."

119 *Spacey . . . grew up in California:* Ibid.

120 *built by James Burbage in 1576:* Lee, *Life of William Shakespeare*, 36.

120 *English comedy made its first appearance:* Boas, *Shakespeare and His Predecessors*, 21–22. I want to make it clear that I mean "pre-Elizabethan extremist" in a very positive way.

121 *The first written reference to Shakespeare:* Schoenbaum, *Shakespeare's Lives*, 22.

121 *a somewhat dissolute playwright:* Greenblatt, *Will in the World*, 216.

121 *Pandosto for The Winter's Tale:* Lee, *Life of William Shakespeare*, 250–51.

121 *the ur-Hamlet:* Ibid., 221.

121 *direct references to Marlowe's work:* Weis, *Shakespeare Unbound*, 146–488; and Black, "Hamlet Hears Marlowe."

121 *Marlowe's earlier The Jew of Malta:* Lee, *Life of William Shakespeare*, 68.

121 *influenced Antony and Cleopatra:* Logan, *Shakespeare's Marlowe*, ch. 7, 169–96.

121 *confident that they personally knew each other:* Greenblatt, *Will in the World*, 199.

122 *Olivier directed the young Peter O'Toole:* "Routine Performance of Hamlet," review, *Times* (London), no. 55839, Oct. 23, 1963, 14.

122 *The Second City began in 1959:* Rohter, "Second City Looks Back in Laughter."

122 *DJ Kool Herc:* Starr and Waterman, *American Popular Music*, 83, 86, 200.

123 *are 1.8 times as many people working in grocery stores:* U.S. Census Bureau, County Business Patterns 2008, www.census.gov/econ/cbp.

123 *in New York that ratio is more than reversed:* U.S. Census Bureau, 2007 County Business Patterns, New York County (Manhattan), Bronx County, Queens County, Richmond County (Staten Island), and Kings County (Brooklyn).

123 *employment in Manhattan restaurants increased by 55 percent:* In 1998, 57,680 people worked in restaurants in New York County (Manhattan). By 2007, this had increased 44 percent to 83,257 people. U.S. Census Bureau, County Business Patterns, www.census.gov/econ/cbp, New York County, 1998 and 2007.

123 *Adam Smith noted that the division of labor:* Smith, *Wealth of Nations,* 1791, vol. 1, 26.

123 *credited as the first restaurateur:* Spang, *Invention of the Restaurant,* 11.

124 *to avoid the catering guild's harsh rules:* Ibid., 24.

124 *La Grande Taverne de Londres opened in Paris:* "Restaurant," *Encyclopædia Britannica.*

124 *"an elegant room . . . superior cooking":* Brillat-Savarin, *Physiology of Taste,* 231.

124 *Delmonico's of Manhattan:* Lately Thomas, *Delmonico's.*

124 *Auguste Escoffier:* Escoffier, *Memories of My Life.*

125 *first London restaurant to get three stars:* www.albertroux.co.uk, Biography, Le Gavroche.

125 *two hundred thousand Londoners who were born in India:* Spence, *A Profile of Londoners,* 18; and Greater London Authority, Data Management and Analysis Group, "ONS mid-2007 Ethnic Group Population Estimates," GLA Demography Update, 11-2009, Oct. 2009, p. 2.

125 *gave stars to two Indian restaurants in London:* Robin Young, "First to Pull a Michelin Star."

125 *Rasoi Vineet Bhatia: Zagat 2011 London Restaurants,* review of Rasoi Vineet Bhatia, 27, 144; review of Restaurant Gordon Ramsay (at 68 Royal Hospital Road), 28, 82.

126 *working in clothing and accessories stores:* U.S. Census Bureau, County Business Patterns, www.census.gov/econ/cbp, New York County (Manhattan), 1998 and 2008.

127 *spend 42 percent more on women's clothing:* Bureau of Labor Statistics, *Consumer Expenditure Survey, 2008,* www.bls.gov/cex, table 2400: "Population Size of Area of Residence: Average Annual Expenditures and Characteristics."

127 *spend 25 percent more on footwear:* Ibid.

127 *housed 1.4 million people over the age of fifteen:* U.S. Census Bureau, American Community Survey, Data Profile for New York County, 2008, generated using American FactFinder.

127 *a third (460,000) were married:* Ibid.

127 *About half . . . were divorced:* Ibid.

127 *one half of people over fifteen are married:* U.S. Census Bureau, American Community Survey, Data Profile for the United States, 2008, generated using American FactFinder.

127 *Manhattanites are much more likely . . . to be singles:* U.S. Census Bureau, PCT7, Sex by Marital Status by Age for the Population 15 Years and Over, United States and New York County, Census 2000 Summary File 3, data generated using American FactFinder.

128 *the most economically successful couples:* Costa and Kahn, "Power Couples."

128 *Theodore Dreiser came to Chicago:* Dreiser, *Sister Carrie,* introduction by Richard Lingeman.

128 *Carrie Meeber:* Dreiser, *Sister Carrie.*

130 *Some cities . . . unusually high real incomes:* The ACCRA cost-of-living indexes for Rochester, Honolulu, San Diego, and Dallas are 96.7, 162.8, 136.4, and 92.1, respectively. The average cost of living for all areas included is indexed to 100, then each place is given an index relative to 100, so the higher the index number, the higher the cost of living. The median household incomes for Rochester (Minnesota), Honolulu, San Diego, and Dallas are $66,197, $60,531, $62,668, and $40,796, respectively. The ACCRA-adjusted median household income is calculated by dividing the household income for each place by its ACCRA cost-of-living index (divided by 100). The ACCRA-adjusted median household incomes for these places are $68,458, $37,189, $45,943, and $44,285, respectively, showing how low the real incomes of San Diego and Honolulu are compared with those of Rochester and Dallas. American Chamber of Commerce Research Association, Council for Community and Economic Research, ACCRA Cost-of-Living Index—Historical Dataset, 1Q1990–2009, http://hdl.handle.net/1902.1/14823, Council for Community and Economic Research, Arlington, VA; and U.S. Census Bureau, American Community Survey, Data Profile for Rochester (MN), Honolulu, San Diego, and Dallas, data generated using American FactFinder.

130 *most expensive . . . were in coastal California:* Glaeser et al., "Consumer City."

131 *relationship between city size and real wages:* Glaeser and Gottlieb, "Urban Resurgence."

131 *accept lower real wages to live in New York:* Ibid.

132 *population that commutes from central city to suburb:* Baum-Snow, "Transportation Infrastructure."

CHAPTER 6: WHAT'S SO GREAT ABOUT SKYSCRAPERS?

135 *Haussmann, who rebuilt the city:* All on Haussmann's Paris from Jordan, *Transforming Paris.*

136 *Tower of Babel:* Genesis 11:4, King James Version.

137 *In worldly Bruges, wool topped worship:* John Weale, *Quarterly Papers on Architecture,* vol. 1, London: Iohan Weale, 1844.

137 *the 284-foot spire of Trinity Church:* Goldberger, "God's Stronghold."

137 *Eiffel Tower:* "The Eiffel Tower," *New York Times,* Apr. 21, 1889, p. 13, ProQuest Historical Newspapers, Document ID: 106346206.

137 *move upward was a moderate evolution:* Landau and Condit, *New York Skyscraper,* 5–18.

138 *Tall buildings became possible in the nineteenth century:* Goodwin, *Otis,* 45.

138 *Archimedes allegedly built one:* Ibid., 8.

138 *Louis XV had his own personal lift:* Taub, "Elevator Technology."

138 *Matthew Boulton and James Watt:* Landau and Condit, *New York Skyscraper,* 35–36.

138 *Otis . . . took the danger out of vertical transit:* Goodwin, *Otis,* 12–13.

138 *first two buildings to install powered safety elevators:* Ibid., 17; and Landau and Condit, *New York Skyscraper,* 36.

138 *the elevator enabled pathbreaking structures:* Landau and Condit, *New York Skyscraper,* 62.

139 *whether Jenney was really the inventor of the skyscraper:* Turak, "Home Insurance Building."

139 *Jenney's proto-skyscraper was a patchwork:* Bascomb, *Higher,* 94–97.

139 *Other builders . . . further developed the idea:* Landau and Condit, *New York Skyscraper,* 268, 302, 334, and passim.

139 *They were great architects . . . fireproofing innovator Peter B. Wight:* Vermiel, *The Fireproof Building.*

140 *Pulitzer's World Building had some steel columns:* Ibid., 199.

140 *surpassed by the Park Row Building:* Ibid., 252.

140 *iconic Flatiron Building in 1907:* Ibid., 303.

140 *Metropolitan Life tower, then the tallest building:* Ibid., 361.

140 *In 1913, the Woolworth Building reached 792 feet:* 792 feet, 1 inch, to be exact. Ibid., 382.

140 *tallest building until the boom of the late 1920s:* Ibid., 395–96.

140 *Like a proper Horatio Alger hero:* "Romance in Lives of City Builders: New Building Peaks Adjacent to East River Waterfront," *New York Times,* Feb. 24, 1929.

140 *working full-time in retail, he kept selling papers:* "By-the-Bye in Wall Street," *Wall Street Journal,* Dec. 5, 1932.

140 *Treasury bond, which he kept pinned to his shirt:* Ibid.

140 *still in his early thirties, led the management side:* "State Board Trying to End Cloak Strike: Employers' Committee Meets To-morrow to Consider a Joint Conference; No Settlement, They Say," *New York Times,* July 17, 1910.

141 *the Protocol of Peace:* Greenwald, "'More than a Strike.'"

141 *a less bloody and likely more profitable middle ground:* Ibid.

141 *sank all of his capital into a twelve-story loft building:* Tarshis, "Thirty-one Commercial Buildings."

141 *Bedrock may have:* Barr et al., "Bedrock Depth."

141 *he erected thirty-one edifices:* Tarshis, "Thirty-one Commercial Buildings."

141 *Lefcourt used those Otis elevators in soaring towers:* Ibid.

141 *"he demolished more historical structures":* "By-the-Bye in Wall Street," *Wall Street Journal,* Dec. 5, 1932.

141 *wealth was estimated at $100 million:* "E. Lefcourt Dies Suddenly at 55: Was Credited with Building More Skyscrapers Than Any Other Individual," *New York Times,* Nov. 14, 1932.

141 *celebrated by opening a national bank:* "In and Out of the Banks," *Wall Street Journal,* Sept. 12, 1928.

141 *optimism was unfazed by the stock market crash:* "Lefcourt Plans for 1930 Large: Propose $50,000,000 Expenditure for New Buildings—Other Projects," *Wall Street Journal,* Dec. 2, 1929.

142 *died in 1932 worth only $2,500:* "A. E. Lefcourt Left $2,500, No Realty: Builder of 20 Skyscrapers Had Property Valued at $100,000,000 in 1928," *New York Times,* Dec. 15, 1932.

142 *Two economists tried . . . where density was easier to develop:* Rosenthal and Strange, "Attenuation of Human Capital Spillovers."

142 *artists connected in the Brill Building:* Inglis, "'Some Kind of Wonderful.'"

142 *"save Fifth Avenue from ruin":* "Saving Fifth Avenue: Building Height Restriction to Prevent It Becoming a Canyon," *New York Times,* July 20, 1913.

142 *antigrowth activists . . . city as a whole:* Ibid.

143 *landmark 1916 zoning ordinance:* New York City, "About NYC Zoning."

143 *New York's many ziggurat-like structures:* Landau and Condit, *New York Skyscraper,* 395.

143 *Five of New York City's ten tallest buildings:* Emporis.com, www.emporis.com/en/wm/ci/bu/?id=101028. They are, tallest first, Empire State Building, 1931; Bank of America Tower, 2009; Chrysler Building, 1930; New York Times Tower, 2007; American International Building, 1932; Trump Building, 1930; Citigroup Center, 1977; Beekman Tower, 2010; Trump World Tower, 2001; and GE Building, 1933.

143 *race to produce the tallest structure:* Bascomb, *Higher,* 139–53.

143 *amended more than twenty-five hundred times:* Makielski, *Politics of Zoning.*

143 *resulting 420-page code:* New York City, City Planning Commission, Zoning Maps and Resolution.

143 *thirteen different types . . . of commercial districts:* Ibid.

144 *picayune detail of the code:* Ibid., 25.

145 *"piece of built-in rigor mortis":* Alexiou, *Jane Jacobs,* 91.

145 *a fight with Jane Jacobs:* Asbury, "Board Ends Plan."

146 *Jacobs published her masterpiece:* Jacobs, *Death and Life,* Random House, 1961.

146 *between one and two hundred households per acre:* Jacobs, *Death and Life,* 208–17.

148 *Several papers have shown that new construction is lower:* For example, Glaeser and Ward, "The Causes and Consequences of Land Use Regulation: Evidence from Greater Boston," 265–78; and Katz and Rosen. "The interjurisdictional effects of growth controls on housing prices," 149–60.

148 *One of the cleverest papers . . . less new construction and higher price:* Albert Saiz, "The Geographic Determinants of Housing Supply," 1253–96.

148 *The building's architect, like Jane Jacobs, saw height:* Moore, *Life and Times of Charles Follen Mckim,* 274; and Ballon and McGrath, *New York's Pennsylvania Stations,* 54.

148 *preparing to raze its old New York station:* Jacobs, *Death and Life,* Random House, 1961.

149 *subtitle of the* New York Times *article:* Bennett, "City Acts to Save Historical Sites."

149 *Landmarks Preservation Commission became permanent:* Landmarks Preservation Committee, www.nyc.gov/html/lpc/html/about/mission.shtml; and "A Landmark Law," *New York Times,* Apr. 27, 1965.

149 *twenty-five thousand landmarked buildings:* New York City Landmarks Preservation Commission, Mid-century Modern Midtown Office Tower Becomes a Landmark, Apr. 13, 2010, No. 10-04, www.nyc.gov/html/lpc/downloads/pdf/10_04_springs_mills.pdf.

149 *More than 15 percent of Manhattan's nonpark land:* Glaeser, "Preservation Follies," 62. This figure was calculated using New York City Map (http://gis.nyc.gov/doitt/nycitymap/) and GIS (Geographic Information System) software to determine historic district and park boundaries and land areas.

149 *proposed putting a twenty-two-story glass tower:* Pogrebin, "Upper East Side Tower."

149 *Tom Wolfe . . . would betray its mission:* Wolfe, "(Naked) City."

149 *In response to his critics . . . "on the way to being solved":* Gillette, "Has Tom Wolfe Blown It?"

150 *almost 74 percent wealthier:* Author's calculations using Geolytics Neighborhood Change Database 1970–2000 Tract Data Short Form Release 1.1, CD-ROM (Brunswick, NJ: Geolytics, 2002) and landmark district information from http://gis.nyc.gov/doitt/nycitymap; and Glaeser, "Preservation Follies."

150 *three quarters of the adults living in historic districts:* Glaeser, "Preservation Follies," 62.

150 *are 20 percent more likely to be white:* Author's calculations; Glaeser, "Preservation Follies," 62.

150 *In the postwar boom years . . . 11,000 units each year:* U.S. Census Bureau, Manufacturing, Mining and Construction Statistics, Residential Building Permits, www.census.gov/const/www/permitsindex.html.

150 *Between 1980 and 1999 . . . 3,120 units per year:* Ibid.

150 *price of a Manhattan housing unit increased by 284 percent:* Haines, "Historical, Demographic, Economic, and Social Data: The United States, 1790–2002."

150 *an additional square foot of living space on the top of a tall building is less than $400:* Glaeser et al., "Why Is Manhattan So Expensive?"

151 *80 percent of structures erected in the 1970s had more than twenty stories:* Ibid.

151 *fewer than 40 percent of the buildings erected in the 1990s were that tall:* Ibid.

153 *Parisians crowded into narrow streets and ancient buildings:* Jordan, *Transforming Paris,* 93–96.

153 *Paris had had land-use regulations for centuries:* Papayanis, *Planning Paris,* 14.

153 *When Henry IV . . . most perfect piazza:* Sutcliffe, *Paris,* 19–22.

154 *forty-four times the total budget of Paris in 1851:* Pickney, "Rebuilding of Paris," 45.

154 *height limit was increased:* Sutcliffe, *Paris,* 66, 91.

155 *Gustave Caillebotte's famous 1877 picture:* Gustave Caillebotte, *Paris Street; Rainy Day,* 1877, oil on canvas, 212.2 × 276.2 cm, Charles H. and Mary F. S. Worcester Collection, 1964.336, Art Institute of Chicago, www.artic.edu/artaccess/AA_Impressionist/pages/IMP_4.shtml.

155 *heights were limited to ninety-eight feet:* Sutcliffe, *Paris,* 123.

156 *Paris City Council lifted the city's height restrictions:* Ibid., 166.

156 *The Montparnasse Tower was widely loathed:* "Few Parisians consider the skyscrapers of La Defense or the 56-story tower at Montparnasse to be worthy of their city." LaFranchi, "New Look on the Left Bank."

156 *height limit of 83 feet in central Paris:* Sutcliffe, *Paris,* 185.

156 *close to 40 million square feet of commercial space:* Urban Land Institute, Award Winner Project.

157 *small apartments sell for a million dollars:* For instance, on the real estate Web site www.frenchentree.com, I found a 968-square-foot apartment in the sixth arrondissement selling for over $1.25 million.

158 *three people each day were pushed out of that train to their death:* Blakely, "17 People Die Every Day Commuting to Work in Mumbai, India."

158 *Average commute times in Mumbai:* American Community Survey, 2008 Data Profile for the United States, generated using American FactFinder; and Beniwal, "Commuting Time in Mumbai."

159 *maximum floor area ratio of 1.33:* Sridhar, "Impact of Land Use Regulations."

159 *three of the six buildings in Mumbai that rise above 490 feet:* Emporis.com, www.emporis.com/en/wm/ci/bu/sk/li/?id=102037&bt=2&ht=2&sro=0.

160 *about 30 square feet per person:* The China figure is from Shanghai. Sridhar, "Impact of Land Use Regulations."

CHAPTER 7: WHY HAS SPRAWL SPREAD?

165 *The Houston metropolitan area had a million . . . after Atlanta and Dallas:* U.S. Census Bureau, Population Estimates, "Combined Statistical Area Population and Estimated Components of Change: April 1, 2000 to July 1, 2009," www.census.gov/popest/metro/metro.html. Fastest growth is based on total population added, not percentage growth.

165 *Twenty-four million people visit:* Simon Malls, "About the Houston Galleria," www.simon.com/mall/default.aspx?ID=805.

165 *modeled on hallowed urban space:* Swartz, "Born Again," 48.

166 *average single-family home in 2008 sat on more than an acre:* U.S. Census Bureau, Residential Construction Branch, Characteristics of New Housing, "Lot Size of New Single-Family Houses Sold (Excluding Condominiums)," www.census.gov/const/C25Ann/malotsizesold.pdf.

166 *only 13 percent of the nation is in that age category:* U.S. Census Bureau, American Community Survey, 2008 Data Profile for the United States and the County of New York, generated using American Fact-Finder.

168 *Pack animals . . . human geography:* Lay, *Ways of the World,* 7.

168 *Pack animals made cities possible:* Bairoch, *Cities and Economic Development,* 11–14.

168 *Wheels seem to have originated in Mesopotamia:* Lay, *Ways of the World,* 27.

168 *The Incas never developed the wheel:* Diamond, *Guns, Germs, and Steel,* 248.

168 *Paving returned . . . since the Roman era:* Lay, *Ways of the World,* 62, 112.

168 *breeding and training . . . elite transport technology:* Ibid., 20.

169 *father of the bus:* Ibid., 128.

169 *the paving and the population:* Ibid.

169 *first public transit in New York City:* Burrows and Wallace, *Gotham;* and "New York City Transit—History and Chronology," Metropolitan Transit Authority, www.mta.info/nyct/facts/ffhist.htm.

169 *the omnibus easily doubled that range:* Glaeser et al., "Why Do the Poor Live in Cities?"

169 *An omnibus ride may have cost . . . so they kept walking:* Gin and Sonstelie, "The Streetcar and Residential Location in Nineteeth Century Philadelphia," 92–107.

170 *around masses of horse-drawn vehicles:* Burrows and Wallace, *Gotham,* 420–21.

170 *Before the bus:* Folpe, *It Happened on Washington Square,* 6–7.

170 *built the first functioning train in 1804:* Lay, *Ways of the World,* 137; Mason, *Matthew Boulton,* 63–65.

170 *underground rail system:* Fischler, *Subways of the World,* 10.

171 *invested in elevated rail networks:* Burrows and Wallace, *Gotham,* 1053–55; and Donald L. Miller, *City of the Century,* 268–70.

171 *of 12 miles per hour to jobs downtown:* Burrows and Wallace, *Gotham,* 1054.

171 *suburbs built on steam:* Conn, *Metropolitan Philadelphia,* 125, 175–76.

171 *powering an urban train with electricity:* Lay, *Ways of the World,* 134.

171 *streetcars that ran down the Passeig de Gràcia:* "Barcelona," *Encyclopædia Britannica.*

172 *four-stroke internal combustion engine . . . Motorwagen:* Lay, *Ways of the World,* 152–53.

172 *had 23 million cars:* Suits, "Demand for New Automobiles."

173 *soaring speed of 25 miles per hour:* Lay, *Ways of the World,* 194, 314.

173 *Federal Highway Act of 1921:* Ibid., 118, 314.

173 *along the "Mother Road":* Steinbeck, *Grapes of Wrath.*

173 *forty-six thousand miles of roads:* (as of 2000) U. S. General Accounting Office, Report to the Chairman, Committee on Transportation and Infrastructure, House of Representatives, GAO-02-571, Status of the Interstate Highway System, *Highway Infrastructure: Interstate Physical Conditions Have Improved, but Congestion and Other Pressures Continue,* May 2002, www.gao.gov/new.items/d02571.pdf, p. 8.

174 *Income and population growth have been significantly higher in those metropolitan areas:* Gilles Duranton and Matthew Turner, "Urban Growth and Transportation," 2010, http://individual.utoronto.ca/gilles/Papers/GrowthTransport.pdf.

174 *"reduces its population by about 18 percent":* Baum-Snow, "Did Highways Cause Suburbanization?"

174 *William Levitt:* Gans, *Levittowners.*

175 *fits of literary condescension:* Ibid., 8.

175 *"first and foremost functional for his daily needs":* Ibid., 186.

175 *possibly apocryphal story:* Aaseng, *Business Builders,* 62.

175 *twenty-six separate steps:* Ibid.

175 *thousands of homes quickly in one area:* "Line Forms Early in Sale of Houses," *New York Times,* Mar. 7, 1949, p. 21, repr. in Nicolaides and Wiese, eds., *Suburb Reader.*

176 *splurging on housing subsidies:* Gans, *Levittowners,* 13–14, 22.

176 *GI Bill . . . for middle-income buyers:* U.S. Government Printing Office, Congressional Research Service, A

Chronology of Housing Legislation and Selected Executive Actions, 1892–2003, Mar. 2004, www.gpo.gov/fdsys/pkg/CPRT-108HPRT92629/html/CPRT-108HPRT92629.htm.

176 *the McMansions of their day:* Hayden, "Building the American Way," 276.

176 *disproportionately to middle-class enclaves:* U.S. General Accounting Office, Resources, Community, and Economic Development Division, House of Representatives, *Community Development: The Extent of Federal Influence on "Urban Sprawl" Is Unclear,* Apr. 30, 1999, GAO/RCED-99-87 Research on "Urban Sprawl," www.gao.gov/archive/1999/rc99087.pdf.

176 *overwhelmingly single-family houses:* U.S. Census Bureau, U.S. Census 2000, Data Profile for the United States, Summary File 3, generated using American FactFinder.

177 *half of the jobs . . . away from the city center:* Kneebone, "Job Sprawl."

177 *inverse connection between density and car usage:* Glaeser and Kahn, "Sprawl," 2499–2500.

177 *Accord . . . a hundred square feet on its own:* According to Honda's Web site, a 2010 Honda Accord has a length of 194.1 inches and a width of 72.7 inches, for an area of 98 square feet: http://automobiles.honda.com/accord-sedan/specifications.aspx?group=dimensions.

178 *typical parking space:* Parking regulations in Massachusetts, for instance, require parking spaces to measure at least 9 feet by 18 feet, or 162 square feet: www.mass.gov/Cago/docs/Municipal/sb_parking.rtf.

178 *structured parking, which can cost more than $50,000:* Marshall and Emblidge, *Beneath the Metropolis,* 181.

178 *average gas tax in France:* Glaeser and Kahn, "Sprawl," 2499–2500.

178 *Comparing seventy cities . . . 40 percent:* Glaeser and Kahn, "Sprawl."

178 *Today, 84 percent of passenger transport:* European Road Federation, *European Road Statistics 2009,* table 6.3: "Inland Transport Modal Split by Country in EU-27," p. 43.

178 *In Italy . . . 5 and 5.66:* European Automobile Manufacturing Association, *Automobile Industry Pocket Guide,* "Trends in Motorisation," p. 4, www.acea.be/images/uploads/files/20090529_motorisation.pdf.

178 *there are 7.76 cars for every 10 Americans:* Ibid.

178 *European Environment Agency . . . "low density residential areas":* European Environment Agency, *Urban Sprawl in Europe,* fig. 2, p. 12.

179 *in the United States . . . forty-eight minutes:* Glaeser and Kahn, "Sprawl," 2499–2500.

179 *That time cost . . . for buses and subways:* Glaeser et al., "Why Do the Poor Live in Cities?" 12.

180 *The Woodlands:* General history of The Woodlands from Galatas and Barlow, *The Woodlands.*

180 *on twenty-eight thousand sylvan acres:* The Woodlands. http://www.thewoodlands.com/masterplan.htm.

180 *over ninety-two thousand people live in The Woodlands:* The Woodlands Development Company. *The Woodlands, Texas Demographics,* January 1, 2010. http://www.thewoodlandstownship-tx.gov/DocumentView.aspx?DID=667.

180 *Levittown . . . three times as dense as this Texas suburb:* U.S. Census Bureau, American Community Survey, 2006–2008 Data Profile Levittown Census Designated Place, New York, generated using American FactFinder.

180 *About 28 percent of The Woodlands:* The Woodlands. http://www.thewoodlands.com/greenspace.htm.

181 *more than doubled . . . over 40 percent between 2000 and 2008:* The Woodlands Development Company. *The Woodlands, Texas Demographics.* January 1, 2010. http://www.thewoodlandstownship-tx.gov/DocumentView.aspx?DID=667.

181 *More than half of the adults . . . given their income levels:* U.S. Census Bureau, American Community Survey, 2006–2008 Data Profile for the Woodland Census Designated Place, generated using American FactFinder; and The Woodlands Development Company. *The Woodlands, Texas Demographics.* January 1, 2010. http://www.thewoodlandstownship-tx.gov/DocumentView.aspx?DID=667.

181 *average home value there is about $200,000:* Ibid.

182 *Almost half of The Woodlands' households have children under eighteen:* The Woodlands Development Company. *The Woodlands, Texas Demographics.* January 1, 2010. http://www.thewoodlandstownship-tx.gov/DocumentView.aspx?DID=667.

182 *average commute time in The Woodlands as 28.5 minutes:* Ibid.

183 *Fifty-six percent of the jobs in Houston . . . city center:* Kneebone, "Job Sprawl Revisited: The Changing Geography of Metropolitan Employment."

183 *more than a million other people:* The calculations in this section first appeared in Glaeser, "Houston, New York Has a Problem,'" *City Journal;* U.S. Census Bureau, Population Estimates, "Combined Statistical Area Population and Estimated Components of Change: April 1, 2000 to July 1, 2009," www.census.gov/popest/metro/metro.html.

183 *In Wayne County . . . $60,000:* U.S. Census Bureau, American Community Survey, 2008 Data Profile for Wayne County, Michigan, and Harris County, Texas, generated using American FactFinder.

184 *unemployment rate . . . 13.2 percent:* Bureau of Labor Statistics, *Unemployment Rates for States, Monthly Ranking, Seasonally Adjusted,* June 2010, www.bls.gov/web/laus/laumstrk.htm.

184 *Houston . . . above 90 degrees:* National Climatic Data Center, "Mean Number of Days with Maximum Temperature 90 Degrees F or Higher," http://lwf.ncdc.noaa.gov/oa/climate/online/ccd/max90temp.html.

184 *American family earned about $60,000:* U.S. Census Bureau, American Community Survey, 2006 Data Profile for the United States, generated using American FactFinder.

184 *average registered nurse . . . $50,000 in New York:* Author's calculations using Ruggles et al., *Microdata Series.*

184 *average retail manager . . . $28,000 in New York:* Ibid.

185 *average owner-occupied housing unit in the Houston area:* $119,400, to be exact. U.S. Census Bureau, American Community Survey, 2006 Data Profile for Houston–Sugar Land–Baytown, Texas, Metropolitan Statistical Area, and 2006 Data Profile for City of Houston; both generated using American FactFinder.

185 *three quarters of the homes in the city:* U.S. Census Bureau, American Community Survey, 2006 Data Profile for city of Houston, generated using American FactFinder.

185 *median price of a Houston home sold:* National Association of Realtors, "Median Sales Price of Existing Single-Family Homes for Metropolitan Areas," www.realtor.org/wps/wcm/connect/497de980426de7ccb96eff03cc9fa 30a/REL10Q1T_rev.pdf?MOD=AJPERES&CACHEID=497de980426de7ccb96eff03cc9fa30a.

185 *In 2006, the Census . . . in New York City as $496,000:* U.S. Census Bureau, American Community Survey, 2006 Data Profile for City of Los Angeles and City of New York, generated using American FactFinder.

185 *on Staten Island for about $340,000:* Realtor.com, searched Aug. 31, 2010.

185 *New Brighton . . . $375,000:* Ibid.

185 *These houses don't have . . . square feet of living space:* Ibid.

185 *condominium with two or three bedrooms:* Ibid.

185 *If the family can muster . . . (for a $160,000 home):* Author's calculations, assuming a 30-year fixed interest rate of 6.75 percent.

186 *Houston residents . . . property taxes . . . for a $160,000 home:* Author's estimates, using TAXSIM.

186 *In New York . . . state income and city income taxes:* Ibid.

186 *up to $8,500 per year on transportation:* Bureau of Labor Statistics, *Consumer Expenditure Survey, 2006,* www .bls.gov/cex; and personal communication, Oct. 2007.

186 *average Houston commute is 26.4 minutes:* U.S. Census Bureau, American Community Survey, 2008 Data Profile for City of Houston, generated using American FactFinder.

186 *In Queens, the average commute is 42.7 minutes:* U.S. Census Bureau, American Community Survey, 2008 Data Profile for County of Queens, NY, generated using American FactFinder.

186 *In Staten Island . . . multimode marathon:* U.S. Census Bureau, American Community Survey, 2008 Data Profile for County of Richmond, NY, generated using American FactFinder.

186 *The ferry ride itself . . . Manhattan destination:* From the official Web site, www.siferry.com.

187 *people dislike time spent on mass transit:* Small and Verhoef, *Economics of Urban Transportation.*

187 *biggest price gaps are in groceries:* ACCRA Cost of Living Index for Houston and Queens: 88 and 149.4.

187 *A T-bone steak . . . in New York:* Ibid.

187 *real income of the Queens residents is a little less than $19,750:* Ibid.

187 *The same figure for Houston . . . is $31,250:* Ibid.

187 *even without a brilliant child, the Houston resident:* Houston Association of Realtors, School Finder, School District Detail, Spring Branch ISD, generated at www.har.com/school/dispDistrictDetail.cfm?id=101920.

188 *bizarre doubling of home prices in Las Vegas:* Case-Shiller Home Price Indices, July 21, 2010.

188 *two thirds of the variation in metropolitan prices . . . by 3 percent:* Author's calculations using U.S. Census Bureau, Census 2000, County and City Data Book 2000, table C-7, "Cities—Government Finances and Climate," www.census.gov/prod/2002pubs/00ccdb/cc00_tabC7.pdf.

188 *For every $1.00 . . . by $1.20:* Author's calculations using U.S. Census Bureau, Census 2000.

188 *California's Santa Clara County . . . pay plenty to live there:* Santa Clara average $116,079, median $88,846; U.S. average $71,498, median $52,029. U.S. Census Bureau, American Community Survey, 2008 Data Profile for County of Santa Clara, California, and for the United States, generated using American FactFinder.

188 *close to $800,000, more than four times the U.S. average:* Ibid.

189 *remained the most expensive place in the continental:* Only Honolulu was more expensive. National Association of Realtors, "Median Sales Price of Existing Single-Family Homes for Metropolitan Areas," www.realtor.org/ wps/wcm/connect/497de980426de7ccb96eff03cc9fa30a/REL10Q1T_rev.pdf?MOD=AJPERES&CACHEID=4 97de980426de7ccb96eff03cc9fa30a.

189 *only about sixteen thousand new single-family homes:* U.S. Census Bureau, Manufacturing, Mining and Construction Statistics, Residential Building Permits, www.census.gov/const/www/permitsindex.html.

189 *less than one third of the U.S. average building rate:* Ibid.

189 *If Silicon Valley . . . would be about 40 percent lower:* Santa Clara County today has about 390,000 homes, so an extra 200,000 homes would be a 50 percent increase in the housing stock. Typically, estimates of the elasticity of housing demand are around −.7; see Polinsky and Ellwood, "Empirical Reconciliation of Micro and Grouped Estimates of the Demand for Housing," which implies that a 50 percent increase in housing supply would be associated with a 40 percent reduction in housing price.

189 *did permit more than two hundred thousand new single-family homes:* U.S. Census Bureau, Manufactur-

ing, Mining and Construction Statistics, Residential Building Permits, www.census.gov/const/www/permitsin-dex.html.

189 *household income in Detroit ... half the U.S. average:* U.S. Census Bureau, American Community Survey, 2008 Data Profile for City of Detroit and for the United States, generated using American FactFinder.

190 *peak of the recent bubble ... rose by 64 percent:* Case-Shiller Home Price Indices (July 21, 2010).

190 *In Dallas, prices rose by only 8 percent:* Ibid.

190 *three years that followed the bubble's peak ... only 5.5 percent:* Ibid.

190 *prices in Houston have stayed remakably constant ... $153,100 in 2009:* National Association of Realtors, "Median Sales Price of Existing Single-Family Homes for Metropolitan Areas," www.realtor.org/wps/wcm/co nnect/497de980426de7ccb96eff03cc9fa30a/REL10Q1T_rev.pdf?MOD=AJPERES&CACHEID=497de980426d e7ccb96eff03cc9fa30a.

190 *Harris County ... cushioned the drop:* U.S. Census Bureau, Manufacturing, Mining and Construction Statistics, Residential Building Permits, www.census.gov/const/www/permitsindex.html.

190 *From 1996 to 2006 ... least supply-constrained cities:* Glaeser et al., "Housing Supply and Housing Bubbles."

190 *In the boom of the 1980s ... in the elastic places:* Ibid.

190 *Texas builders ... $75 a square foot:* Gyourko and Saiz, "Construction Costs."

190 *Texas and California ... more than 1,600 square feet of land:* U.S. Census Bureau, State and County Quickfacts, http://quickfacts.census.gov/qfd/states; and U.S. Census Bureau, International Database, World Population Summary, www.census.gov/ipc/www/idb/worldpopinfo.php.

190 *America's abundance of land ... physical costs of construction:* Gyourko and Saiz, "Construction Costs."

191 *construction costs are ... more expensive in Los Angeles:* U.S. Census Bureau, American Community Survey, 2006–2007 Data Profile for the City of Houston and the City of Los Angeles, generated using American Fact-Finder; and Gyourko and Saiz, "Construction Costs."

191 *In Harris County ... and 2 people per acre respectively:* Haines, "Historical, Demographic, Economic, and Social Data: The United States, 1790–2002"; and U.S. Census Bureau, American Community Survey, 2008 Data Profile for Harris County, Texas, Westchester County, New York, and Santa Clara County, California, generated using American FactFinder.

191 *natural barriers to building ... help explain the differences:* Saiz, "Geographic Determinants."

191 *Together with Bryce Ward and Jenny Schuetz ... multiunit developments:* Glaeser et al., "Regulation and the Rise in Housing Prices."

192 *founded by two real estate developers:* Haley, *Sam Houston.*

192 *fresh water and invigorating ocean breezes:* Schadewald, "Salute to the Allen Brothers."

194 *the $15 billion Big Dig ... drive to Logan:* Stern, "Boston's Big Dig Wraps Up."

194 *More than 85 percent ... detached dwellings own them:* U.S. Census Bureau, U.S. Census 2000, Data Profile for the United States, Summary File 3, generated using American FactFinder.

194 *Homes depreciate ... their important asset:* Shilling et al., "Measuring Depreciation."

195 *In Manhattan, 76 percent of housing units are rentals:* U.S. Census Bureau, American Community Survey, 2008 Data Profile for New York County (Manhattan), generated using American FactFinder.

195 *Big-city schools ... suburban school districts:* Loveless, "How Well Are American Students Learning?"

196 *decrease in the size of the home mortgage interest deduction: Report of the President's Advisory Panel on Federal Tax Reform.*

CHAPTER 8: IS THERE ANYTHING GREENER THAN BLACKTOP?

199 *"fitly procure our food from the stream":* Thoreau, *I to Myself,* 52.

199 *"the flames spread with rapidity":* Ibid., 52.

199 *"I have set fire to the forest":* Ibid., 54.

199 *a "dammed rascal" and a "flibbertigibbet":* Ibid., 52; and Thoreau, *Journal,* vol. 2, 25.

200 *"seldom thanked colleagues for their services":* Thoreau, *Walden and Resistance.*

201 *clustering together in high-rises and walking to work:* Jacobs, *Death and Life,* Random House; and David Owen, *Green Metropolis.*

201 *ecofriendly households ... a once beautiful landscape:* Seuss, *Lorax.*

202 *"detests the town and yearns for the sacred grove":* Horace, *Satires and Epistles,* 283.

202 *Wordsworth, Coleridge, Keats, Shelley:* For example, in Ferguson et al., *Norton Anthology of Poetry:* Wordsworth, "I Wandered Lonely as a Cloud," p. 801; Coleridge, "Frost at Midnight," pp. 810–12; Keats, "Bright Star," p. 940; and Shelley, "Mont Blanc," pp. 866–70.

202 *"go to nature in all singleness of heart":* Ruskin, *Works,* vol. 3, 624.

202 *an early advocate of town planning:* Ruskin, *Genius,* 1997, 353.

202 *"from any part of the city ... a few minutes walk"* Ruskin, *Genius,* 353.

202 *"belt of beautiful garden and orchard":* Ibid.

203 *giving up a decent meal for a "sight of the far horizon":* bid.

203 *more than 3 million are recreational second homes:* U.S. Department of Housing and Urban Development and U.S. Census Bureau, Current Housing Reports, *American Housing Survey for the United States: 2007*, H150/07, Sept. 2008, www.census.gov/prod/2008pubs/h150-07.pdf, table 1A-1.

203 *Ebenezer Howard . . . made Ruskin's vision concrete:* It was originally published under the title *Tomorrow: A Peaceful Path to Real Reform.*

203 *the Green Belt is hardly within walking distance:* Estimated using Journey Planner on www.tfl.gov.uk/tube.

203 *Olmsted specialized in bringing bucolic vistas:* Rybczynski, *Clearing in the Distance.*

205 *five new buildings opened that soared above 849 feet:* Empire State Building, 1931; Chrysler Building, 1930; American International Building, 1932; Trump Building, 1930; and GE Building, 1933. Emporis.com, www .emporis.com/en/wm/ci/bu/?id=101028.

205 *tallest skyscraper in Western Europe today:* The tallest building in Western Europe, at about 849 feet, is Commerzbank Tower, in Frankfurt, Germany. Emporis.com, www.emporis.com/en/bu/sk/st/tp/ct/?id=100001.

205 *that tall for another thirty-six years:* The Chase Tower, in Chicago, 849 feet, was built in 1969. Emporis.com, www.emporis.com/en/bu/sk/st/tp/wo.

205 *Global temperatures have been rising continuously:* Archer and Rahmstorf, *Climate Crisis*, 3, 41.

206 *carbon inventory of new housing:* Glaeser and Kahn, "Greenness of Cities." An earlier version of this analysis appeared in Glaeser, "Green Cities, Brown Suburbs."

206 *In 2006, the United States produced . . . emitted by Europe and Latin America:* U.S. Energy Information Administration, International Energy Annual 2006, H. lco2 World Carbon Dioxide Emissions from the Consumption and Flaring of Fossil Fuels, 1980–2006,'" www.eia.doe.gov/pub/international/iealf/tablehlco2.xls.

206 *Together, homes and cars . . . our motor vehicles:* Glaeser and Kahn, "Greenness of Cities."

207 *Using a gallon of gas . . . in a city or a suburb:* Ibid.

207 *area density and distance to the city center:* Ibid.

207 *average household . . . 687 gallons of gas per year:* Ibid.

207 *gas consumption per family per year declines by 106 gallons:* Ibid.

207 *to deliver 2.6 billion trips to its riders:* Ridership data from MTA, "The MTA Network," www.mta.info/mta/ network.htm; fuel information from Kennedy, "New York's Bus Cleanup"; and electricity data from Metropolitan Transit Authority, *Greening Mass Transit.*

208 *fewer than 850 gallons of gas per year:* Glaeser and Kahn, "Greenness of Cities."

208 *twice as likely to take mass transit as to drive to work:* In 2008, 5 percent of Americans used public transportation to get to work, and 75.5 percent drove themselves to work. In the same year, 23.3 percent of New Yorkers drove themselves to work, while 54.8 percent used public transportation. U.S. Census Bureau, American Community Survey, 2008 Data Profile for the City of New York and the United States, generated using American FactFinder.

208 *On average, when population doubles . . . their residents use the most gas:* Glaeser and Kahn, "Greenness of Cities."

208 *biggest city-suburb gaps are in older areas:* Ibid.

208 *also occur in places like Atlanta and Nashville:* Ibid.

208 *urbanites use less electricity:* Ibid.

208 *Electrical appliances account for two thirds of residential energy use:* The Census Bureau gives us a convenient snapshot of electricity usage. It asks 5 percent of the U.S. population how much their household is spending on electricity. Using state-level price data from the Department of Energy, we can then convert that spending into electricity usage. With a little bit of statistics, we can use this data to estimate how much electricity an average family buys in different parts of the country. Because apartment dwellers often don't directly pay for their own electricity, we have to use the government's Residential Energy Consumption Survey to fill in the gaps. To figure out the total carbon emissions from electricity, we need to multiply average electricity usage in a place by the carbon emissions associated with creating electricity in that region. Glaeser and Kahn, "Greenness of Cities."

209 *lowest electricity-using metropolitan areas:* Ibid.

209 *lead the pack in electricity consumption:* Ibid.

209 *The average single-family detached home consumes:* Department of Energy, U.S. Energy Information Administration, Residential Energy Consumption Survey (RECS), 2005 Consumption & Expenditures Tables, Table US8. Average Consumption by Fuels Used, 2005, http://www.eia.doe.gov/emeu/recs/2005/c&e/summary/pdf/ tableus8.pdf.

209 *The average suburban household consumes:* Ibid.

209 *central-city residents use less electricity:* Glaeser and Kahn, "The Greenness of Cities."

209 *More centralized . . . like Dallas or Phoenix:* Ibid.

209 *natural gas is America's primary source of warmth:* Department of Energy, U.S. Energy Information Administration, Office of Integrated Analysis and Forecasting, "Emissions of Greenhouse Gases in the United States 2008," Dec. 2009, table 7, U.S. Carbon Dioxide Emissions from Residential Sector Energy Consumption, 1990–2008, www.eia.doe.gov/oiaf/1605/ggrpt/pdf/0573(2008).pdf.

209 *Detroit and Grand Rapids . . . even at night:* Glaeser and Kahn, "The Greenness of Cities."

209 *it should be no surprise that cities are greener than suburbs:* Ibid.

210 *But the differences between . . . its equivalent in Memphis:* Ibid.

210 *Older places . . . higher emissions:* Ibid.

210 *about 2 people living on each acre in Santa Clara County:* Haines, "Historical, Demographic, Economic, and Social Data: The United States, 1790–2002"; and U.S. Census Bureau, American Community Survey, 2008 Data Profile for Marin and Santa Clara Counties, California, generated using American FactFinder.

210 *Montgomery County in Maryland has about 3 people per acre:* Haines, "Historical, Demographic, Economic, and Social Data: The United States, 1790–2002"; and U.S. Census Bureau, American Community Survey, 2008 Data Profile for Montgomery County, Maryland, generated using American FactFinder.

210 *Cook County, Illinois, has almost 9 people per acre:* Haines, "Historical, Demographic, Economic, and Social Data: The United States, 1790–2002"; and U.S. Census Bureau; American Community Survey, 2008 Data Profile for Cook County, Illinois, generated using American FactFinder.

210 *Manhattan has 111 people per acre:* Haines, "Historical, Demographic, Economic, and Social Data: The United States, 1790–2002"; and U.S. Census Bureau, American Community Survey, 2008 Data Profile for New York County, generated using American FactFinder.

210 *Santa Clara County more than tripled:* Haines, "Historical, Demographic, Economic, and Social Data: The United States, 1790–2002."

211 *Santa Clara County grew by only 17.8 percent:* Ibid.; and U.S. Census Bureau, American Community Survey, 2008 Data Profile for Santa Clara County, California, generated using American FactFinder.

211 *median sales price passed $800,000:* National Association of Realtors, "Median Sales Price of Existing Single-Family Homes for Metropolitan Areas," 2nd Quarter 2010, www.realtor.org/wps/wcm/connect/497de980426d e7ccb96eff03cc9fa30a/REL10Q1T_rev.pdf?MOD=AJPERES&CACHEID=497de980426de7ccb96eff03cc9fa30a.

211 *these places remain the two most expensive:* Ibid.

211 *kept high by draconian limits on new construction:* Marin County Development and Zoning Code, www.marin.ca.gov/depts/CD/main/comdev/CURRENT/devCode.cfm.

211 *one quarter of the land in the Bay Area:* California, Government of, Association of Bay Area Governments, San Francisco Bay Area Housing Needs Plan 2007–2014, p. 3. According to the Greenbelt Alliance, 1.1 million of these acres are protected. About Greenbelt Alliance: www.greenbelt.org/downloads/resources/factsheets/AboutGA_08.pdf.

211 *about 8.7 million acre-feet of water:* California Water Plan Update 2005, vol. 2, ch. 22, p. 1.

211 *uses 34 million acre-feet of water each year for irrigation:* Ibid., vol. 2, ch. 3, p. 1.

212 *The 1970 California Environmental Quality Act:* California, Government of, California Environmental Quality Act (CEQA), Statute and Guidelines 2009.

212 *but also projects permitted by local government:* Friends of Mammoth v. Board of Supervisors.

212 *generated 583 environmental impact reviews:* Author's calculations using the databases at www.ceqanet.ca.gov, California's clearinghouse for California Environmental Quality Act (CEQA) documents, and www.epa.gov/oecaerth/nepa/eisdata.html, the U.S. Environmental Protection Agency's Environmental Impact Statement Database.

213 *"Red" Ken Livingstone:* Hoksen, *Ken,* 90, 240, 288–302, 317; Fiona Hamilton, "Boris Makes an Early Start."

213 *"single biggest problem facing humanity" . . . "greatest threat to mankind":* Ben Webster, "Congestion Charge Will Rise to £25"; Prince of Wales, "Speech . . . Bali to Poznan."

213 *The prince was born in 1948 in Buckingham Palace:* www.princeofwales.gov.uk/personalprofiles/theprinceofwales/biography.

213 *Livingstone was born three years earlier in Lambeth:* Hoksen, *Ken,* 1.

213 *more formal education than any British king:* Dimbleby, *Prince of Wales,* 25, 79, 89, 103–4.

213 *Livingstone's education was spotty:* Hoksen, *Ken,* 5–7.

213 *"cultivating tumors in the smaller rodents":* Foggo, "Ken, the Animal Tester of X Block."

213 *rising in the London-Lambeth Labour Party:* Hoksen, *Ken,* 38–80.

213 *Prince Charles was being a dutiful royal:* Dimbleby, *Prince of Wales,* 159, 214, 217.

213 *young prince's Cinderella wedding:* Ibid., 284–85, 288–90.

213 *head of the Greater London Council:* Carvel, *Citizen Ken,* 18.

213 *Ken Livingstone refused to attend:* Willis, "Royal Wedding"; and Hoksen, *Ken,* 99.

214 *Livingstone argued loud and long:* Rowbotham, "London's 'Red Ken' Arrives."

214 *He fought for more housing, but he opposed skyscrapers:* Hoksen, *Ken,* 408, and Sudjic, "Thoroughly Modernising Mayor."

214 *patron of sustainable agriculture and a foe of modernism:* Dimbleby, *Prince of Wales,* 312.

214 *an opportunity to push for organic farming:* Ibid., 439. Explanation of the Duchy of Cornwall at www.duchyofcornwall.org/naturalenvironment.htm, linked from the Prince of Wales Web site.

214 *tough attack on modernist architecture:* Dimbleby, *Prince of Wales,* 314–17.

214 *offered a nostalgic vision:* Prince of Wales, Speech . . . Royal Institute of British Architects.

214 *"a monstrous carbuncle on the face":* Ibid.

214 *"Why has everything got to be vertical":* Ibid.

214 *"a giant glass stump":* Ibid.

214 *but the prince won, sort of:* "Victoriana vs. Mies in London," *New York Times,* May 3, 1984, p. C18.

214 *"an early Victorian market town":* Worsley, "A Model Village Grows Up Gracefully."

214 *forces behind the New Urbanist movement:* Watson et al., *Learning from Poundbury,* 8.

214 *New Urbanism "stand[s] for . . . our built legacy":* Charter of the New Urbanism, www.cnu.org/charter.

214 *more conservationist than the New Urbanist communities of America:* Compare the Web site of Poundbury, www.duchyofcornwall.org/designanddevelopment_poundbury_livinginpoundbury.htm, with its note that "It is intended to be a sustainable development" and that it is "designed to maintain the quality of the environment" and its photographs of green space, with the Web site of Celebration, Florida, www.celebration.fl.us/towninfo.html, with its emphasis on its "strong sense of self" and photographs of people at play.

215 *In Celebration, 91 percent of people who leave their homes to work take cars:* U.S. Census Bureau, Census 2000, P30, Means of Transportation to Work for Workers 16 Years and Over, Summary File 3, generated using American FactFinder.

215 *More people (64.5 percent) drive to work in Poundbury:* Watson, *Learning from Poundbury,* 37.

215 *Three quarters of Poundbury's residents drive on their shopping trips:* Ibid.

215 *About 70 percent of the homes in Celebration are single-family:* U.S. Census Bureau, Census 2000, H30, Units in Structure, Summary File 3, generated using American FactFinder.

215 *only 17 percent of Poundbury's homes are apartments:* Watson, *Learning from Poundbury,* 19.

215 *pay £5 each time they entered an inner corridor of London:* Leape, "London Congestion Charge."

215 *congestion charging has appealed to economists:* For instance, Vickrey, "Congestion Theory," 251; Vickrey, "Pricing of Urban Street Use"; Vickrey, "Pricing in Urban and Suburban Transport"; and Walters, "Private and Social Cost of Highway Congestion."

215 *by moving people out of cars and into subways:* Behar, "Livingstone Wins Fight."

215 *He also saw it as progressive legislation:* Giles, "A Logical Effort to Ease the London Gridlock"; see also: "Traffic Decongestant," *Economist,* Feb. 15, 2003.

216 *greater than 20 percent reduction in driving:* Lewis Smith, "Traffic Still Light."

216 *congestion dropped by 30 percent over the next two years:* Leape, "London Congestion Charge."

216 *postmodernist Number 1 Poultry Building:* Lillyman et al., *Critical Architecture,* 143.

216 *Climate Group's Low Carbon Champions Award:* "London Leaders Lauded," www.edie.net/news/news_story .asp?id=10857.

216 *a furor when he flew his entourage:* Philip Webster, "Miliband Attacks Prince for Flying."

217 *embraced higher-density building to protect London's Green Belt:* Design for London, "Housing for a Compact City."

217 *"overblown phallic sculptures":* Prince of Wales, Speech . . . "Tall Buildings."

217 *half of America's homes in 2000 were built between 1970 and 2000:* U.S. Census Bureau, American Community Survey, 2008 Data Profile for the United States, generated using American FactFinder.

218 *carbon consumption would increase by 139 percent:* In 2006, per capita emissions in the United States were 19.78 metric tons. In France, they were 6.60 metric tons; in China, 4.58 metric tons; and in India, 1.16 metric tons. Total emissions in 2006 were 29.195 billion metric tons. If we subtract China's 2006 emissions from this total (1.314 billion people times 4.58 metric tons per capita for a total of 6.018 billion tons) as well as India's (1.112 billion people times 1.16 metric tons per capita for a total of 1.293 billion tons), and then add China's total emissions if they were at the U.S. per capita level (1.314 billion people times 19.78 metric tons for a total of 25.998 billion tons) as well as India's (1.112 billion people times 19.78 metric tons per capita for a total of 21.988 billion tons), the new world total would be 69.8601 billion tons, an increase of 139 percent.

218 *about 20 metric tons of carbon dioxide per person per year:* U.S. Energy Information Administration, International Energy Annual 2006, table H.1cco2, "World Per Capita Carbon Dioxide Emissions from the Consumption and Flaring of Fossil Fuels, 1980–2006," www.eia.doe.gov/pub/international/iealf/tableh1cco2.xls.

218 *Canadians . . . almost the same amount per person:* Ibid.

218 *English emit a little less than 10 tons:* Ibid.

218 *Italians . . . 8 tons of carbon dioxide per person annually:* Ibid.

218 *The Chinese . . . almost 5 tons:* Ibid.

218 *If the Chinese . . . increasing world carbon emissions by 69 percent:* Total emissions in 2006 were 29 billion tons. If we subtract China's 2006 emissions from this total (1.314 billion people times 4.58 metric tons per capita for a total of 6.018 billion tons) and then add China's total emissions if they were at the U.S. per capita level (1.314 billion people times 19.78 metric tons for a total of 25.998 billion tons), the new world total would be 48.98 billion tons, an increase of 69 percent. U.S. Energy Information Administration, International

Energy Annual 2006, table H.1cco2, "World Per Capita Carbon Dioxide Emissions from the Consumption and Flaring of Fossil Fuels, 1980–2006," www.eia.doe.gov/pub/international/iealf/tableh1cco2.xls.

218 *But if energy consumption in India and China levels off . . . cutbacks in the United States and elsewhere:* If, instead, we used France's 6.60 metric ton per capita figure, China's revised emissions would be 8.668 billion tons (1.314 billion people times 6.60 metric tons per capita) and India's would be 7.334 billion tons (1.112 billion people times 6.60 metric tons per capita), for a revised world total of 37.887 billion tons, or an increase of about 30 percent. U.S. Energy Information Administration, *International Energy Annual 2006*, table H.1cco2, "World Per Capita Carbon Dioxide Emissions from the Consumption and Flaring of Fossil Fuels, 1980–2006," www.eia.doe.gov/pub/international/iealf/tableh1cco2.xls.

218 *city-by-city analysis of China's household carbon emissions:* Zheng et al., "Greenness of China."

218 *While the typical household . . . brownest places in China:* Glaeser and Kahn, "Greenness of Cities"; and Zheng et al., "Greenness of China."

220 *fifty thousand people per square mile:* Mumbai, *Mumbai Human Development Report 2009*, 238; and American Community Survey, 2008 Data Profile for the City of New York, generated using American FactFinder.

220 *Kolkata and Bangalore:* Kolkata: "Seoul 6th Most Densely Populated City," *Korea Times*, Dec. 26, 2007. Bangalore: Annemarie Schneider and Curtis E. Woodcock, "Compact, Dispersed, Fragmented, Extensive? A Comparison of Urban Growth in Twenty-five Global Cities Using Remotely Sensed Data, Pattern Metrics, and Census Information," *Urban Studies* 45 (Mar. 2008): 659–92, doi:10.1177/0042098007087340.

220 *Shenzhen . . . fifteen thousand people per square mile:* "Around China," *China Daily*, www.chinadaily.com.cn, Apr. 29, 2010.

220 *Shanghai and Beijing . . . (about 2,600 people per square mile) as Los Angeles:* Los Angeles population in 2008 was 3,803,383, and land area is 469 square miles, for a density of 8,109.5 per square mile. American Community Survey, 2008 Data Profile for the City of New York and the City of Los Angeles, generated using American FactFinder.

220 *Chinese car ownership:* "Chinese Agency Highlights Problems of Rising Car Ownership," BBC Worldwide Monitoring, Asia Pacific, July 19, 2010.

220 *by producing a $2,500 car:* Timmons, "A Tiny Car."

CHAPTER 9: HOW DO CITIES SUCCEED?

223 *"Happy families are all alike":* Tolstoy, *Anna Karenina*, 3.

224 *Tokyo became one of the largest cities:* "Tokyo," *Encyclopædia Britannica*.

224 *his new castle home, Edo, became the country's effective capital:* "Japan," *Encyclopædia Britannica*.

225 *half of Japan's rice revenue:* Ades and Glaeser, "Trade and Circuses."

225 *The more centralized a nation's government, the larger its capital city:* Ibid.

225 *largest cities in dictatorships . . . 35 percent:* Ibid.

225 *in stable democracies . . . 23 percent:* Ibid.

225 *Edo had a million people:* Seidensticker, *Low City, High City*, 13.

225 *the Meiji Restoration reestablished imperial power:* Ibid., 26–28.

225 *moved his court from Kyoto to Edo, renaming it Tokyo:* Ibid., 26.

225 *shogun's castle became the imperial palace:* Ibid., 28–29.

225 *when Japan was still poor, its people were remarkably well educated:* Maddison, "Statistics on World Population."

225 *substantially more than in France, the Netherlands, or Spain:* France had 6, Netherlands 5.42, and Spain 3.4. Barro and Lee, "Educational Attainment."

226 *Ministry of International Trade and Industry:* Chalmers Johnson, *MITI and the Japanese Miracle*.

226 *usually picked losers rather than winners:* Beason and Weinstein, "Growth, Economies of Scale."

227 *The success of the British East India Company . . . buccaneering ambition:* Boulger, *Life of Sir Stamford Raffles*; and Wurtzburg, *Raffles of the Eastern Isles*, 16.

227 *passionate about flora and fauna, keeping a sun bear cub as a pet:* Raffles, *History of Java*; and Wurtzburg, *Raffles of the Eastern Isles*, 113–14, 197–98, 569–71.

227 *He later became . . . the tip of the Malay Peninsula:* Wurtzburg, *Raffles of the Eastern Isles*, 256–70, 643–44, 648; and "Singapore," *Encyclopædia Britannica*.

228 *and 25 million people may have died:* Ebrey et al., *East Asia*, 308.

228 *Twelve years later . . . an independent city-state:* Yew, *Singapore Story*.

228 *His 217-square-mile domain:* Ibid.; population in 1965 from Maddison, "Statistics on World Population."

228 *incomes in Singapore were about one fifth:* Maddison, "Statistics on World Population."

228 *more than 8 percent growth per year, among the highest:* Author's calculations using Maddison, "Statistics on World Population."

228 *Singapore was a poor shantytown:* Yew, *From Third World to First*, 120.

228 *one of the highest per capita gross domestic products:* Maddison, "Statistics on World Population."

228 *more than $70 just to enter the casino:* "The Dragon's Gambling Den," *Economist,* July 10, 2010.

228 *average adult in Singapore had only three years of schooling:* Barro and Lee, "Educational Attainment."

229 *Singapore's thirteen-year-olds led the world:* Boston College, "Highlights of Results from TIMSS."

229 *A large literature now documents the perverse tendency of natural resource windfalls:* Frankel, "The Natural Resource Curse: A Survey."

229 *high salaries and even higher penalties for malfeasance:* Yew, *From Third World to First,* 182–98.

229 *world's best logistics for trade and transport:* United Nations Industrial Development Organization, Industrial Development Report 2009, p. 69; and World Bank, *Connecting to Compete,* 26.

230 *Until recently, it had to import ... recycling the wastewater:* "Singapore's Deep Tunnel Sewerage System Wins Global Water Awards 2009," *Marketwire,* Apr. 28, 2009.

230 *adopted congestion pricing in 1975:* Goh, "Congestion Management."

230 *Commute times run around thirty-five minutes:* Payscale.com, www.payscale.com/research/SG/Country= Singapore/Commute_Time.

230 *forty-two of its buildings rise above 490 feet:* Emporis.com: Singapore high-rises—www.emporis.com/en/wm/ ci/bu/sk/li/?id=100422&bt=5&ht=2&sro=0; London high-rises—www.emporis.com/en/wm/ci/bu/sk/li/?id= 100637&bt=5&ht=2&sro=0; and Paris high-rises—www.emporis.com/en/wm/ci/bu/sk/li/?id=100603&bt= 5&ht=2&sro=0.

231 *second-fastest GDP growth of any country:* Maddison, "Statistics on World Population."

231 *one of the two or three most prosperous nations in sub-Saharan Africa:* Ibid.

231 *Gaborone was founded in 1965 ... a tenth of the country's population:* Botswana, "Stats Update Dec. 2009."

231 *Botswana's success rests on ... its human capital:* "Khama, Sir Seretse," *Encyclopædia Britannica.*

231 *average years of schooling in Botswana:* Barro and Lee, "Educational Attainment."

231 *Gaborone's growth has paralleled Botswana's:* They do census on the "1" year, so it's 1971–2001. Botswana, table 1.6, "Distribution of Population in Urban Settlements."

231 *humane and moderately effective:* Botswana, "MASA: Anti-Retroviral Therapy."

231 *raising the life expectancy substantially for those with HIV:* Dorrington et al., *Demographic Impact of HIV/AIDS.*

232 *explained, in a statistical sense, by education levels in 1940:* 2000 is the year with the latest comprehensive Census data across 256 metropolitan areas. When share of adults with a college degree in 2000 is regressed on share of adults with college degrees in 1940, the r-squared is 53 percent and the coefficient is over three. Glaeser et al., "Inequality in Cities."

232 *If less than 5 percent ... 19 percent of that area's population had a college degree in 2000:* Author's calculations using data from U.S. Census Bureau, 1940 and 2000 Census.

232 *If more than 5 percent ... 29 percent had a college degree in 2000:* Author's calculations using data from U.S. Census Bureau, 1940 and 2000 Census.

232 *"raise a Bulwork against the kingdom of AntiChrist":* Vaughan, *Puritan Tradition,* 26

232 *founded the Boston Latin School in 1635:* Ibid., 27; Boston Latin School, "History (375 Years), Celebrating a Public Treasure," www.bls.org/podium/default.aspx?t=113646.

232 *allocated £400 ... for a college:* Morison, *Three Centuries of Harvard;* and Quincy, *History of Harvard.*

232 *Another £375 and four hundred books:* Morison, *Three Centuries of Harvard,* 9.

232 *"most literate society then existing":* McCullough, *Reformation,* 520.

233 *In 1647, a famine ... fortune during the Colonial era:* Rutman, "Governor Winthrop's Garden Crop."

233 *The city exported ... food and wood to the Caribbean:* Ibid., 131–32.

233 *Boston's first-mover advantage ... as China and South Africa:* Ibid.

234 *an understanding of Manchester's power looms:* "Lowell, Francis Cabot," *Encyclopædia Britannica.*

234 *religious mosaic founded new colleges:* Tufts: "The Founding of Tufts University," www.tufts.edu/home/get_to _know_tufts/history; Boston College: "History: From the South End to Chestnut Hill," www.bc.edu/about/ history.html, Feb. 5, 2010; Boston University: "Timeline," www.bu.edu/timeline; and Wellesley: "College History," web.wellesley.edu/web/AboutWellesley/CollegeHistory.

234 *Vannevar Bush:* "Raytheon: A History of Global Technology Leadership," www.raytheon.com/ourcompany/ history.

234 *Raytheon's current headquarters:* The Raytheon Web site has a Google map confirming location on the reservoir near Route 128; address: Raytheon Company, 870 Winter Street, Waltham, MA 02451-1449.

234 *engineers from MIT and Harvard created companies:* Dorfman, "High Technology Economy."

234 *Wang had 30,000 employees and DEC had over 120,000:* Wang: "An American Tragedy," *Economist,* Aug. 22, 1992, 56–58. DEC: Edgar H. Schein, *DEC Is Dead, Long Live DEC: The Lasting Legacy of Digital Equipment Corporation* (San Francisco: Berrett-Koehler, 2003), 152.

234 *lost the edge that comes from urban density:* Saxenian, *Regional Advantage.*

235 *first business trusts in 1827:* Adams, *Boston Money Tree.*

235 *the first investment trusts:* Markham, *Financial History of the United States,* 324.

235 *birth of management consulting:* Arthur D. Little "About Us/History," www.adl.com/9.html.

235 *Little was a training ground for smart people:* Treynor bio: Treynor, *Treynor,* xviii. Black bio: *New York Times,* Aug. 31, 1995; and Henriques, "Fischer Black." BCG: Boston Consulting Group, "BCG History: 1963," www .bcg.com/about_bcg/history/History_1963.aspx. Bain: Bain and Company, "History Based on Results," www .joinbain.com/this-is-bain/measurable-results/history-based-on-results.asp.

235 *Foreign firms . . . Necco Wafers:* Treffinger, "Alchemy Will Turn a Candy Factory into Biotech Offices."

236 *Minneapolis, which lost 30 percent of its population:* Gibson, "Population of the 100 Largest Cities."

236 *per capita personal income in the Minneapolis metropolitan area:* U.S. Department of Commerce, Bureau of Economic Analysis, "Personal Income for Metropolitan Areas, 2009," Monday, August 9, 2010. http://www.bea .gov/newreleases/regional/mpi/2010/pdf/mpi0810.pdf.

236 *seventh-best-educated metropolitan area:* U.S. Census Bureau, American Community Survey, 2008 Data Profile for the Minneapolis–St. Paul–Bloomington, MN-WI Metropolitan Statistical Area, generated using American FactFinder.

236 *Medtronic:* "Medtronic Annual Revenue Up 8 Percent to $14.6 Billion," May 19, 2009, wwwp.medtronic .com/Newsroom/NewsReleaseDetails.do?itemId=1242677732763&lang=en_US; expansion: www.medtronic .com/about-medtronic/locations/index.htm; employee count: www.medtronic.com/about-medtronic/diver sity/index. htm; history: "Our Story: The Garage Years," www.medtronic.com/about-medtronic/our-story/ index.htm.

236 *Walt Lillehei:* Medtronic, "Our Story: The Pacemaker Years," www.medtronic.com/about-medtronic/our-story/ our-first-pacemakers/index.htm.

236 *Bob Ulrich:* Wakin, "Hit, Strummed or Plucked."

237 *trained two mathematicians:* I am specifically referring to Francesco Brioschi, secretary to the minister of education and founder of the Politecnico, and to Gabrio Casati, an education minister, founder of the Accademia of Milan, which was later merged into the University of Milan, and promulgator of the Casati Law, which organized Italian postunification education. See: *The Men of the Time: or Sketches of Living Notables,* 1852, 161.

237 *Pirelli . . . use of rubber:* Polese, "In Search of a New Industry."

237 *telegraph cables insulated with rubber:* Ibid.

237 *headquarters is an architectural icon:* Foot, *Milan Since the Miracle,* 118.

237 *two design magazines:* Nelson, *Building a New Europe,* 161–62.

237 *designed ceramics, bottles, and chairs:* Ibid., 58–59; Foot, *Milan Since the Miracle,* 113.

237 *also made Milan's population plummet:* "Milan," *Encyclopædia Britannica.*

238 *population increased between 2000 and 2008:* Istat, Demography in Figures.

238 *Milan's per capita productivity is the highest:* In this case, I am using productivity to mean value added per capita. Author's calculations using Istat, Regional Accounts and National Economic Accounts.

238 *three quarters of Milan's workers are in services:* Author's calculations using Istat, Regional Accounts.

238 *Miuccia Prada and Patrizio Bertelli:* Galloni, "Miuccia and Me"; "Learning from Prada," *RFID Journal,* June 24, 2002, www.rfidjournal.com/article/view/272/1; and for Pocone, "Prada, Miuccia," *Britannica Book of the Year, 2003, Encyclopædia Britannica.*

238 *The Versaces:* Spindler, "Gianni Versace."

238 *A quarter of the Vancouver area's residents:* Canada: Statistics Canada, Population 15 Years and Over; and Canada: Statistics Canada, Greater Vancouver.

239 *top of global quality-of-life rankings:* For instance, Mercer's Quality of Living Worldwide City Rankings, www .mercer.com/qualityoflivingpr#City_Ranking_Tables, or the *Economist* Intelligence Unit, Global Liveability Report, www.eiu.com/site_info.asp?info_name=The_Global_Liveability_Report_Press_Release&rf=0; and Canada: Statistics Canada, Greater Vancouver.

239 *Its Januaries average 37 degrees . . . cooler than the other two cities:* Estimated temperature for Vancouver from a tourism site: http://vancouver.ca/aboutvan.htm; U.S. cities temperature from U.S. Census Bureau, County and City Data Book 2000, table C-7, "Cities—Government Finances and Climate," www.census.gov/ prod/2002pubs/00ccdb/cc00_tabC7.pdf.

239 *Vancouver was a logging town with . . . well-educated citizens:* Morley, *Vancouver,* 33–34, 58–61, 79, 84–89, 145, 222.

239 *population stagnated . . . 50 percent:* Vancouver Public Library, "City of Vancouver Population."

239 *Arthur Erickson . . . plenty of open space:* "A Tribute to Arthur Erickson," *AI Architect,* http://info.aia.org/ aiarchitect/thisweek09/0612/0612n_arthur.cfm; "Arthur Erickson, Lauded Canadian Architect, Dies," *Architectural Record,* 197, no. 7: 24; "Massey, Raymond," *Encyclopædia Britannica;* "Massey, Vincent," *Encyclopædia Britannica;* "MacMillan Bloedel Building," www.arthurerickson.com/txt_macm.html; and UBC Robson Square, "About Us: History," www.robsonsquare.ubc.ca/about/history.html.

240 *Erickson became a national icon:* Martin, "'Greatest Architect.'"

240 *twenty structures with more than twenty stories:* Emporis.com, "James KM Cheng Architects Inc.," www .emporis.com/application/?nav=company&lng=3&id=101306.

240 *Good planning . . . deserted at night:* Emporis.com, "Buildings of Vancouver," www.emporis.com/en/wm/ci/ bu/?id=100997.

240 *A full 40 percent of the city's population is foreign-born:* Canada: Statistics Canada, Greater Vancouver.

240 *a quarter of its citizens were born in Asia:* Canada: Statistics Canada, Population by Selected Ethnic Origins.

240 *its immigrants are disproportionately skilled:* Author's calculations using Canada: Statistics Canada, Immigrant Status and Period of Immigration; and Canada: Statistics Canada, Educational Portrait of Canada.

241 *better educated than native Canadians:* Galarneau and Morissette, "Immigrants' Education."

241 *nearly half of the Canadians with a PhD were born somewhere else:* Canada: Statistics Canada, Educational Portrait of Canada.

241 *more than two hundred thousand immigrants:* Canada: Statistics Canada, Components of Population Growth.

241 *bulk of visas are granted to so-called independent immigrants:* Becklumb, "Canada's Immigration Program."

241 *A fifth of its residents are ethnic Chinese:* Canada: Statistics Canada, Population by Selected Ethnic Origins.

242 *grand mansions . . . high crime rate:* The Web page www.explorechicago.org/city/en/things_see_do/attractions/ tourism/former_home_of_muhammad.html confirms Ali's former address, 4944 S. Woodlawn Ave., Chicago, IL 60615, where he moved to be closer to his mentor at the Nation of Islam, Elijah Muhammad.

242 *Chicago lost almost 18 percent of its population:* Gibson, "Population of the 100 Largest Cities."

242 *Chicago had five mayors, none of whom was able:* Miranda, "Post-machine Regimes."

242 *one of the few large Midwestern cities that has grown:* Gibson, "Population of the 100 Largest Cities"; and U.S. Census Bureau, American Community Survey, 2008 Data Profile for the City of Chicago, generated using American FactFinder.

242 *despite the facts . . . weather can be brutal:* U.S. Census Bureau, American Community Survey, 2008 Data Profile for the City of Chicago, generated using American FactFinder.

242 *Financial entrepreneurs . . . compared with Manhattan:* This sentence is based on the author's conversation with Mr. Griffin.

242 *Chicago issued 68,000 housing permits:* U.S. Census Bureau, Manufacturing, Mining and Construction Statistics, Residential Building Permits, www.census.gov/const/www/permitsindex.html.

242 *Boston issued 8,500 housing permits:* Ibid.

243 *three times as many housing permits as San Jose:* Ibid.

243 *Among Chicagoans, 10.8 percent live in housing built since 1990:* U.S. Census Bureau, American Community Survey, 2008 Data Profile for the Cities of Chicago, New York, and Boston, generated using American FactFinder.

243 *rents are 30 percent higher in Boston than in Chicago, and housing prices are about 39 percent higher:* U.S. Census Bureau, American Community Survey, 2008 Data Profile for the Cities of Chicago and Boston, generated using American FactFinder.

243 *median sales price of a condominium:* National Association of Realtors, Median Sales Price of Existing Condo-Coops Homes for Metropolitan Areas for Second Quarter 2010, www.realtor.org/research/research/metroprice.

243 *In downtown Chicago, $650,000 . . . twice as much:* Realtor.com, searched Sept. 1, 2010.

243 *almost 40 million new square feet of office space:* Calculations performed by Joseph Gyourko using REIS office real estate market data.

243 *about 30 percent cheaper than rents in Boston or San Francisco:* Calculations performed by Joseph Gyourko using REIS office real estate market data.

243 *Atlanta metropolitan area added 1.12 million people:* U.S. Census Bureau, Population Estimates, "Combined Statistical Area Population and Estimated Components of Change: April 1, 2000, to July 1, 2009," www.census .gov/popest/metro/metro.html.

244 *typically 20 percent cheaper than even Chicago's:* Calculations performed by Joseph Gyourko using REIS office real estate market data.

244 *same share of adults with college degrees as Minneapolis:* U.S. Census Bureau, American Community Survey, 2008 Data Profile for the Cities of Atlanta, Boston, and Minneapolis, generated using American FactFinder.

244 *More than 47 percent . . . Middlesex County, Massachusetts:* U.S. Census Bureau, American Community Survey, 2008 Data Profile for Fulton County, Georgia; Westchester County, New York; Fairfield County, Connecticut; Santa Clara County, California; and Middlesex County, Massachusetts; generated using American FactFinder.

244 *Emory and Georgia Tech: A Thousand Wheels Are Set in Motion: The Building of Georgia Tech at the Turn of the Century: 1888–1908,* "The Hopkins Administration, 1888–1895," www.library.gatech.edu/gtbuildings/ hopkins.htm.

244 *Hope Scholarship program:* Kiss and Schuster, "Hope Scholarships."

244 *Fulton County's share of college graduates:* U.S. Census Bureau, American Community Survey, 2008 Data Profile for Fulton County, Georgia, and the United States; and U.S. Census 2000, Data for Fulton County, Georgia, and the United States; both generated using American FactFinder.

245 *Dubai came under . . . the Middle East:* "Dubayy," *Encyclopædia Britannica.*

245 *Jebel Ali Free Zone:* Ibid.

245 *Burj Al Arab:* "Sailing into a New Luxury at Famous Dubai Hotel," *Toronto Star,* Sept. 11, 2004, Travel.

246 *A 2,684-foot mixed-use building:* Davis, "Dubai Hits the Heights."

246 *Dubai Mall . . . one of the biggest in the world:* Official site says *one* of the biggest in the world: www .thedubaimall.com/en/section/faq; dimensions: www.thedubaimall.com/en/news/media-centre/news-section/ the-dubai-mall-opens-largest.html.

246 *Sheikh Mohammed had envisioned . . . Business Bay:* "Richard Spencer in Dubai: Developer to Resume Work on Dubai's Troubled World," *London Daily Telegraph,* Dec. 18, 2009, City.

246 *Dubailand:* Dubailand is unfinished at the moment. Kolesnikov-Jessop, "Theme Park Developers."

246 *market seems to have found his exuberance somewhat irrational:* "Dredging the Debt: Dubai's Debt Mountain," *Economist,* Oct. 31, 2009.

CONCLUSION: FLAT WORLD, TALL CITY

247 *"Cities are the abyss of the human species":* Rousseau, *Émile,* 52.

247 *Monet and Cézanne . . . Belushi and Aykroyd:* "Cézanne, Paul," *Encyclopædia Britannica;* and "Dan Aykroyd," Blues Brothers Central, www.bluesbrotherscentral.com/profiles/dan-aykroyd.

251 *In every decade but one . . . urban growth slowed dramatically:* U.S. Census Bureau, *1990 Census of Population and Housing,* "1990 Population and Housing Unit Counts: United States," (CPH-2), p. 5, www.census.gov/ population/www/censusdata/files/table-4.pdf.

252 *American, or Know-Nothing, Party:* "Know-Nothing Party," *Encyclopædia Britannica.*

252 *Ku Klux Klan:* Jackson, *Ku Klux Klan.*

253 *college graduates . . . $31,000 per year:* U.S. Census Bureau, Census in Schools, Educational Attainment, www .census.gov/schools/census_for_teens/educational_attainment.html.

253 *college is associated with an over 80 percent increase in earnings:* Ibid. Much of the economic literature on the returns to schooling has focused on trying to correct for unobserved factors that push the earnings of the skilled up, by comparing only identical twins, for example; see Ashenfelter and Krueger, "Estimates of the Economic Return to Schooling."

253 *As the number of college graduates . . . no matter how educated they are:* Glaeser and Gottlieb, "Place-Making Policies."

253 *Among nations . . . wages by less than 20 percent:* Barro and Lee, "Educational Attainment"; and Maddison, "Statistics on World Population."

254 *"If a nation expects to be ignorant and free":* Padover, *Thomas Jefferson on Democracy.*

254 *The link between education and democracy:* Glaeser et al., "Why Does Democracy Need Education?"

254 *better-educated members of the Warsaw Pact:* Ibid.

254 *A study of compulsory-schooling laws:* Milligan et al., "Does Education Improve Citizenship?"

254 *research on charter schools in Boston and New York:* Kane et al., *Informing the Debate*; and Hoxby and Murarka, "Charter Schools."

254 *Research has uncovered huge gaps in effectiveness:* Kane and Staiger, "Estimating teacher impacts on student achievement: An experimental evaluation."

255 *In 1800, six of the twenty largest cities:* Gibson, "Population of the 100 Largest Cities."

256 *children displaced from New Orleans by Katrina:* The gains from leaving the city are equal to about 37 percent of the test-score gap between whites and African Americans. Sacerdote, "When the Saints Come Marching In."

257 *spending up to $200 billion rebuilding New Orleans:* Heath, "Katrina Claims Stagger Corps."

257 *$400,000 for every man, woman and child:* U.S. Census Bureau, American Community Survey, 2006 Data Profile for the City of New Orleans and the New Orleans MSA, generated using American FactFinder.

257 *putting infrastructure in a place that lost its economic rationale:* A recent article estimates $142 billion in federal funds have been spent. Sasser, "Katrina Anniversary."

261 *status quo bias:* Kahneman et al., "Experimental tests of the endowment effect and the Coase theorem," 1325–48.

262 *impact bias:* Gilbert, *Stumbling on Happiness.*

263 *circuitous route keeps speeds down:* Dennis, "Gas Prices, Global Warming."

264 *more than 60 percent of Americans are home owners:* U.S. Census Bureau, Current Population Survey, Housing Vacancies and Homeownership Annual Statistics: 2009, table 1A, "Rental Vacancy Rates, Homeowner Vacancy Rates, Gross Vacancy Rates, and Homeownership Rates for Old and New Construction," www.census.gov/hhes/ www/housing/hvs/annual09/ann09ind.html.

264 *The average deduction . . . between $40,000 and $70,000:* Poterba and Sinai, "Tax Expenditures for Owner-Occupied Housing."

265 *and 85 percent of such dwellings are renter-occupied:* U.S. Census Bureau, Data Profile for the United States, Census 2000 Summary File 3, generated using American FactFinder.

265 *the infrastructure component of the 2009 stimulus bill was as stacked against urban America:* www.recovery .gov/?q=content/rebuilding-infrastructure.

265 *Per capita stimulus spending . . . in the rest of the country:* The least dense states are Alaska, Wyoming, Montana, North Dakota, and South Dakota. U.S. Government, State/Territory Totals by Award Type, www.recovery.gov/Transparency/RecipientReportedData/Pages/RecipientAwardSummarybyState.aspx. Population from U.S. Census Bureau, United States—States, Geographical Comparison Tables, GCT-T1-R, 2009 population estimates generated using American FactFinder.

265 *control 10 percent of the Senate with only 1.2 percent of the population:* U.S. Census Bureau, United States—States, Geographical Comparison Tables, GCT-T1-R, Population Estimates, generated using American FactFinder.

265 *But that doesn't make . . . as of December 2009:* Bureau of Labor Statistics, *Regional and State Employment and Unemployment—December 2009,* www.bls.gov/news.release/archives/laus_01222010.htm.

266 *last twenty years . . . ten least dense states:* Glaeser and Gottlieb, "Place-Making Policies."

266 *"funding is not based on need or performance":* White House Office of Management and Budget, Program Assessment: Highway Infrastructure, www.whitehouse.gov/omb/expectmore/summary/10000412.2007.html.

267 *U.S. gas taxes are too low:* Parry et al., "Automobile Externalities and Policies."

269 *"set the stage for the evolution of humanlike intelligence":* Pinker, *How the Mind Works,* 192.

BIBLIOGRAPHY

Aaseng, Nathan. *Business Builders in Real Estate*. Minneapolis: Oliver Press, 2002.

Acemoğlu, Daron. "Why Do New Technologies Complement Skills? Directed Technological Change and Wage Inequality." *Quarterly Journal of Economics* 113, no. 4 (Nov. 1998): 1055–89.

Achenbach, Joel. *The Grand Idea: George Washington's Potomac and the Race to the West*. New York: Simon & Schuster, 2004.

Adams, Russell B., Jr. *The Boston Money Tree*. New York: Crowell, 1977.

Ades, Alberto F., and Edward L. Glaeser. "Trade and Circuses: Explaining Urban Giants." *Quarterly Journal of Economics* 110, no. 1 (Feb. 1995): 195–227.

Aitken, Hugh G. J. *The Continuous Wave: Technology and American Radio 1900–1932*. Princeton, NJ: Princeton University Press, 1985.

Albion, Robert Greenhalgh. *The Rise of New York Port [1815–1860]*. New York: Scribner's, 1939.

Alexiou, Alice Sparberg. *Jane Jacobs: Urban Visionary*. New Brunswick, NJ: Rutgers University Press, 2006.

Amaker, Norman C. "*Milliken v. Bradley*: The Meaning of the Constitution in School Desegregation Cases." *Hastings Constitutional Law Quarterly* 2, no. 2 (Spring 1975): 349–72.

American Chamber of Commerce Research Association. ACCRA Cost of Living Index—Historical Dataset (1Q1990–2009), Arlington, VA: Council for Community and Economic Research [distributor] version 1, http://hdl.handle.net/1902.1/14823.

American FactFinder, U.S. Census Bureau, http://factfinder.census.gov.

Ankeny, Brent, and Robert Snavely. "Renovate Joe or Build Rink? Wings Likely to Decide by Year's End, Ilitch Says." *Crain's Detroit Business*, June 19, 2006, p. 1.

Ansary, Tamim. *Destiny Disrupted: A History of the World through Islamic Eyes*. New York: PublicAffairs, 2009.

Archer, David, and Stefan Rahmstorf. *The Climate Crisis: An Introductory Guide to Climate Change*. Cambridge University Press, 2010.

Arias, Elizabeth. "United States Life Tables, 2006." *National Vital Statistics Reports* 58, no. 21 (June 28, 2010), Centers for Disease Control and Prevention, www.cdc.gov/nchs/data/nvsr/nvsr58/nvsr58_21.pdf.

Arns, R. G. "The Other Transistor: Early History of the Metal-Oxide Semiconductor Field-Effect Transistor." *Engineering Science and Education Journal* 7, no. 5 (Oct. 1998): 233–40.

Asbury, Edith Evans. "Board Ends Plan for West Village: Residents Win Fight to Save 16 Blocks from Being Bulldozed in 'Deal'; Wagner's Stand Cited: Aides Say His Opposition Bars Project—Lifting of Slum Label Sought." *New York Times*, Oct. 25, 1961.

Ashenfelter, Orley, and Alan Krueger. "Estimates of the Economic Return to Schooling from a New Sample of Twins." *American Economic Review* 84, no. 5 (Dec. 1994): 1157–73

Bairoch, Paul. *Cities and Economic Development: From the Dawn of History to the Present*, tr. Christopher Braider. University of Chicago Press, 1988.

Bakhit, Mohammad Adnan. *History of Humanity: From the Seventh Century BC to the Seventh Century AD*. Paris: UNESCO; and London: Routledge; 2000.

Ballon, Hillary, and Norman McGrath. *New York's Pennsylvania Stations*. New York: W. W. Norton & Company, 2002.

"Baltimore Tries Drastic Plan of Race Segregation," *New York Times*, Dec. 25, 1910.

Barman, Roderick J. *Citizen Emperor: Pedro II and the Making of Brazil, 1825–1891.* Stanford: Stanford University Press, 1999.

Barr, Jason, Troy Tassier, and Rossen Trendafilov. "Bedrock Depth and the Formation of the Manhattan Skyline, 1890–1915." New York: Columbia University Working Paper, January 2010.

Barro, Robert J., and Jong-Wha Lee. "International Data on Educational Attainment: Updates and Implications." Cambridge, MA: Harvard Center for International Development, Working Paper no. 42, Apr. 2000, www.cid .harvard.edu/ciddata/ciddata.html.

Bascomb, Neal. *Higher: A Historic Race to the Sky and the Making of a City.* New York: Doubleday, 2003.

Baumol, William J. "Entrepreneurship: Productive, Unproductive, and Destructive," *The Journal of Political Economy* 98, no. 5, part 1 (Oct. 1990): 893–921.

Baum-Snow, Nathaniel. "Changes in Transportation Infrastructure and Commuting Patterns in U.S. Metropolitan Areas, 1960–2000." *American Economic Review,* 100, no. 2 (May 2010): 378–82.

———. "Did Highways Cause Suburbanization?" *Quarterly Journal of Economics* 122, no. 2 (2007): 775–805.

Beasley, William G. "The Foreign Threat and the Opening of the Ports." In *The Cambridge History of Japan,* vol. 5, *The Nineteenth Century,* ed. Marius B. Jansen, ch. 4. Cambridge, UK: Cambridge University Press, 1989.

Beason, Richard, and David Weinstein. "Growth, Economies of Scale and Targeting in Japan (1955–1990)." *Review of Economics and Statistics* 78, no. 2 (May 1996): 286–95.

Beatty, Jack. *The Rascal King: The Life and Times of James Michael Curley, 1874–1958.* Reading, MA: Addison Wesley, 1992.

Becker, Gary S. "Crime and Punishment: An Economic Approach." *Journal of Political Economy* 76, no. 2 (Mar.–Apr. 1968): 169–217.

Becklumb, Penny. "Canada's Immigration Program," rev. Sept. 10, 2008. Ottawa: Library of Parliament, Law and Government Division, www2.parl.gc.ca/content/lop/researchpublications/bp190-e.pdf.

Behar, Darren. "Livingstone Wins Fight over £5 Car Charge." *Daily Mail* (London), Aug. 1, 2002.

"Bengal Leads Hunger List, Poor Land-Man Ratio Blamed." *Financial Express,* Apr. 4, 2007.

Beniwal, Vrishti. "Commuting Time in Mumbai the Maximum, Says Study." *Financial Express,* Aug. 16, 2007.

Bennett, Charles G. "City Acts to Save Historical Sites: Wagner Names 12 to New Agency—Architects Decry Razing of Penn Station." *New York Times,* Apr. 22, 1962.

Berger, Joseph. "Hell's Kitchen, Swept Out and Remodeled." *New York Times,* Mar. 19, 2006.

Bernstein, Peter L. *Against the Gods: The Remarkable Story of Risk.* New York: Wiley, 1996.

———. *Wedding of the Waters: The Erie Canal and the Making of a Great Nation.* New York: Norton, 2005.

Berrien, Jenny, and Christopher Winship. "Lessons Learned from Boston's Police-Community Collaboration." *Federal Probation* 63, no. 2 (Dec. 1999), Academic Search Premier, EBSCOhost.

Besley, Timothy, and Robin Burgess. "Can Labor Regulation Hinder Economic Performance? Evidence from India." *Quarterly Journal of Economics* 119, no. 1 (Feb. 2004): 91–134.

Bertaud, Alain. "Mumbai FSI Conundrum: The Perfect Storm—the Four Factors Restricting the Construction of New Floor Space in Mumbai," July 15, 2004, http://alain-bertaud.com/AB_Files/AB_Mumbai_FSI_conun drum.pdf

Bertoni, Steven, Keren Blankfeld, Katie Evans, Russell Flannery, Duncan Greenberg, Naazneen Karmali, Benjamin Klauder, et al. "Billionaires." *Forbes* 185, no. 5: 69–76.

"Billionaires' Favorite Hangouts." *Forbes* 181, no. 6: 120ff.

"The Birth of the University." *History of Stanford.* Stanford University, www.stanford.edu/about/history/index.html (accessed July 20, 2010).

Black, James. "Hamlet Hears Marlowe; Shakespeare Reads Virgil." *Renaissance and Reformation,* 18, no. 4 (1994): 17–28.

Blakely, Rhys. "17 People Die Every Day Commuting to Work in Mumbai, India." *Times* (London), Apr. 1, 2009.

Bloomberg, Michael, and Matthew Winkler. *Bloomberg by Bloomberg.* New York: Wiley, 1997.

Boas, Frederick S. *Shakespeare and His Predecessors.* New York: Scribner's, 1900.

Bond Street Association. http://www.bondstreetassociation.com/.

Boorstin, Daniel Joseph. *The Discoverers.* New York: Random House, 1985.

Boston College. "Highlights of Results from TIMSS" [Third International Mathematics and Science Study], Nov. 1996, http://timss.bc.edu/timss1995i/TIMSSPDF/P2HiLite.pdf.

Boston Latin School. "History (375 Years), Celebrating a Public Treasure," www.bls.org/podium/default.aspx?t= 113646.

Boswell, James. *The Life of Samuel Johnson, LL.D.* London: Printed by Henry Baldwin, for Charles Dilly, 1791.

Botswana, Republic of. "MASA: Anti-Retroviral Therapy," www.gov.bw/Global/MOH/Masa_ARV_Program.pdf.

Botswana, Republic of, Central Statistics Office. "Stats Update December 2009." www.cso.gov.bw/images/stories/ StatsUpdates/update_dec09.pdf.pdf.

————. Table 1.6, "Distribution of Population in Urban Settlements: 1971–2001 Censuses," www.cso.gov.bw/index.php?option=com_content&task=view&id=147&Itemid=94.

Boulger, Demetrius Charles. *The Life of Sir Stamford Raffles.* London: Horace Marshall & Son, 1899.

Braunhut, Herman Jay. "Farm Labor Wage Rates in the South, 1909–1948," *Southern Economic Journal* 16, no. 2 (Oct. 1949): 189–96.

Brillat-Savarin, Jean Anthelme. *The Physiology of Taste,* trans. M. F. K. Fisher. New York: Courier Dover Publications, 2002.

Brinkley, Douglas. *Wheels for the World: Henry Ford, His Company, and a Century of Progress.* New York: Viking, 2003.

Brody, Howard, Michael Russell Rip, Peter Vinten-Johansen, Nigel Paneth, and Stephen Rachman. "Map-Making and Myth-Making in Broad Street: The London Cholera Epidemic, 1854." *Lancet* 356, no. 9223 (July 1, 2000): 64–68.

Bundles, A'Lelia. *On Her Own Ground: The Life and Times of Madam C. J. Walker.* New York: Scribner, 2001.

Burns, E. Bradford. *A History of Brazil,* 3d ed. New York: Columbia University Press, 1993.

Burrough, Bryan, and John Helyar. *Barbarians at the Gate: The Fall of RJR Nabisco.* New York: HarperCollins, 2003.

Burrows, Edwin G., and Mike Wallace. *Gotham: A History of New York City to 1898.* New York: Oxford University Press, 1999.

Busso, Matias, and Patrick Kline. "Do Local Economic Development Programs Work? Evidence from the Federal Empowerment Zone Program." *American Economic Journal: Economic Policy,* forthcoming.

"By-the-Bye in Wall Street." *Wall Street Journal,* Dec. 5, 1932.

Cahalan, Margaret Werner. "Historical Corrections Statistics in the United States, 1850–1984." Rockville, MD: U.S. Department of Justice, Bureau of Justice Statistics, 1986, www.ncjrs.gov/pdffiles1/pr/102529.pdf.

Caillebotte, Gustave. *Paris Street; Rainy Day,* 1877, oil on canvas, 212.2 × 276.2 cm, Charles H. and Mary F. S. Worcester Collection, 1964.336, Art Institute of Chicago, www.artic.edu/artaccess/AA_Impressionist/pages/IMP_4.shtml.

California Department of Public Health. *Los Angeles County's Health Status Profile for 2010,* www.cdph.ca.gov/programs/ohir/Documents/losangeles.xls.

————. *San Francisco County's Health Status Profile for 2010,* www.cdph.ca.gov/programs/ohir/Documents/sanfrancisco.xls.

California Department of Water Resources. *California Water Plan Update 2005,* vol. 2, ch. 3, "Agricultural Water Use Efficiency," /www.waterplan.water.ca.gov/docs/cwpu2005/vol2/v2ch03.pdf; vol. 2, ch. 22, "Urban Water Use Efficiency," www.waterplan.water.ca.gov/docs/cwpu2005/vol2/v2ch22.pdf (accessed Aug. 11, 2010).

California, Government of. Association of Bay Area Governments, San Francisco Bay Area Housing Needs Plan 2007–2014, www.abag.ca.gov/planning/pdfs/SFHousingNeedsPlan.pdf.

————. California Environmental Quality Act (CEQA), Statute and Guidelines 2009, http://ceres.ca.gov/ceqa/stat.

Canada: Statistics Canada. Components of Population Growth, by Province and Territory, www40.statcan.gc.ca/l01/cst01/demo33a-eng.htm.

————. Educational Portrait of Canada, 2006 Census: Immigration, "Immigrants Account for a Large Proportion of Doctorate and Master's Degree Holders, www12.statcan.ca/census-recensement/2006/as-sa/97-560/p13-eng.cfm.

————. Greater Vancouver, 2006 Community Profiles, www12.statcan.gc.ca/census-recensement/2006/dp-pd/prof/92-591/details/Page.cfm?Lang=E&Geo1=CD&Code1=5915&Geo2=PR&Code2=59&Data=Count&SearchText=Greater%20Vancouver&SearchType=Begins&SearchPR=01&B1=All&Custom=.

————. Immigrant Population by Place of Birth, by Census Metropolitan Area, 2006 Census, Vancouver, www40.statcan.gc.ca/l01/cst01/demo35g-eng.htm.

————. Immigrant Status and Period of Immigration (9), Work Activity in 2005 (14), Highest Certificate, Diploma or Degree (7), Age Groups (9), and Sex (3) for the Population 15 Years and Over of Canada, Provinces, Territories, Census Metropolitan Areas, and Census Agglomerations, 2006 Census—20% Sample Data, www12.statcan.gc.ca.

————. Population 15 Years and Over by Highest Degree, Certificate or Diploma (1986 to 2006 Census), www40.statcan.gc.ca/l01/cst01/EDUC42-eng.htm.

————. Population by Selected Ethnic Origins, by Census Metropolitan areas, 2006 Census, Vancouver, www40.statcan.gc.ca/l01/cst01/demo27y-eng.htm.

Canagarajan, Sudharshanv, John Ngwafon, and Saji Thomas. "The Evolution of Poverty and Welfare in Nigeria, 1985–92." Policy Research Working Paper Series 1715. World Bank, 1997.

Cannato, Vincent J. *The Ungovernable City: John Lindsay and His Struggle to Save New York.* New York: Basic Books, 2001.

Card, David. "Estimating the Return to Schooling: Progress on Some Persistent Econometric Problems." *Econometrica* 69, no. 5 (Sept. 2001): 1127–60.

"Carlos Slim Helú, Biography of," www.carlosslim.com/biografia_ing.html (accessed Aug. 4, 2010).

Cartledge, Paul. *Ancient Greece: A History in Eleven Cities.* New York: Oxford University Press, 2009.

Carvel, John. *Citizen Ken.* London: Chatto & Windus/Hogarth Press, 1984.

Case-Shiller Home Price Indices, Standard & Poor's, www.standardandpoors.com/indices/sp-case-shiller-home-price-indices/en/us/?indexId=SPUSA-CASHPIDFF--P-US----.

Catan, Thomas. "Spain's Bullet Train Changes Nation—and Fast." *Wall Street Journal*, Apr. 20, 2009.

Chandler, Tertius. *Four Thousand Years of Urban Growth: A Historical Census*. Lewiston, NY: Mellon House, 1987.

Chasteen, John Charles. *Born in Blood and Fire: A Concise History of Latin America*. New York: Norton, 2001.

"Chinese Agency Highlights Problems of Rising Car Ownership," BBC Worldwide Monitoring, Asia Pacific, July 19, 2010.

Chinitz, Benjamin. "Contrasts in Agglomeration: New York and Pittsburgh." *American Economic Review* 51, no. 2 (May 1961): 279–89.

Collins, William J. "The Political Economy of State Fair Housing Laws before 1968," *Social Science History* 30 (2006): 15–49.

Columbia University, Office of Public Affairs. "Nobelist William S. Vickrey: Practical Economic Solutions to Urban Problems," Oct. 8, 1996, www.columbia.edu/cu/pr/96/18968.html.

Congo, République Démocratique du. *Enquête Démographique et de Santé 2007*. Macro International, Calverton, MD, Aug. 2008, www.measuredhs.com/pubs/pdf/FR208/FR208.pdf.

Conn, Steven. *Metropolitan Philadelphia: Living with the Presence of the Past*. Philadelphia: University of Pennsylvania Press, 2006.

Costa, Dora L., and Matthew E. Kahn. "Power Couples: Changes in the Locational Choice of the College Educated, 1940–1990." *Quarterly Journal of Economics* 115, no. 4 (Nov. 2000): 1287–1315.

Couch, Carl J., David R. Maines, and Shing-Ling Chen. *Information Technologies and Social Orders*. New Brunswick, NJ: Transactions, 2006.

Cronon, William. *Nature's Metropolis: Chicago and the Great West*. New York: W. W. Norton, 1991.

Currid, Elizabeth. *The Warhol Economy: How Fashion, Art, and Music Drive New York City*. Princeton, NJ: Princeton University Press, 2007.

Cutler, David M., and Edward L. Glaeser. "Are Ghettos Good or Bad?" *Quarterly Journal of Economics* 112, no. 3 (Aug. 1997): 827–72.

Cutler, David M., Edward L. Glaeser, and Karen Norberg. "Explaining the Rise in Youth Suicide." Chapter in Jonathan Gruber, ed. *Risky Behavior Among Youths: An Economic Analysis*. Chicago: University of Chicago Press, 2001.

Cutler, David M., Edward L. Glaeser, and Jacob L. Vigdor. "The Rise and Decline of the American Ghetto." *Journal of Political Economy* 107, no. 3 (June 1999): 455–506.

Cutler, David M., and Grant Miller. "Water, Water Everywhere: Municipal Finance and Water Supply in American Cities." In *Corruption and Reform: Lessons from America's Economic History*, Edward L. Glaeser and Claudia Goldin, eds., pp. 153–84. Chicago: University of Chicago Press, 2006.

Davey, Monica. "Detroit Mayor's Tough Love Poses Risks in Election." *New York Times*, Sept. 25, 2009.

Davis, Heather Greenwood. "Dubai Hits the Heights Again: World's Tallest Tower Goes over the Top with Luxury Complex." *Toronto Star*, Jan. 7, 2010, Travel.

de Long, J. Bradford, and Andrei Shleifer. "Princes and Merchants: European City Growth Before the Industrial Revolution." *Journal of Law and Economics* 36 (Oct. 1993).

DeNavas-Walt, Carmen, Bernadette D. Proctor, and Jessica C. Smith. U.S. Bureau of the Census, Current Population Reports, *Income, Poverty, and Health Insurance Coverage in the United States: 2008*, September 2009, Table 4: "People and Families in Poverty by Selected Characteristics: 2007 and 2008," p. 14.

Dennis, Jan. "Gas Prices, Global Warming Renewing Interest in High-Speed Rail." Associated Press, Sept. 7, 2007.

Derbyshire, Wyn. *Six Tycoons: The Lives of John Jacob Astor, Cornelius Vanderbilt, Andrew Carnegie, John D. Rockefeller, Henry Ford, and Joseph P. Kennedy*. London: Spiramus, 2008.

Design for London. "Housing for a Compact City," June 2003, www.london.gov.uk/archive/mayor/auu/docs/housing_compact_city_1.pdf.

Diamond, Jared. *Guns, Germs and Steel: The Fates of Human Societies*, rev. ed. New York: Norton, 2005.

Dimbleby, Jonathan. *The Prince of Wales*. Boston: Little, Brown, 1994.

DiPasquale, Denise, and Edward L. Glaeser. "The Los Angeles Riot and the Economics of Urban Unrest." *Journal of Urban Economics* 43, no. 1 (Jan. 1998): 52–78.

Dobbie, Will, and Roland G. Fryer. "Are High Quality Schools Enough to Close the Achievement Gap? Evidence from a Social Experiment in Harlem." National Bureau of Economic Research Working Paper 15473, Nov. 2009.

Doms, Mark, Timothy Dunne, and Kenneth R. Troske. "Workers, Wages, and Technology." *Quarterly Journal of Economics* 112, no. 1 (Feb. 1997): 253–90.

Donohue, John J., III. "Fighting Crime: An Economist's View." *Milken Institute Review*, 1st quarter 2005, http://works.bepress.com/cgi/viewcontent.cgi?article=1016&context=john_donohue.

Donohue, John J., III, and Steven D. Levitt. "The Impact of Legalized Abortion on Crime." *Quarterly Journal of Economics* 116, no. 2 (May 2001): 379–420.

Dorfman, Nancy S. "Route 128: The Development of a Regional High Technology Economy." *Research Policy* 12 no. 6 (1983): 299–316.

Dorrington, R. E., T. A. Moultrie, and T. Daniel. *The Demographic Impact of HIV/AIDS in Botswana.* Gaborone: UNDP and NACA, Botswana, 2006, www.gov.bw/Global/NACA%20Ministry/Demographic_Report.pdf.

"The Dragon's Gambling Den," *Economist,* July 10, 2010.

"Dredging the Debt: Dubai's Debt Mountain," *Economist,* Oct. 31, 2009.

Dreiser, Theodore. *Sister Carrie.* New York: Doubleday, Page & Co., 1900.

Dubai Mall, www.thedubaimall.com/en.

Durack, David T., Robert J. Littman, R. Michael Benitez, and Philip A. Mackowiak. "Hellenic Holocaust: A Historical Clinico-Pathologic Conference." *American Journal of Medicine* 109, no. 5 (Oct. 1, 2000): 391–97.

Durant, Will, and Ariel Durant. *The Story of Civilization,* vol. 4, *The Age of Faith: A History of Medieval Civilization—Christian, Islamic, and Judaic—from Constantine to Dante,* A.D. *325–1300.* New York: Simon & Schuster, 1950.

Duranton, Gilles, and Matthew Turner. "The Fundamental Law of Road Congestion: Evidence from the U.S." University of Toronto Department of Economics Working Paper 370, 2009.

Duranton, Gilles, and Matthew Turner: "Urban Growth and Transportation," (2010). http://individual.utoronto.ca/gilles/Papers/GrowthTransport.pdf.

Dussault, Raymond. "Jack Maple: Betting on Intelligence." *Government Technology,* Apr. 1, 1999.

Ebrey, Patricia, Anne Walthall, and James Palais. *East Asia: A Cultural, Social, and Political History.* Boston: Houghton Mifflin, 2008.

Economist Intelligence Unit, Global Liveability Report, www.eiu.com/site_info.asp?info_name=The_Global_Live ability_Report_Press_Release&rf=0.

Edgerton, Robert B. *The Troubled Heart of Africa: A History of the Congo.* New York: St. Martin's. 2003.

Elliott, Orrin Leslie. *Stanford University: The First Twenty-Five Years.* Palo Alto, CA: Stanford University Press, 1937.

Encyclopædia Britannica Online, www.britannica.com.

Escoffier, Auguste. *Memories of My Life,* trans. Laurence Escoffier. New York: Van Nostrand Reinhold, 1997.

European Automobile Manufacturing Association. *The Automobile Industry Pocket Guide.* "The Trends in Motorisation," data for 2006, www.acea.be/images/uploads/files/20090529_motorisation.pdf.

European Environment Agency. *Urban Sprawl in Europe: The Ignored Challenge.* Report No. 10/2006. Nov. 24, 2006, www.eea.europa.eu/publications/eea_report_2006_10/eea_report_10_2006.pdf.

European Road Federation. *European Road Statistics 2009,* www.irfnet.eu/media/stats/ERF-2009%20European%20Union%20Road%20Statistics%20BOOKLET_V07_update.pdf.

"'Fairchildren' Who Came to Dominate the World of Technology." *Financial Times* (London), Oct. 31, 2007, Business Life.

Farrell, William E. "D.A.'s Assail Rockefeller Drug Penalties." *New York Times,* Feb. 7, 1973, p. A4.

Federal Bureau of Investigation. *Crime in the United States, 2008,* Sept. 2009, www.fbi.gov/ucr/cius2008/index.html.

Federal Bureau of Investigation. *Famous Cases.* "Willie Sutton," www.fbi.gov/libref/historic/famcases/sutton/sutton.htm.

Ferguson, Margaret, Mary Jo Salter, and Jon Stallworthy, eds. *Norton Anthology of Poetry,* 5th ed. New York: Norton, 2005.

Ferreira, Francisco H. G., Peter Lanjouwr, and Marcelo Neri. "A Robust Poverty Profile for Brazil Using Multiple Data Sources." *Revista Brasileira de Economia* 57, no.1 (Mar. 2003): 59–92.

Ferrie, Joseph P., and Werner Troesken. "Water and Chicago's Mortality Transition, 1850–1925." *Explorations in Economic History* 45, no. 1 (Jan. 2008): 1–16.

Fischler, Stan. *Subways of the World.* Minneapolis: MBI, 2000.

Fisman, Raymond. "Estimating the Value of Political Connections." *American Economic Review* 91, no. 4 (Sept. 2001): 1095–1102.

Foggo, Daniel. "Ken, the Animal Tester of X Block." *Times* (London), Feb. 17, 2008, Home News.

Folpe, Emily Kies. *It Happened on Washington Square.* Baltimore: Johns Hopkins University Press, 2002.

Foot, John. *Milan Since the Miracle: City, Culture and Identity.* Oxford: Berg, 2001.

47th Street Business Improvement District, The Diamond District, www.diamonddistrict.org/home.html.

Frankel, Jeffrey A. "The Natural Resource Curse: A Survey," National Bureau of Economic Research Working Paper no. 15836, 2010.

Friends of Mammoth v. Board of Supervisors, Sac. No. 7924 Cal. 3d, 8, 247 (Supreme Court of California).

Galarneau, Diane, and René Morissette. "Immigrants' Education and Required Job Skills." Statistics Canada, *Perspectives,* Dec. 2008, www.statcan.gc.ca/pub/75-001-x/2008112/pdf/10766-eng.pdf.

Galatas, Roger, and Jim Barlow. *The Woodlands: The Inside Story of Creating a Better Hometown.* Washington, DC: Urban Land Institute, 2004.

Galloni, Alessandra. "Miuccia and Me." *Wall Street Journal Magazine,* Mar. 2010.

Gandhi, Mahatma. *Mahatma Gandhi: The Essential Writings,* ed. Judith Margaret Brown. New York: Oxford University Press, 2008.

Gans, Herbert J. *The Levittowners: Life and Politics in a New Suburban Community.* New York: Columbia University Press, 1982.

Gari, L. "Arabic Treatises on Environmental Pollution up to the End of the Thirteenth Century." *Environment and History* 8, no. 4 (2002): 475–88.

Gaspar, Jess, and Edward L. Glaeser. "Information Technology and the Future of Cities." *Journal of Urban Economics* 43, no. 1 (Jan. 1998): 136–56.

Gelzinis, Peter. "Commissioner Connecting: Neighbors Notice as Hands-on Meaasures Take Root in Neighborhoods." *Boston Herald,* Aug. 22, 2007, News.

Geolytics Neighborhood Change Database 1970–2000 Tract Data Short Form Release 1.1, CD-ROM. (Brunswick, NJ: Geolytics, 2002.

Gergen, Christopher, and Gregg Vanourek. *Life Entrepreneurs: Ordinary People Creating Extraordinary Lives.* San Francisco: Wiley, 2008.

Geyl, Pieter. *The Revolt of the Netherlands 1555–1609.* London: Cassel, 1932.

Gibson, Campbell. "Population of the 100 Largest Cities and Other Urban Places in the United States: 1790 to 1990." U.S. Census Bureau, Working Paper No. 27, June 1998, www.census.gov/population/www/documentation/twps0027/twps0027.html.

Gibson, Campbell, and Kay Jung. "Historical Census Statistics on Population Totals by Race, 1790 to 1990, and by Hispanic Origin, 1970 to 1990, for Large Cities and Other Urban Places in the United States." U.S. Census Bureau, Population Division, Working Paper No. 76, Feb. 2005; detailed tables for Illinois, Michigan, and New York: "Race and Hispanic Origin for Selected Large Cities and Other Places: Earliest Census to 1990"; and New York—Race and Hispanic Origin for Selected Large Cities and Other Places: Earliest Census to 1990; www.census.gov/population/www/documentation/twps0076/twps0076.html.

Gilbert, Daniel. *Stumbling on Happiness.* New York: Vintage Books, 2007.

Giles, Chris. "A Logical Effort to Ease the London Gridlock." *Financial Times* (London), Jan. 24, 2003, Comment & Analysis.

Gillette, Felix. "Has Tom Wolfe Blown It?" *Village Voice,* Jan. 10, 2007, www.proquest.com.ezp-prod1.hul.harvard.edu.

Gillmor, C. Stewart. *Fred Terman at Stanford.* Palo Alto, CA: Stanford University Press, 2004.

Gin, Alan, and Jon Sonstelie. "The Streetcar and Residential Location in Nineteenth Century Philadelphia." *Journal of Urban Economics,* Elsevier 32, no. 1 (July 1992) 92–107.

Glaeser, Edward L. "Are Cities Dying?" *Journal of Economic Perspectives* 12, no. 2 (Spring 1998): 139–60.

———. "Can Buffalo Ever Come Back?" *City Journal,* Fall 2007.

———. "Green Cities, Brown Suburbs." *City Journal,* Winter 2009.

———. "Growth: The Death and Life of Cities." In *Making Cities Work: Prospects and Policies for Urban America,* Robert P. Inman, ed. Princeton, NJ: Princeton University Press, 2009.

———. "Houston, New York Has a Problem." *City Journal,* Summer 2008.

———. "Preservation Follies." *City Journal,* Spring 2010.

———. "Reinventing Boston: 1640–2003." *Journal of Economic Geography* 5, no. 2 (Nov. 2005): 119–53.

———. "Urban Colossus: Why Is New York America's Largest City?" Federal Reserve Bank of New York, *Economic Policy Review,* Dec. 2005.

Glaeser, Edward L., and Spencer Glendon. "Who Owns Guns? Criminals, Victims, and the Culture of Violence." *American Economic Review* 88, no. 2 (May 1998), Papers and Proceedings of the 110th Annual Meeting of the American Economic Association, 458–62.

Glaeser, Edward L., and Joshua D. Gottlieb. "The Economics of Place-Making Policies." *Brookings Papers on Economic Activity* 2008.1: 155–253.

———. "Urban Resurgence and the Consumer City." *Urban Studies* 43, no. 8 (July 2006): 1275–99.

Glaeser, Edward L., and Joseph Gyourko. "Urban Decline and Durable Housing." *Journal of Political Economy* 113, no. 2 (Apr. 2005): 345–75.

Glaeser, Edward L., Joseph Gyourko, and Albert Saiz. "Housing Supply and Housing Bubbles." *Journal of Urban Economics* 64, no. 2 (Sept. 2008): 198–217.

Glaeser, Edward L., Joseph Gyourko, and Raven E. Saks. "Urban Growth and Housing Supply." *Journal of Economic Geography* 6, no. 1 (Jan. 2006): 71–89.

———. "Why Is Manhattan So Expensive? Regulation and the Rise in Housing Prices." *Journal of Law and Economics* 48, no. 2 (Oct. 1, 2005): 331–69.

Glaeser, Edward L., and Matthew E. Kahn. "From John Lindsay to Rudy Giuliani: The Decline of the Local Safety Net." *Economic Policy Review* 5, no. 3 (Sept. 1999).

———. "The Greenness of Cities: Carbon Dioxide Emissions and Urban Development." *Journal of Urban Economics* 67, no. 3 (May 2010): 404–18.

———. "Sprawl and Urban Growth." In *Handbook of Regional and Urban Economics,* ed. J. Vernon Henderson and Jacques-François Thisse, vol. 4, ch. 56, pp. 2481–2527. Amsterdam: Elsevier, 2004.

Glaeser, Edward L., Matthew E. Kahn, Richard Arnott, and Christopher Mayer. "Decentralized Employment and the Transformation of the American City." Brookings-Wharton Papers on Urban Affairs, 2001.

Glaeser, Edward L., Matthew E. Kahn, and Jordan Rappaport. "Why Do the Poor Live in Cities? The Role of Public Transportation." *Journal of Urban Economics* 63, no 1 (2008): 1–24.

Glaeser, Edward L., Hedi D. Kallal, José A. Scheinkman, and Andrei Shleifer. "Growth in Cities." *Journal of Political Economy* 100 no. 6 (Dec. 1992): 1126–52.

Glaeser, Edward L., William R. Kerr, and Giacomo A. M. Ponzetto. "Clusters of Entrepreneurship." *Journal of Urban Economics*, Special Issue: *Cities and Entrepreneurship*, vol. 67, no. 1 (Jan. 2010): 150–68.

Glaeser, Edward L., and Janet E. Kohlhase. "Cities, Regions, and the Decline of Transport Costs." *Papers in Regional Science* 83, no. 1 (2003): 197–228.

Glaeser, Edward L., Jed Kolko, and Albert Saiz. "Consumer City." *Journal of Economic Geography* 1, no. 1 (Jan. 2001): 27–50.

Glaeser, Edward L., Giacomo A. M. Ponzetto, and Andrei Shleifer. "Why Does Democracy Need Education?" *Journal of Economic Growth* 12, no. 2 (2007): 77–99.

Glaeser, Edward L., Matt Resseger, and Kristina Tobio. "Inequality in Cities." *Journal of Regional Science* 49, no. 4 (Oct. 2009): 617–46, http://ssrn.com/abstract=1487265 or doi:10.1111/j.1467-9787.2009.00627.x.

Glaeser, Edward L., and Bruce Sacerdote. "Why Is There More Crime in Cities?" *Journal of Political Economy* 107, no. 6, part 2 (*Symposium on the Economic Analysis of Social Behavior in Honor of Gary S. Becker,* Dec. 1999): 225–58.

Glaeser, Edward L., and Albert Saiz. "The Rise of the Skilled City." *Brookings-Wharton Papers on Urban Affairs,* 2004: 47–105.

Glaeser, Edward L., and Raven E. Saks. "Corruption in America." *Journal of Public Economics* 90, no. 6–7 (Aug. 2006): 1053–72.

Glaeser, Edward L., and José Scheinkman. "Neither a Borrower nor a Lender Be: An Economic Analysis of Interest Restrictions and Usury Laws." *Journal of Law and Economics* 41, no. 1 (Apr. 1998): 1–36.

Glaeser, Edward L., Jenny Schuetz, and Bryce Ward. "Regulation and the Rise in Housing Prices in Greater Boston: The Impacts of Regulation on Housing Production and Prices in the Region Based on Data from 187 Communities in Massachusetts." Pioneer Institute for Public Policy Research and Rappaport Institute of Greater Boston Research, Jan. 2006.

Glaeser, Edward L., and Jesse M. Shapiro. "Cities and Warfare: The Impact of Terrorism on Urban Form." *Journal of Urban Economics*, Elsevier 51, no. 2 (March 2002): 205–24.

Glaeser, Edward L., and Andrei Shleifer. "The Curley Effect: The Economics of Shaping the Electorate." *Journal of Law, Economics, and Organization* 21, no. 1 (Apr. 2005): 1–19.

Glaeser, Edward L., and Kristina Tobio. "The Rise of the Sunbelt." *Southern Economic Journal* 74, no. 3 (Jan. 2008): 609–43.

Glaeser, Edward L., and Bryce A. Ward. "The Causes and Consequences of Land Use Regulation: Evidence from Greater Boston." *Journal of Urban Economics* 65, no. 3 (May 2009): 265–78.

Godshalk, David Fort. *Veiled Visions: The 1906 Atlanta Race Riot and the Reshaping of American Race Relations.* Chapel Hill: University of North Carolina Press, 2009.

Goh, Mark. "Congestion Management and Electronic Road Pricing in Singapore." *Journal of Transport Geography* 10, no. 1 (Mar. 2002): 29–38.

Goldberger, Paul. "God's Stronghold at Mammon's Door: After 150 Years, Trinity's Spire Still Looms Amid Wall St. Towers." *New York Times,* May 14, 1996.

Goldin, Claudia, and Lawrence F. Katz. *The Race Between Education and Technology.* Cambridge, MA: Belknap/ Harvard University Press, 2008.

Gómez-Ibáñez, José A., and Fernanda Ruiz Nuñez. "Inefficient Cities." Harvard University, Working Paper, Mar. 2007.

Gondola, Ch. Didier. *The History of Congo.* Westport, CT: Greenwood Press. 2003.

Goodman, Grant K. *Japan and the Dutch: 1600–1843.* Richmond, UK: Curzon Press, 2000.

Goodwin, Jason. *Otis: Giving Rise to the Modern City.* Chicago: Ivan R. Dee., 2001.

Greenblatt, Stephen. *Will in the World: How Shakespeare Became Shakespeare.* New York: Norton, 2004.

Greenwald, Richard A. "'More than a Strike': Ethnicity, Labor Relations, and the Origins of the Protocol of Peace in the New York Ladies' Garment Industry." *Business and Economic History* 27, no. 2 (Winter 1998): 318–32.

Groner, Isaac N., and David M. Helfeld. "Race Discrimination in Housing." *Yale Law Journal* 57, no. 3 (Jan. 1948): 426–58.

Guinness World Records 2008. New York: Bantam Dell, 2007.

Gussow, Mel. "Kevin Spacey's New Role, Overseas and Behind the Scenes." *New York Times,* May 25, 2004.

Gyourko, Joseph, and Albert Saiz. "Construction Costs and the Supply of Housing Structure." *Journal of Regional Science* 46, no. 4 (Oct. 2006): 661–80.

Haines, Michael R. "Historical, Demographic, Economic, and Social Data: The United States, 1790–2002," version 1, Feb. 25, 2005, Inter-university Consortium for Political and Social Research, http://hdl.handle.net/1902.2/2896.

Haley, James L. *Sam Houston.* Norman: University of Oklahoma Press, 2004.

Hall, Sir Peter. *Cities in Civilization.* New York: Pantheon Books, 1998.

Hamilton, Alan. "You're Scraping Wrong Part of the Sky, Prince Tells Architects," *Sunday Times* (London), Feb. 1, 2008.

Hamilton, Fiona. "Boris Makes an Early Start with Demands on Action to Cut Crime." *Times* (London), May 5, 2008, Home News.

Harlem Children's Zone. "History," www.hcz.org/about-us/history.

Hartemink, Alfred E. "Soil Map Density and a Nation's Wealth and Income." In *Digital Soil Mapping with Limited Data,* ed. Alfred E. Hartemink, Alex McBratney, and Maria de Lourdes Mendonça-Santos, pp. 53–66. New York: Springer, 2008.

Harvey, Rowland Hill. *Samuel Gompers: Champion of the Toiling Masses.* Palo Alto, CA: Stanford University Press, 1935.

Haughwout, Andrew, Robert Inman, Steven Craig, and Thomas Luce. "Local Revenue Hills: Evidence from Four U.S. Cities." *Review of Economics and Statistics* 86, no.2 (2004): 570–85

Hayden, Dolores. "Building the American Way: Public Subsidy, Private Space." In *The Suburb Reader,* ed. Becky M. Nicolaides and Andrew Wiese. New York: Routledge, 2006.

Heath, Brad. 2007. "Katrina Claims Stagger Corps: La., New Orleans Want $277 Billion." *USA Today,* Apr. 9, 2007, News.

Henig, Jeffrey R., "New York City: Paying the Tab," review of *Political Crisis/Fiscal Crisis: The Collapse and Revival of New York City,* by Martin Shefter. *Washington Post,* Nov. 10, 1985.

Henion, Andy. "People Mover Grows Up: Proposal Would Extend Route to New Center." *Detroit News,* Dec. 23, 2006, Metro A.

Henriques, Diana B. "Fischer Black, 57, Wall Street Theorist, Dies." *New York Times,* Aug. 31, 1995.

Hessel, Evan. "Conspicuous Consumption." *Forbes* 175, no. 6: 180.

Hoksen, Andrew. *Ken: The Ups and Downs of Ken Livingstone.* London: Arcadia Books, 2008.

Holmes, Steven A. "The 1989 Elections: Mayors and Referendums; Voters Say Yea to Incumbents, Nay to More Taxes." *New York Times,* Nov. 9, 1989.

Holmes, Thomas J. "The Effect of State Policies on the Location of Manufacturing: Evidence from State Borders." *Journal of Political Economy* 106, no. 4 (Aug. 1998): 667–705.

Horace. *The Satires and Epistles of Horace,* trans. Smith Palmer Bovie. Chicago: University of Chicago Press, 2002.

Howard, Ebenezer. *Tomorrow: A Peaceful Path to Real Reform.* London: Sonnenschein, 1898.

Howard, Nicole. *The Book: The Life Story of a Technology.* Westport, CT: Greenwood Press, 2005.

Hoxby, Caroline M., and Sonali Murarka. "Charter Schools in New York City: Who Enrolls and How They Affect Their Students' Achievement." National Bureau of Economic Research Working Paper Series, vol. w14852, Apr. 2009, http://ssrn.com/abstract=1376155.

Hoyt, Homer. *One Hundred Years of Land Values in Chicago: The Relationship of the Growth of Chicago to the Rise of Its Land Values, 1830–1933.* Washington, DC: Beard Books, 1933.

Hudgins, Bert. "Evolution of Metropolitan Detroit." *Economic Geography* 21, no. 3 (July 1945): 206–20.

Hyland, William. *Richard Rogers.* New Haven, CT: Yale University Press, 1998.

India, Government of. "Climatological Data of Important Cities." India Meteorological Department, Ministry of Earth Sciences, www.imd.gov.in/doc/climateimp.pdf.

India, Government of, National Crime Records Bureau. *Crime in India 2008,* ch. 2, "Crime in Megacities," http://ncrb.nic.in.

India, Planning Commission of. "Poverty Estimates for 2004–05," 2007, www.planningcommission.gov.in/news/prmar07.pdf.

Inglis, Ian. "'Some Kind of Wonderful': The Creative Legacy of the Brill Building." *American Music* 21, no. 2 (Summer 2003): 214–35.

Institut Pasteur. HIV/AIDS research at the Institut Pasteur: "The discovery of the AIDS virus in 1983." http://www.pasteur.fr/ip/easysite/go/03b-000027-00i/the-discovery-of-the-aids-virus-in-1983.

Iriye, Akira. "Japan's Drive to Great-Power Status." In *The Cambridge History of Japan,* vol. 5, *The Nineteenth Century,* ed. Marius B. Jansen, ch. 12, 765–82. Cambridge, UK: Cambridge University Press, 1989.

Istat—Institute of National Statistics (Italy). Demography in Figures, http://demo.istat.it/index_e.html.

———. National Economic Accounts, http://en.istat.it/dati/dataset/20100604_00.

———. Regional Accounts, http://en.istat.it/dati/dataset/20100114_01.

Jackson, Kenneth. *The Ku Klux Klan in the City: 1915–1930.* New York: Oxford University Press, 1967.

Jacob, Sarah. "Now, Social Networking Gets a Voice, Bubbly Allows for Audio Blogging." *Economic Times,* Mar. 23, 2010.

Jacobs, Jane. *The Death and Life of Great American Cities.* New York: Random House, 1961.

———. *The Economy of Cities.* New York: Random House, 1969.

Jaffe, Adam B., Manuel Trajtenberg, and Rebecca Henderson. "Geographic Localization of Knowledge Spillovers as Evidenced by Patent Citations." *Quarterly Journal of Economics* 108, no. 3 (Aug. 1993): 577–98.

Jervis, John Bloomfield. *Description of the Croton Aqueduct*. New York: Slamm and Guion, 1842.

Johnson, Chalmers. *MITI and the Japanese Miracle: The Growth of Industrial Policy, 1925–1975*. Palo Alto, CA: Stanford University Press, 1982.

Johnson, Steven. *The Ghost Map: The Story of London's Most Terrifying Epidemic—and How It Changed Science, Cities, and the Modern World*. New York: Riverhead Books, 2006.

Jordan, David P. *Transforming Paris: The Life and Labors of Baron Haussmann*. New York: Free Press, 1995.

Kahneman, D., J. L. Knetsch, and R. H. Thaler. "Experimental Tests of the Endowment Effect and the Coase Theorem." *Journal of Political Economy* 98 no. 6 (1990): 1325–48. http://www.journals.uchicago.edu/doi/abs/10.1086/261737.

Kain, John F., and Joseph J. Persky. "Alternatives to the Gilded Ghetto." *Public Interest* 14 (Winter 1969): 74–83.

Kain, John F., and John M. Quigley. "Housing Market Discrimination, Home-Ownership, and Savings Behavior." *American Economic Review* 62, no. 3 (June 1972): 263–77.

Kane, Thomas, Atila Abdulkadiroglu, Josh Angrist, Sarah Cohodes, Susan Dynarski, Jon Fullerton, and Parag Pathak. *Informing the Debate: Comparing Boston's Charter, Pilot, and Traditional Schools*. Boston Foundation, Jan. 2009, www.gse.harvard.edu/%7Epfpie/pdf/InformingTheDebate_Final.pdf.

Kane, T. J., and D. O. Staiger. "Estimating teacher impacts on student achievement: An experimental evaluation." National Bureau of Economic Research Working Paper no. 14607, 2008.

Katz, Lawrence F., and Kenneth T. Rosen. "The Interjurisdictional Effects of Growth Controls on Housing Prices." *Journal of Law and Economics* 30, no.1 (1987): 149–60.

Kazadi, Walter, John D. Sexton, Makengo Bigonsa, Bompela W'Okanga, and Matezo Way. "Malaria in Primary School Children and Infants in Kinshasa, Democratic Republic of the Congo: Surveys from the 1980s and 2000," *American Journal of Tropical Medicine and Hygiene* 71, no. 2 suppl. (Aug. 2004): 97–102.

Kellermann, Arthur L., Frederick P. Rivara, Grant Somes, Donald T. Reay, Jerry Francisco, Joyce Gillentine Banton, Janice Prodzinski, Corinne Fligner, and Bela B. Hackman. "Suicide in the Home in Relation to Gun Ownership." *New England Journal of Medicine* 327, no. 7 (Aug. 13, 1992): 467–72

Kennedy, Randy. "New York's Bus Cleanup Brings Other Cities on Board." *New York Times*, June 16, 2002, Metropolitan Desk.

Kiss, Gary, and Elizabeth Schuster. "Hope Scholarships." *Atlanta Journal-Constitution*, Dec, 8, 2008.

Kleck, Gary. *Point Blank: Guns and Violence in America*. Piscataway, NJ: Aldine Transaction, 2009.

Kling, Jeffrey R., Jeffrey B. Liebman, and Lawrence F. Katz. "Experimental Analysis of Neighborhood Effects." *Econometrica* 75, no. 1 (Jan. 2007): 83–119.

Kneebone, Elizabeth. "Job Sprawl Revisited: The Changing Geography of Metropolitan Employment." Metropolitan Policy Program at the Brookings Institute, Apr. 2009, www.brookings.edu/reports/2009/0406_job_sprawl_kneebone.aspx.

Knowles, David. *The Evolution of Medieval Thought*. New York: Vintage Books, 1962.

Kolesnikov-Jessop, Sonia. "Theme Park Developers Turn Their Attention to Asia, Where Business Is Growing." *New York Times*, Dec. 26, 2009, Business/Financial.

Koskoff, David E. *Joseph P. Kennedy: A Life and Times*. Englewood Cliffs, NJ: Prentice-Hall, 1974.

Krueger, Alan B. "How Computers Have Changed the Wage Structure: Evidence from Microdata, 1984–1989." *Quarterly Journal of Economics* 108, no. 1 (Feb 1993): 33–60.

Kumar, Satish. "The Whole Truth of a Home Economy." In *Mahatma Gandhi: 125 Years*, ed. Manmohan Choudhuri and Ramjee Singh. Varanasi, India: Sarva Seva Sangh Prakashan, Gandhian Institute of Studies, 1995.

LaFranchi, Howard. "New Look on the Left Bank in Paris." *Christian Science Monitor*, Aug. 14, 1989.

Landau, Sarah Brandford, and Carl W. Condit. *The Rise of the New York Skyscraper 1865–1913*. New Haven: Yale University Press, 1996.

Langley, Monica. *Tearing Down the Walls: How Sandy Weill Fought His Way to the Top of the Financial World . . . and Then Nearly Lost It All*. New York: Free Press, 2003.

Lay, Maxwell Gordon. *Ways of the World: A History of the World's Roads and of the Vehicles That Used Them*. New Brunswick, NJ: Rutgers University Press, 1992.

Leape, Jonathan. "The London Congestion Charge." *Journal of Economic Perspectives* 20, no. 4 (Autumn 2006): 157–76.

"Learning from Prada." *RFID Journal*, June 24, 2002, www.rfidjournal.com/article/view/272/1.

Lee, Sidney. *A Life of William Shakespeare*. London: Smith Elder, 1898.

Levick, Barbara. *Vespasian*. New York: Routledge, 1999.

Levine, Robert M. *The History of Brazil*. Westport, CT: Greenwood Press, 1999.

———. *Vale of Tears: Revisiting the Canudos Massacre in Northeastern Brazil, 1893–1897*. Berkeley: University of California Press, 1992.

Levinson, Marc. *The Box: How the Shipping Container Made the World Smaller and the World Economy Bigger*. Princeton, NJ: Princeton University Press, 2006.

Levitt, Steven D. "The Effect of Prison Population Size on Crime Rates: Evidence from Prison Overcrowding Litigation." *Quarterly Journal of Economics* 111, no. 2 (May 1996): 319–51.

———. "The Limited Role of Changing Age Structure in Explaining Aggregate Crime Rates." *Criminology* 37, no. 3 (Aug. 1999): 581–98.

———. "Understanding Why Crime Fell in the 1990s: Four Factors That Explain the Decline and Six That Do Not." *Journal of Economic Perspectives* 18, no. 1 (Winter 2004): 163–90.

Lewis, Michael M. *Liar's Poker: Rising Through the Wreckage on Wall Street.* New York: Norton, 1989.

Lillyman, William J., Marilyn F. Moriarty, and David J. Neuman. *Critical Architecture and Contemporary Culture.* New York: Oxford University Press, 1994.

Logan, Robert A. *Shakespeare's Marlowe: The Influence of Christopher Marlowe on Shakespeare's Artistry.* Hampshire, UK: Ashgate, 2007.

Loveless, Tom. *The 2008 Brown Center Report on American Education: How Well Are American Students Learning?* Washington, D.C.: Brown Center on Education Policy, Brookings Institution, 2008.

Lucas, Adam. "The Role of the Monasteries in the Development of Medieval Milling." In *Wind and Water in the Middle Ages: Fluid Technologies from Antiquity to the Renaissance,* ed. Steven A. Walton. Tempe: Arizona Center for Medieval and Renaissance Studies, 2006.

Lychagin, Sergey, Joris Pinkse, Margaret E. Slade, and John Michael Van Reenen. "Spillovers in Space: Does Geography Matter?" National Bureau of Economic Research Working Paper Series, vol. w16188, July 2010.

Lyons, Jonathan. *The House of Wisdom: How the Arabs Transformed Western Civilization.* New York: Bloomsbury, 2010.

Maddison, Angus. "Statistics on World Population, GDP, and Per Capita GDP, 1–2008 A.D." Mar. 2010, links at www.ggdc.net/maddison.

Maier, Thomas. *The Kennedys: America's Emerald Kings.* New York: Basic Books, 2004.

Makielski, Stanislaw J., Jr. *The Politics of Zoning: The New York Experience.* New York: Columbia University Press, 1966.

Markham, Jerry W. *A Financial History of the United States: From Christopher Columbus to the Robber Barons 1492–1900.* Armonk, NY: M. E. Sharpe, 2002.

Marshall, Alex, and David Emblidge. *Beneath the Metropolis: The Secret Lives of Cities.* New York: Carroll & Graf, 2006.

Martin, Sandra. "'The Greatest Architect We Have Ever Produced.'" Toronto *Globe and Mail,* May 22, 2009, p. S8.

Mas, Alexandre, and Enrico Moretti. "Peers at Work." *American Economic Review* 99, no. 1 (Mar. 2009): 112–45.

Mason, Shena. *Matthew Boulton: Selling What All the World Desires.* New Haven, CT: Yale University Press, 2009.

Maurseth, Per Botolf, and Bart Verspagen. "Knowledge Spillovers in Europe: A Patent Citations Analysis." *Scandinavian Journal of Economics* 104, no. 4 (Dec. 2002): 531–45.

McClain, James L. *Japan: A Modern History.* New York: Norton, 2002.

McConnell, Kathryn. "Could the Next Silicon Valley Be in [sic] Developing Country? Nonprofit Group Fosters Mentorship Support for High-Potential Businesses." America.gov, Jan. 22, 2009, www.america.gov/st/develop english/2009/January/20090122143528AKllennoCcM0.4231378.html?CP.rss=true.

McCullough, Diarmaid. *The Reformation.* New York: Penguin, 2005.

McElroy, Joanne, ed. *Key Statistic Bulletin No. 6,* Apr. 2009, Liverpool City Council, www.liverpool.gov.uk/Images/tcm21-151075.pdf.

McNeill, William H. *History of Western Civilization: A Handbook,* 6th ed. University of Chicago Press, 1986.

———. *Plagues and Peoples.* Garden City, NY: Doubleday, 1976.

———*Venice: The Hinge of Europe, 1081–1797* Chicago: University of Chicago Press, 1974.

McWhirter, Cameron. "Homes Give Way to Urban Prairie." *Detroit News,* June 21, 2001.

Meade, Teresa. "'Civilizing Rio de Janeiro': The Public Health Campaign and the Riot of 1904." *Journal of Social History* 20, no. 2 (Winter 1986): 301–22, www.jstor.org/stable/3787709.

Mehta, Stephanie N. "Carlos Slim, the Richest Man in the World." *Fortune,* Aug. 20, 2007.

Men of the Time; or, Sketches of Living Notables. London: David Bogue, 1852.

Mercer's Quality of Living Worldwide City Rankings, www.mercer.com/qualityoflivingpr#City_Ranking_Tables.

Meredith, Robin. "G.M. Buys a Landmark of Detroit for Its Home." *New York Times,* May 17, 1996.

Metropolitan Transit Authority. *Greening Mass Transit and Metro Regions: The Final Report of the Blue Ribbon Commission on Sustainability and the MTA,* www.mta.info/sustainability/pdf/SustRptFinal.pdf.

Meyer, Milton W. *Japan: A Concise History,* 4th ed. Lanham, MD: Rowman & Littlefield, 2009.

Meyer, Stephen Grant. *As Long as They Don't Move Next Door: Segregation and Racial Conflict in American Neighborhoods.* Lanham, MD: Rowman & Littlefield, 2001.

Milgrom, Paul R., Douglass C. North, and Barry R. Weingast. "The Role of Institutions in the Revival of Trade: The Medieval Law Merchant, Private Judges, and the Champagne Fairs." *Economics and Politics* 1 (1990): 1–23.

Miller, Donald L. *City of the Century: The Epic of Chicago and the Making of America.* New York: Simon & Schuster, 1996.

Miller, Matthew, Deborah Azrael, and David Hemenway. "Household Firearm Ownership and Suicide Rates in the United States." *Epidemiology* 13, no. 5 (Sept. 2002): 517–24.

Milligan, Kevin, Enrico Moretti, and Philip Oreopoulous. "Does Education Improve Citizenship? Evidence from the U.S. and the U.K." *Journal of Public Economics* 88, no. 9–10 (Aug. 2004): 1667–95.

Minchinton, Walter E. "Bristol: Metropolis of the West in the Eighteenth Century." *Transactions of the Royal Historical Society*, Fifth Series, vol. 4 (1954): 69–89.

Miranda, Rowan A. "Post-machine Regimes and the Growth of Government: A Fiscal History of the City of Chicago, 1970–1990." *Urban Affairs Review* 28, no. 3 (Mar. 1993): 397–422.

Monkkonen, Eric. *Homicides in New York City, 1797–1999* (and various historical comparison sites; computer file in several formats). Los Angeles: University of California, Los Angeles (producer), 2000; and Ann Arbor, MI: Interuniversity Consortium for Political and Social Research (distributor), 2001.

Moore, Charles. *The Life and Times of Charles Follen Mckim.* Boston and New York: Houghton Mifflin, 1929.

Moore, Jim. "The Puzzling Origins of AIDS." *American Scientist* 92, no. 6 (Nov.–Dec. 2004): 540–47.

Morison, Samuel Eliot. *Three Centuries of Harvard 1636–1936.* Cambridge, MA: Belknap Press/Harvard University Press, 1937.

Morley, Alan. *Vancouver: From Milltown to Metropolis.* Vancouver: Mitchell Press, 1961.

Morris-Suzuki, Tessa. *The Technological Transformation of Japan: From the Seventeenth to the Twenty-first Century.* Cambridge, UK: Cambridge University Press, 1994.

Mott, Frank Luther. *Golden Multitudes: The Story of Best-Sellers in the United States.* New York: Macmillan, 1947.

Mumbai, Office of the Executive President, State Planning Board, Government of Maharashtra. *Mumbai Human Development Report 2009.* New Delhi: Oxford University Press, 2010, http://mhupa.gov.in/W_new/Mumbai%20 HDR%20Complete.pdf.

Mumford, Lewis. *The City in History: Its Origins, Its Transformations, and Its Prospects.* Boston: Houghton Mifflin Harcourt, 1961.

Munn, Mark H. *The School of History: Athens in the Age of Socrates.* Berkeley: University of California Press, 2000.

Murdoch, James. *A History of Japan*, vol. 3., *The Tokugawa Epoch, 1652–1868*, rev. Joseph H. Longford. Hertford, UK: Stephen Austin and Sons, 1996.

Murray, Christopher J. L., Sandeep C. Kulkarni, Catherine Michaud, Niels Tomijima, Maria T. Bulzacchelli, Terrell Iandiorio, and Majid Ezzati. "Eight Americas: Investigating Mortality Disparities Across Races, Counties, and Race-Counties in the United States," Dataset S1. Life Expectancy at Birth by County. *Public Library of Science: Medicine* 3, no. 9 (2006): 1513–24.

Murray, James M. *Bruges, Cradle of Capitalism, 1280–1390.* New York: Cambridge University Press, 2005.

National Advisory Commission on Civil Disorders, Report of the, (Kerner Report), Washington, D.C., 1968.

National Center for Injury Prevention and Control, www.cdc.gov/injury/index.html, and WISQARS (Web-based Injury Statistics Query and Reporting System), www.cdc.gov/injury/wisqars.

National Climatic Data Center. "Mean Number of Days With Maximum Temperature 90 Degrees F or Higher," http://lwf.ncdc.noaa.gov/oa/climate/online/ccd/max90temp.html.

Needels, Karen E. "Go Directly to Jail and Do Not Collect? A Long-Term Study of Recidivism, Employment, and Earnings Patterns Among Prison Releases." *Journal of Research in Crime and Delinquency* 33, no. 4 (Nov. 1996): 471–96.

Nelson, George. *Building a New Europe: Portraits of Modern Architects.* New Haven, CT: Yale University Press, 2007.

Nelson, Richard R., and Edmund S. Phelps. "Investment in Humans, Technological Diffusion, and Economic Growth." *American Economic Review* 56, no. 1–2 (Mar. 1966): 69–75.

Nevins, Allan, and Frank Ernest Hill. *Ford*, vol. 1, *The Times, the Man, the Company;* vol. 2, *Expansion and Challenge, 1915–1933;* vol. 3, *Decline and Rebirth, 1933–1962.* New York: Scribner's, 1954–63.

New York City, Department of City Planning. "About NYC Zoning," http://home2.nyc.gov/html/dcp/html/zone/ zonehis.shtml.

New York City, Department of City Planning, City Planning Commission. Zoning Maps and Resolution, Dec. 15, 1961, www.nyc.gov/html/dcp/pdf/zone/zoning_maps_and_resolution_1961.pdf.

New York City Department of Health and Mental Hygiene, Bureau of Vital Statistics. *Summary of Vital Statistics 2008*, Jan. 2010, http://home2.nyc.gov/html/doh/downloads/pdf/vs/2008sum.pdf; *Summary of Vital Statistics 2007*, http://home2.nyc.gov/html/doh/downloads/pdf/vs/2007sum.pdf; *Summary of Vital Statistics 2000*, http://home2 .nyc.gov/html/doh/downloads/pdf/vs/2000sum.pdf; and *Summary of Vital Statistics 1961*, http://home2.nyc.gov/ html/doh/downloads/pdf/vs/1961sum.pdf.

Nguyen, Lananh. "Online Network Created by Harvard Students Flourishes." *Tufts Daily*, Apr. 12, 2004.

Nicholson, Tom, and James C. Jones. "Detroit's New Towers of Hope." *Newsweek*, Mar. 28, 1977.

Nicolaides, Becky M., and Andrew Wiese, eds. *The Suburb Reader.* New York: Routledge, 2006.

Nolan, Jenny. "How the Detroit River Shaped Lives and History." *Detroit News*, Feb. 11, 1997.

Obama, Barack. "Remarks of Senator Barack Obama: Changing the Odds for Urban America." Washington, DC, July 18, 2007, www.barackobama.com/2007/07/18/remarks_of_senator_barack_obam_19.php.

O'Hare, Greg, and Michael Barke. "The Favelas of Rio de Janeiro: A Temporal and Spatial Snalysis." *GeoJournal* 56, no. 3: 225–40.

Owen, David. *Green Metropolis: Why Living Smaller, Living Closer, and Driving Less Are the Keys to Sustainability.* New York: Riverhead Books, 2009.

Owen, David Elystan. *Canals to Manchester.* Manchester, UK: Manchester University Press, 1977.

Padover, Saul K. *Thomas Jefferson on Democracy.* New York: Appleton-Century, 1939.

Pagden, Anthony. *Worlds at War: The 2,500-Year Struggle Between East and West.* New York: Random House, 2009.

Papayanis, Nicholas. *Planning Paris Before Haussmann.* Baltimore: Johns Hopkins University Press, 2004.

Parry, Ian W. H., Margaret Walls, and Winston Harrington. "Automobile Externalities and Policies." *Journal of Economic Literature* 45, no. 2 (June 2007): 373–99.

Patel, Shirish B. "Dharavi: Makeover or Takeover?" *Economic and Political Weekly* 45, no. 24 (June 12, 2010): 47–54.

Pelfrey, William. *Billy, Alfred, and General Motors: The Story of Two Unique Men, a Legendary Company, and a Remarkable Time in American History.* New York: Amacom, 2006.

Piccadilly Arcade. http://piccadilly-arcade.com/.

Pickney, David H. "Money and Politics in the Rebuilding of Paris, 1860–1870." *Journal of Economic History* 17, no. 1 (Mar. 1957): 45–61.

Pinker, Steven. *How the Mind Works*, 1st ed. New York: Norton, 1997.

Pirenne, Henri. *Medieval Cities: Their Origins and the Revival of Trade*, trans. F. D. Halsey. Princeton, NJ: Princeton University Press, 1952.

Plato. *The Republic of Plato*, trans. Benjamin Jowett and Thomas Herbert Warren, 3d ed. New York: Random House, 1973.

Plaza, Beatriz. "The Return on Investment of the Guggenheim Museum Bilbao." *International Journal of Urban and Regional Research* 30, no. 2 (June 2006).

Plöger, Jörg. "Bilbao City Report." Centre for Analysis of Social Exclusion, Economic and Social Research Council (UK), 2007, http://eprints.lse.ac.uk/3624/1/Bilbao_city_report_%28final%29.pdf (accessed July 29, 2010).

———. "Leipzig City Report." Centre for Analysis of Social Exclusion, Economic and Social Research Council (UK), case report 42, 2007, http://eprints.lse.ac.uk/3622/1/Leipzig_city_report_(final).pdf.

Plunz, Richard. *A History of Housing in New York City.* New York: Columbia University Press, 1990.

Pogrebin, Robin. "Plan for an Upper East Side Tower Meets with Disapproval." *New York Times*, Oct. 17, 2006.

Polese, Francesca. "In Search of a New Industry: Giovanni Battista Pirelli and His Educational Journey Through Europe, 1870–1871." *Business History* 48, no. 3 (2006): 354–75.

Polinsky, A. Mitchell, and David T. Ellwood. "An Empirical Reconciliation of Micro and Grouped Estimates of the Demand for Housing." *Review of Economics and Statistics* 61, no. 2 (May 1979): 199–205.

Portes, Alejandro. "Housing Policy, Urban Poverty, and the State: The Favelas of Rio de Janeiro, 1972–1976." *Latin American Research Review* 14, no. 2 (Spring 1979): 3–24.

Poterba, James, and Todd Sinai. "Tax Expenditures for Owner-Occupied Housing: Deductions for Property Taxes and Mortgage Interest and the Exclusion of Imputed Rental Income." *American Economic Review* 98, no. 2 (May 2008): 84–89.

Power, Garrett. "Apartheid Baltimore Style: The Residential Segregation Ordinances of 1910–1913." *Maryland Law Review* 42 (1983): 289–328.

President's Advisory Panel on Federal Tax Reform, Report of the. "Simple, Fair, and Pro-Growth: Proposals to Fix America's Tax System," Nov. 2005, www.taxpolicycenter.org/taxtopics/upload/tax-panel-2.pdf.

PricewaterhouseCoopers. "Which Are the Largest City Economies in the World and How Might This Change by 2025?" *PricewaterhouseCoopers UK Economic Outlook*, Nov. 2009, https://www.ukmediacentre.pwc.com/imageli brary/downloadMedia.ashx?MediaDetailsID=1562.

Pride, Richard A. "Public Opinion and the End of Busing: (Mis)Perceptions of Policy Failure." *Sociological Quarterly* 41, no. 2 (Spring 2000): 207–25.

Prince of Wales. Speech by HRH the Prince of Wales for the Bali to Poznan Corporate Leaders Group on Climate Change Conference, St. James's Palace, London, July 16, 2008, www.princeofwales.gov.uk/speechesandarticles/a_ speech_by_hrh_the_prince_of_wales_for_the_bali_to_poznan_c_1864009205.html.

———. Speech by HRH the Prince of Wales at the 150th Anniversary of the Royal Institute of British Architects (RIBA), Royal Gala Evening at Hampton Court Palace, May 29, 1984, www.princeofwales.gov.uk/speechesand articles/a_speech_by_hrh_the_prince_of_wales_at_the_150th_anniversary_1876801621.html.

———. Speech by HRH the Prince of Wales Titled "Tall Buildings," Invensys Conference, QE2 Centre, London, Dec. 11, 2001, www.princeofwales.gov.uk/speechesandarticles/a_speech_by_hrh_the_prince_of_wales_titled_ tall_buildings_in_62434944.html.

Quinn, Thomas C., Jonathan M. Mann, James W. Curran, and Peter Piot. "AIDS in Africa: An Epidemiologic Paradigm." *Science*, New Series 234, no. 4779 (Nov. 21, 1986): 955–63.

Quincy, Josiah. *History of Harvard*, vol 1. New York: Arno, 1977.

"Race Riots." *Encylopedia of Chicago*, http://encyclopedia.chicagohistory.org/pages/1032.html.

Raff, Daniel M. G., and Lawrence H. Summers. "Did Henry Ford Pay Efficiency Wages?" *Journal of Labor Economics* 5, no. 4, part 2 (Oct. 1987): S57–86.

Raffles, Thomas Stamford. *History of Java*, 2 vols. London: Black, Parbury and Allen, 1817.

Ranjan, Amit. "Bixee, Pixrat Acquired . . . First Web 2.0 Acquisition in India." Webyantra, Dec. 5, 2006, www.weby antra.net/2006/12/05/bixeepixrat-acquiredfirst-web20-acquisition-in-india/.

Recovery.gov. Track the Money, www.recovery.gov/?q=content/rebuilding-infrastructure.

Reubens, Beatrice G. "Burr, Hamilton, and the Manhattan Company, Part I: Gaining the Charter." *Political Science Quarterly* 72, no. 4 (Dec. 1957): 578–607.

Rich, Wilbur C. *Coleman Young and Detroit Politics: From Social Activist to Power Broker*. Detroit: Wayne State University Press, 1989.

Rocco, Elena. "Trust Breaks Down in Electronic Contexts but Can Be Repaired by Some Initial Face-to-Face Contact." In *Proceedings of the SIGCHI Conference on Human Factors in Computing Systems*, 496–502. Los Angeles: Special Interest Group on Computer-Human Interaction, 1998.

Rohter, Larry. "Second City Looks Back in Laughter." *New York Times*, Dec. 16, 2009, Arts/Cultural.

Roosevelt, Theodore. *The Rough Riders: An Autobiography* (reprint) Louis Auchincloss, ed. New York: Library of America, 2004.

Rosenthal, Stuart S., and William C. Strange. "Agglomeration, Labor Supply, and the Urban Rat Race." Center for Policy Research, Syracuse University Working Paper no. 106, 2003.

Rosenthal, Stuart S., and William C. Strange. "The Attenuation of Human Capital Spillovers." *Journal of Urban Economics* 64, no. 2 (Sept. 2008): 373–89.

Rousseau, Jean-Jacques. *Émile: or, On Education*, ed. Allan Bloom. New York: Basic Books, 1979.

Routledge, Christopher. *Cains: The Story of Liverpool in a Pint Glass*. Liverpool: Liverpool University Press, 2009.

Rowbotham, Jill. "London's 'Red Ken' Arrives." *Brisbane Courier-Mail* (Queensland, Australia), Sunday, May 12, 1985.

Rowley, Hazel. *Richard Wright: The Life and Times*. New York: Holt, 2001.

Rucker, Walter C., and James N. Upton. *Encyclopedia of American Race Riots*. Westport, CT: Greenwood, 2007.

Ruggles, Steven, J. Trent Alexander, Katie Genadek, Ronald Goeken, Matthew B. Schroeder, and Matthew Sobek. *Integrated Public Use Microdata Series*, ver. 5.0 (machine-readable database). Minneapolis: University of Minnesota, 2010.

Ruskin, John. *The Genius of John Ruskin: Selections from His Writings*, ed. John D. Rosenberg. New York: Routledge, 1980; Charlottesville: University Press of Virginia, 1997.

———. *The Works of John Ruskin*. London: G. Allen, 1903.

Russell, Josiah C. "That Earlier Plague." *Demography* 5, no. 1 (1968): 174–84.

Rutman, Darrett B. "Governor Winthrop's Garden Crop: The Significance of Agriculture in the Early Commerce of Massachusetts Bay." *William and Mary Quarterly*, 3d series, vol. 20, no. 3 (July 1963), 396–415.

Rybczynski, Witold. *A Clearing in the Distance: Frederick Law Olmsted and America in the Nineteenth Century*. New York: Scribner, 1999.

Sacerdote, Bruce. "When the Saints Come Marching In: Effects of Hurricanes Katrina and Rita on Student Evacuees." National Bureau of Economic Research Working Paper No. 14385, Oct. 2008.

Sachs, Jeffrey D. "Breaking the Poverty Trap." *Scientific American*, Sept. 2007.

Sachs, Jeffrey D., and Howard J. Shatz. "U.S. Trade with Developing Countries and Wage Inequality." *American Economic Review* 86, no. 2 (May 1996): 234–39.

"Sailing into a New Luxury at Famous Dubai Hotel." *Toronto Star*, Sept. 11, 2004, Travel.

Saiz, Albert. "The Geographic Determinants of Housing Supply." *The Quarterly Journal of Economics*, 125, no. 3 (Aug. 2010): 1253–96.

Sasser, Bill. "Katrina Anniversary: How Well Has Recovery Money Been Spent?: Money from Charitable Foundations and $142 Billion in Federal Funds Have Produced a Substantial Recovery in Metro New Orleans, Says a Report Released Ahead of Hurricane Katrina Anniversary." *Christian Science Monitor*, Aug. 27, 2010.

Saulney, Susan. "To Save Itself, Detroit Is Razing Itself." *New York Times*, June 20, 2010.

Saunders, Doug. "Slumming It Is Better Than Bulldozing It: Asian Leaders Tearing Down Long-Standing Slums to Build Housing Projects Are Repeating Western Mistakes of the 1950s and 1960s." Focus Column, Reckoning—"Going Ghetto: Urban 'Improvements' That Aren't." *Toronto Globe and Mail*, Jan. 12, 2008.

Saxenian, AnnaLee. *Regional Advantage: Culture and Competition in Silicon Valley and Route 128*. Cambridge, MA: Harvard University Press, 1994.

Schadewald, Bill. "A Speculative Salute to the Allen Brothers." *Houston Business Journal*, Sept. 12, 2008.

Schivelbusch, Wolfgang. "The Policing of Street Lighting." *Yale French Studies*, no. 73, Everyday Life, ed. Alice Kaplan and Kristin Roth, pp. 61–74. New Haven, CT: Yale University Press, 1987.

Schlosser, Julie. "Harder than Harvard." *Fortune*, Mar. 17, 2006.

Schoenbaum, Samuel. *Shakespeare's Lives*, rev. ed. Oxford, UK: Clarendon Press, 1991.

Schultz, Theodore W. "The Value of the Ability to Deal with Disequilibria." *Journal of Economic Literature* 13, no. 2 (June 1975): 827–46.

Seidensticker, Edward. *Low City, High City: Tokyo from Edo to the Earthquake*. New York: Knopf, 1983.

Seuss, Dr. (Theodor Seuss Geisel). *The Lorax*. New York: Random House, 1971.

Shilling, James D., C. F. Sirmans, and Jonathan F. Dombrow. "Measuring Depreciation in Single-Family Rental and Owner-Occupied Housing." *Journal of Housing Economics* 1, no. 4 (Dec. 1991): 368–83.

Shurkin, Joel N. *Broken Genius: The Rise and Fall of William Shockley, Creator of the Electronic Age*. New York: Palgrave Macmillan, 2008.

"Singapore's Deep Tunnel Sewerage System Wins Global Water Awards 2009." *Marketwire*, Apr. 28, 2009.

Skoufias, Emmanuel, and Roy Katayama. "Sources of Welfare Disparities Across and Within Regions of Brazil: Evidence from the 2002–03 Household Budget Survey." World Bank Poverty Reduction Group, Policy Research Working Paper 4803, Dec. 2008.

Small, Kenneth, and Erik Verhoef. *The Economics of Urban Transportation*. New York: Routledge, 2007.

Smith, Adam. *An Inquiry into the Nature and Causes of the Wealth of Nations*, 3d ed. Basel: J. J. Tourneisen and J. L. LeGrand, 1791; New York: Cosimo, 2007.

Smith, Lewis. "Traffic Still Light in London Charge Zone." *Times* (London), Mar. 1, 2003.

Smith, Russell A. "The Taft-Hartley Act and State Jurisdiction over Labor Relations." *Michigan Law Review* 46, no. 5 (Mar. 1948): 593–624.

Spang, Rebecca L. *The Invention of the Restaurant: Paris and Modern Gastronomic Culture*. Cambridge, MA: Harvard University Press, 2000.

Spelman, William. *Criminal Incapacitation*. New York: Plenum Press, 1994.

Spence, Lorna. *A Profile of Londoners by Country of Birth: Estimates from the 2006 Annual Population Survey*. Greater London Authority, Data Management and Analysis Group, DMAG Briefing 2008-05, Feb. 2008, http://static .london.gov.uk/gla/publications/factsandfigures/dmag-briefing-2008-05.pdf.

Spindler, Amy M. "Gianni Versace, 50, the Designer Who Infused Fashion with Life and Art." *New York Times*, July 16, 1997.

Sridhar, Kala Seetharam. "Impact of Land Use Regulations: Evidence from India's Cities." *Urban Studies* 47, no. 7 (June 2010): 1541–69.

Starr, Larry, and Christopher Waterman. *American Popular Music*. New York: Oxford University Press, 2003.

Steinbeck, John. *The Grapes of Wrath*. New York: Viking Press, 1939.

Stern, Seth. "$14.6 Billion Later, Boston's Big Dig Wraps Up." *Christian Science Monitor*, Dec. 19, 2003.

Stevens, J. E. "Anaesthesia in Japan: Past and Present." *Journal of the Royal Society of Medicine* 79, no. 5 (May 1986): 294–98.

Stigler, George Joseph. *The Organization of Industry*. Chicago: University of Chicago Press, 1968.

Strube, Michael J. "What Did Triplett Really Find? A Contemporary Analysis of the First Experiment in Social Psychology." *American Journal of Psychology* 118, no. 2 (Summer 2005): 271–86.

Sturgeon, Timothy J. "How Silicon Valley Came to Be." In *Understanding Silicon Valley: The Anatomy of an Entrepreneurial Region*, ed. Martin Kenny. Palo Alto, CA: Stanford University Press, 2000.

Sudjic, Deyan. "A Thoroughly Modernising Mayor: Ken Livingstone Was a Dogged Opponent of Richard Rogers 20 Years Ago; Now They're the Best of Friends—What's Going On?" *Observer*, July 8, 2001.

Sugita, Genpaku. *Dawn of Western Science in Japan: Ranaku Kotohajime*, tr. Ryozo Matsumoto and Eiichi Kiyooka. Tokyo: Hokuseido Press, 1969.

Sugrue, Thomas J. *The Origins of the Urban Crisis: Race and Inequality in Postwar Detroit*. Princeton, NJ: Princeton University Press, 2005.

Suits, Daniel B. "The Demand for New Automobiles in the United States 1929–1956." *Review of Economics and Statistics* 40, no. 3 (Aug. 1958): 273–80.

Sukehiro, Hirakawa. "Japan's Turn to the West." In *The Cambridge History of Japan*, vol. 5, *The Nineteenth Century*, ed. Marius B. Jansen, ch. 7, 432–98. Cambridge, UK: Cambridge University Press, 1989.

Sutcliffe, Anthony. *Paris: An Architectural History*. New Haven, CT: Yale University Press, 1993.

Swartz, Mimi. "Born Again." *Texas Monthly* 19, no. 10 (Oct. 1991): 46–50.

Tarshis, Arthur. "Thirty-one Commercial Buildings Erected by A. E. Lefcourt in Two Decades." *New York Times*, May 18, 1930, Real Estate.

Taub, Eric A. "Elevator Technology: Inspiring Many Everyday Leaps of Faith." *New York Times*, Dec. 3, 1998.

TAXSIM. National Bureau of Economic Research, Internet TAXSIM Version 8.2 Home Page, www.nber.org/~taxsim/ taxsim-calc8/index.html.

Taylor, George Rogers. *The Transportation Revolution, 1815–1860*. New York: Rinehart, 1951.

Taylor, Philip M. *Munitions of the Mind: A History of Propaganda from the Ancient World to the Present Day*. Manchester, UK: Manchester University Press, 2003.

Thomas, Hugh. *The Slave Trade: The Story of the Atlantic Slave Trade 1440–1870*. New York: Simon & Schuster, 1997.

Thomas, June Manning. "Planning and Industrial Decline: Lessons from Postwar Detroit." *Journal of the American Planning Association* 56, no. 3 (Sept. 1990): 297–310.

Thomas, Lately. *Delmonico's: A Century of Splendor.* Boston: Houghton Mifflin, 1967.

Thompson, Heather Ann. *Whose Detroit? Politics, Labor, and Race in a Modern American City.* Ithaca, NY: Cornell University Press, 2004.

Thoreau, Henry David. *I to Myself: An Annotated Selection from the Journal of Henry David Thoreau*, ed. Jeffrey S. Cramer. New Haven, CT: Yale University Press, 2007.

———. *The Journal of Henry D. Thoreau.* Boston: Houghton Mifflin, 1906.

———. *Walden.* New York: Routledge, 1904.

———. *Walden and Resistance to Civil Government*, ed. Willaim Rossi, 2d ed. New York: Norton, 1996.

Tilly, Charles, Louise Tilly, and Richard Tilly, *The Rebellious Century: 1830–1975.* Cambridge: Harvard University Press, 1975.

Timmons, Heather. "A Tiny Car Is the Stuff of 4-Wheel Dreams for Millions of Drivers in India." *New York Times*, Mar. 24, 2009, Business/Financial.

Tollens, Eric. "Current Situation of Food Security in the D. R. Congo: Diagnostic and Perspectives." Katholieke Universiteit Leuven, Faculty of Agricultural and Applied Biological Sciences, Working Paper, Aug. 2003, www.agr.kuleuven.ac.be/aee/clo/wp/tollens2003b.pdf.

Tolstoy, Leo. *Anna Karenina*, trans. Constance Black Garnett. New York: Random House, 1939.

Treffinger, Stephen. "Alchemy Will Turn a Candy Factory into Biotech Offices." *New York Times*, June 19, 2003, House & Home/Style.

Treynor, Jack L. *Treynor on Institutional Investing.* New York: Wiley, 2008.

"A Tribute to Arthur Erickson." *AI Architect*, http://info.aia.org/aiarchitect/thisweek09/0612/0612n_arthur.cfm.

Triplett, Norman. "The Dynamogenic Factors in Pacemaking and Competition." *American Journal of Psychology* 9, no. 4 (July 1898): 507–33.

Troesken, Werner. "Typhoid Rates and the Public Acquisition of Private Waterworks, 1880–1920." *Journal of Economic History* 59, no. 4 (Dec. 1999): 927–48.

Turak, Theodore. "Remembrances of the Home Insurance Building." *Journal of the Society of Architectural Historians* 44, no. 1 (Mar. 1985): 60–65.

Tyler, Gus. *Look for the Union Label: A History of the International Ladies' Garment Workers' Union.* New York: M. E. Sharpe, 1995.

Ungar, Mark. "Prisons and Politics in Contemporary Latin America." *Human Rights Quarterly* 25, no. 4 (Nov. 2003): 909–34, www.jstor.org/stable/20069699.

U.S. Bureau of Labor Statistics, Economic News Releases, *County Employment and Wages*, "Table 1. Covered establishments, employment, and wages in the 327 largest counties, first quarter 2010." http://www.bls.gov/news/release/cewqtr.t01.htm. Last Modified Date: October 19, 2010.

U.S. Census Bureau, www.census.gov, numerous pages cited in full in individual notes; extensive use was made of American FactFinder, http://factfinder.census.gov.

U.S. Department of Agriculture, Economic Research Services, *Major Uses of Land in the United States, 2002*, "Urban and Rural Residential Uses." http://www.ers.usda.gov/publications/EIB14/eib14g.pdf.

U.S. Department of Agriculture, National Agricultural Statistics Service, Crops by State (95111), cn186629.csv. http://usda.mannlib.cornell.edu/MannUsda/viewDocumentInfo.do?documentID=1269.

U.S. Department of Commerce, Bureau of Economic Analysis, "Personal Income for Metropolitan Areas, 2009," Monday, August 9, 2010. http://www.bea.gov/newsreleases/regional/mpi/2010/pdf/mpi0810.pdf.

U.S. Department of Housing and Urban Development and U.S. Census Bureau, Current Housing Reports, *American Housing Survey for the United States: 2007*, H150/07, Sept. 2008, www.census.gov/prod/2008pubs/h150-07.pdf.

U.S. Energy Information Administration, Department of Energy, Residential Energy Consumption Survey (RECS), www.eia.doe.gov/emeu/recs.

U.S. Energy Information Administration, International Energy Annaual 2006, "H.1co2 World Carbon Dioxide Emissions from the Consumption and Flaring of Fossil Fuels, 1980–2006." www.eia.doe.gov/pub/international/iealf/tableh1co2.xls.

U.S. Environmental Protection Agency, Environmental Impact Statement Database, www.epa.gov/oecaerth/nepa/eisdata.html.

United Nations, Department of Economic and Social Affairs, Population Division, World Urbanization Prospects: 2009, File 12, Population of Urban Agglomerations with 750,000 Inhabitants or More in 2009, by Country, 1950–2025. http://esa.un.org/unpd/wup/CD-ROM_2009/WUP2009-F12-Cities_Over_750K.xls.

United Nations Habitat, *State of the World's Cities 2010/2011—Cities for All: Bridging the Urban Divide, 2010.* http://www.unhabitat.org/pmss/listItemDetails.aspx?publicationID=2917.

Urban Land Institute, Development Case Studies, ULI Award Winner Project Summary, http://casestudies.uli.org/Profile.aspx?j=7607&p=5&c=7.

Vancouver Public Library. "City of Vancouver Population." www.vpl.vancouver.bc.ca/research_guides/item/6848/C779.

Vaughan, Alden T. *The Puritan Tradition in America, 1620–1730*. Hanover, NH: University Press of New England, 1997.

Vedder, Richard. "Right-to-Work Laws: Liberty, Prosperity, and Quality of Life." *Cato Journal* 30, no. 1 (Jan. 1, 2010): 171–80.

Vermiel, Sarah E. *The Fireproof Building: Technology and Public Safety in the Nineteenth-Century American City*. Baltimore: Johns Hopkins University Press, 2000.

Vickrey, William S. "Congestion Theory and Transport Investment." *American Economic Review* 59, no. 2 (1969): 251–60.

———. "Pricing in Urban and Suburban Transport." *American Economic Review* 52, no. 2 (May 1963): 452–65.

———. "A Proposal for Revising New York's Subway Fare Structure." *Journal of the Operations Research Society of America* 3, no. 1 (Feb. 1955): 38–68.

———. "Statement on the Pricing of Urban Street Use." In Hearings, U.S. Congress, Joint Committee on Metropolitan Washington Problems, Nov. 11, 1959, pp, 466–77.

Viegas, Jennifer. *Pierre Omidyar: The Founder of Ebay*. New York: Rosen, 2007.

Wakin, Daniel J. "If It's Hit, Strummed or Plucked, It'll Be Here." *New York Times*, Feb. 2, 2008, Arts/Cultural.

Wallis, John Joseph, Price V. Fishback, and Shawn Everett Kantor. "Politics, Relief, and Reform: The Transformation of America's Social Welfare System During the New Deal." In *Corruption and Reform: Lessons from America's Economic History*, ed. Edward L. Glaeser and Claudia Goldin, pp. 153–84. University of Chicago Press, 2006.

Walters, Alan A. "The Theory and Measurement of Private and Social Cost of Highway Congestion." *Econometrica* 29, no. 4 (Oct. 1961): 676–99.

Ware, Leland B. "Invisible Walls: An Examination of the Legal Strategy of the Restrictive Covenant Cases." *Washington University Law Quarterly* 67, no. 3 (1989): 737–72.

Warner, Sam Bass. *The Private City: Philadelphia in Three Periods of Its Growth*. Philadelphia: University of Pennsylvania Press, 1968; repr. 1996.

Watkins, Kevin. "Beyond Scarcity: Power, Poverty and the Global Water Crisis." United Nations Development Programme, Human Development Report, 2006, http://hdr.undp.org/en/media/HDR06-complete.pdf.

Watson, Georgia Butina, Ian Bentley, Sue Roaf, and Pete Smith. *Learning from Poundbury: Research for the West Dorset District Council and Duchy of Cornwall*. School of the Built Environment, Oxford Brookes University, 2004.

Webster, Ben. "Congestion Charge Will Rise to £25 for 'Chelsea Tractors.'" *Times* (London), July 13, 2006, Home News.

Webster, Philip. "Miliband Attacks Prince for Flying to Collect Green Award in New York." *Times* (London), Jan. 20, 2007, Home News.

Weis, René. *Shakespeare Unbound: Decoding a Hidden Life*. New York: Holt, 2007.

Weiss, H. Eugene. *Chrysler, Ford, Durant, and Sloan: Founding Giants of the American Automotive Industry*. Jefferson, NC: McFarland, 2003.

White House Office of Management and Budget, Program Assessment: Highway Infrastructure, www.whitehouse.gov/omb/expectmore/summary/10000412.2007.html.

White, John. *The Birth and Rebirth of Pictorial Space* 2nd ed. Boston: Boston Book and Art Shop, 1967.

Whitford, David. "A Factory Gets a Second Chance." *Fortune* 160, no. 7 (Oct. 12, 2009): 74–80.

Williams, Susan. *Food in the United States, 1820s–1890*. Westport, CT: Greenwood, 2006.

Willis, David K. "The Royal Wedding." *Christian Science Monitor*, July 6, 1981.

Wilkerson, Isabel. "Years Late, Detroit's Monorail Opens." *New York Times*, Aug. 1, 1987.

Wilson, William Julius. *The Declining Significance of Race: Blacks and Changing American Institutions*. Chicago: University of Chicago Press, 1978.

WISQARS (Web-based Injury Statistics Query and Reporting System), www.cdc.gov/injury/wisqars.

Wolfe, Tom. "The (Naked) City and the Undead." *New York Times*, Nov. 26, 2006.

The Woodlands. http://www.thewoodlands.com/masterplan.htm and http://www.thewoodlands.com/greenspace.htm.

The Woodlands Development Company. The Woodlands, Texas Demographics. January 1, 2010. http://www.thewoodlandstownship-tx.gov/DocumentView.aspx?DID=667.

World Bank. *Connecting to Compete: Trade Logistics in the Global Economy*. Washington, DC, 2007.

———. "Nigeria: Expanding Access to Rural Infrastructure: Issues and Options for Rural Electrification, Water Supply, and Telecommunications." Energy Sector Management Assistance Program, Technical Paper 091, 2005, www-wds.worldbank.org/external/default/WDSContentServer/WDSP/IB/2006/04/28/000090341_20060428141651/Rendered/PDF/359940UNI0ESM01ural1Access01PUBLIC1.pdf.

———. World Development Indicators and Global Development Finance, Population in the Largest City (percent of urban population), data extracted July 26, 2010, databank.worldbank.org.

World Health Organization, Global Alert and Response (GAR). "Typhoid Fever in the Democratic Republic of the Congo—Update," Jan. 19, 2005, www.who.int/csr/don/2005_01_19/en/index.html.

Worsley, Giles. "A Model Village Grows Up Gracefully: The Prince of Wales's Pet Project Received a Drubbing When It was First Mooted, But Now Poundbury Is Coming into Its Own." *Daily Telegraph* (London), Jan. 30, 2001.

Wright, Richard. *Black Boy.* New York: Harper & Row, 1945.

———. "I Tried to Be a Communist." *Atlantic Monthly,* Aug. 1944.

Wrigley, Edward Anthony, and Roger S. Schofield. *The Population History of England 1541–1871: A Reconstruction.* Cambridge, MA: Harvard University Press, 1981.

Wurtzburg, C. E. *Raffles of the Eastern Isles.* Singapore: Oxford University Press, 1954, 1986.

Wylie, Jeanie. *Poletown: Community Betrayed.* Urbana: University of Illinois Press, 1989.

Xu, Jiaquan, Kenneth D. Kochanek, Sherry L. Murphy, and Betzaida Tejada-Vera. "Deaths: Final Data for 2007." *National Vital Statistics Report* 58, no. 19 (May 2010), Centers for Disease Control, www.cdc.gov/nchs/data/nvsr/nvsr58/nvsr58_19.pdf.

Yew, Lee Kwan. *From Third World to First: The Singapore Story, 1965–2000.* Tarrytown, NY: Marshall Cavendish, 2000.

———. *The Singapore Story: Memoirs of Lee Kuan Yew.* Singapore Press Holdings, 1998.

Young, Coleman A. *The Quotations of Mayor Coleman A. Young.* Detroit: Wayne State University Press, 2005.

Young, Coleman A., and Lonnie Wheeler. *Hard Stuff: The Autobiography of Coleman Young.* New York: Penguin, 1994.

Young, Robin. "Village Pub Is First to Pull a Michelin Star." *Times* (London), Jan. 19, 2001, Home News.

Zagat 2011 London Restaurants. Zagat Survey, September 2010.

Zagorín, Pérez. *Rebels and Rulers 1500–1660,* vol. 2, *Provincial Rebellion: Revolutionary Civil Wars 1560–1660.* Cambridge, UK: Cambridge University Press, 1982, repr. 1984.

Zheng, Siqi, Rui Wang, Edward L. Glaeser, and Matthew E. Kahn. "The Greenness of China: Household Carbon Dioxide Emissions and Urban Development." National Bureau of Economic Research Working Paper no. 15621, 2009.

INDEX

cities as good for, 14, 145, 197, 200–201,
208–9, 217, 222, 267–68
energy consumption and, *see* energy
consumption
garden living and, 202–6
global warming and, 201, 205–6, 213, 218,
220, 221, 268, 269
suburbs and, 14, 145, 200, 201, 208, 209,
268
wetlands, 192
environmental impact reviews, 212
environmentalism, 21, 192, 201–2, 205,
213
in California, 14, 192, 211–12, 221, 262
first phase of, 220–21
global perspective in, 14
Livingstone and, 213–17, 221
Lorax fallacy in, 201–2, 221
Prince Charles and, 213–17
smart, 15, 220–22
unintended consequences of, 210–12,
221
wealth and, 203
The Woodlands and, 180–81, 182
Equitable Life Assurance Society,
142–43
Erickson, Arthur, 239–40
Erie Canal, 44, 45
Escoffier, Auguste, 124–25
Europe, 20, 21–22, 42, 52, 58, 64, 193, 218
car ownership in, 178–79
industrial cities in, 46
plague in, 97–98
sprawl in, 178–79
externalities, 100
exurbs, 13, 15, 167, 180
see also suburbs

Facebook, 33, 34, 37
face-to-face contact, 34–38, 57, 248, 249,
269
Fairchild, Sherman, 32
farming, 72, 75, 219
fashion, garment, and textile industries, 4, 5,
42, 43, 50, 51, 52, 56, 126–27, 238
Federal Highway Act (1921), 173
Federal Housing Administration (FHA), 176,
265
Federal Telegraph Corporation (FTC),
30–31
Fermi, Enrico, 79
Ferrie, Joseph, 101
Ferriss, Hugh, 204–5
Fidelity Investments, 235

finance, 5, 52, 56–57, 234–35, 238, 242,
249
firearms, 115
Fitzgerald, F. Scott, 174
Fitzgerald, John F. "Honey Fitz," 78
Flatiron Building, 140, 161
Florence, 12, 22
Renaissance in, 1, 8, 56, 248, 250
Florida, 209
Florida, Richard, 260
Forbes, 118
Ford, Gerald, 3
Ford, Henry, 8, 46–49, 50, 53, 57, 72, 81, 171,
172–73, 224, 250
Ford, Henry, II, 62, 160
Foster, Norman, 149
Fountainhead, The (Rand), 139
France, 15, 218, 221, 263
car travel in, 178
Paris, *see* Paris
schools in, 89, 195, 254, 258
Franco, Francisco, 52
Freeman Field, 59
free trade, 252
Frick, Henry Clay, 141
friends and social networks, 128
Fryer, Roland, 88
Fuller, George, 139

Gaborone, 230–31
Gandhi, Mohandas K., 7, 9, 13
Gans, Herbert, 175
Garden Cities of Tomorrow (Howard), 203
garment, textile, and fashion industries, 4, 5,
42, 43, 50, 51, 52, 56, 126–27, 238
gasoline:
carbon emissions and, 207
consumption of, 207, 208
price of, 179
taxes on, 178, 267
Gates, Bill, 27
General Motors, 47, 49, 62–63, 256
Geneva, 129
Germany, 47, 178, 263
ghettos, *see* slums and ghettos
Gielgud, John, 121
Giuliani, Rudy, 54, 56, 58, 110–11
globalization, 18, 40, 216, 251–53
New York City and, 4–5
skills and, 29
global trade, 252
global warming, 201, 205–6, 213, 218, 220,
221, 268, 269
Gompers, Samuel, 50